ENCYCLOPEDIA OF
THE HORSE

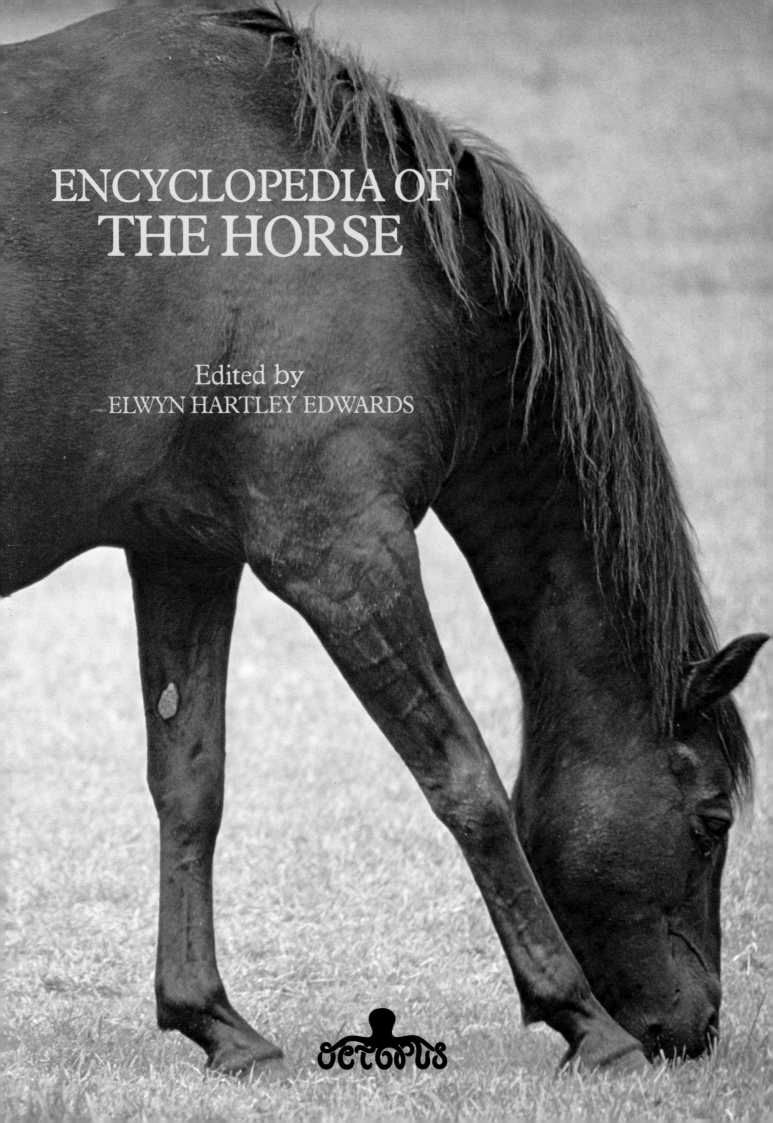

ENCYCLOPEDIA OF THE HORSE

Edited by
ELWYN HARTLEY EDWARDS

Octopus

CONTENTS

First published 1977 by
Octopus Books Limited
59 Grosvenor Street
London W1

© 1977 Octopus Books Limited

Reprinted 1983

ISBN 0 7064 0606 0

Produced by Mandarin Publishers Limited
22a Westlands Road,
Quarry Bay, Hong Kong

Printed in Hong Kong

FOREWORD

Encyclopedias, including horse encyclopedias, take two forms: the first is an expanded dictionary – a series of short articles on a host of topics arranged alphabetically, useful to the experienced horseman who knows just which headings to look for; the second is the form adopted by the editor of this book – a comprehensive series of articles by leading authorities, covering the entire realm of the ridden horse. The result is a most readable book which is not only highly informative to the general reader and an admirable introduction for beginner riders and owners, but is also so complete as to add even to the knowledge of lifetime horsemen and horsewomen.

The general coverage is international in viewpoint and application and in addition there are special articles about riding and horsemanship in America and Australia. The breeds of the world, sensibly including harness and heavy draught horses, are fully covered.

The editor has been eminently successful in achieving his aim; by enlisting the contributions of a notable group of authors he has produced the outstanding illustrated horse encyclopedia in the English language.

International Editor
The Chronicle of the Horse

INTRODUCTION

The domestication of the horse, thought to have been made by tribes inhabiting the steppes bordering the Caspian Sea some 5000 years ago, stands as one of the most significant watersheds in the human progression. Initially the value of horses to early peoples amounted to little more than the convenience of easily accessible supplies of meat, hides for the making of clothing and tents, and dung which could be used as fuel. But it was not long, in terms of history, before the horse had assumed a role of far greater importance as a means of transport, communication and, very importantly, of conquest.

Four hundred years ago the Spanish *conquistadores*, following the discovery of the New World, re-established the horse on the American continent, where the species had become extinct thousands of years before for reasons which can now only be matters for conjecture. By the 19th century America, with the help of horses, had been transformed from a colonial outpost to a world power and up to the early part of our own century world economy was still to a large degree dependent upon natural horsepower.

Today, the horse, superseded by the internal combustion engine in trade, industry and, mercifully, in warfare, survives now chiefly for pleasure riding and provides recreation and sport for an ever growing number of people in all parts of the world.

In this book, which combines the work of numerous authors who are accepted authorities on their subjects, we have presented the role of the ridden horse in its modern context but against the background of history. We have, for instance,

included studies which trace the early development of the species; we have covered the origination, establishment and improvement of the many horse breeds and types; and we have shown how the growth of riding activity has resulted in the wide variety of sports and recreational uses with which the 20th century horse is involved internationally.

In addition, we have introduced an entirely practical element to the book by the inclusion of chapters giving detailed information on methods of horse and pony management, training, breeding and many other topics which we hope will add to an overall understanding of the horse.

It is amusing to reflect that the horse, who for all those centuries was used, misused and abused in every human enterprise as the faithful servant of man, has now, when he no longer plays a part in human progress, exchanged roles with his former masters.

It is we who are now *his* faithful servants.

This book is a tribute to him.

Editor
Riding magazine

PART ONE

THE DEVELOPMENT
OF
THE HORSE

The Pre-Domestic Horse

BEFORE Darwin perfected his theory of evolution all that was known about the origin of the horse, so far as the average horseman was concerned, was contained in the story of Noah and the Ark. From this, a belief that *Equus caballus* was of one single origin was a logical conclusion. Darwin, himself, was, therefore, no innovator in this respect. He demonstrated his tenets of evolution and the origin of species by natural selection, largely by reference to successive equine ancestors in *one line*.

The only pre-Darwinian theory that can still command respect is that of Hamilton Smith who had postulated several wild species of horses contributing to the make-up of *Equus caballus*. He thought they were principally differentiated by coat-colour, which explained the wide spectrum of extant coat colours. That part of his theory, however, cannot be upheld in the light of our present knowledge.

The discovery of the Przewalski horse in 1881, caused it to be hailed as the only

Left The Tarpan – a breed which arose from the crossing of two of the ancestral types after the last Ice Age. Now extinct in its original form, it has been 'reconstructed' by selective breeding in Poland.
Below The Icelandic pony is a modern breed which closely resembles an ancestral type.

begetter of domestic horses, thus supporting, again, the theory of single origin.

It was not until about the turn of the nineteenth/twentieth centuries that the single origin theory, so widely held, suffered a reverse, through the discoveries made by J. Cossar Ewart of Edinburgh. He made a series of hybridization experiments with Equidae at Pennicuik not far from that city, the results of which, and of his study of 'primitive' horses and ponies in Britain and overseas, he best summarized in an article in *Nature* (21 April 1904). He it was who coined the phrase 'Celtic pony' to indicate one of the wild equine sub-species ancestral to the domestic horse. Another heavier, Northern sub-species he called the Norse horse. Other separate ancestors he recognized were the wild horse of Mongolia, *Equus przewalskii* and two more-than-pony-sized races, one with a ram head and one with a straight profile, which he did not endow with names. He did not assign the Arab or related breeds to a separate race, deeming them merely the most easterly representatives of the 'cline' (as it is now called) of which the Exmoor and the Welsh pony were the westernmost. From this it will be seen, that he regarded the geographical distribution of all these races as very wide, and that he envisaged two or three or more of them co-existing in the same district . . . 'as Africa now contains several species of zebras, Europe at the beginning of the Pleistocene period was inhabited by several species of horses'.

Monophylists or partisans of the single-ancestor school still flourish, notably among equine psychologists, professional or amateur, who seek to explain behaviour in terms of situations to which the wild ancestor was exposed: and it is always one kind of wild ancestor, exclusively grass-eating, dwelling on a boundless prairie with neither mountain nor forest in sight.

In my view, the most articulate, the most

logical, and the best-equipped with evidence among prehistorians of the horse are the latter-day followers of Ewart, Speed (also of Edinburgh), Skorkowski in Poland, and Ebhardt in Germany. They have the advantage of being equipped with aids not available to Ewart, such as radiology and the technique of carbon-14 dating, and the results of some archaeological finds of the first importance, such as the

Below Once considered to be an ancestor of the modern horse, the Przewalski, or Mongolian wild horse, is now known to be a distinct species.
Bottom left The Exmoor is a pony of great antiquity and is probably a descendant of the Celtic pony of Type 1 in the classification.
Bottom right The Fjord pony originated in Norway. It is a primitive breed, resembling the northern Eurasian Type 2.

Pazyrik horse burials of the Altai which have been made since his day.

Their classifications of post-glacial Old World horses available to the first domesticators are not dignified by the name of species but as 'Types', as under:
1) substantially, Ewart's Celtic pony, better called the Atlantic pony. The modern breeds most resembling it are the Exmoor and a certain strain of Icelandic.
2) substantially, Ewart's Norse horse and inhabiting northern Eurasia. Modern breeds mostly resembling it are the Norwegian Fjord pony, a certain type of Highland pony, and the Noriker heavy horse of the sub-Alpine region.
3) a horse, not a pony, with a Central Asian habitat. Modern breeds most resembling it are the clay-coloured Sorraia horse of the Spanish-Portuguese border, and, in a more elegant form, the Akhal-Teké of Central

Asia and the Karabakh, both of which are golden-dun. This was the ancestor of the Nisaean and Bactrian breeds (discussed in the next section) and, to the extent of about 50 per cent through the 'Turks', the Bactrian and the Andalucian, of the Thoroughbred.
4) a pony-sized horse of Western Asia. The modern breed most resembling it is the Caspian pony. This latter is thought to be the ancestor of the Arabian and a small handful of allied breeds found chiefly in Persia. But in part this type is bred into a multitude of domestic races, endowing them with many of its qualities, not the least of which is beauty.

Excluded is Przewalski's horse, because of a factor not known in Ewart's day. This is that a species is characterized by an embryonic cell structure peculiar to it, the cell nuclei containing a given number of chromosomes – 'rod-like structures ... regarded as the bearers of hereditary factors' (R. Geurts). The chromosome count of Przewalski's horse differs from that of all domestic horses.

Included is the Tarpan, the wild horse of eastern Europe and western Russia. Extinct in its pure form since the last century but now 're-constituted' in the Polish Tarpan herds, it is regarded as a hybrid occurring in the wild at the point where the habitats of Types 1 and 4 once joined. The Tarpan was the basis of stock used by all the chariot-driving nations of the eastern Mediterranean from the Hittites to the Greeks, and originally of the Celtic tribes. It is the principal ancestor of the small 'peasants' horses' in east Central Europe and the Balkans. Many individuals of these breeds resemble it closely; such as the Hungarian Goral, the Romanian Hucul, the Polish Konik and the Bosniak of Yugoslavia, etc., but even closer facsimiles have been 'back-bred' in Poland and Bavaria, for scientific purposes.

If we had no evidence from fossil bones and teeth at all, it would still be apparent to anyone with an eye for a horse, from the evidence of European cave paintings alone, that in the Old Stone Age a great variety of wild horse types roamed Europe. In the Dordogne, there is the cave of Rouffignac, the roof of which is covered with drawings that depict identically the present day Exmoor ponies. Not far away, at Les Combarelles, there is a drawing of an obese, ram-headed, Clydesdale-looking specimen. At Niaux in the Pyrenees, there is a quite credible Fell pony. At Font de Gaume, near Les Eyzies, there is a New Forest pony in the act of leaping. Go over the mountains into Cantabrian Spain and yet further recognizable types can be seen in these prehistoric galleries, including horses of great quality – virtually 'oriental'.

In speaking of domestic horses the over-worked phrase 'pure-bred' is a relative term. At the head of every pedigree stands an imported stallion of whose history and ancestry in his 'old country', nothing of consequence is known, and a country-bred mare of unrecorded ancestry. 'Pure breeding' occurred only in the wild ancestors: and then, it seems, not absolutely.

Domestication and the Early Horse Peoples

THE preceding section, concerning the pre-domestic horse, might be thought to be within the province of the naturalist. He could be either a biologist or a zoologist, but would be accustomed to working in the past not the present. He would be well-grounded in ecology, and thus able to consider the horse against the background of its environment; the effect on it of climate and vegetation; its own effect on the vegetation; and its relations to other living creatures, be they vegetarians which constituted competition for grazing, or predators which controlled its numbers. These are its 'natural enemies', chief among whom, up to the moment of domestication, is Man.

Of qualified experts in this field there is no lack; the academic staffs of veterinary schools abound in them. But to make any progress in this relatively new discipline, the history of the horse as a domestic animal, and by implication the history of horse-breeding and horse-borne peoples, requires a different set of qualifications

For centuries the horse has played a primary role in the everyday life of many nomadic peoples.

altogether, and they would be outside the experience of the pure naturalist. Ideally, in addition to the knowledge of the equine pre-historian, some acquaintance with practical horsemanship and horsemastership, the former to include driving as well as riding, is an essential. Then something must also be known about soldiering and agriculture, as well as wainwrightship, enough at least to realize what is practicable and what is not practicable in the way of vehicle design. Likewise some historical grasp of the technical aspects of shipbuilding at certain crucial times and places, enough to determine whether it was viable in, say, 200 BC, to transport horses across, say, 200 km (125 miles) of open sea.

In earlier days it all seemed so simple, at least up to the time when Darwin wrote his *Origin of Species*. All literate persons then were acquainted with Holy Writ, at least in Protestant countries. The educated class in Europe and North America, both Catholic and Protestant, were well read in Greek and Latin authors. All that had to be done was to assemble the requisite quotations from the Bible and the Classics, arrange them in the right order, and the back of the work was broken. As for the practical implications of what the literary sources said, they were easily, and mostly correctly, interpreted, because up to the invention of the passenger-carrying railway, and to a certain extent from then until the birth of the internal combustion engine, almost all competent middle-class males knew how to persuade a horse to convey them from point A to point B by one means or another. Not to be able to do this was not simply the equivalent of not being able to drive a car: it was more like not

This 9th century BC Assyrian relief from Nimrud shows the grooming and feeding of chariot teams of Tarpan-type horses in the stables at the camp of Ashurnasirpal II. Horses were much despised by the Hebrews and figure little in the Old Testament.

being able to ride a bicycle. To this extent Dr Syntax and his like could cope more adequately with this involved subject than their modern counterparts.

It might appear simple but in fact it was not so. No one took account of the fact that the Old Testament was written by and for a people who had a taboo against horses. Up to the time of King Solomon, this was about as virulent as the one they had against dogs or pigs. The pious Hebrew looked back to respected patriarchs who rode camels and asses, but horses never. To him the horse was inseparably associated with foreign imperialists – Assyrians or Egyptians or Persians. Hence

the Old Testament is an indifferent historical source for this subject, and can tell us virtually nothing about it before about 900 BC, by which time we have plenty of alternative evidence anyway.

The same objections apply, though to a lesser degree, to classical authors, whose voices speak to us from about 800 BC onwards of the great civilizations of the Mediterranean. But then the horse was not first domesticated about 800 BC, nor in the Mediterranean region.

When was the horse domesticated and where? To the first there is no quick or certain answer. Only that it was certainly as early as the third millennium BC and that as evidence from archaeology slowly accumulates, the favoured date recedes ever further towards the opening centuries of that millennium. As to where, the certainty is that it was in a region north east of the Mediterranean, at least as far distant as the Oxus (Amu Darya) basin, and perhaps as distant as the far end of Siberia, along the shores of the Bering Strait. Or anywhere along that diagonal line. But 'when?' and 'where?' are closely related questions. Just as there are monophylists who believe in a single wild ancestor of the horse, and polyphylists who postulate several of them, so there are diffusionists who believe that the horseman was born in one centre and one only, from which the horse culture spread over all the world. In addition there are those who maintain that horses could be, and in fact were, domesticated, not necessarily in imitation of other tribes but by several peoples not in contact with each other each living in separate regions where wild horses were found.

So then, to be able to read Xenophon in the original is not enough. To be able to interpret the exact practical implications of the Hebrew text of the Book of Job is not enough. A knowledge of ancient Egyptian and Babylonian texts would be a help and mastery of the languages current in the Hittite Empire about 1400 BC more useful still. . . .

That will bring us back to the earliest written text of any significance concerning horses, *The Chariot Training Manual* of Kikkulis the Mittanite. And yet we have irrefutable evidence of the use of horses in

various regions of the Old World, more than sixteen centuries earlier than that. This is the testimony of pictorial art and the remains of artifacts belonging to illiterate peoples, *one* of whom – but which? – first domesticated the horse. The interpretation of this evidence is a branch of archaeology. It can be supplemented by the oral traditions of the peoples dwelling along that diagonal line between the Oxus basin and the Pacific coast of Siberia, a study of which, in the original, demands familiarity with several languages, some of them Indo-European but mostly belonging to the Turkic, Ural-Altaic and Mongolian groups. Oral tradition is valuable because legends contain a core of what once in the remote past was historical fact. But they need interpreting: to take a Western example, the legend of horses being bestowed on some hero by a God of the Sea, such as the Greek Poseidon, or the Irish Mananaan Mac Lir, may signify in mundane terms that horses, or more likely a superior breed of horse, were first brought to Hellas or to Eire by sea. And to arrive at the right interpretation of such legends demands, in the first instance, an anthropologist or a folklorist.

And where will we find the historian possessed of all these skills? Nowhere, for there is no such person. So the task must fall inevitably to those who have much knowledge in some areas, and less in others, or who have some knowledge in most areas. They must take other men's translations and interpretations at their face value, and rely on someone else's summary and exposition for the layman of highly technical reports of research in various natural sciences, from geology to genetics. If we are to construct a prehistory, and an early history, of the horse before and after domestication, it must be built of bricks made of other men's straw and other men's clay, baked in a kiln fired with other men's fuel, and bound with mortar made by yet others. There is no other way. This is the extent of the problem and it must, therefore, preclude any single definitive explanation.

Let us now consider the fortunes of the domestic horse over the first 30 centuries or so, still considering them, in the main, under the headings of the four local races which were defined and discussed in the preceding section.

Type 1: which Ewart called the Celtic Pony, was probably not first domesticated by the Celtic peoples, but by the peoples who preceded them in Northwest Europe; in Scotland, for example, by the Picts. Being capable of a very fast trot with a sweeping action it was admirably adapted for chariot work in pairs, and some years ago a practical demonstration was given by two Exmoor mares harnessed to a replica

of an ancient British chariot, discovered at Llyn Cerig Bach in Wales. The mares performed admirably, although in fact such a team would in ancient times have consisted of stallions, who could have done much better. The rock drawings of Scandinavia which date from the Bronze Age include many pictures of pairs of ponies harnessed to chariots, and these are likely to have been of the same type 1. Here domestication was not the work of the aboriginal Lapps, who stuck to the reindeer, but of Indo-European invaders – ancestors of the Norse – who brought sheep, goats, cattle and crop-farming to the North.

The Celts themselves originally lived, not on the Atlantic coast, but in the lower Danube valley, where the prevalent wild horse was not this type, but the Tarpan. In the early stages of their equestrian history, therefore, the chariots would have been horsed with Tarpans, which as we have seen were a cross between type 1 and type 4. But the great Celtic migration which

came about the middle of the first millenium BC, led up that valley and along the axis Swabia-Burgundy-Brittany. Conquering as they went, they inevitably acquired great numbers of horses along the route, and these would include, as the most important element, the more substantial horses of the Alpine foothills as they skirted around the northern edge of the massif. Thus when they stood poised on the Channel shore for the invasion of Britain, it would have already been inaccurate to describe their horses as 'pure-bred'. What awaited them on this side of the Channel was a more uniform stock, consisting only of type 1 with a small admixture of type 2. Once they had established themselves and begun putting their own stallions to the aboriginal mares, therefore, the 'ancient British horse' would already have contained elements of three out of four types of the primeval wild stock.

Type 2: whatever its exact relationship to Przevalski's horse may be, is most likely the first to have been domesticated. Its habitat overlapped that of the reindeer and it may well be that in Northeast Asia (where it lived) it was first domesticated as a substitute for the reindeer. At least one tribe in that region, the Yakuts, seem to have remained in a transitional stage to this day, riding horses and reindeer alike. At a primitive level of culture, it is probably easier for a reindeer-keeping people to start taming horses from scratch than it would be for anyone else. For instance, in certain weather conditions it might be feasible for men mounted on reindeer or in light reindeer-drawn sledges like the Lapps' *pulkka* to overtake, or get within lasso-range of, horses hampered by snow (this might also be done on ski, or on snow-shoes, but hardly by any other means). Again, reindeer-keepers are the people most likely to be familiar with the use of the lasso. If the hunt took place in summer-time, all, or the majority of, the animals captured intact would be unweaned foals. Next to camel-keepers, reindeer herders would have the readiest adequate supply of milk that can be digested by a foal (cow's milk cannot).

The wheel was unknown in Northeast Asia long after its invention in Southwest Asia, and the newly-domesticated horses could only have been put to work under the pack or the riding saddle or in front of the sleigh. Their performance in the first two roles would have been inferior to that of reindeer in the winter months. In the summer the sleigh could not be used, but the slide-car, a wheelless conveyance called a 'travois' in North America, could be drawn by either horses or reindeer (it was originally drawn by dogs).

Two rock drawings of the early domestication period. *left*: Reindeer-mounted archer hunting, from Tepsei in the Upper Yenisey Valley, Siberia (1st millennium BC). *below*: Horseborne archer, from Ladakh, north India (about 1200 BC). Both animals, in the wild, had forecastable migration routes and could therefore be trapped and then domesticated.

However it was under the saddle that the horse bestowed the greatest mobility on the herdsmen of Mongolia, Manchuria, and eastern Siberia. Its adoption began that long series of horse-borne invasions by archers armed with the double-curved laminated bow, which culminated in the invasion of Europe by the Turks – a tide that did not begin to recede until the end of the seventeenth century of our era.

Again, this cycle began with the taming, almost exclusively, of type 2, but as the flood of conquering horse-archers rolled steadily west and south other varieties were added to the remount herds, just as they were to be later with the Celts. The disturbances spread outwards from the vortex of Mongolia like ripples in a pond, and the first impact on Europe was chiefly felt

in the invasions of Indo-European ('Aryan') and Turkic charioteers, moving westward under pressure from the Mongol horse-archers. Then came other Indo-Europeans, riding and armed with the Tartar-type composite bow. The most famous of these people are the Scythians, and probably it was they who drove the Celts out of the Danube valley and set in train the Celtic pilgrimage to the Atlantic shore. The particular wave threatening to engulf Europe at the dawn of the Christian era consisted of Parthians. They it is whom St John had in mind when he wrote: 'And I looked, and behold a pale horse, and

Mongol achievements against the settled empires of the East and the West were limited until the Mongols had acquired the means of crossing water obstacles too formidable for horses to swim, and of besieging and storming walled towns. Once they had obtained siege engines and pontoon bridges, and the services as engineers of Persian or Chinese deserters, there was really nothing but the sea to stop the horse-archers. This 16th century Mogul miniature shows the crossing of the river Yang-tse-Kiang and the storming of the Chinese fortress of O-Chou by Kublai Khan's armies.

his name that sat on him was Death.' The word rendered as 'pale' in the Authorized version could also be rendered 'light dun', the characteristic colour of types 2 and 3.

Type 3: Beginning with the Persian invasions which were checked at Marathon and Salamis, these horses now began to appear in Europe in considerable numbers. They included the famous Nisaean breed that was so much taller than any mount available to the Greeks of Xenophon's time. That they were all in enemy hands was a position only reversed by Alexander the Great's conquest of Persia, accomplished not alone by the redoubtable Macedonian infantry but also by auxiliary horsemen from the conquered kingdom of Bactria (northern Afghanistan). After the take-over of the Persian Empire it became possible to bring back these Bactrian horses to Macedon to upgrade the Tarpan-type local stock.

Type 4: The same applies to specimens of this type, although from a military point of view this Proto-Arab, as it then was, had the grave disadvantage of being too small for a charger. But certainly it was in the Hellenistic period when Alexander's successors were ruling his fragmented empire in Europe and Asia – and not, as is commonly supposed, in Roman times – that these horses were first available in any considerable numbers in Mediterranean Europe. It was to be many centuries before they were to be called Arabian.

If we conclude that the Caspian Pony is *not* the unmodified descendant of type 4, the Proto-Arab, or that the latter never existed in the wild, then we shall have to look for another possible ancestor for the Arab and its close relations among early domestic stock. This brings us back inevitably to Professor Ridgeway and his *Multiple Origins of the Thoroughbred*. As we have seen in the last section, Lady Wentworth triumphed over him, and he lost face, largely because he was not a zoologist nor an archaeologist and all the 'hard' evidence he was able to produce about Arabian origins was an impressive array of quotations from classical authors. But he wrote at a time when the science of

genetics was less advanced than it is today, and the trump card which neither he nor his antagonist had up their respective sleeves has now dropped out of the cuff of modern biologists.

We already know that doubt has been cast on the claim of Przevalski's horse to be the sole ancestor of all domestic horses, by the fact that its chromosome count is not identical with that of the domestic horse. Ridgeway's intuitive guess was that the Proto-Arab was a hybrid, arising from the union of the Asiatic Wild Horse, or rather its domestic descendants, with some species of zebra that was formerly, but is not now, domesticated, and that this cross could only have come about in North Africa. The chromosome count of a hybrid is the sum of the count of both parents divided by two. If this 'average' comes to an odd number (as most of the feasible ones do) then the hybrid is sterile (e.g. the mule). But in the few cases where it comes to an even number, hybrid can mate fruitfully with hybrid and a new species – or at least sub-species – can be born. The Hungarian author, Miklos Jankovich, has pointed out in a work not yet published in English that, in terms of species now living, not all Equidae have had their chromosome count established. Of those whose count is known, there is a species of zebra whose chromosome count added to that of Przevalski's horse and divided by two is identical with that of the domestic horse. Jankovich therefore has demonstrated, without consciously wishing to reinforce Ridgeway, that in terms of the mechanics – that is the arithmetic – of genetics, his theory of equine origins is perfectly feasible. He refuses to speculate on how such a cross could have arisen, but nobody supposes it could have occurred in the wild, in view of what is known about the distribution of the Asiatic Wild Horse and the various species of zebra. Ridgeway lost the trick by assuming that the horse came to the zebra and not vice versa.

Let us suppose that some species of zebra towards the northern limit of its geographical range – say Ethiopia or the Sudan – *was* once domesticated. We tend to think 'once domesticated, always domesticated', but we are wrong. There are precedents for the taming of animals for just this use, namely riding and driving, and the abandonment of the practice when a more acceptable substitute has been found. Such are for instance the elk (moose) in the sub-arctic regions of

Eurasia, and the onager in Mesopotamia. The only surviving elks and onagers now are running wild or living in zoos, but the rock drawings of the White Sea Coast and the clay tablets of Iraq show them towing men on skis, drawing sleighs and harnessed to the curious Sumerian battlecars. In the dawn of history, the one was displaced by the reindeer and the other by the horse, whereupon they were simply turned back on the tundra or the desert.

We know from many modern instances that zebras *can* be tamed to ride and drive, but it has never been claimed that they are as good to drive as a horse, and there is ample testimony that they are a worse ride, since they have no withers. Suppose that in late prehistoric times men came down the Nile Valley leading pack-laden zebras, to cross the Isthmus of Suez and journey through Sinai and Palestine. Somewhere in the latitude of the Caspian Sea we might expect them to meet men riding or driving or leading the domesticated version of Przevalski's horse. Ridgeway's theory foundered on the archaeological rock; no identifiable remains of horses of the required antiquity could be found in North Africa to prove his point. Likeways no such remains of zebras have been found in Western Asia. But then, for *certain* identification of Equidae a deal of material is required for autopsy, the minimum being a skull with both jaws intact, and one fore and one hind limb below the knee, or hock.

Opposite below The Onager, one of the species of Asiatic wild ass, was once domesticated in Mesopotamia but was later discarded when the more adaptable horse was brought in from the North.
Below Przewalski's horse was originally the wild horse of Mongolia. It seems unlikely that, either as a domesticated animal or in the wild, it ever mated with the Zebra to become an ancestor of the Proto-Arab.

For this much to remain of one skeleton over several thousand years, along a migration route that is mostly through desert country, is too much to be hoped, yet only the bones can tell the true story. Neither the striped hide, nor the huge trumpet-like ears of the zebra nor yet its chromosomes could possibly be preserved. In passing it is worth mentioning that it is the slender cannon bones that distinguish the oriental horses skeletally from other varieties, and in this respect they more resemble asses, onagers, or zebras than Northern horses.

The fact that very occasionally zebra-like markings are found on the legs and more rarely still on other parts of the body, of new-born Arabian foals is neither here nor there. So they are in horses of all breeds, and they are merely an atavistic reminder of the stripes that are believed to have occurred in most Equidae before the Ice Age. Whatever the origin of the horses now called Arabian, they only just fail to be considered in this section, which does not extend beyond the beginning of the Christian era. Classical Greek authors do not mention Arabian horses, and no Latin author up to the time of Augustus does so, in the sense that there was then a recognized Arabian breed. European authors writing in antiquity give the impression rather that the Arab peoples used donkeys almost exclusively in peace-time and camels in war. Horses in Arabia at the beginning of the Christian era were very scarce and this was still the case in the lifetime of Mahomet, who in his holy wars demonstrated their superiority over camels for military purposes. It was the compulsion to spread the faith of Islam by force of arms that led to the expansion of horse-breeding among the desert tribes to its widest feasible limits. Although the Koran might exhort the faithful to produce as many foals as possible for service against the infidel, this could only be done, how-

ever, in the Arabian peninsula, by the same means as had been practised in pre-Islamic times. And so these limits remained fairly narrow. Horses cannot live on camel-thorn; the number that could be reared was in direct proportion to the amount of barley that could be acquired from the Fertile Crescent bordering the desert zone, and the amount of dates that the oases could produce, surplus to human consumption. The only requisite that was available more or less ad lib was the camel's milk – essential for weaning foals under conditions in which the mare only lactated for a couple of months at best.

Horse-breeding and horse-keeping began, in Arabia itself, as a prestige symbol, associated only with the rich and powerful. When it became a religious duty incumbent also on the less rich and less powerful this must have meant three things.

First, that other livestock kept by the Bedouin – his sheep, goats, camels – would have to content themselves with a smaller share of available drinking water and even grittier grazing than before.

Second, that breeders themselves would have to make do with less dates, less barley, less camel's milk and even less fish, since in certain parts of Arabia near the coast, protein in the diet of horses is supplied by dried sprats from which the oil is first extracted.

Third, that the slogan 'quality before quantity' would be hammered home in no uncertain fashion. If piety compels a man to bankrupt himself and starve his family and flocks in order to breed horses, he might as well breed good ones. One cannot but reflect, contemplating the enormously inflated numbers of Arabs bred outside Arabia today, that some such economic stringency and consequent pruning of numbers would be of the greatest benefit to modern Western breeders.

The Growth of Classical Equitation

THE first definitive records of man riding a horse date back to 1600 BC and are depicted on the tomb of Horenhab of Egypt. From long before this, however, there are plaques still in existence that show man sitting on the quarters of an onager. This horse-like animal is now rare but was, in fact, domesticated long before the horse. The next recorded horsemen of any note were the Assyrians, great hunters of the 800s BC. They sat in the centre of the horse's back as opposed to perching on his quarters, and were, in turn, followed by the Persians. But it was a Greek cavalry officer, Xenophon, who provided the first landmark in classical equitation.

Born in Athens in 430 BC, Xenophon's two books, *Hippike* and *Hipparchikos*, provide a wealth of information on a system of riding that is just as applicable today as it was when it was written, and which formed the base of the classical equestrian art. They cover breaking, buying and schooling young horses and Xenophon trained his horses in most of the movements that we know today. As well as balancing and suppling exercises involving changes of pace and direction, turns and circles, he also taught his horses to jump collectedly off their hocks and enjoyed hunting and cross-country riding when he was able to put his manège work into practice.

Xenophon also studied the horse's mind and believed in a system of reward and correction, for 'if you reward him with kindness when he has done what you wish and admonish him when he disobeys, he will be most likely to do what you want. This holds good in every branch of horsemanship'. He insisted on the patient handling of horses, disapproving strongly of any form of force to get the required results, saying 'riders who force their horses by the use of the whip only increase their fear, for they then associate the pain with the thing that frightens them'. But however advanced Xenophon's thinking, his great disadvantage, as a cavalry officer, was his lack of a saddle. As befitted a Spartan officer, he rode bareback, without even a cover on the horse's back, a fact that no doubt encouraged his liking of a well-muscled back. He rode with a long leg and turned down toe, maintaining that man's naked leg gave a greater degree of adhesion to the horse's sweating coat if the two were in direct contact.

Jousts and tourneys had their heyday in the Middle Ages and were the early forms of carousels which were to come into their own during the Renaissance.

In battle, however, the adhesion was not sufficient to withstand the enemy's charge and it was not until the invention of the saddle, built high at both pommel and cantle, and used initially by a group of Nubian mercenaries from the Nile valley, that the course of mounted warfare was changed. This was because the high cantle provided a base against which the mounted soldier could brace his back when closing with bodies of infantry. With the invention of the stirrup, first used by the Huns of Mongolia in the fourth century AD, the use of the Horse advanced rapidly, although we know little of the use to which they were put in the Dark Ages which followed.

The Middle Ages, however, saw the beginning of Charlemagne's Age of Chivalry, with jousts and tourneys between teams of knights who, initially at least, rode light Arab or Barb-type horses and wore light chain mail. The tourneys were also the beginning of an early form of musical ride or carousel which was to be seen much later. Although they now used stirrups, the knights still rode with a long leg and with their feet pushed forward. They held the reins high in their left hand together with the shield, leaving their right hand free to handle the sword. Curb bits were much in evidence but the principal means of control was by the use of the leg. The influence of the mounted knight, ever skilful in defence but not so good in attack, persisted until 1346 when the disciplined use of the bow and arrow decimated the French troops at Crecy, forcing the knights to take measures to protect both themselves and their horses. The solution was to encase themselves and their mounts in cumbersome armour, which meant in turn that the horses had to be larger and heavier and in consequence they became slower and less mobile. Increasingly, they became virtual sitting targets, until their end came in 1525 with the Battle of Pavia.

The age of the mounted knights did however produce a high degree of school-

Xenophon, the Greek cavalry officer who laid the foundations of classical equitation and whose teachings are just as applicable today.

ing in the horse, albeit imposed by mechanical means. Long curb bits were employed and so were long, sharp spurs in order to control the quarters without necessitating the leg being moved too much. The battles and jousts continued – knights being mounted on heavy, lumbering horses – long after their influence in battle was finished. But while this form of riding was operating in the West, the cavalry of the East was in fact fast and mobile. They favoured a forward seat and rode with a loose rein on Arab-type horses.

Riding was first recognized as an art form in its own right, on an equal footing with the classical arts of music, painting, literature and so on, in the Renaissance

period of 1500–1600. Then no nobleman's education was considered complete until he had acquired an appreciation of the art of equitation and could ride well. Movements, in imitation of those that it was thought were practised in battle by the armoured knights were performed, the pirouette, piaffe and passage forming the basis of the work on the ground, while the levade, courbette and the capriole formed the basics of the airs above the ground. Elegant Baroque riding halls – of which the last remaining one is the Spanish Riding School in Vienna built in 1735 by Fischer von Erlach (although first built of wood in 1572, prior to that the area it covered was laid out as a training ground in 1565) – sprang up all over Europe to house the stately carousels performed by members of the aristocracy. Xenophon and his works were rediscovered and High School riding had begun, although the horses were, initially, rather heavy.

Although Count Cesare Fiaschi's book written in 1559 advocates, like Xenophon, the use of patience when dealing with horses and recommends the use of hands, legs and voice used in combination, in practice it would appear that the required result was achieved by breaking the horse's resistance by any barbaric method that presented itself. Hedgehogs or cats tied to the horse's tail, a hot iron applied in the same place, or an iron bar with sharp hooks on the end to be dug into the quarters, were all used to encourage horses to go forward, and the only reward would appear to have been a relaxation of the punishment currently being inflicted. The natural aids were defined, an addition to the more usual ones being a clicking of the tongue, but considerable emphasis was given to the artificial aids or 'helps', of the bridle, the stirrup – made frequently with a sharp inner edge – the spur and the rod. Stress was laid on not harming the mouth, however, although long severe curb bits were frequently used, as were spiked nosebands.

Fiaschi recommended the use of a mild jointed bit with no curb chain, which acted on the bars of the mouth and had no port. He taught in Naples, his most successful and best-known pupil being Federico Grisone to whom credit is usually given for being the First Master. His book, *Gli Ordini de Cavalcare*, published in 1550 shortly before that of his tutor, and his own popularity, may well be the reason for this claim to fame. Whatever the cause, Grisone's pupils were invited to other parts of Europe where his system of training and riding was propounded and his word spread. His book was translated into English on the instructions of Queen Elizabeth I.

Grisone's successor and the most famous of his pupils was Giovanni Baptista Pignatelli who also taught at the Academy of Naples. He developed Grisone's methods still further and incorporated some circus training and movements into his work. He observed in the methods of the circus performers that although a high degree of obedience and balance was necessary from their horses, physical force achieved by mechanical means and severe bits was not employed to get the desired result. He was not slow to see the advantages in this form of riding and training and gradually, using some of the circus methods, the whole picture of classical riding took on a lighter appearance, and many of the more severe 'aids' were abandoned. Horses of a lighter Spanish build became popular and to cope with the demand for this type of horse studs were set up, the best known being the stud at Lipizza. It was founded with nine stallions and 24 mares in 1580 by the emissary of Archduke Charles, the Freiherr von Khevenhiller, and it established the breed which we now know as the Lipizzaner.

Pignatelli's pupils continued to disseminate the teachings of their master throughout Europe in the early seventeenth century. The Chevalier de St

Lipizzaner stallions in the magnificent hall at the Spanish Riding School of Vienna during one of their performances in the classical art of equitation.

Antoine became the first Master of the Horse to James I, while Pignatelli's most famous pupil, Antoine de Pluvinel, (1555–1602) went to France to teach King Louis XIII. His book *L'Instruction du Roy* was published in 1623.

De Pluvinel carried on the teachings of his Master, all the time trying to fine down the aids so as to make them almost unnoticeable. He was a much more sympathetic teacher both with his horses and his pupils, not believing in the use of a long curb or curb chain and never introducing a bit into a horse's mouth until it was sufficiently schooled to accept it readily. His schooling methods too, were more refined and he used a number of suppling exercises in preparation for the more advanced movements such as passage and changes of leg at every two or three strides. Very rarely did he resort to the persuasions of the whip and spur, the latter being an aid he considered 'a confession of failure'.

De Pluvinel was the first of the Masters to make use of the pillars in the *manège*, teaching his pupils to sit their horses without reins while they performed the High School airs. He was also a very practical horseman, realizing the importance of getting the horse fit before attempting to work him hard and he was constantly concerned that all items of saddlery really fitted properly. He started schooling his young horses by lungeing them from the cavesson. Not until they were performing calmly, was a bridle and saddle introduced and finally a lightweight rider put on top. He used educated and experienced horsemen to teach the horses their elementary schooling and laid great stress on patient handling and gentleness. Work on two tracks and various figure riding on large circles and at various gaits and tempos was introduced,

Above An engraving showing the pillars being used. De Pluvinel was the first of the Masters to make use of the pillars in the *manège*.
Right William Cavendish, Duke of Newcastle. He trained at the School of Naples and was the only English Master.

bringing with it a new and enlightened approach to the schooling of horse and rider.

While de Pluvinel was practising this new approach to riding and schooling in France, William Cavendish, Duke of Newcastle (1592–1676), who had been trained in the School of Naples, had started a riding school in Belgium, later transferring it to Bolsover Castle in England. Although he was a classically educated man, reading easily in Italian, French and Latin, he was a hard taskmaster and believed that horses obeyed their riders' wishes out of fear rather than respect. However he did not often resort to severe punishment, and, like de Pluvinel, made extensive use of the cavesson and lunge rein. Unlike de Pluvinel though, he did not place much faith in the pillars as a means of teaching the horse, believing that their use stopped free forward movement. His

own forte was *manege* work but he expected his horses, as well as his pupils, to be masters of all trades, and indeed two of his most famous pupils, Charles II and Prince Rupert, were principally concerned with racing and cavalry respectively.

Newcastle was one of the first horsemen to realize that horses had memories and to see that this fact could be turned to advantage. He wrote in his book, *A New Method to Dress Horses and Extraordinary Invention and Work them According to Nature* published in 1658, that 'often repetition fortifies the memory'. He realized equally that this memory could also be a disadvantage if the horse was initially taught wrongly. He like to use long spurs so that the rider had to move very little in the saddle and he carried two switches, one in each hand (as is still done in the Spanish Riding School today), in order to tell his horse on which leg to strike off, and he also

used the voice extensively as an aid. The only English Master, Newcastle found great difficulty in persuading the British people that classical equitation was an art form and that there was more to riding than racing and hunting – a fact that the British as a whole have still to appreciate.

As the new enlightened approach to horsemanship spread across Europe, the way became paved for the Frenchman who was to become known as the 'Father of Classical Equitation', Francois Robichon de la Gueriniere (1688–1751). This man's influence changed the course of classical equitation and his teachings are at the base of modern equitation. It was largely as a result of his work that two great streams of

Illustrations from *Ecole de Cavalerie*, written by de la Guérinière and published in 1733. The teachings of de la Gueriniere remain as the basis of modern equitation.

Le Pas.   *Le Trot.*

classical equitation sprang up in Europe, one based on the French Schools of Versailles and Saumur, and the other on the Spanish Riding School of Vienna. His riding school at the Tuileries, which had previously housed the Royal Stables before they were moved to Versailles, was founded by Louis XIV and was managed by de la Guérinière from 1730 onwards. It was soon to become famous all over Europe, mainly through the refinements in his schooling methods and the better stamp of horses (mostly English Thoroughbreds), that were used there. De la Guérinière perfected a system of suppling and gymnastic exercises designed to cultivate and extend the horse's natural movements and paces, and to make it respond willingly to its rider's wishes without any form of physical force or cruelty being inflicted. His book *Ecole de Cavalerie*, published in 1733, describes his methods and these suppling exercises in detail. He invented the shoulder-in and used it extensively as a suppling exercise, also further developing two- and four-track work as well as making extensive use of the lateral movements. During de Pluvinel's time the aids had gradually become more refined and de la Guérinière furthered these refinements in the way the seat and legs were used in combination and in his definition and extensive use of the rein aids. He designed a modern form of saddle in which the high pommel and cantle that had hitherto been used were reduced and knee and thigh rolls were incorporated. It was similar to that still used in the Spanish Riding School today.

Meanwhile, in Versailles, de Nestier who is reported to have exhibited on horseback the *belle assiette* of the time, had become riding master to Louis XV but at the outbreak of the Revolution he, together with the Director of the Great Stables, de Salvert, and the rest of the *écuyers*, was driven into exile. As military supremacy became increasingly important the first cavalry school was set up in Saumur by the Duc de Choiseul, and although it was closed down through lack of funds, another was set up in 1744 at Versailles, with one of Francois de Salvert's pupils,

Lubersac, at its head. Seven years later a 'Military School' was created in Paris which, although it lasted only 37 years, left its influence on French equitation. The first Director was d'Auvergne who was to change the rider's position, making it less formal and stiff, and in fact making military equitation 'less academic, simpler, more natural and bolder, more military indeed and yet no less brilliantly taught and practised'.

The war years did little to further equitation in France but with the return of Louis XVIII, the School of Versailles was re-established for academic equitation under the direction of Viscount Pierre Marie d'Abzac. This man's principal claim to fame, his own talents apart, was his training of Count d'Aure. The National School of Equitation created in 1793 at Versailles changed its name three years later to The School for Mounted Troop Instruction, its

Two engravings Depicting *haute école* as it was at the time of de la Guérinière. *left*: The shoulder in – one of de la Guérinière's important innovations and a splendid exercise for straightening the horse. *right*: The *courbette* – one of the high school airs perfected by the Duke of Newcastle.

function being to train men to be officers in the shortest possible time. It did, however, train Cordier who was later to become the first *ecuyer en chef* of the School of Saumur, when The School for Mounted Troop Instruction was moved there and academic equitation again took over at Versailles. The first of the Carousels for which the School of Saumur is famous was presented under Cordier in 1828. This was just two years before the School of Versailles closed its doors for ever, leaving Saumur to take over and perpetuate the traditions of the French School.

Le Galop désuni du devant à droite.   *Le Galop désuni du derriere à droite.*

One whose ambition was to become *écuyer en chef* at Saumur after the retirement of Cordier's pupil, Novital, was a butcher's son from Versailles, François Baucher, (1796–1873). Although he was never to fulfil this ambition, Baucher founded a school in Le Havre and later another in Rouen, running the two concurrently. At the same time, he wrote his book *Dictionnaire Raisonné d'Equitation* which was published in 1833. Baucher was an obsessive seeker after truth, constantly accepting and rejecting theories until he discovered the right one. His only platform for propounding his theories was the circus ring to which he had been introduced by Franconi. Realizing, however, that the circus was bad for his image, depicting him as an entertainer rather than as a serious teacher and trainer, he persuaded the Duc d'Orléans to let him train a couple of regiments using his own methods. The Duke agreed, but before he could complete this task d'Orléans was killed in a carriage accident, and Baucher's training programme was stopped. He returned to the circus producing ever more outlandish acts and then, fortuitously, met Lt. L'Hotte in Lyon to whom he expounded his pure classical teachings. It was during a rehearsal for one of his circus acts that a chandelier crashed down on him

A herd of Lipizzaners running free. The best known Lipizzaner stud is at Lipizza, and was founded in 1850 by the emissary of Archduke Charles with nine stallions and 24 mares.

leaving him almost crippled and without the full use of his legs. To make up for this deficiency, he invented his own 'slipper equitation', that is, 'hand without leg–leg without hand'. Baucher was undoubtedly a brilliant teacher and a genius, using a systematic training of the horse to destroy resistance. His methods and achievements have left their mark on French equitation, not least by the use of the flying change of leg at every stride which was invented by him and written off by his contemporaries as 'nothing but a cantered amble'.

Baucher's contemporary, who did in fact succeed Novital as *écuyer en chef,* was Antoine Cartier, Viscount D'Aure, born in Toulouse in 1799. He was a strong and gifted horseman but did not possess Baucher's gift for teaching. He opposed resistance in the horse with resistance, thereby, leading his mount mechanically into the required movements. D'Aure dispensed with many of the teachings of the School of Versailles and stopped teaching his pupils on perfectly trained horses. Instead he treated each horse as an individual and left his pupils to find out which particular aids achieved the best results on each particular horse. He also introduced racing and cross-country riding into Saumur and placed greater emphasis on the all-round performance of both horse and rider.

The man who brought both the teachings of Baucher and D'Aure together was Alexis Francois L'Hotte, the 'icy tin soldier' who was an admirer and pupil of

Baucher's until the teacher's death, and later came under D'Aure as a cavalry officer at Saumur. He adopted D'Aure's methods as enthusiastically as he had done Baucher's, but when at the end of his first year he was warned that he would not be promoted unless he disavowed Baucher and his teachings, he refused to do so. Nevertheless, he was promoted and he taught his men and their horses in D'Aure's methods, while teaching his own horses according to Baucher. A brilliant horseman and an efficient officer, his book 'Questions Equestres' was gathered from notes made after each lesson and conversation that he had with both of his teachers, and it expounded his motto of 'calm, forward and straight'. He took over as *écuyer en chef* at Saumur and by combining the teachings of both D'Aure and Baucher, became probably the most complete and versatile horseman not only of his day but of the century. He finally retired to run his own school at Luneville, to which selected horsemen were invited to spectate.

Another versatile, if somewhat unorthodox, horseman who performed in the circus, was James Fillis, an Englishman who lived most of his time in France and who later became *écuyer en chef* at the Cavalry School in Leningrad. He was an all-round horseman who specialized in manège work and taught his pupils without stirrups in order that they might gain a deep, flexible seat. He placed great importance on balance and suppleness as opposed to grip, a point he makes clear in

his book *Breaking and Riding*. Although Fillis practised a number of unorthodox movements for the circus ring, such as the reversed pirouette with the feet crossed, the passage to the rear, and the canter backwards on three legs, he also introduced jumping into his performances for which, unlike his other movements when he used a double bridle, he used a snaffle. The position he adopted was to lean back on the descent from the jump, slip the reins to allow the horse free movement of his head, while keeping his legs in contact with the horse throughout the jump in order to obtain a *bascule*. Fillis was probably the last of the great horsemen to use this position over fences, for Federico Caprilli (1868–1908), a captain at the Italian Cavalry School at Tor di Quinto, evolved the forward seat and established its use in the cavalry school at just about the same time as Fillis died in 1900. The reason for the necessity of the forward seat as Caprilli saw it, was in accordance with the classical principle of keeping the rider above the horse's centre of gravity when going across country at speed, and to do this, his weight must be moved forward. The system of cross-country riding used today is a combination of Caprilli's system and the purely classical method.

During the nineteenth century, there were frequent interchanges between the two Great Schools of Europe; the Comte de Montigny for instance commanded the Spanish Riding School from 1842–1845 before becoming *écuyer* at Saumur. Few

The splendidly elegant Baroque riding hall of the Spanish Riding School. The present School, situated on the corner of Josephsplatz, was officially opened by the Emperor Charles in September 1735 and is the last home of the classical art of equitation.

documents exist concerning the early beginnings of the Spanish Riding School, but the Imperial Court in Vienna, through its associations with the Hapsburg family (one member ruling over Austria and the other over Spain and Naples), had long been concerned with equitation, and horses frequently changed hands between the two sides of the family. Spanish horses were introduced in 1562 to found the Court Stud at Kladrub and three years later an exercise area was built near the Hofburg. This was later replaced by a covered school, which kept out the worst of the weather. Work was not actually started on the present School on the corner of Josephsplatz, until 1726 and the first Chief Instructor after the School's move was Adam von Weyrother. The School was officially opened by the Emperor Charles VI in September 1735 and subsequently a number of festivals, balls and exhibitions were held there in addition to the daily routine of training the horses. Carousels, too, were popular, the most spectacular being that held in November 1814 to which all the Kings of Europe were invited. A brochure, published in 1833, stated that 'The Imperial Royal Court Riding School accepts trainees only by special permission of the Office of the Chief Master of the Horses, and everyday you can ride your own horse there between the hours of 12 and 3 in the afternoon'. After 1894, the School was devoted solely to the training of horse and rider in Haute Ecole but entrance to the School was exclusive being restricted to officers and members of the aristocracy, and fees were high. The French Revolution and the Napoleonic Wars, whilst putting an end to the classical art in most European countries did not have a similar effect on Vienna. Indeed the School continued to adhere strictly to its principles and succeeded in developing the art further during the nineteenth century under the direction of Max Ritter von Weyrother and his subsequent instructors.

The training of horse and rider at the Spanish Riding School, then as now, follows the pattern laid down by de la Guérinière, with an overlay of Field-Marshal Franz Holbein von Holbeinsberg and Chief Rider Johann Meixmer's 'Directives for the Implementation of a Methodical Procedure in the Training of Riders and Horses at the Imperial Spanish Riding School', which was drawn up in 1898. In this, it is made clear that the 'High Art of Riding' comprises three distinct parts. These are the first stage, in which the horse is ridden in 'as natural a position as possible with free forward movement along straight lines'; 'campaign riding' which involves riding the collected horse at all gaits including turns and circles in perfect balance; and riding the horse in a more collected position with the haunches deeply bent and performing all the gaits and jumps which make up the 'Airs'.

With the collapse of the Austro-Hungarian Monarchy in 1918 the Spanish Riding School was taken into State possession and the future of the School seemed in doubt. Due largely to the efforts of the Chief Rider, Moritz Herold, who gave lectures to visiting education societies and had postcards printed of the School's High School airs, which he sold to raise funds for the ailing school, it was saved. In July 1920 the first public performance of the Spanish Riding School was given. Since then the School has given regular public performances throughout the summer, autumn and winter months, attracting visitors from all over the world to see the highly-schooled Lipizzaners performing the classical art of equitation in what is its last home in the world.

The Growth of Western Riding

IN the Iberian peninsula, during the late fifteenth century, there were two distinct styles of horsemanship. In the north, as in Western Europe, men rode *a la brida*, straight-legged, feet rather forward, in the saddle with a high pommel and cantle. The bit was a very severe curb, with a high port and arms as much as 37 cm (15 in) long. The whole was the product of battle-tactics which had long been obsolete – the lance-charge of the heavily armoured knight. In this, he braced himself between stirrups and cantle to take the shock of impact; he needed a severe bit to control his heavyweight horse with his left hand (impeded by a shield), while his right hand was busy with a weapon. Throughout Western Europe and much of North America this style of horsemanship prevailed for centuries after its original purpose had disappeared, a sad reflection on the intelligence and originality of horsey people.

In the south of the peninsula, where Moorish influence was strong, men rode in the style of the steppes and desert, described by a contemporary English author as 'riding short in the Turkey fashion'. They did so because their principal weapons were the bow and the curved scimitar, both used to best effect if the rider stands up in the stirrups. Young horses were initially trained by Arabs and Moors with a bitless device acting on the nose, and only when they answered to this were they fitted with a ring-bit. The bitless bridle was known to them as a *hakma*, to Spaniards as a *jaquima*, and to us as a hackamore. The ring-bit was called *la gineta* after the name of a Moorish tribe, and the Moorish school of horsemanship, to some extent adapted by Spaniards for

light cavalry, was *a la gineta*. The more accomplished Iberian horsemen could ride well 'in both saddles', i.e. *a la brida* and *à la gineta*; but at a time when Spaniards were turning their eyes towards the New World, it seems that most of them rode *a la brida*.

When Columbus first crossed the Atlantic in 1492, he took a number of gentlemen adventurers as his mounted escort. Before embarking on such a doubtful enterprise, these men exchanged their costly chargers on advantageous terms for quadrupeds which were more expendable, but even these, against Amerindians who had never seen horsemen, proved as formidable as tanks would be to an army of the eighteenth century. It is reasonable to suppose that the first horses taken to the mainland – Mexico in 1509 – were of far better quality. For some reason unknown to us, *a la brida* equitation prevailed among the new settlers in North America, but some of those who settled in Brazil and the Argentine rode *a la gineta*, as some of their descendants still do today. There must have been some synthesis between the two schools, however, because 200 years later, Mexican riders were training young horses on the hackamore before fitting them either with a ring-bit or a very severe curb with a high port and long arms known as a spade-bit.

From the horses of the *conquistadores*, descended the mustangs, through animals abandoned by early explorers or through those that strayed from ranches and missions. By the nineteenth century they were roaming in herds over the great plains west of the Mississippi. They proved a good foundation-stock; for Spanish horses, with Arab and Barb blood, had been highly prized by the Crusaders and the knights of mediaeval Europe. Mustangs had hard feet, sound legs, and were extremely tough and self-reliant. On the dry, curly buffalo-grass of the prairies they increased and multiplied, but two or three centuries of sparse grazing and hard conditions, with no selective breeding, impaired them in size and beauty. By the nineteenth century the typical mustang tended to be hammer-headed, ewe-necked, mutton-withered, roach-backed, cow-hocked and tied-in below the knee. These defects were generally ignored by artists, but cruelly displayed in early photographs.

The horse transformed the life-style of the plains Indians. Previously their efforts at cultivation had been desultory and in their efforts as hunters they had always been at a disadvantage in pursuing the animals of the open prairie on foot. Mounted, they could kill buffalo by the thousand. In addition the horse meant wealth and nobility in war; he was currency, status-symbol and bride-price. In a couple of generations the plains tribes, especially the Comanches, became horsemen as complete as Scythians, Mongols and Huns. They virtually lived on horseback, and when a war-leader died, his favourite horses were sacrificed in the belief that they would accompany him to the Happy Hunting Grounds.

Some Indians rode horses stolen, or

even bought, from Mexicans, using the Mexican saddle and an armour of tough bull's hide in imitation of the Spaniard's morion and cuirass. They would pay up to $300 dollars for a good made pony. Most, however, caught and trained wild mustangs. The method was to gallop into a herd, lariat coiled over the arm, and cast it over a likely animal's neck. The rider then vaulted off his own pony and ran after the captive, letting out rope as slowly as possible until the mustang dropped, half-throttled, to the ground. Then the forelegs could be hobbled and a thong tied round the lower jaw. The lariat was loosened, giving the mustang a chance to rise to its feet, buck, rear and plunge; but the hobble and thong soon brought it under control. As the animal quietened down, the Indian advanced, hand over hand along the rope,

Horses were introduced to the Americas by the *conquistadores* who, under Cortes in the 16th century, took Spanish dominion to the New World. From the few horses they took with them grew the enormous bands of mustangs – and a transformation in the life of the Indians. *left*: A *conquistador*, by Frederic Remington. *top*: A buffalo hunt. The native Indian tribes soon learned that they could hunt more effectively with the new mobility their horses gave them, and evolved their own methods of training and riding the mustangs they caught. Most of the tribes did not excel in horsemastership – it was easier to catch and train a new horse than to care for a lame or sick animal. *right*: The formal style of riding of the Spaniards was soon superseded by the Indians' acrobatic performances, as this Remington engraving of a raiding party attacking a wagon train shows.

Not much has changed in the way the wild horses are captured. This one could have been caught a hundred years ago by an Indian using a lariat rather than by this modern cowboy at a round-up in Oregon. Once much in demand, for they made the best cowponies, the mustangs bred in the wild until their numbers were so great that they became a nuisance and now their numbers have to be controlled.

until he could first touch, then stroke the animal's muzzle and eyes. Soon the captive lost its fear, or realized the hoplessness of further resistance; and in two or three hours after capture – according to George Catlin, an eye-witness – could be led or ridden back to camp.

Another method was to control the newly-caught mustang with a thin thong around its muzzle which, when jerked, exerted cruel pressure on the nose. The Indian first talked to the pony, his grunts, deep in the chest, apparently intriguing and soothing the terrified animal. Then he passed his hands and a blanket all over the pony's body, punishing any protest by a jerk of the thong. He rested his weight on the pony's back, then swung a leg over and was mounted in an instant.

In admiring these feats, it is well to remember that it would usually be the laggard of the herd, not the best animal, which was caught, and that the mustang was only about 13 h.h., while the Indian was a strapping young warrior.

Indians rode on the white man's saddle, on home-made imitations of it, on pads fitted with stirrup-leathers or bare back. Usually they rode with an almost straight leg, but in races the boys rode short, crouched over the pony's neck like a modern jockey. Control was by a rawhide thong, half-hitched round the lower jaw. The Spaniards adopted from the Moors,

and the Indians from the Spaniards, the habit of mounting their horses from the off-side.

A trick which, according to Catlin, most young braves could do, was to drop down on the off-side of his mount, at full gallop, his left leg crooked over the horse's back and his right arm through a leather loop braided to the mane, while he shot arrows over the back or under the neck. It sounds more spectacular than lethal, for the shooting could hardly have been accurate except at point-blank range. The rider however was protected by the pony's barrel, and a raiding party might be taken for a wild herd until it got close enough to attack.

In general, Indians were good riders but bad horsemasters, paying not the least attention to lameness or galls so long as an animal could still be ridden. When a pony foundered, it was abandoned or killed and eaten; mustangs were plentiful – another could easily be caught. But of the Indians' mobility there is no doubt. It was based on the *remuda*, each brave on a raid having a number of spare ponies herded by boys, so that as soon as one was tired he could change to another. The disadvantaged pursuing troopers had only one horse apiece.

The only tribe noted for good horsemastership was the Nez Percés. In one of the later Indian wars this tribe, led by its famous Chief Joseph, rode 2,575 km (1,600 miles) to evade converging forces and escape into Canada. The women, children and baggage averaged 34 km (21 miles) a day, the men much more, besides fighting 13 battles and skirmishes. They were finally brought to bay and surrendered almost within sight of the border.

The first American rancher was a Puritan gentleman named John Pynchon who, when Cromwell was Lord Protector, with

his cowboys (as they were already called) drove a herd of fat cattle from his farm at Springfield down to Boston for shipment to the West Indies. Around Springfield, ranching techniques developed on a small scale, and spread to the 'cowpens' in several southern states. The cowboy's favourite tool, or weapon, was the 4·5 m (15 ft) long stock-whip with which he could kill a man, throw a steer or snap the head off a rattlesnake. Hence the expression 'Georgia cracker'.

When their manifest destiny brought Americans to Texas, they found there a different tradition of ranching, developed by the wealthy Charros and their Mexican vaqueros. These people were riding the progeny of Cortes's horses, on saddles which were basically those of the mediaeval knight with the pommel lengthened into a horn for roping. The cattle were lean, wild, leggy Longhorns. As immigrants flooded into the west at the close of the Civil War, it became apparent that the toughest beef would find a buyer if only it could be brought to market. It was discovered, too, that the Longhorn could survive a winter on the prairie and would put on weight as it was moved over the plains in spring and summer.

In 1867, a bold entrepreneur built a complex of stockyards on the railway at Abilene to which cattle could be driven in great herds from Texas and then railed east or west to the consumer. So began the 'cattle kingdom'. It was ended in the 1880s by over-production, a slump in prices, wire, sheep-farming, the farmers themselves and a succession of very hard winters. But on the screen and in fiction it has never ended.

The cowboys of the 1860s, apart from Mexican vaqueros, were nearly all Texans: indeed the two terms were almost synonymous. The ranchers, big and small, grazed their cattle on the open range; the cowboys herded them, rounded them up, branded them and drove them up the Chisholm and other trails to the railhead. Although some of the cowboys must have had experience of eastern cowpens, they copied the methods of the Mexicans and furthermore they adopted the Mexican saddle, bridle, bit, lariat, riding gear and vocabulary of horsemanship.

Since they were sometimes derided for putting a $40 saddle on a $10 horse, it is well to have a close look at both. To begin with, most of their ponies were mustangs, captured wild or bred from captured stock. Despite its small size and common appearance, the mustang was a very good cowpony. It had extraordinary endurance, living just on grass and a handful of oats: it seemed to be resistant to heat, cold, hunger and thirst, and though it was slow and grossly overloaded for its size, it could nevertheless cover amazing distances in a short time. As an example of its ability, one purebred mustang that raced against larger and faster horses from Galveston, Texas, to Rutland, Vermont – a distance of 2,880 km (1,800 miles) – came in two weeks before its nearest rival.

The mustang seemed to inherit, or develop very quickly, the essential quality of 'cow-sense'; like a sheepdog, it just knew what a cow would do next, so that a pony with a rider on its back could establish an extraordinary moral ascendancy over the savage Longhorns, which would kill a man on foot. Finally the mustang, once broken, was nearly always a quiet ride. For an objective witness to this, take my ancestor, J. H. Lefroy who, while surveying Western Canada in the 1840s, rode

nothing but mustangs. He said of them: 'Though scarcely at all broken in, these horses are good-tempered, completely free from vice and much more easily managed than our own.'

No doubt there were buckjumpers and other hot rides among the mustang stock, kept by cowboys who rode well and liked to show off, but these would be viewed with disfavour by the trail-boss who had no wish to see cattle 'spooked' and stampeded by a fiery steed. What was wanted for the long trail to Abilene was a pony which walked or loped slowly alongside the herd, head low, seemingly bored and boring, but essentially undramatic. As an indication of what was required, the cowboy songs, soothing to the cattle, were timed to a pony's slow walk; they could not be sung in time with a gallop or even a trot. On the trail each cowboy had seven such ponies – two for the mornings, two for the afternoons, his best two for night-work, and one to carry him to and from chapel or the saloon on Sundays. Like the Indian's, his mobility was based on the *remuda* system, spare horses being herded along by the outfit's horse-wrangler.

Ponies were broken by crude and cruel methods. A youngster would be 'forefooted' (roped round both forefeet) as he ran round the corral, so that he was brought down with such violence that the stuffing, and sometimes the front teeth, were knocked out of him. While on the ground he was saddled (rolled from side to side to tighten the cinch) and then he was mounted. Or he might be saddled and mounted when tied to a post or held by a strong man with a rope round the lower jaw. Once mounted, he probably started

bucking, and every time he bucked he was hit on the nose with a quirt (a short, stout stick with a braided leather lash). Soon he would stop bucking, at which point he was deemed broken; and so he was, in every sense of the word, unless the bronc-buster was broken first. If a pony did not respond to these methods, he was turned loose as an outlaw, or kept on the ranch to take the 'mickey' out of the first stranger who claimed he could ride. No further training in the modern sense was considered necessary, apart from being taught the specialist tricks of the stockhorse's trade. Why bother? Broncs were cheap and expendable, and so were bronc-busters.

There were more sophisticated methods of breaking practised by professional, itinerant 'horse-tamers'. In general these were based on the tactful application of overwhelming force, so that the horse learned painlessly that resistance was futile. But horse-tamers were expensive, and often resented by cowboys who took pride in their toughness and preferred to do things the 'hard way'. One Texan rancher devised a highly efficient method of teaching unbacked ponies to walk and trot quietly by tying them to the slowly revolving arms of a threshing-machine, the gentle force of which was quite irresistible. This system worked, and produced better horses, quicker than any orthodox bronc-buster, but all the rancher's cowboys, jealous of their image, walked out on him, having

Another scene with a timeless quality about it. In much the same way as sheepdogs can anticipate the actions of the flock, a good cowpony will be a real partner to his rider in herding the cattle.

been ridiculed by other outfits for riding 'machine-broken' horses.

The early Mexican and Texan stock-saddles had a flat seat. So did the McLelland which was a simplified adaptation of the stock-saddle without the roping-horn, used by the U.S. cavalry. But gradually the stock-saddle acquired a sharp slope from front to rear which pushed the rider's seat back against the cantle. The stirrups were slung rather far forward, so that the stockman, like the knight in armour, was braced between stirrups and cantle. Modern horsemen deprecate this, but no-one then realized that for the horse's comfort and best performance, the rider's weight must be directly above the horse's centre of gravity: otherwise he is 'unbalanced'. To modern eyes, the cowboy sat too far back with his feet too far forward, but be that as it may, the early stock-saddle had undeniable advantages for indifferent riders.

'The cowboy an indifferent rider!?' Well, the average cowboy must have been, for no-one is a born horseman, any more than a born electrician, although some have the physical and mental attributes to profit more from teaching and experience than others. He must have been worse than the average cavalry trooper who had six months' riding school training behind him, for it is doubtful if anyone on a ranch had much time to teach a new hand to ride. Experience for the most part, meant riding slowly behind a herd, 16 km (10 miles) a day, 'eating dust' while better horsemen led the way or rode alongside the herd to prevent animals straying. In time most cowboys probably became good riders – or they became farmhands or bar-tenders – but it would have taken time.

An indifferent rider, after a few hours in the saddle, likes to rest his aching back against the cantle and push his feet forward. He feels safer in a deep seat, and from the deep-seated stock-saddle, with 'swells' to hold the thighs in place, it is almost impossible to fall, providing the horse is reasonably well behaved. The insecure rider likes to have something to grab in a crisis, and even the best modern performers will not hesitate to grab the horn if, for instance, a cutting-horse makes

Our Olympia Heavy High Grade Cowboy Saddle.

$31.85

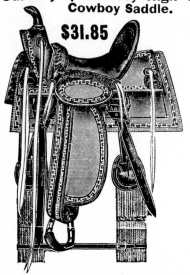

a sharp turn. (It is certainly far better than jerking the reins.) On a long ride in a flat saddle the beginner slides about, giving his horse a sore back; he could not slide about in a stock-saddle. The stock-saddle is criticized for standing too far off the horse's back, modern equestrians liking to sit as close to the horse as possible, but it was

The cowboy's saddle was designed to be comfortable on a long day's ride, to prevent inexperienced riders from causing galls and to make it easier to sit a difficult horse such as the bucking bronco (*top*). His saddle was the cowboy's trademark, and he took particular pride in having the best and most elaborate that he could afford (*left*).

made that way so it would fit (over a folded blanket), horses of almost any size or conformation without galling their back or withers.

Because of its size and weight, the stock-saddle had two cinches, fore and aft, which held it firmly in place. These were made of horsehair or lamp-wick, which would not gall the belly. To take the terriffic strain of roping, Americans improved the Mexican saddle by a fork and horn of tempered steel. But the great and outstanding virtue of the stock-saddle was that it and its rider's weight, were distributed by the skirts over two or three times the rib-area covered by the eastern hunting-saddle. Thus, despite its weight, it was very easy on the horse for long rides. Three examples out of hundreds may be quoted to emphasize this. A constable of the North-West Mounted Police, on a 19 kg (42 lbs) stock-saddle rode from Regina to Wood Mountain Post, 209 km (132 miles) in daylight without changing horses. Most of the cowboys and Mounted Police constables moving between Fort Macleod and Calgary covered this distance, 173 km (108 miles) in a day. Kit Carson and a party of three Mexican gentlemen rode from Los Angeles to San Francisco, 960 km (600 miles), in six days without changing horses. Outlaw gangs such as the Robbers' Roost thought nothing of covering even longer distances, although they had spare horses stationed along their escape-route.

The cowboy seldom galloped, except for fun, or to head back contrary steers or get round a stampeding herd. On long distances he walked, trotted and cantered in turn. His seat at the canter, feet slightly forward, leaning slightly back, was comfortable and relaxed for him, if not entirely so for his horse. Since his stirrups were, to modern eyes, slung too far forward, in order to rise at the trot, he had to balance himself by thrusting his buttocks back against the cantle and raking his body well forward – an ugly seat. Some horses were taught to amble, which was a very comfortable gait for the rider and popular among those of riper years, but a tiring one for the horse. On the rare occasions on which he was compelled to jump – perhaps over a deadfall trap, or up a bank – the roping-horn prevented him leaning forward, since any attempt to do so would drive it into his midriff, or worse! At that time eastern riders also leaned back, and not forward, for a jump, under the impression that they were helping by lightening the horse's forehand.

Generally using a severe curb or spade-bit, the cowboy rode with a loose rein and made no attempt at collection. Any pull on the rein would probably be rewarded by the horse rearing out of sheer pain or giving the rider a bloody nose. Besides, a horse ridden on a loose rein over rough ground, left to pick his own way, is less likely to stumble than one on a tight rein. The evangelist, John Wesley, who rode very long distances, always bought stumblers because he could get them cheap; then he rode with a loose rein, reading the Bible as he went. Within a few weeks they ceased to stumble, and he sold them for a good price – profit and piety combined. An old-time western horsewoman told me that with a loose rein she has ridden across ground crawling with rattlesnakes and her horse, left to himself, kept out of trouble. All western horses were taught to neck-rein.

Although no attempt was made to supple and school a horse in the modern sense, he had of course to be taught his trade – that of remaining calm and steady under a whirling lariat, and bracing himself back against the pull of a roped steer. The star turn of any ranch was the good cutting-horse. As we have seen mustangs were particularly good because of their 'cow-sense', and some were extraordinarily expert. A quote

from a veteran rancher bears witness to this: 'If we were cutting yearlings out of a mixed herd, all I had to do was to show Old Harvey the first one. After we had brought it out, Old Harvey would go back and bring out all the others, one by one'. Down on record is another cutting-horse called Red Bird, who, on his rider's orders, worked a jack-rabbit out of a herd of cattle. A good cutting-horse had only to be shown the wanted animal, and would then do the job himself, even without a bridle.

I cannot discover if the stock-horses of the old west were usually shod. Cavalry horses, being larger, certainly were; Indian ponies, mustangs with iron-hard hooves, were not. I have found occasional references to forges on ranches, but none to mobile forges or anvils travelling with the chuck-wagon. I am inclined to think that the boss's better horses might have been shod to work at home, but on the trail the cowboys rode unshod horses. A list of all the articles a well-equipped rider should carry on a long journey at the end of the last century did not include spare shoes, nails or tools for cold-shoeing.

Of course there were plenty of Western riders who never worked with cattle,

among them the cavalry troopers, Texas Rangers and other law enforcement officers, hunters, trappers, miners, prospectors, homesteaders and livery stable keepers. But all rode, and all in Western style, with Western tack, and were part of the Western tradition. Most famous were the Pony Express riders of the early 1860s. The riders were 'young, skinny, wiry fellows, not over 18, willing to risk death daily'. And on joining they had to swear not to get drunk, use profane language, ill-treat animals or do anything incompatible with being a gentleman. The horses were selected for speed and endurance, and bought at high prices. Although stock-saddles seem to have been used (the lighter McLelland might have been better) everything else was done to cut down weight. The Express averaged at 15 km (9 miles)

Above The famous Pony Express riders had to brave human predators as well as animals and the elements, providing a remarkable postal service before the advent of railways. *Below* America's rodeo sports originated in local competitions held to amuse cowboys and prove their prowess when the day's work was done: steer wrestling is always popular.

respond favourably to the rugged methods of the old-time bronc-buster. Besides, they could no longer be bought for $10 nor be hired for $5 a horse. So more time, patience and skill began to be devoted to training the stock-horse. However, this was not entirely an innovation. Texans taking cattle to the West Coast a century ago were astonished at what could be achieved with time by the Californian hackamore experts. It is claimed that their methods were used by the conquistadores, who learned them from the Moors, and perfected by charros who had been liquidated in Mexican revolutions but survived in California. Patience and gentleness were the keynotes of hackamore training.

The hackamore is a bitless bridle which acts on the nose, not the mouth. It is shaped rather like the frame of an old-fashioned tennis racket; wide and rounded at the end which encircles the horse's nose, and pointed at the end which lies behind the chin-groove. The rear-end is weighted by a heavy rawhide knot which acts as a counterweight to hold the noseband clear of the nose when the reins are loose: as the reins are tightened, pressure is applied to the tender skin above the nostrils. The reins are attached, together, just in front of the knot. What appears in pictures to be a third rein is actually a tie-rope, coiled on the saddle. The horse is stopped by pressure on the nose and steered by neck-reining, with no help from the rider's legs.

After about ten months, the breaking hackamore is replaced by a much lighter model known as a two-rein bosal and a bit. The rider holds all four reins in one hand,

The hackamore is a bitless bridle which acts by putting pressure on the horse's nose. It has always been a popular bit for Western riding; this one is of a different design to that described above but acts in the same way.

an hour over 40 km (25 mile) stages, with two minutes for changing horses. A rider's round-trip of 110–160 km (70–100 miles) was covered twice a week. At every staging-post were the best of oats, stables, bedding and ostlers. It was all very expensive, and eventually it became priced out of business.

With the decline of the cattle kingdom and free range, ranching conditions altered. The long trail was a thing of the past; much of a cowboy's work consisted of riding along great lengths of fence-line looking for, and repairing, breaks. Fewer horses were needed, and it became more convenient to have something faster than a 13·2 h.h. pony. More emphasis began to be placed on pleasure-riding, and casual contests between cowboys for fun and a few dollars, developed into the highly organized rodeo industry, with full-time professionals competing for big money prizes. Later still, the internal combustion engine put many ranch-horses out of business. All this resulted in the gradual phasing-out, or breeding-up, of the mustang by imported Arabs, Morgans, Quarter-horses and Thoroughbreds. The stock-horse improved enormously in size,

A modern Western saddle. The seat is a little less deep, and the rider can now sit more nearly over the horse's centre of gravity.

speed and appearance, though some would still claim that no 'improved' stock-horse can touch the mustang for 'cow-sense' and endurance.

The old stock-saddle was altered by sloping the horn forward, (making it less of a hazard to the rider's masculinity), levelling the seat and bringing back the stirrups so as to make possible a balanced seat over the horse's centre of gravity. (Not all modern saddles have been so improved.) Milder bits than the spade-bit or ring-bit were found to be perfectly suitable for Western horses. Snaffles, Pelhams, the half-breed which is a modified spade, the cutting-bit which is a mild curb with swept-back cheekpieces, even the Weymouth double-bridle all came into use. The ring-bit is now rarely seen north of the Mexican border, but some spade-bit enthusiasts still maintain that what could be an instrument of torture with rough hands, is a perfect instrument for the painless and sensitive control of a horse when used by an expert.

Larger, hot-blooded horses would not

with the bit-reins very loose, so that the horse is still ridden by nose-pressure, applied now by the bosal. After another year the bosal is replaced by an even lighter model, without nose-pressure reins, and the horse is now ridden on the bit. Throughout the horse's career however, the Californian rings the changes between bosal and bit, for if kept too long on either, a horse becomes heavy on the hand or hard-mouthed. Traditionally the Californian uses the spade-bit. The charros, themselves born with silver spoons in their mouths, believed that their horses too preferred silver and gold to steel, and used bits made of these precious metals. Now spade-bits with a copper inlay are used to serve the same purpose.

The spade-bit, with its very high port, acts on the roof as well as on the bars of the mouth, so with a really good rider the horse is kept correctly bent by these two opposing, but very light, pressures. The port is often fitted with copper rollers or 'crickets' conducive to a horse's contentment since he can play with them as he goes along, and is encouraged to hold the bit, without pain, in the correct position. The noise of the cricket is a familiar feature of spade-bit country. The horse is ridden on the very lightest of reins, controlled not so much by the ironmongery in his mouth, as by respect for the reins imparted by his early training on the hackamore. This is proved by the ban, in Western riding-horse competitions, of any form of noseband, even though no reins be attached to it.

Many Westerners believe that the hackamore is a Californian affectation, and that a spade's a spade, an instrument of torture in any hands. Hackamore spade-bit riding certainly remains a specialized form of Western horsemanship, practised chiefly in California. Most Western horses now have a preliminary training – although subject to the idiosyncracies of individual trainers – very much like that of hunters, hacks, show-jumpers, polo-ponies and event-horses. That is to say, they are lunged, long-reined, backed, ridden first in a snaffle and schooled for months to render them obedient, supple and balanced at all paces. Only then are they considered fit for specialized training in roping, cutting, barrel-racing or any other work on the ranch or at the rodeo. The end-product is a far better horse for modern purposes, and one that is pleasanter to ride, than the mustang broken by a bronc-buster in half an hour. But it is not necessarily more efficient for the purposes of a cowboy a century ago, and it is certainly a lot more expensive.

A description of Western horsemanship would be incomplete without mention of the distinctive riding clothes of the west, that are so different from the breeches and narrow boots of flat-saddle riders. Whatever its present purpose (and there may now be an element of fancy-dress involved)

The cowboy's dress and equipment evolved as the most practical and comfortable for the work he had to do, from protective leg chaps to his neckerchief and wide-brimmed hat.

it was developed for practical reasons. The nineteenth-century cowboy wore a wide-brimmed hat with a much flatter crown than the modern Stetson. This sheltered him from sun and rain, protected his head and face when he forced his way – head down – through thorn-scrub, and served as a pillow at night. A large silk or cotton square, knotted loosely round the neck, was sweat-rag, bandage, water-filter, dust-mask and mosquito-net. A flannel shirt, with close-fitting cuffs, was as warm, yet less sweaty and constrictive than a jacket. In winter a sheepskin coat might be necessary. The cowboy's trousers were not skin-tight as seen on 'Glorious Technicolor', but loose, tucked into boots with high heels, which could be dug into the ground to help hold a roped steer and would not slip through the wide wooden stirrup. Leather chaps gave a good grip on the saddle, were used as a groundsheet at

night, and protected the legs against the friction of long distance riding, as well as thorns, kicks, snake-bites and rain. The spurs had huge rowels, more humane than prick-spurs, making a distinctive clink which a horse would recognize as his master came to catch him at night.

The lariat was used for roping cattle, for tying between trees to make a temporary corral, for stringing up horse-thieves and any number of other purposes. It was usually made of rawhide or cotton or, sometimes, plaited horsehair. The last were very expensive, but did not kink and were believed by Mexican vaqueros to have the invaluable property, when laid round the bed roll, of keeping off rattlesnakes. Most cowboys wore a gun as a badge of their profession and to despatch a horse or a cow with a broken leg. Contrary to another great tradition – most were very bad shots; practice ammunition was expensive.

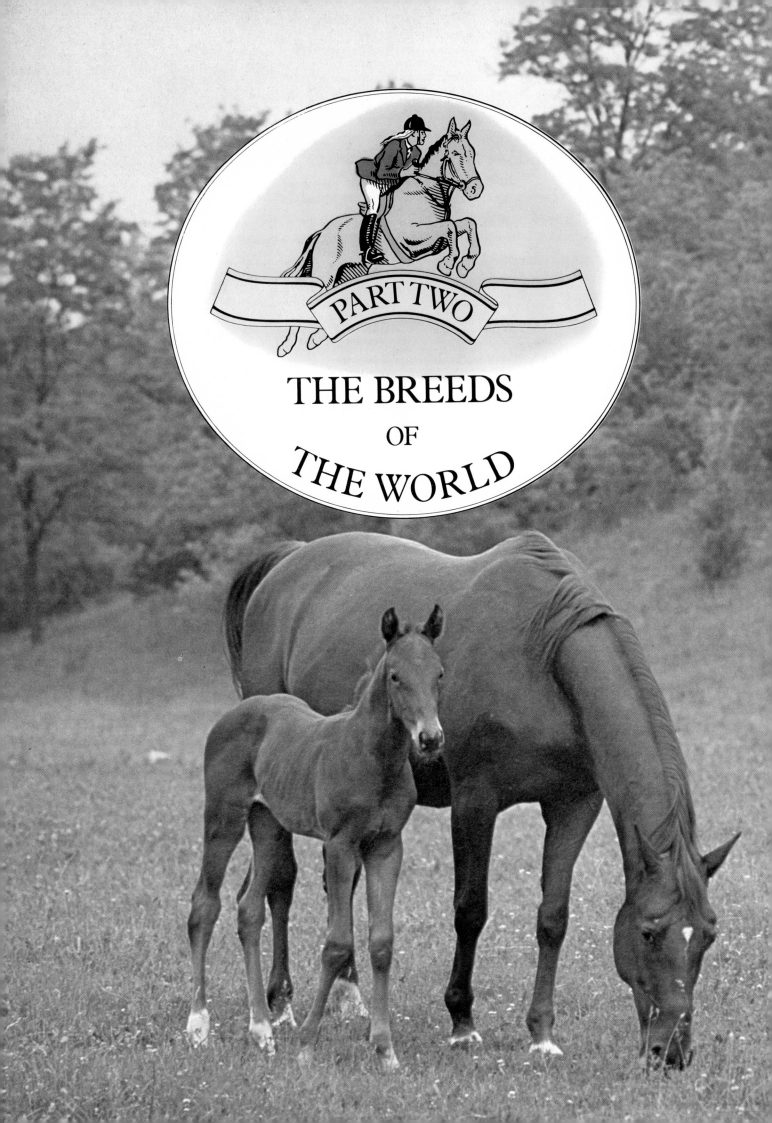

PART TWO

THE BREEDS
OF
THE WORLD

The Influence of the Arabian

THE Arabian horse is the oldest pure breed in the world. In its close association with the people of lands where it was found, it shared and helped to shape their history, as well as the manner of their lives.

The beauty of the Arabian has been the inspiration of artists from time immemorial; his achievements in war, and his endurance in the service of his masters have

oldest blood stock of all. It is a Tap Root, not a derivation from anything else at all. It has the gift, possessed alone by true root stock, of absolute dominance in breeding and unrivalled power of impressing its own character on any other breed with irresistible force. The Arab is the chief and noblest origin of our national racehorse, of the best breeds of North Africa, and of light breeds all over the world.'

In this section a number of the more important breeds that have been influenced significantly by the Arab, or which are derived from Arabian blood, are examined.

In India, for centuries past, the horse has served as a beast of burden; sharing this task with the bullock and the buffalo. The only transport for peasants in the countryside was a wheeled vehicle. Heavy carts were drawn by bullocks, and sometimes water-buffaloes. The small two-wheeled *ekka* (meaning literally 'a vehicle for one',

Bhutia pony, the Spiti and the Kabuli – all hill-ponies of obvious Mongolian origin. In the Western Provinces more refined types existed – the Manipuri, Kathiawari, and Marwari – traditionally said to be descended from a shipload of Arabians wrecked on the west coast.

The earliest recorded date of the coming of the Arabian into India is about 1290. Marco Polo writing of his travels says: 'It is from this Port of Aden that the merchants obtain pure Arabian destriers of which they make such great profit in India, for you must know that they sell in India a good many horses for 100 marks of silver or more'.

Another quote from this traveller, writing in 1292 of his visit to a port in the southern Province of Madras, states, 'It is said at this city the ships touch that come from the West as from Hormuz and from Kis [an island in the Persian Gulf] and from Aden and all Arabia laden with

become legends handed down from generation to generation; warriors and chiefs have been remembered because of the fame of their horses.

Yet perhaps it is unfortunate that it is legendary beauty and speed that have so long been associated with the Arab, rather than the qualities which he has transmitted and which prove his true value as a horse – stamina, hereditary soundness, intelligence and perfect temperament based on his unique love of human companionship.

Fine as these characteristics are, there is, from the breeder's point of view, a still greater value in the Arab. Lady Wentworth sums it up in these words 'The Arab is the

although usually packed with three or four passengers) was the only other means of transport. Later came the *bund-ghari*, a four-seated covered box drawn by two ponies.

The ponies used in these vehicles were of mixed ancestry. In appearance they were small, from 12 to 14 h.h., thin and weedy, with all the attributes of poor feeding and overwork – yet their greatest attribute was their ability to exist and work under conditions which no other breed of horse could have survived. Their generic name was 'Country-bred', a term which needs some explanation.

The only indigenous breeds found in the Northern Provinces of India are the

horses and with other things for sale'. In 1350 Indian history records that the Rajput, Sultan Allah-ud-Din, distributed 500 Arab horses as gifts on his son's marriage. The Moghul rulers who brought with them the Persian tradition of owning horses of beauty as well as size were the first to import Arabian sires with the aim of improving the Indian breeds. The Emperor Akhbar did so and his successors continued his policy for two centuries. Early miniatures and paintings, like that of the Emperor Shah Jehan (1628) riding an Arabian of perfection, portray the type they brought to India.

Arabians of varying quality and origin continued to be imported regularly from

Iran, Iraq and the Persian Gulf until late into the nineteenth century. Several of the Princely States had their own studs although less attention was paid to pedigres than to speed and looks. By gradual infiltration over this vast continent, the Arabian spread its dominance. Thus the Country-bred was evolved and is now the breed most common in India.

All types show Arab characteristics in a refinement of head and silky manes and coats. They are noted for their endurance, sure-footedness on rough going, and ability to exist on a sparse diet. The Country-bred's qualities are said to include 'an uncertain temper'. This is not true of all Country-breds, but when one considers

that they have endured generations of starvation and mis-handling; have lived in conditions that no other breed of horse could survive; have undertaken tasks that robbed them of their vigour, and literally have been expected to 'work till they dropped', it is not altogether surprising that although they serve man, they do not 'trust his hand'.

The Country-bred ranges in appearance and size from the bedraggled little *tutoo*, sometimes no more than 12 h.h. to the agile, compact 14 to 15 h.h. polo pony, racer, carriage-horse, cross-country hunter, and the mounts for the army and police.

In 1902, the British Government, observing a certain deterioration in the

Opposite An Egyptian Arab displaying the typical characteristics of the breed in his neat ears, widely spaced eyes, tapering muzzle, and aristocratic head.
Above Arab mares and foals at the stables of the Emir in Bahrain on the Persian Gulf. Arabs are bred all over the world as well as in their original native desert lands.

Country-bred following the importation of the big Australian Walers and English carriage-horses, established a stud in Ahmednagar, administered by the Army Remount Department. Its aim was to provide the services of good Arabian and Thoroughbred stallions free to breeders and thus improve the Country-bred stock.

This well-run organization is still carried on, and a similar stud has been established in recent years at Saharanpur in the Province of Uttar Pradesh in Northern India.

On the opposite side of the world, in Poland, the Arabian influence is even more pronounced.

As a horse-breeding nation Poland is actually second to none, and in its agricultural environment, the horse has for centuries played an important part in the lives of its people. The Poles have been most successful in breeding horses for specific purposes; for the army, for agriculture, for racing, for work in harness, and, more recently, for hunting and international equestrian events.

These specialized breeds are, in the main, based on Arabian blood, for the importation of Oriental horses has a long history in Poland, and some of the most famous studs in Europe existed in the country before the First World War. The catastrophe of war destroyed the valuable legacy of the years, but the stock, although depleted, was restored gradually through the initiative of Polish breeders. The Second World War again devastated the horse-breeding centres in Poland, but fortunately by this time representatives of Polish-bred stock had been exported, and thus survived in many other countries.

The Wielkopolski is a comparatively new type which is rapidly growing in favour. It is a mixture of Arab, Thoroughbred and Trakehner bloodlines and is a horse with a fine outlook. Standing about 15.2 h.h., it looks like a well-bred hunter and is a most useful and versatile individual of which Poland is justly proud.

Germany (both East and West) has a long tradition of horse-breeding and West Germany today is notable for the advances made in producing high-quality competitive horses. Foremost among these is the Hanoverian that is descended from the German Great Horse of the Middle Ages – the war-horse who carried the heavily armoured knights into battle.

The modern Hanoverian owes its greater refinement to the introduction of English Thoroughbred blood between the

Above Poland is a great breeding nation – and exports Arabs like these on a stud in the American state of Oregon.
Below Lipizzaners may come in other colours, but the white is the colour most favoured. This and the horse's noble bearing both show its part Arab origins.
Below right The Morgan breed was established in one generation, in Massachusetts at the end of the 18th century. Now it is a popular breed, retaining the Arab characteristics it has inherited.
Below far right The Akhal-Teké, like the Arab from which it descends, is a smallish horse of great stamina.

years 1714 and 1837. The Hanoverian king, George I, and his successors took a natural interest in the horses bred in their own country of Hanover and sent over many good Thoroughbreds to improve the

stock there. The English Thoroughbred of this period was the close descendant of the foundation Arabian sires – the Darley Arabian, the Godolphin Arabian and the Byerley Turk.

The Hanoverian Stud Book says that 'the object of the breeders is to produce strong half-breds of high quality, the lighter specimens of which will make sturdy riding horses; and the heavy ones fairly strong coach horses'. This aim has been achieved in all respects. The State Stud at Celle, founded in 1735, is still the official centre of this breed.

Almost as popular is the Trakehner, or East Prussian horse, one of the most successful of the European breeds in every sphere of activity. It descends from a cross based on the Smudish horses of Lithuania, and infusions of Arab and Thoroughbred blood. The Smudish horse was a breed of ancient origin held in esteem in the Baltic States, varying in height from 13 to 15 h.h.

The Trakehnen Stud in East Prussia was founded by William I of Prussia in 1732. He gave the land and the foundation stock to the Imperial Government, and supplied the Stud with high-class Arabian stallions imported from Poland, and from his own Royal Stud at Wurtemburg. Thoroughbred sires were introduced at a later date, and the increase in height combined with quality and good conformation, widened the scope of the uses to which these horses could be put, thus adding greatly to their popularity. The Trakehnen Stud still stands as the centre of the famous breed which it originated.

One of the best-known horses in the world and almost as romantic as the Arabian is the Lipizzaner. The noble white stallions are world famous for their displays at the Spanish Riding School in Vienna, Austria, but Lipizzaners are also

bred elsewhere in Europe, notably in Yugoslavia, Czechoslovakia and Hungary. The breed originally came from the Lipizza Stud, near Trieste, founded in 1580 by the Archduke Charles, son of the Emperor Ferdinand I. The breed, besides being used for riding, makes excellent harness horses and is much in demand for ceremonial occasions. The original stock was founded on a mixture of strains – notably the Austrian Kladruber, Spanish Jennet, and Arabian, and the type was fixed by careful breeding, in studs specifically devoted to the preservation and improvement of the breed. Count Esterhazy had such a stud at Tata and it contained stock from the Imperial Stud at Weil, as well as Arab Shagya stock from Babolna, in Hungary.

The Lipizzaner is a very handsome horse of compact build, standing not above 15 h.h. He does not have the long, elegant neck of the Arabian, but compensates with splendid legs and good bone. The head is small and convex in outline, with large, well-set eyes. Bays and browns are found among them and take their part in the dressage groups, but the white is most favoured as being typical of the breed and is perhaps the best indication of the Arabian blood in their ancestry. If any further proof were needed of its legacy of Arabian ancestry, it would surely be the mobility of carriage, combined with its intelligent responses to the most exact training.

The Hungarian Shagyas, instrumental in the development of the Lipizzaner, are bred at the Hungarian State Stud at Babolna. Their ancestry goes back to the ancient black breeds of Hungary and Transylvania, which were renowned for their speed, courage and endurance and had their origins in the small-headed Tarpan.

In the aftermath of Turkish invasions, from about 1526 to 1720, horses of Oriental blood entered the country, and from then on the horse-breeding industry became a serious concern of the State. The Government Military Stud of Mezöhegyes was established in 1784 and that of Babolna in 1789, the latter becoming the centre for the breeding of Arabians.

The Shagya takes its name from an 'original full-blood Arabian' purchased in 1836 from a Bedouin tribe. The descendants of this horse, bred to carefully selected mares, have founded an 'Arabian race' of part-breds. They are part-breds who, for a century or more, have been mated with pure, or part-bred, Arabians but whose pedigrees also indicate Hungarian, Transylvanian and Spanish blood.

The Shagya is an attractive horse, standing about 15 h.h., and of marked Arab type, mostly grey in colour. They are very hardy and are beautiful movers, proved equally good in harness or under saddle. They are used widely in Hungary and exported all over the world.

The USSR, as might be imagined from the vast extent of the territories involved, has the greatest number of horse and pony breeds in the world – most of them owing something, in some instances a very great deal, to the Arabian horse.

Two very notable Russian breeds are the golden Akhal-Teké, a saddle horse of great endurance, and the Orlov Trotter.

The Akhal-Teké derives from the crossing of Arab and Turkoman, or other Central Asian breeds. It has a refined head and neck and a short, level back. Rather lacking in depth but with good bone and action, it stands 14.2 to 15 h.h., and makes an ideal small hack. Its steady trot and kind temperament also made the Akhal-Teké very popular in Russia as a harness horse. The type is fixed and is now classed as a special breed, with its own stud book.

Trotting is a very popular sport in Russia, far more so than conventional racing, and the Orlov was developed specifically for this purpose. The breed was founded in 1775 by Count Alexis Orlov-Tchestmensky, using the pure-bred Arab Smetanka. Mated with a Danish cartmare, Smetanka sired the stallion Polkan, who in 1784 sired Barss, whose dam was a strongly-built Dutch mare.

All the Orlov Trotters are descended from the three sons of Barss; Lubeznoy, Dobroy, and Lebed. The dam of Lubeznoy was by an Arab out of a Mecklenburg mare; Dobroy's dam was a Thoroughbred English mare, and that of Lebed was by Felkerzamchik out of a Mecklenburg mare. Felkerzamchik was by Smetanka out of a Thoroughbred English mare.

The Orlov Trotter is a big horse, standing about 17 h.h., but it shows evidence of Arab blood in its small well-shaped head and the predominance of greys.

American horse-culture, by comparison with the rest of the world, is young, but in an incredibly short space of time it has produced a remarkable variety of breeds. America, too, has the distinction of having the largest population of pure-bred Arabians.

One of the several families of horses bred in America of which they are justly proud is the Morgan. The breed takes its name from a little bay stallion 'Justin Morgan' bred in Vermont in 1793. His blood has never been positively known, though it is believed that Arab and Thoroughbred predominated. Perhaps the most convincing proof of this is the fact that this little horse stamped his progeny from generation to generation with a uniformity of type that only pure breeding could have achieved.

The Morgans were the first trotting breed in America, but in the course of time have become the most popular all-purpose horse. They are hardy, good-tempered and attractive in type and colour. Bays still predominate, although brown and chestnut are not uncommon.

Another famous breed of trotters that has superseded the Morgan in this sphere of racing is the Standardbred. Bred entirely for speed and stamina, it is a bigger horse than the Morgan, standing 15 to 15.2 hands. It is a very specialized breed and owes its origin to an obscure horse foaled in 1849 at the village of Sugar Loaf in Orange County, New York. His pedigree, however, was not obscure, he had three crosses of the English Thoroughbred Messenger (whose sire was the famous Mambrino) in his immediate pedigree as well as the imported Norfolk trotter, Bellfounder, believed to carry the blood of the Darley Arabian. He was bought as a foal by William M. Rysdyke, and named Hambletonian. Hambletonian's fame grew with the phenomenal success of his progeny on the race-track, and succeeding generations added to his fame.

In South America, the Arab's inference may be seen in the Criollo, or Argentine Cow-pony – a breed believed to be the descendants of the Arab and Barb strains brought to South America by the Spanish invaders. Criollos are noted for their hardiness and calm temperaments, and their

A new generation carrying Arab blood. *top left*: A standardbred, one of the popular American breeds. *bottom left*: A Welsh Mountain pony, one of the most attractive of the British pony breeds. *top right*: Twin foals, an unusual achievement for their Arab dam.

dun colouring, matching the sandy wastes of their natural environment, is characteristic of the breed.

Britain can justly claim to have the most beautiful 'native' ponies in the world, deriving from original wild stock that were localized on the moors, hills and forests. These native ponies were to the peasants, the farmers and the ordinary citizens a means of transport and travel, while they were a beast of burden and an indispensible aid in agriculture. With the passage of time and the importation of heavy horses of various breeds, however, there must have been a certain amount of neglect of the small pony, in favour of the larger animal of more practical use in war or the pursuits of horsemanship. The ever-increasing 'enclosure' of land also had its effect on the numbers and conditions under which the pony herds existed.

In 1540, a dramatic and what might have been catastrophic change occurred in the history and fortunes of the pony breeds. The ponderous King Henry VIII decreed the elimination of all stock under 14 h.h., as one of his rules for the improvement of horse-breeding. 'Forasmuch as the breed

of good and strong horses is a great help and defence to the realm' was his motive, but the implementation of such an order could not have been carried out without co-operation between verderers and private owners, which was hardly likely to come about. The immediate consequence was the elimination of large numbers of the weedy, unfit and under-sized.

There was too, an unforeseen and favourable consequence. Breeders now had no alternative but to introduce and foster height in their ponies and the surest way to do this was to introduce an out-cross. There were many small Thoroughbreds and Arabian stallions in Britain by this time, few of them over 14 h.h. when racing was growing in popularity. There are records of outside stallions being introduced to pony-herds, but of their breeding the records are obscure.

In 1756, a Dorsetshire farmer bought a Thoroughbred named Marske at an auction and kept him in the New Forest district where he served the mares for four years. He had been previously owned by H.R.H. the Duke of Cumberland, in whose ownership, he had sired a colt who made racing history – the famous Eclipse. Another Arab to have influence on the New Forest breed was the Arab stallion Zoreb, lent by Queen Victoria in 1852. He ran with the New Forest mares for eight years. In 1885, the Queen lent two more Arabian stallions to the Forest.

The New Forest pony is now a fixed type and has its own stud book. An ideal riding pony of good proportions and a very easy action, it stands about 14 h.h. Its surefootedness and calm temperament make it equally useful in harness.

Possibly the most attractive of the pony breeds in Britain, the Welsh Mountain Pony, is unmistakably of Arab lineage. It stands no more than 12 h.h., is compact with good flat bone and has no hint of coarseness. The head in particular shows the Arabian characteristics of large eyes, wide forehead, and concave outline tapering to a fine muzzle.

Its alert and friendly temperament, and stamina, are attributes which the Welsh Mountain Pony shares with the Arab. Its action is showy and gay, and with its long neck and well-set head it makes an ideal child's riding-pony, in which role it has been very successful in the show-ring.

The introduction of Arab blood to this breed was officially recorded in 1838. Con-

temporary records continued to report the presence of Arab stallions running with privately-owned pony herds in the Welsh hills, and it was from such a herd that the little mare Moonlight emerged. Her son Dyoll Starlight, and his son Greylight, founded a dynasty which has earned distinction all over the world as the perfect type of small pony. Volume I of the Welsh Stud Book lays down the following standard required of the breed:

'The Welsh Mountain Pony in its purest state is under 12 hands, and can best be described by stating that it is an Arab in miniature, and any judge of horses upon seeing these ponies must at once perceive the great similarity they bear to the Arab. The pony has the perfect Arab type of head, and also setting on of tail the instant it moves.'

Another uniquely British product is the Hackney Horse, which is related to the American Standardbred. Both have a common ancestor in the Norfolk Trotter, a breed evolved in about 1729, combining the blood of an Arabian stallion and a Yorkshire Hackney, and in fact the majority of Hackney sires trace back to the Darley Arabian. The Hackney's action is a spectacular high-stepping trot in perfect rhythm and its well-proportioned head and high-set tail are always carried with an air of distinction and alertness. Although a comparatively big horse of about 15 h.h. its size never detracts from the overall picture of perfect control and rhythmic action.

One of the most valued breeds influenced by the introduction of Arab blood, and second only to the Thoroughbred in distinction is the Anglo-Arab. As its name implies, it stems from the two purest sources, the Arabian and the Thoroughbred. In Britain, the Arab Horse Society is responsible for the Stud Register, and defines the breed as follows: 'Anglo-Arabs are the cross from a Thoroughbred stallion and Arab mare or vice-versa, with their subsequent re-crossing: that is to say they have no strains of blood other than Thoroughbred and Arab in their pedigrees.'

Perhaps the most noteworthy contributions of its Arabian progenitor are stamina and good temperament, which makes the Anglo-Arab a most versatile horse. It is supremely good as a hack and as a dressage horse, and is most successful across country and in Three-Day Events.

France was a pioneer in the development of this breed and in appreciation of its value and capabilities. As testimony to this there are 26 Anglo-Arab studs in France from which stallions are leased to country districts. Notable among them are Pau, Aurillac and Pompadour all of which have bred some famous horses, and in fact the Anglo-Arab stock from these studs are the best in the world. Anglo-Arabs are now bred in every country that promotes horsemanship.

Finally, in the Thoroughbred horse, the world's most esteemed breed, the value of Arabian blood is demonstrated at its highest. Lady Wentworth writes in *Horses of Britain*: 'The English Thoroughbred,

though foreign by blood, is called 'English' because of the long time it has been bred and developed in England, and 'Thoroughbred' because it originated from the Arabic 'Kehailan' of which 'Thoroughbred' is the literal translation, and which is the generic term for the Arabian breed, meaning pure-bred all through'.

How did this horse 'foreign by blood' and of Eastern origin achieve its domination of all other breeds – first in Europe and finally throughout the world?

The Arabian, sometimes called Barb or Turk, indicating that it came from the East, was ridden into Europe as long ago as the thirteenth century – the accompaniment as it were, to the movements of men in war, invasion, or the fruits of conquest. Its subsequent use was dictated by the needs of the country to which it was brought, and although stamina and temperament must have placed it in some special category, it is doubtful whether speed or the value of its blood would have been recognized as being of the first importance. Nevertheless, it was the influence of that blood that modified and gave distinction to the indigenous breeds of Europe.

The earliest record of Arabians in Britain being raced in a match is in 1377, although we know nothing of their breeding or their descendants. From time to time contemporary documents mention an 'Eastern' horse being presented to Royalty, or brought into the country, but it is not until the end of the seventeenth century that we have authentic records of the Oriental stock in the country, together with their performance, pedigrees, and value. This marks the beginning of the history of the English Thoroughbred.

The importation of Arabians into England, variously described as Barbs, Turks, or Arabs, was constant throughout the Tudor period. The owners of these horses were men of wealth and influence who, having had the opportunity to travel abroad, had seen the superiority of the Eastern breeds over the heavy coursers and ambling breeds of England.

The speed, elegance, and quality of the imported Eastern sires encouraged the sport of racing, and the fame of individual horses, both as progenitors and as race-winners, began to be recorded. There is no exact information of the breeding of the mares put to these foundation sires. There are records of imported 'Oriental' mares,

Thoroughbreds at a stud in Germany. The first Thoroughbreds came from England, but as their fame spread they began to be bred all over the world.

and 'the Royal Mares', who were presumably the finest of the collection of Arabians bred, purchased, or presented to Royalty, but whatever their origin, the quality of their progeny was the best proof of their high breeding.

Queen Elizabeth I had a racing establishment at Greenwich, where it is recorded that she kept 40 Oriental horses. Her successors carried on the tradition of Royal studs for the breeding of racehorses, and under the Stuarts many more studs belonging to private individuals were founded for the breeding of 'fine horses' sired by Arabians.

The evolution of the English Thoroughbred must in its early stages have been an experiment. As the interest in racing grew, the demand for ever-increasing speed, and for a bigger horse with greater scope grew with it. It was discovered that the fastest horses were not the pure Arabians but the larger individuals resulting from the English-bred Arabians and home-bred mares of Oriental descent.

By the end of the eighteenth century the identity of the Thoroughbred had been established. The first studbook was published in 1791 by Mr James Weatherby and in it were entered the pedigree and stud records of those sires and dams who were the foundation of the breed.

The greatest contribution stemmed from three imported Arabian sires:
The Byerley Turk (about 1684–90)
The Darley Arabian (1700)
The Godolphin Arabian (1730)

All Thoroughbreds in the world today trace their ancestry in direct male line through about 30 generations to these three sires – imported into England between 250 and 300 years ago.

There are other Arabians whose names are remembered as landmarks in the breeding and perfection of the Thoroughbred. For example, The Helmsley Turk, the Lister Turk; the Leedes Arabian, the Alcock Arabian (from which every grey Thoroughbred in the world is descended); the Darcy White Turk, and the Darcy Yellow Turk. All have contributed to the making of a horse, predominantly bred for speed, of perfect conformation and noble quality – the English Thoroughbred.

▲ Cleveland Bay

Clydesdale ▼

Principal Horse Breeds

EUROPE

Great Britain

The Cleveland Bay

One of the oldest English breeds, the Cleveland Bay was used as a pack horse in the seventeenth and eighteenth centuries when it was known as the Chapman Horse. It originated in the Cleveland district of north-east Yorkshire and has been relatively free from outside influence, although some Thoroughbred blood was introduced around the end of the eighteenth century. It is a handsome horse with a large, convex head, a longish neck, good shoulders, deep girth and strong, though fairly long, back. The quarters are strong and the legs short with good bone and feet. Bay coloured, it stands at 16 to 16·2 h.h. and can be ridden, driven or used for light draught work. Notable characteristics are its intelligence, sensible temperament, strength, stamina and longevity. It is a natural jumper and when crossed with the Thoroughbred will produce a really top-class hunter, a show-jumper or a carriage horse.

The Clydesdale

The Clydesdale is a heavy horse originating in the Clyde Valley, Lanarkshire, where the local mares were crossed with heavier Flemish stallions, first imported at the beginning of the eighteenth century. The considerable demand for a strong draught horse suitable for farm work and for transporting coal from the Scottish mines meant the breed quickly flourished. It is less massive than the Shire, averaging 16·2 h.h., and the commonest colours are bay and brown, though grey and black also occur. There is usually a lot of white on the face and legs, which carry profuse feather, and sometimes on the body. Great emphasis has been given to breeding horses with sound legs and feet and, for such a big animal, the Clydesdale is extremely active. It has a kindly disposition and, like the Shire, has been exported to many countries requiring good draught horses.

The Cob

The Cob is a 'stuffy', short-legged type of horse, standing up to 15·2 h.h., with a small head set on an elegantly arched neck, a short, deep body and ample quarters. He should give a comfortable ride and have an infinitely placid, obedient temperament. A good Cob makes a wonderful ride for elderly or nervous riders and, as a hunter, what he lacks in speed he will make up for in handiness and good manners. There is no basic breeding pattern for producing a good cob, and many of the best are the result of chance crosses. As with the Hack and the Hunter, many of the best Cobs may be seen in the show ring. The Cob always used to be shown with docked tail and hogged mane, a fashion which emphasized his stocky appearance. The Docking and Nicking Act, passed in Britain in 1948, made the practice of docking horses' tails illegal. It is, however, still usual to hog a Cob's mane.

The Hack

Just as any horse which follows hounds can be called a Hunter, so any horse used for leisure riding can be called a Hack. As with the Hunter, however, the Hack which approaches nearest to the ideal in type, conformation and manners is that exhibited in the show ring. The show Hack must not exceed 15·3 h.h. and must have impeccable manners, absolute obedience to the rider, smooth and elegant paces and be as near to perfection in conformation as possible: in short, he should be the perfect riding horse, a pleasure both to ride and to behold. In England, it is Thoroughbred horses that usually make the most successful show Hacks.

The Hackney

The Hackney horse is a descendant of the old Norfolk Roadster, a renowned trotting horse developed in the eighteenth century. The best Roadsters were descendants of a horse called Shales, who was a son of the Thoroughbred – Blaze, by Flying Childers, and can thus be traced back to The Darley Arabian. The Hackney, therefore, has both Arab and Thoroughbred blood in its veins, and it is not surprising that it came into demand in the nineteenth century as a producer of good quality military and carriage horses. Today the Hackney is chiefly to be seen being driven in the show ring for which its extravagant, elevated trot and spirited disposition are ideally suited. The neat head, carried high on an arched neck, and the high-set tail, add to the overall impression of vigour and alertness. The usual colours are bay, brown, black and chestnut and the average height a little over 15 h.h.

▲ Cob
▼ Hack

▼ Hackney

▲ Hunter

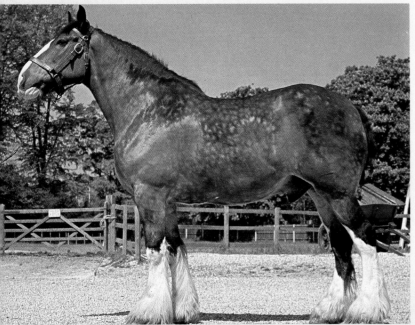

▲ Shire

Suffolk ▼

The Hunter

A Hunter is a horse which is suitable for carrying a person to hounds and the breed or type of horse required will vary according to the type of country and the quarry hunted, as well as the needs and ability of the rider. However, a type of horse has emerged in some countries, notably Great Britain, Ireland and the United States, that may be considered the most suitable for hunting at its best. The English Hunter is a horse of good conformation, often with Thoroughbred blood in its veins, capable of carrying its rider comfortably, safely and expeditiously for several hours over a variety of terrain, at various paces, and over any obstacles that may come its way. In the show ring, horses are judged according to the weight they are best suited to carry and much importance is placed on conformation (the better the conformation the more sound the horse is likely to remain throughout a season's hunting), manners and action. By riding the exhibits himself, the judge can assess their suitability for the job of following hounds. In some countries, the United States for instance, the horses are required to prove their jumping ability in the ring. One of the best types of Hunter produced is the Thoroughbred/Irish Draught cross.

The Shire

One of the largest horses in the world, the Shire originated in the 'Shires' of England and is a descendant of the Old English Black Horse whose ancestors were the 'great horses' of mediaeval times. It stands up to 18 h.h., and may be bay, brown, black or grey in colour. An immensely strong, big-barrelled horse, with long legs carrying much feather, it nevertheless has a fine head in comparison to its overall size. Despite its great size and strength (an average Shire will weigh 1 tonne and is capable of moving a 5-tonne load) it is the gentlest of beasts and is a good worker in agriculture and as an urban draught horse. With the ever increasing mechanization of the twentieth century, the Shire and other heavy breeds, could easily have been allowed to die out, but fortunately there has in recent times been a great revival of interest in these magnificent animals. No show classes are more popular with spectators than those for the 'heavies'. Shires still work the land in some parts of the country and several brewers use them to pull drays in the city streets.

The Suffolk

A heavy draught horse originating in East Anglia at the beginning of the sixteenth century, all modern Suffolks can trace back to one horse, foaled in 1760, and the breed is remarkably pure. The modern Suffolk is a compact horse with a big body set on short, clean legs. Although it stands between 16 and 16·2 h.h. and weighing about 1 tonne, it is a very active horse and is still used on farms in some areas, as well as appearing in the show ring. Without exception, it is chestnut in colour and may be one of seven shades ranging from nearly brown to a pale 'mealy' shade. The breed is noted for its longevity and ability to thrive on meagre rations and is exceptionally gentle.

The Thoroughbred

The racehorse par excellence and one of the most beautiful horses in the world, the Thoroughbred has a fine head set on an elegant neck, good sloping shoulders, deep girth, powerful quarters, and strong legs with plenty of bone. The breed was evolved in England by crossing Eastern stallions with native mares and the English racing enthusiasts of the seventeenth and eighteenth centuries soon succeeded in producing their ultimate objective – the fastest horse in the world. Three stallions are accepted as being the 'founding fathers', namely the Byerley Turk, imported in 1689, the Darley Arabian, imported in 1705, and the Godolphin Arabian, imported in 1728. These three horses established the Herod, Eclipse and Matchem blood lines which are of paramount importance in British Thoroughbred breeding. English horses were soon being exported all over the world and wherever racing is popular the Thoroughbred has become established. Many countries have developed their own stamp of Thoroughbred. In the United States, for instance, there has been much emphasis on speed and precocity, although the country is not entirely lacking in middle-distance stock, witness such great horses as Mill Reef, Allez France and Dahlia, all of whom have raced in Europe. In Europe the accent is more on stamina. Italy, in particular, specializes in producing middle and long-distance horses. With the exception of his own progenitor, the Arab, the Thoroughbred has had more influence on other breeds than any other horse, and has been used to improve horse and pony breeds throughout the world. It is successful in all branches of equestrian sport where courage and stamina are prime requisites. The usual colours are brown, bay and chestnut, though any solid colour is permissible, and the height can vary from as little as 14·2 h.h. to well over 17 h.h. The average is about 16·1 h.h.

Ireland

The Irish Draught
A light draught horse, this breed is of uncertain origin, although it is possible that its forebears were Connemaras bred up in size on the good grasslands of southern Ireland. An Irish Draught horse book was first opened in 1917. The breed suffered serious losses during the First World War, many of the best mares being requisitioned by the army. More recently the export trade in horses to the Continent has caused further depletion in numbers until legislation to curb this trade was passed in the mid-1960s. An excellent farm worker, its chief value, nevertheless, is in producing top-class hunters and show-jumpers when put to Thoroughbred stallions. The height varies between 15 and 17 h.h. and the best examples have excellent shoulders and good sound legs with only a little hair on the fetlocks. The action is free and straight and most are natural jumpers. The usual colours are grey, bay, brown and chestnut.

France

The Ardennais
The Ardennais is a stocky, compact draught horse originating in the Ardennes region where the severe climate of the region produces immensely tough horses of medium height, ideally suited to farm work (see also the Belgian Ardennes). After the second world war, horses were imported from other European countries, including Belgium and the Netherlands, to help build up the depleted French stock. It is a horse of great gentleness and docility and is suitable for all types of draught work. Standing up to 15·3 h.h., it has enormous bones and the usual colours are bay, roan or chestnut.

The Auxois
This is the modern version of the old Burgundian heavy horse which is known to have existed at least as far back as the Middle Ages. Since the nineteenth century infusions of Percheron, Boulonnais and Ardennais blood have been added and the present-day breed, called the Auxois, is a heavier type than the old horse of north-east Burgundy. Like its near relatives it is an extremely hardy, willing worker with the equable temperament typical of this type of draught horse. In appearance the Auxois resembles the Ardennais and the Trait du Nord, being a strong horse with relatively little feather. The average height is 15·2 to 16 h.h. and selective breeding produces predominantly bay or red roan horses.

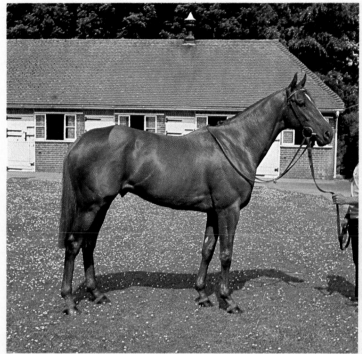

▲ Thoroughbred

▲ Irish Draught

Ardennais ▼

▲ Boulonnais

▲ Breton

French Anglo-Arab ▼

The Boulonnais

The Boulonnais comes from northern France and is a descendant of the ancient north European heavy horse. It is thought to have received infusions of Eastern blood as early as the time of the Roman invasion of Britain, when Numidian cavalry were stationed on the coast of Boulogne. Eastern blood was certainly introduced during the times of the Crusades and the Andalucian also had its effect on the breed which evinces oriental characteristics to this day. It is a heavy draught horse standing 16 to 16·3 h.h., but with great intelligence and activity. Very like the Percheron, it is elegant and well proportioned and it may be grey, bay or chestnut in colour.

The Breton

The original Breton horse is a small draught or carriage horse indigenous to Brittany in north-west France, but by crossing it with various other breeds three distinct types emerged. These are the Draught Breton, containing infusions of Percheron, Ardennais and Boulonnais blood; the Postier, a horse with a good, active trot, containing Norfolk Trotter and Hackney blood; and the Corlay (now rare, if not actually extinct), a lighter type of carriage or riding horse, containing Arab and Thoroughbred blood. The Draught stands up to 16 h.h. and the Postier to about 15 h.h. The usual colours are roan (blue and red), chestnut and bay, with occasional blacks. The Breton is a hirsute individual not unlike the primitive Steppe horse and has been used (notably in North Africa), to upgrade primitive types and produce a useful work horse. It is an active horse of good disposition.

The Charollais Half-Bred

Formerly used as a cavalry horse, the Charollais Half-Bred is now used in equestrian sports, particularly as a hunter. The breed originated by crossing Thoroughbreds and Anglo-Normans, and together with two other very similar types, the Bourbannais and Nivernais half-breds, is known under the collective term Demi-Sang Charollais. The Charollais stands between 15 and 16·2 h.h. and may be of any solid colour. It is a sensible sort of horse, that is renowned for its soundness.

The Comtois

The Comtois is a light draught horse of the Franco-Swiss borderland where it is said to have existed since the sixth century AD. Its environment has made it sure-footed, active and extremely hardy and it is ideally suited to working in hill country. It stands between 14·3 and 15·3 h.h. and is a rather plain horse, with a large head set on a straight neck. It has a long back, and the strong hindquarters of a hill-bred animal.

The French Anglo-Arab

The term Anglo-Arab refers simply to a combination of Arab and Thoroughbred blood and Anglo-Arabs are bred all over the world. In France, however, the breed is of particular importance as a quality riding horse which has achieved much success in the various equestrian sports. Many have reached Olympic level in competition. In the breeding of the French Anglo-Arab the progeny must possess a minimum 25 per cent of Arab blood and the most usual combination is to put a pure-bred Arab stallion to a Thoroughbred or Anglo mare. Many of the stallions used at the French state studs specializing in Anglo-Arab breeding (notably that at Pompadour) are imported from North Africa and Syria. The breed traces back to the second Empire when France began to import large numbers of English Thoroughbreds for racing. The National Stud then had the idea of crossing some of these with their broodmares who possessed much Eastern blood. Selective breeding has taken place ever since and the modern Anglo combines the typically Arabian qualities of soundness and endurance with the scope and, to a lesser extent, the speed of the Thoroughbred. Anglos are not usually as excitable as Thoroughbreds. Their average height is 16 to 16·3 h.h. and the predominant colours are bay, brown and chestnut.

The French Trotter
A world-class harness racehorse, the French Trotter was developed in the nineteenth century by putting Thoroughbred, half-bred and Norfolk Roadster stallions, imported from England, to Norman mares. Two English horses who had particular influence were Young Rattler and The Heir of Linne, both foaled in the first half of the nineteenth century. Ninety per cent of modern French trotters trace back to five descendants of these two prepotent stallions, namely, Conquerant, Lavater, Normand, Phaeton and Fuchsia. More recently American Standardbred blood has been introduced but the French Trotter is a rather bigger, more upstanding horse than the American Standardbred – and necessarily so, for in France ridden trotting races, which have largely died out elsewhere, are still popular. It is a raw-boned type of horse, standing up to 16·2 h.h., with the typically sloping, muscular quarters of the trotting horse. Predominant colours are black, brown, bay and chestnut.

The Limousin Half-Bred
This is one of the many good half-bred horses produced in France which come under the general heading *Cheval de Selle Français* (not to be confused with the Anglo-Norman). Within this heading, horses are divided into regional groups, the Limousin coming under the title *Demi-Sang du Centre*, as does the Charollais. These half-breds are intended to be used as all-round sporting horses and the Limousin is a result of crossing good Limousin mares with Thoroughbred, Arab and Anglo-Arab stallions over a long period. The resultant half-breds, some of which also contain Anglo-Norman blood, somewhat resemble the Anglo-Arab, but show a more definite likeness to their Eastern forebears. The average height is 16 h.h. and the usual colours chestnut and bay.

The Percheron
Originating in the Perche region of France – hence its name – only those horses bred in the Departments of Perche (Sarthe, Eure et Loir, Loir et Cher and Orne) are admitted into the Percheron Stud Book. Horses bred in other regions have their own stud books. It is still possible to discern the modern Percheron's Arab ancestry and it is a more highly-strung horse than the other 'heavies', needing more careful handling to produce the good results of which it is so eminently capable. It is a well proportioned, grey or black heavy horse, standing anything between 15·2 and 17 h.h., which despite its size has both beauty and grace of movement. It has a fine head for a horse of such powerful proportions and combines stamina and endurance with much freedom of movement. It is a popular breed all over the world, including the U.S.A. and Great Britain. The British Percheron has been crossed with the Thoroughbred to produce a heavyweight hunter type.

The Poitevin
The Poitevin derives from horses imported from several countries, including The Netherlands and Denmark, and was originally used for work on the marshlands of the Poitou region, for which its large feet made it extremely suitable. Its chief use today, however, is in the production of mules which are obtained by mating jack asses with the best of the Poitevin mares. The Poitevin itself is a poor equine specimen combining many conformational defects with very limited mental capacity, and in fact, is so limited in scope and intelligence that it makes a poor work horse. Its head is heavy, its neck short and straight, its shoulders straight, its back long and its quarters sloping. Standing between 16·2 and 17 h.h., it is usually dun, although some bays and browns occur.

▲ French Trotter

Percheron ▼

The Selle Français

The term Selle Français (French Saddle Horse) is of very recent origin, dating only from 1965, although the stud book of the Selle Français is a continuation of the Anglo-Norman stud book. The name 'Norman horse' was in use some thousand years ago and referred to a heavy draught animal which subsequently became a war horse. With the demise of the heavily-armoured knight and the advent of the more agile military mount, it returned to being a draught animal. Later, in the seventeenth century, the Norman horse received infusions of German blood as well as some Arab and Barb, producing as a result, a sturdy saddle horse. In the eighteenth and nineteenth centuries, English Thoroughbred and Norfolk Trotter blood was introduced and the Anglo-Norman came into being. More recent infusions of Thoroughbred blood have resulted in a good quality hunter type which is today called the Selle Français. It stands between 15·2 and 16·3 h.h. and is a strong horse of good conformation and temperament, well suited to competitive sports such as show-jumping and eventing. Any colour is permissible but chestnut is predominant.

The Trait du Nord

A horse of fairly recent origin (a stud book was first opened in 1919 after the breed had been fixed at the beginning of this century), the Trait du Nord comes from the same area as the Ardennais and contains Ardennais, Belgian and Dutch blood. A very powerful but gentle draught horse which, like the Ardennais, is exceptionally hardy, it is in fact a bigger, heavier version of that breed. It has a large head set on a huge neck, a strong muscular body and hindquarters and averages about 16 h.h. The usual colours are bay, chestnut and roan.

Germany

The Bavarian Warm Blood

This horse can be traced back beyond the time of the Crusades. It was known, until recently, as the Rottaler since it originated in the Rott Valley of Bavaria, a region noted for horse-raising and as a war horse it was considered the equal of the Friesian. Various British blood was introduced during the eighteenth century, including Cleveland Bay and Thoroughbred, and Norman and Oldenburg horses have also influenced the breed. Today it is a heavyweight riding horse, standing about 16 h.h., chestnut in colour, and with a steady, reliable temperament.

The Beberbeck

This type was bred at the Beberbeck Stud near Kassel from the eighteenth century until 1930, when the stud closed. Arabs and Thoroughbreds were mated with local mares to produce a good quality cavalry horse which was also capable of light draught work. The Beberbeck is still bred today although in reduced numbers, and it resembles a heavier version of the Thoroughbred. Standing about 16 h.h., with predominant colours of chestnut and bay, it is a useful, weight-carrying riding horse of good temperament.

The Hanoverian

The foremost German 'warm-blood' horse, the Hanoverian traces back to the seventeenth century when Spanish, Oriental and Neapolitan stallions were imported into Germany and crossed with local mares. Members of the House of Hanover promoted the breed, and George II of England opened the Landgestüt at Celle in 1735 where 14 black Holstein stallions were installed. For a time infusions of Thoroughbred blood were made in order to imbue the breed with more courage and stamina. The aim was to produce a really good

▲ Selle Français   Trait du Nord ▼

all-rounder suitable for riding, driving and draught work. Since the mid-1940s, the aim has been more towards producing a good competition horse, to which end, Trakehner and more Thoroughbred blood have been used to help upgrade the breed. Today it is in particular demand as a dressage horse and in show-jumping. It is a big, strong, upstanding horse, standing 16 to 17 h.h., of good conformation, tending perhaps towards plainness. Active and bold, it has the courage of the Thoroughbred although not his speed. All solid colours are permissible, the usual being brown, chestnut, bay and black. The horse known as the Westfalisches Pferd or Westphalian is the Hanoverian under another, regional, title.

The Holstein

The Holstein is a somewhat heavier stamp of riding horse than the Hanoverian, and traces back to the fourteenth century war horse. Spanish and Eastern blood made it lighter and in the nineteenth century Yorkshire Coach Horses and English Thoroughbreds were imported to upgrade the breed still further and produce horses suitable for both light harness and saddle work. More Thoroughbred blood has been added since the second world war and the Holstein is today an all-round saddle horse, particularly noted as a show-jumper. It is powerfully built, with strong quarters, good depth of girth and short legs with plenty of bone. The usual colours are black, brown and bay and the average height, 15·3 to 16·2 h.h. It is a good-tempered horse possessed of intelligence and willingness to work.

▲ Hanoverian

Holstein ▼

49

▲ Oldenburg

Rhineland Heavy Draught ▼

The Oldenburg
This is the heaviest of the German 'warm bloods' and it can be traced back to the seventeenth century Oldenburg, when it was based on the Friesian horse. The breed was originally developed as a good strong carriage horse and over the years Spanish, Neapolitan and Barb blood were added, followed at a later stage by Thoroughbred, Cleveland Bay, Norman and Hanoverian. During the twentieth century, when the need for carriage horses dwindled, more Thoroughbred and Norman blood was introduced, resulting in the production of an all-purpose saddle horse. It is very tall, standing between 16·2 and 17·2 h.h., but in spite of its height it is a short-legged horse with good bone. Notable too, for its strong back and depth of girth, it matures early and has a kind, yet bold nature.

The Rhineland Heavy Draught
Originating in the Rhineland – hence its name 'Rhineland' or 'Rhenish' – this horse was bred along the lines of the Belgian horse, and was developed during the nineteenth century when there was a great demand for heavy draught horses. It is very bulky, and powerfully built, standing 16 to 17 h.h., with massive quarters and shoulders, a deep, broad back, crested neck, and short, strong legs. Good-natured, and noted for its early maturity, it may be either red roan with black points or flaxen mane and tail, or chestnut. As with many other heavy draught animals, it is in much less demand nowadays, but it can still be found, albeit in decreasing numbers, in Lower Saxony and Westphalia.

The Schleswig Heavy Draught
Developed in Schleswig-Holstein in the nineteenth century, the breed traces back to Denmark's Jutland horse, to which was added Yorkshire Coach Horse and Thoroughbred blood. Up until the Second World War much use was made of Danish stallions, but more recently Boulonnais and Breton blood has been introduced to iron out the noticeable conformational defects of slab-sides, long back and soft feet. It is a medium sized, compact horse, standing 15·2 to 16 h.h. and, being a willing worker, was formerly much in demand as a tram and bus horse. The predominant colour is chestnut, though bays and greys also occur and it has a very placid disposition.

▼ Hans Winkler on Halla — a Trakehner

▼ Schleswig Heavy Draught

The Trakehner

King Friedrich Wilhelm I founded the Stud of Trakehnen in 1732 and it was here that the East Prussian Horse, known today as the Trakehner, was developed. At the beginning of the nineteenth century, Arab blood was introduced but as time went on, more and more Thoroughbred stallions were used. By 1913 over 80 per cent of the stud's mares were by Thoroughbred stallions. The East Prussian horse made an excellent cavalry remount, as well as being capable of light farm work, and was renowned for its great endurance. At the end of the second world war, when the Germans retreated from Poland, some 1,200 of the 25,000 horses registered in the Trakehner Stud Book reached what is now West Germany after a three-month trek from East Prussia (now part of Poland where its influence is still to be found in the breed known as the Wielkopolski). Today the Trakehner is bred privately in Germany and is a top-class saddle horse, of excellent conformation, having much of the Thoroughbred about it. It stands 16 to 16·2 h.h. and may be of any solid colour. It is a lively but kind horse and possesses the depth of stamina for which its ancestors were noted. It usually makes a good jumper. Halla, the mare ridden to so many victories by Hans Winkler, is a fine representative of the breed.

The Württemberg

The Württemberg horse traces back to the end of the sixteenth century and was developed by putting local mares to Arab stallions from the famous Marbach stallion depot. To produce the sort of horse needed for working the small mountain farms of the Würrtemberg area, East Prussian and Norman blood was later introduced, followed by infusions of Oldenburg and Nonius. A stud book was not opened until 1895, when the required type had eventually been achieved, largely through the influence of the Anglo-Norman stallion named Faust. Recently, still more East Prussian blood has been introduced and the present-day Württemberg is a strong, cobby type standing up to about 16 h.h., suitable for work both in harness and under saddle. A strongly built horse with sound legs and feet, it is a good worker and an economical feeder. The usual colours are black, brown, chestnut and bay.

Hungary

The Furioso

This is a handsome saddle or carriage horse based on two English foundation sires – the Thoroughbred Furioso, foaled in 1836, and the Norfolk Roadster North Star, foaled in 1844 – who were mated with the local mares of Nonius type. Infusions of Thoroughbred blood continued and the result is a horse of sufficient quality to take part in all modern equestrian sports including steeplechasing (half-bred horses are often used for 'chasing in this part of the world where the sport is not as highly developed as elsewhere). A horse of reasonably good conformation, with free, slightly exaggerated action, the average height is 16 h.h. and the usual colours black and brown.

The Gidran Arabian

Siglavy Gidran was imported into Hungary from Arabia in 1816 and founded the strain known as the Gidran Arabian. Like the Shagya, it has the characteristics of the Arab while not being of pure Arab descent. There are now two distinct types of Gidran: the Middle European and the Southern and Eastern European. The first is a horse of more substance than the second, which is more akin in appearance to the Eastern type of Arab. The heavier type is often used in harness while the lighter type is an all-purpose competition horse. The usual colour is chestnut, although bay, grey and black sometimes occur.

▲ Trakehner

▲ Württemberg   Furioso ▼

▲ Murakoz

▲ Nonius

▲ Shagya Arabian

Lipizzaner ▼

The Murakoz

A draught horse, bred in the river Mura region of Hungary (and also in Poland and Yugoslavia), this breed has been developed during this century by crossing native mares with Percheron, Belgian Ardennes and Noriker stallions as well as with home-bred horses. In the 1920s a fifth of all horses in Hungary were Murakoz, but the breed suffered many losses in the Second World War and has not regained its former numbers. It is a fast-moving horse of some quality and is noted as being good tempered, sound and an economical feeder. It is usually chestnut with flaxen mane and tail, but bays, browns, greys and blacks do occur. The average height is 16 h.h. and the horse is a good agricultural worker.

The Nonius

Like the Furioso, of which it is the precursor, the Nonius was developed at the Mezöhegyes Stud in Hungary. The foundation sire is said to be a French stallion called Nonius (foaled in 1810), itself the result of a mating between an English half-bred stallion and a Norman mare. Nonius was captured during the Napoleonic wars and taken to Hungary where he sired 15 outstanding stallions from a variety of mares, including Arabian, Holstein, Lipizzaner and Anglo-Norman. The breed flourished and became very popular and today is a good riding or carriage horse of medium to heavy weight, standing anything from 14·2 to 16 h.h. It is a late developer and is, consequently, a horse of some longevity. The usual colours are black, brown and bay and it is a tough, compact horse, of equable temperament, equally suitable for agricultural work and competitive sports.

The Shagya Arabian

The Shagya Arabian is not, strictly speaking, a 'pure' Arab strain since some of the foundation mares were of dubious descent. The breed takes its name from a Syrian horse, Shagya, who was imported to the Babolna Stud along with several other Arabs in 1836 for restocking purposes, and became a very prepotent sire. Like Shagya, many of the modern horses are grey, and the breed possesses the usual Arabian characteristics and temperament, with an average height of 15 h.h. Although the Shagya is principally an all-purpose riding horse, it is also used in harness.

Austria

The Lipizzaner

This breed is noted for its docility and intelligence and has become world famous for its connection with the Spanish Riding School of Vienna. The modern Lipizzaner traces back to the Spanish Andalucian horses imported into Yugoslavia by the Archduke Charles who founded a stud at Lipizza in 1580. The stud continued to import Spanish horses until the seventeenth century but as the importation of Spanish stock began to dwindle other blood was introduced, notably that of the Arabian stallion, Siglavy. Today Lipizzaners are bred in Austria, at the famous Piber Stud which supplies the Spanish Riding School, and in several East European countries, particularly Yugoslavia and Czechoslovakia. As a breed, they are compact horses, with strong backs and quarters and short, strong legs. They reach an average height of around 15 to 15·2 h.h., and the predominant colour is grey, although some bays and browns occur. Many Lipizzaner foals are born black or brown and take a long time – sometimes up to ten years – to acquire their grey coats. Because they mature slowly, Lipizzaners are often able to work in their twenties and, besides being used for high-school work, they make excellent carriage horses. Its docile temperament makes the Lipizzaner an ideal horse for crossing with other, more highly-strung breeds.

The Noriker

The Noriker, or South German Cold Blood, takes its name from the state of Noricum, which formed part of the Roman Empire and corresponded roughly in outline to modern Austria. The Noriker is probably descended from the tough ponies of the Hafling district of Austria, but owes its present size – 16 to 16·2 h.h. – to later infusions of Neapolitan, Burgundian and Spanish blood. The term Noriker now includes the Pinzgauer, a spotted horse which was formerly designated a separate breed. The present-day Noriker is a sure-footed draught horse of equable temperament, with a broad chest, heavy head set on a short, thick neck, good feet and clean legs. Predominant colours are bay and chestnut and the breed is found throughout South Germany as well as in Austria. It is well suited for work in these mountainous regions and careful selection of stallions – weight pulling, walking and trotting trials must be undergone before a stallion may stand at stud – ensures that the standard of the breed is maintained and improved.

Bulgaria

The Danubian

This breed has been developed this century at the state stud near Pleven, by putting Nonius stallions to Anglo-Arab mares. The result is a good type of half-bred which, although not of outstanding quality, cannot be considered 'common'. Usually black or a dark shade of chestnut, the Danubian is a compact horse standing about 15·2 h.h., with a strong neck, powerful quarters, and a deep body, set on comparatively slender legs. Strong and active, the Danubian is used both as a draught and saddle horse, but its performance in the latter role is improved when crossed with the Thoroughbred.

The East Bulgarian

Based originally on Thoroughbred, Arab and half-bred blood, the East Bulgarian type was fixed in the early twentieth century, since when only Thoroughbred blood has been used for upgrading. Although, in common with many other European warmblood horses, this breed is still expected to work on the land as well as under saddle, it is successful in competitive sports as diverse as dressage and steeplechasing. In appearance it is not unlike a good stamp of Anglo-Arab, with a straight face. Standing up to 16 h.h., it is chestnut or black in colour, with a good, co-operative temperament and active paces. Selective breeding has brought about improvements in the competitive disciplines, although the East Bulgarian cannot compare, when it comes to a trial of speed, with the Thoroughbred.

The Pleven

This breed, of recent origin resulting from the crossing of Russian Anglo-Arabs with local Arab and cross-bred horses, was developed at the state-owned Dimitrov farm near Pleven, from which it takes its name. In the early part of this century Hungarian Arab blood of the Gidran type was added and the breed was deemed fixed in 1938, although since then some carefully selected English Thoroughbred blood has been introduced. Not surprisingly the Pleven has an 'Araby' appearance, although it stands somewhat higher than the average Arabian, at around 15·2 h.h. It is chestnut in colour, and although it has a kindly temperament, it is none the less a bold, spirited ride. As with the East Bulgarian horse, the Pleven may still be expected to serve as a dual-purpose animal and in some areas can be seen doing light agricultural work as well as being ridden. However its natural jumping ability also makes it a good competitive horse and the best horses are used as show jumpers.

▲ Noriker   Pleven ▼

Czechoslovakia

The Kladruber

The Kladruber is a big, upstanding horse similar in appearance to the Andalucian, with the same convex shape to the face, but standing rather higher than its Spanish antecedent. The Emperor Maximilian II founded a stud at Kladruby in Bohemia in 1572, using Spanish foundation stock and the horses bred there became known as Kladrubers. They were used for drawing the imperial carriages. Much inbreeding took place, although infusions of Neapolitan blood were made from time to time and horses were exchanged between the various state studs (all the horses derived, however, from Spanish stock). It was not until the 1920s that the first successful cross was made and this was with a Shagya Arabian. Over the last 50 years or so the Kladruber, which formerly stood at an average height of 18 h.h., has become smaller and correspondingly more active. The average height is now 16·2 to 17 h.h. and although it is still a harness horse, it is also used to produce cross-bred riding horses, whose equable dispositions make them particularly suited to dressage. Only grey and black Kladrubers have been bred since the early nineteenth century and today the old Kladruby Stud produces only greys, the blacks being kept at a nearby, but separate, stud.

▲ Kladruber

▲ Einsiedler

Freiberger ▼

Switzerland

The Einsiedler

Also sometimes known as the Swiss Anglo-Norman this is a dual-purpose horse closely related to the Anglo-Norman. Its name derives from the stud of Kloster Einsiedel. The average height is 15·3 to 16·2 h.h. and it is a versatile horse, of good temperament. Its active and true paces make a good all-round riding and driving horse, and a particularly good cavalry mount. The conformation is usually good, with plenty of depth through the girth, powerful quarters and strong legs. Any solid colour is permissible, the most usual being chestnut and bay.

The Franches-Montagne

This small draught horse originated in the Jura region of Switzerland, when about a century ago Anglo-Norman stallions were imported and crossed with the local mares. There may also have been infusions of English half-bred hunter and Ardennes blood during the early days of the breed. Since then, however, the breed has remained remarkably pure. Being small, active and very sure-footed, it is ideally suited to work on the hill farms and is a very popular agricultural horse. At one time it was also much in demand as a military draught horse. It is a heavily-built cob-type horse with a powerful body set on short, strong legs and the average height is around 15 h.h. It invariably possesses a good temperament and makes a very versatile work horse. Any solid colours are permissible.

The Freiberger

The Freiberger is a saddle horse which has been developed comparatively recently at the Avenches Stud in Switzerland. It is based on the cold-blood Franches-Montagne but has been progressively upgraded by heavy infusions of Shagya Arabian blood from Hungary's Babolna stud, and also some Norman blood, so that today it shows more Arabian characteristics than Franches-Montagne. It is an attractive riding horse standing 15·2 to 16 h.h. with an Arabian-looking head, good shoulders and quarters, short back, deep girth and strong legs with plenty of bone. It is an active, intelligent horse possessed of great stamina.

Poland

The Malapolski
A recently developed breed containing a good deal of oriental blood, the Malapolski is similar to the Wielkopolski, but lighter. It is bred mainly in the south-west of Poland and has similar regional variations to the Wielkopolski. The Malapolski is basically a quality riding horse, averaging 15 h.h., although the Sadecki which may be bigger, is also strong enough to undertake light draught work. An exceptionally sound horse, with great stamina and an equable temperament, any solid colour is permissible.

The Polish Arab
Arabian horses have been bred in Poland since the mid-sixteenth century. During the Turkish wars horses of Eastern origin, including pure-bred Arabs, were captured by the Poles and, later, Polish breeders imported more Eastern stock. Over the years exported Polish Arabs have had a profound effect on other Arab-breeding countries.

The Sokolsky
A powerful light draught horse of north-east Poland, this breed's sound constitution and very economical feeding habits have made it popular as a farm worker. It is now bred in the U.S.S.R. as well as in Poland. It has a rather large head, notably good, sloping shoulder, and a shortish body, carried on short, strong, clean legs. The temperament is calm and patient and it is a hard-working animal. The average height is 15 to 16 h.h. and the predominant colour chestnut.

The Wielkopolski
Wielkopolski is a composite name for what used to be two separate breeds, the Poznan and the Masuren. The Poznan contained Arab, Hanoverian and Thoroughbred blood and the Masuren was based on the Trakehner. Although all the Polish 'warm-bloods' are now known as Wielkopolskis, those bred in certain areas are still regarded as being of specific types. The Wielkopolski is a good quality riding horse standing around 16 h.h., of sound constitution and sensible temperament. It is a notably good mover and can be both ridden and driven. Any solid colour is permissible.

Italy

The Italian Heavy Draught
A medium size draught horse, standing 15 to 16 h.h., the Italian Heavy Draught horse used to be an extremely popular agricultural worker but has, in these days of increasing mechanization, come to be bred more and more for meat. It is an active horse, bred throughout central and northern Italy and has Breton ancestry. It is often a very striking dark liver chestnut with flaxen mane and tail, although other colours (notably roan and chestnut) do occur. The head is fine for so heavy a horse, and is set on a short neck. Other characteristics are a deep chest and girth, a compact body and strong quarters, with feet tending to be boxy.

The Maremmana
A rather common heavy saddle or light draught horse, the Maremmana is indigenous to Italy. Its chief uses are as a mount for the Italian mounted police and for the Italian cattle herdsmen, the *butteri*. It is a hardy horse and an economical feeder, standing about 15·3 h.h., and as a good steady worker it makes a useful farm horse. Any solid colours are permissible.

▲ Wielkopolski

▲ Polish Arab · · · · · · · · · · · · · · · · Italian Heavy Draught ▼

55

▲ Dutch Draught

The Murgese

The modern Murgese horse, which takes its name from the famous horse-breeding region of Murge near Puglia, dates from the 1920s, the old breed having died out 200 years ago. It is a light draught or riding horse in which oriental blood is obviously present, although this cannot be positively identified. The average height is 15 to 16 h.h. and the usual colour, chestnut. When Murgese mares are put to Thoroughbred and Arab stallions they produce a good stamp of riding horse.

The Salerno

A good saddle horse bred in the Maremma and Salerno districts, this breed was formerly the favourite mount of the Italian cavalry. Standing about 16 h.h., it is a sensible horse possessed of intelligence and jumping ability and although there is now less demand for cavalry mounts it still finds favour as an all-round riding horse. It traces back to the Neapolitan and is a horse of good conformation. Any solid colour is permissible.

The Netherlands

The Dutch Draught

This heavy draught horse has been developed since the First World War specifically as a suitable horse for working on both the sand and clay lands of agricultural Holland. Zealand-type mares were chosen and crossed with Brabant stallions and later with Belgian Ardennes. The resultant Dutch Draught is a massively built horse that closely resembles the Brabant. Despite its weight it is an active horse, with a kind disposition, great stamina and quite a turn of foot when required. It stands up to 16·3 h.h. and its colouring is usually chestnut, bay or grey.

The Friesian

The Friesian is one of Europe's oldest breeds, and takes its name from Friesland, where a heavy horse existed as far back as 1000 BC. Throughout the seventeenth century, the Friesian was much sought after as a weight-carrying saddle horse. Then the popularity of trotting races in the nineteenth century, coupled with the Friesian's trotting prowess, led to the production of a lighter, faster horse less suited to the agricultural work hitherto required of it. As a result the breed went into something of a decline. Fortunately a breeding plan was adopted just in time and with the aid of imported Oldenburg stallions the breed was revived. Today it is flourishing. The Friesian is attractive, and sweet natured, and its willingness and active pace make it an ideal all-round working horse. It also finds much favour at horse shows and in circuses. Small in stature, standing around 15 h.h., it is compact and muscular, with a fine head, strong body, short legs with some feather on the heels, and hard feet. The colour is exclusively black, with no white markings.

▲ Friesian

Gelderland ▼

The Gelderland

This popular horse traces back to the last century when a variety of imported stallions, notably Norfolk Roadsters and Arabs, were mated with native mares in the Gelderland province to produce an upstanding carriage horse. Later, East Friesian, Oldenburg and Hackney blood was added and in this century infusions of Anglo-Norman blood have been made. The modern Gelderland is a strong, active sort, standing about 15·2 h.h., usually chestnut or grey in colour, with skewbalds making an occasional appearance. As well as being a first-class carriage horse, with its great presence and eye-catching action, it can also make a useful riding horse. Some Gelderlands also make good jumpers.

The Groningen

Similar in appearance to the Oldenburg from which it derives, the Groningen is now a very rare breed. It was produced by crossing Friesians, East Friesians and Oldenburgs and the result was an attractive carriage horse standing 15·2 to 16 h.h., with great depth of girth and powerful quarters and shoulders set on short, strong legs. An economical feeder, it is a horse of sound constitution and equable temperament. The usual colours are black, dark brown and bay.

Belgium

The Belgian Ardennes

The modern Ardennes horse is thought to be the descendant of the draught horses praised by Julius Caesar in his *De Bello Gallico*. It has in more recent times received infusions of Brabant (Belgian Heavy Draught) blood. Standing up to about 15·3 h.h., it is a compact, heavily-built horse, with a wide, deep chest, a big broad head and a huge barrel carried on short, massively-built legs. There is a pronounced crest to the neck and the legs carry a good deal of feather. Predominant colours are bay, roan and chestnut. It has an exceptionally gentle temperament, and makes a willing draught horse, well suited to hilly country. (See also the French Ardennais.)

The Brabant (Belgian Heavy Draught)

Originally known as the Flanders horse, the Brabant, or Belgian Heavy Draught Horse, is the product of centuries of selective breeding. Today the Brabant stands between 16·1 and 17 h.h. and is usually red roan or chestnut, although greys, duns, bays and browns still occur. It is a handsome, powerful horse, with a short back, deep girth and short legs with a good deal of feather. The head is square and small in proportion to the body. A willing, good-tempered draught horse, with a notably active walk, over the years, the Brabant has had much influence on other European heavy horses.

Norway

The Døle Trotter

The Døle Trotter is a somewhat lighter offshoot of the Døle-Gudbrandsdal pony. It stands about 15 h.h., sometimes a little higher, but retains the pony appearance of the Døle. Trotting stallions have been crossed with Døle mares to develop the active trot characteristic of the pony and the resultant trotter is a tough, active individual that performs well in harness.

Sweden

The North Swedish

An active, medium-sized heavy horse tracing back to the native horse of the region, this breed is closely related to the Døle pony of Norway. It is a powerful horse with a large head, short neck, long, deep body, short, strong legs with plenty of bone and good, lively, long-striding action. Of renowned longevity and kind temperament, it is also exceptionally resistant to equine disease. The latter, coupled with the fact that it is an economical feeder, makes it a popular horse for working on the farmland and in the forests. The usual colours are dun, brown, chestnut and black and the average height 15·1 to 15·3 h.h.

▲ Groningen

▲ Brabant   North Swedish ▼

▲ Swedish Ardennes

Swedish Warm Blood ▼

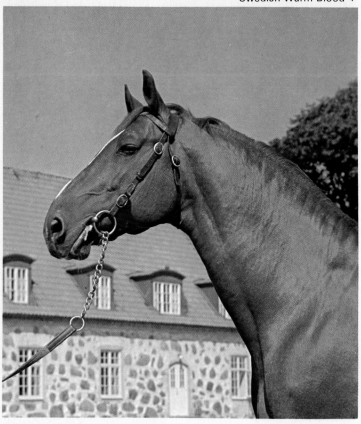

▼ Frederiksborg

The North Swedish Trotter

The trotter is of the same breed, but a lighter version of the North Swedish Horse and is the result of selective breeding within the breed to develop the natural trotting ability. It has a short neck, longish body, the sloping croup characteristic of the trotting horse, short legs with some feather and a thick mane and tail. The stride is long and active and although the breed cannot be compared with the American Standardbred and European trotting horses it is a popular harness racehorse. It stands about 15·1 to 15·3 h.h. and is usually black, brown, chestnut, bay or dun.

The Swedish Ardennes

This heavy draught horse was bred from imported Belgian Ardennes horses crossed with the North Swedish Horse, after the first Belgian Ardennes had been introduced into Sweden about a hundred years ago. A fixed type was quickly developed with the Ardennes becoming the dominating influence. Mechanization has led to a decline in numbers in recent years but the Swedish Ardennes is still a much liked horse both in its country of origin and in those countries which have imported it. The average height is 15·2 to 16 h.h. and the usual colours black, bay, chestnut and brown. It is a good-natured horse, quiet to handle but energetic in its paces, with a crested neck, and a deep and very muscular body, which is set on short, strong legs carrying little feather.

The Swedish Warm Blood

The Swedish Warm Blood is a saddle horse of some quality, and the result of selective breeding going back for some 300 years. In the early years, Spanish, Friesian and oriental blood was imported and more recently infusions of Thoroughbred, Arab, Hanoverian and Trakehner have been made. It is a strong, sound riding horse of good temperament and good conformation with plenty of depth through the girth and short strong legs. It makes a very good competition horse and has a particular aptitude for dressage. Standing about 16·2 h.h. and usually up to a fair amount of weight, all solid colours are permissible.

Denmark

The Frederiksborg

King Frederik II set up the Royal Frederiksborg Stud in 1562, stocking it with Andalucians imported from Spain. Later Neapolitan, Eastern and British blood was added and the Frederiksborg was developed. It became a highly esteemed military charger as well as being considered a good school horse in the days of the great European riding schools. It has also always been used for light harness work and today still fulfils the dual roles of draught and riding horse. King Frederik's stud no longer exists, having closed its doors in 1839, following the injudicious sale of much of its best stock for the purpose of upgrading other breeds. But private breeders have kept the Frederiksborg alive and today it is found all over Denmark. It is a strong, active horse of medium height (around 15·3 h.h.) with particularly powerful shoulders and chest, and good limbs with plenty of bone. The face is often convex in outline, showing it to be a horse of Spanish origin and the predominant colour is chestnut. Its good temperament makes it a very useful working horse.

The Jutland

The Jutland horse takes its name from the island of Jutland and has existed for some thousand years. In the Middle Ages it was used to carry the heavily-armoured knights of the period into battle. The modern breed, greatly influenced by a Suffolk stallion called Oppenheim LXII who was exported

58

from Britain to Denmark in 1860, is a heavy draught horse of massive proportions. It has great depth of chest and girth and short, feathered legs, and averages 15·2 to 16 h.h., but in spite of its enormous strength, the Jutland is a very gentle animal, co-operative and easy to handle when working. It is unfortunately on the decline owing to increased mechanization and a consequent lessening of demand for good draught horses. The predominant colour is chestnut, but roans, bays and blacks are also seen.

The Knabstrup
The Knabstrup traces back to a spotted mare called Flaebehoppen who, in 1808 was put to a Frederiksborg stallion and founded a line of spotted, lighter-built horses. In recent times the accent in breeding has been on coat pattern rather than good conformation and it is doubtful whether the Knabstrup as a breed any longer exists, although there are spotted horses similar to it still in Denmark. Standing at about 15·3 h.h., it was particularly popular as a circus horse.

Finland

The Finnish
The only officially recognized breed of horse in Finland, the Finnish horse is descended from two closely related breeds, the Finnish Draught and the Finnish Universal. These two breeds contain a mixture of many warm and cold-blood types which were imported into Finland and crossed with the country's native ponies. The present-day Finnish horse is a good all-rounder, being used as a draught horse and under saddle and excelling at such diverse occupations as timber hauling and trotting races. Trotting is very popular in Finland and the best trotters are the result of selective breeding. The Finnish horse stands up to 15·2 h.h. and is a strong sort with good bone, usually coloured chestnut, bay, brown and black. Having been bred primarily with performance in mind he is a little lacking in quality but although he lacks in looks he gains in staying power, temperament and constitution.

▲ Finnish   Knabstrup ▼

▲ Andalucian

Alter-Real ▼

Spain

The Andalucian

This famous old breed traces back, at least to the Moorish occupation of Spain, when Barbs from North Africa were introduced to the Iberian peninsula. The horse which resulted from the mingling of the indigenous stock with the invaders' Barbs was to become the foremost horse of Europe and remained so until the eighteenth century. It had a great influence on other European breeds, most notably the Lipizzaner. Cordoba was a very early centre of organized breeding and remains one of the principal centres today along with Seville and Jerez. As far back as the fifteenth century the Carthusian monks of Jerez were devoting their attention, and considerable means, to the breeding of horses with great purity of bloodlines. The Andalucian is a very strong and active horse of enormous presence, and it combines agility and fire with a very docile temperament. Usually white, grey or bay, it has a luxuriant mane and tail and spectacular, high-stepping action. It stands about 15·2 h.h.

The Hispano (Spanish Anglo-Arab)

The Hispano or Spanish Anglo-Arab is the result of putting Spanish Arab mares to English Thoroughbreds. Such matings have produced an attractive saddle horse with more highly pronounced Arabian characteristics than the average Anglo-Arab. It stands about 16 h.h. and is usually bay, chestnut or grey. Its attributes of intelligence, great courage and agility have made it popular as a competition horse in every branch of equestrian sport. It is also used as a mount in the *acoso y derribo* contests in which riders test the fighting bulls by bringing them down with a thrust from a long pole. The horses used in this exercise need to be extremely athletic, for the more spirited bulls will rise and charge their assailants at some speed. Despite being a spirited animal, the Hispano is of a very tractable disposition.

Portugal

The Alter-Real

This horse is based on the Andalucian and is similar to it in appearance. It originated in the mid eighteenth century at the Vila de Portel Stud in Portugal's Alentejo Province, which imported some 300 mares from the Jerez region of Spain. The breed flourished, and was much in demand as an *haute école* horse, until the Napoleonic invasion of 1821 when the stud was sacked by the French and the stock dispersed. In subsequent years the remaining Alters were crossed with a motley collection of horses ranging from Arabs to Hanoverians. It was not until the beginning of the twentieth century that steps were taken to reintroduce Andalucian blood and re-establish the former type. The Alter has survived these vicissitudes and is still today a good saddle horse especially suited to *haute école*, although with its difficult, high-strung temperament it needs careful handling. The action has great elevation and, as a result, lacks extension. It is a compact horse, standing 15 to 16 h.h., usually bay or brown, sometimes grey.

The Lusitano

Very like the Andalucian in appearance, the Lusitano is an old breed of obscure origin but probably containing Andalucian and oriental blood. It is a good looking, compact horse with an alert expression and a wavy mane and tail. The average height is 15 to 16 h.h. and the predominant colour grey. An intelligent, agile horse of great courage, it was formerly in demand as a cavalry horse and is today much prized in the bullring. The Portuguese mounted bullfighters,

known as rejoneadores, require highly schooled, athletic mounts, since the entire fight is carried out on horseback. Unlike the sorry specimens used by picadors in the Spanish bullfight, the rejoneador's horse is a very valuable animal, trained to a high degree in *haute école*.

NORTH AMERICA

U.S.A.

The Albino
Albino is a type of colouring which can occur in horses anywhere in the world, just as it occurs in other creatures. In America, however, Albinos are bred deliberately and are frequently considered a distinct breed, although some people would argue that they are a colour type rather than a breed. Selective breeding has certainly taken place in the States since the beginning of the twentieth century and Albino colouring is regularly achieved. The characteristic pale colouring of the Albino is the result of a congenital lack of pigmentation which produces pink skin, a pure white coat, and very often pale-coloured eyes. While undoubtedly being an eye-catching horse, the Albino is subject to certain disadvantages as a result of its colouring. The skin tends to be sensitive to the sun and the vision is often weak and may even be defective. As a result many horsemen avoid animals of such colouring. The American Albino is said to be descended from one sire called Old King who is thought to have contained Morgan and Arab blood. Apart from their unique colouring, Albinos have no very marked characteristics and may be a variety of sizes and shapes.

The American Quarter Horse
The American Quarter Horse is North America's most popular breed and one which has been exported to countries throughout the world. It was developed by early English colonists in Virginia and the Carolinas and is the result of crossing mares of Spanish descent with imported English stallions. The breed was used as an all-purpose riding and harness horse but was also raced over short distances. The improvized race tracks usually consisted of rough paths cleared out of undergrowth, although the main village street often served as a convenient venue for races. The Quarter Horse took its name from the quarter-mile sprints in which it competed and at which it was so adept. When Thoroughbred racing ousted the Quarter Horse variety, the breed was more and more used as a cow pony and over the years developed a remarkable instinct for herding and cutting out cattle. In recent times however there has been a big revival of interest in Quarter Horse racing over short distances and the future of the breed seems assured. It is an attractive, compact horse of kind disposition and good conformation, with massive, powerful quarters, strong shoulders, and a short, muscular back. The average height is about 15·2 h.h. and any solid colour is permissible, although chestnut is predominant. Its intelligence and great agility make it an exceptionally good mount for working cattle or as a popular all-purpose pleasure horse.

▲ Albino

American Quarter Horse ▼

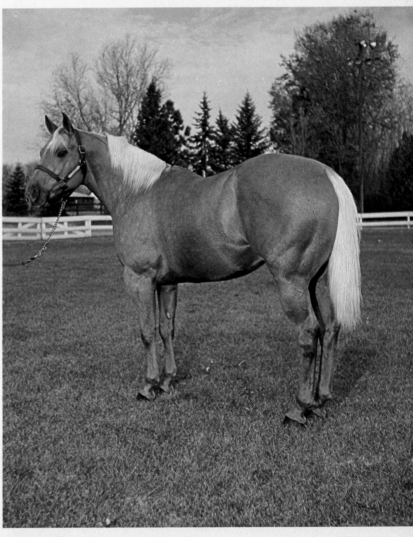

▲ American Saddle Horse

▲ American Standardbred

Appaloosa ▼

The American Saddle Horse

An elegant saddle horse, originally known as the Kentucky Saddler, this breed was developed by the Kentucky plantation owners of the nineteenth century who needed a horse that would carry them comfortably for many hours a day as they went about the task of overseeing their vast plantations. The foundation sire was a Thoroughbred called Denmark, foaled in 1839, and the breed also contains elements of Morgan and old Narragansett Pacer blood. Selective breeding was undertaken to produce a showy horse with easy gaits, an equable temperament and great stamina. Today the American Saddle Horse is bred primarily for the show ring where he can compete in three types of classes: in light harness, as a three-gaited saddler or as a five-gaited saddler. In the light harness class, the paces required are the walk and an animated park trot. In the ridden classes the saddle horse is required either to perform at walk, trot and canter (three-gaited saddler) or at walk, trot, canter, 'slow-gait' and 'rack'. The five-gaited saddler is the aristocrat of the breed and best demonstrates the extravagant, elevated action beloved of its admirers. The 'slow-gait' is a prancing movement in four time, while the 'rack' is its full-speed equivalent. The Saddle Horse has a small, elegant head set on a long, muscular neck, and strong shoulders, back and quarters. The legs are strong and muscular. The showy appearance of the horse is accentuated by the artificially high tail carriage (obtained by nicking the dock muscles and setting the tail in a crupper); and various other means, such as growing the feet long, and fastening weights round the coronet to develop the extravagant action. Predominant colours are bay, brown, chestnut and black and the average height is 15 to 16 h.h.

The American Standardbred

One of the world's finest harness racehorses, the Standardbred originated in America nearly 200 years ago. It traces back to an imported English Thoroughbred, Messenger, who was crossed with the Narragansett pacer, a type of horse deriving from horses of Dutch origin taken to the New World by the early settlers. Messenger, who was a descendant of the Darley Arabian, produced progeny with marked trotting ability and it was one of his descendants, the prepotent Hambletonian, who was responsible for Messenger being designated the breed's foundation sire. Ninety nine per cent of modern Standardbreds trace back to four of Hambletonian's sons – George Wilkes, Dictator, Happy Medium and Electioneer. The term Standardbred derives from the time standard, which was adopted to test the ability of harness racers before admitting them into the American Trotter Register. In the early days the breed received infusions of Morgan and Clay blood (the latter were horses descended from imported Barbs). The modern Standardbred is a courageous and tough horse, sometimes rather plain, with a longish body, great depth of girth and extremely powerful hindquarters. The legs are fairly short and very strong and the action is free and straight. Many Standardbreds both trot and pace (i.e. move the legs in lateral, as opposed to diagonal, pairs) and those which show a natural tendency to pace at an early age are trained in that gait. The Standardbred is bred on a large scale in the United States and Puerto Rico and has had a great influence on trotting strains throughout the world. It is a medium sized horse standing up to around 15·2 to 16 h.h. and the predominant colours are bay, brown, black and chestnut.

The Appaloosa

This breed of saddle horse originated in the Palouse Valley of north-west America and was bred by the Nez Perce Indians who inhabited the valley until 1877. It is descended from horses taken to South America by the Spanish conquistadores during the sixteenth century. The Appaloosa is noted for its spotted coat which may be an all-over spotted pattern, consisting of dark spots on a white background (leopard); light spots on a dark background (snowflake); and spots on the quarters and loins only (spotted blanket). Other variations include marble, frost and white blanket, the latter in fact not being spotted at all, but consisting of white quarters and loins on an otherwise dark coat. The usual ground colour is roan although any colour combination which fits one of the six pattern types mentioned is permissible. The skin of the nose, lips and genitals of the Appaloosa is mottled and there is white sclera round the eyes. The feet are often vertically striped and the mane and tail are sparse. The Appaloosa is one of the most popular horses in America, and today finds much favour as an all-round saddle horse. Because of its remarkable colouring it is much used as a circus and parade horse. It is a compact horse, standing up to about 15·2 h.h., with notably powerful quarters. It is very agile, of exceptionally tractable disposition, and possesses both speed and stamina. It also jumps well.

▲ Missouri Fox Trotter

The Missouri Fox Trotter
The Missouri Fox Trotter is descended from Thoroughbred, Arab and Morgan horses. Selective inbreeding produced a saddle horse with a peculiar broken gait called the 'fox-trot' from which the breed takes its name. The horse walks briskly with its forefeet and trots with its hind feet, and can achieve speeds of up to 16 km/h (10 mph). The gait is a comfortable one and the horse was originally used as an all-purpose mount in the hill country of Missouri and Arkansas. It is a strong, compact horse with an attractive head, short strong back and plenty of depth through the girth. The height can be anything up to 16 h.h. and any colour, including the more exotic ones such as palomino, are permissible. In recent years infusions of American Saddle Horse and Tennessee Walking Horse blood have been added and there are today show classes for this unusual breed.

The Morgan
This strong little horse possesses great physical strength and to this day takes part in the weight-pulling contests which made Justin Morgan, the breed's foundation sire, famous. Justin Morgan was named after his second owner who acquired him towards the end of the eighteenth century. He is thought to be of Thoroughbred and Arab extraction, and it is possible he also had Welsh blood in his veins too. He was a horse of quite incredible endurance, used as a farm horse, in harness and for timber hauling, and although he stood only 14 h.h. he excelled in weight-pulling contests. In spite of his hard working life he became a prepotent sire and although the modern Morgan has more refinement it is still notable for the same qualities that Justin Morgan possessed. Today the Morgan stands up to 15·2 h.h. and makes an ideal all-round pleasure horse. Of good conformation, possessing strong shoulders, short, strong legs, hard feet and an attractive head set on a muscular, crested neck, it is frequently shown both under saddle and in harness. It is an exceptionally active and versatile horse, with boundless stamina and a kindly nature. The usual colours are bay, chestnut, brown and black.

▲ Morgan   Mustang ▼

The Mustang
The Mustang is a scrub-type of horse which is descended from the sixteenth century conquistadores' horses. Some of these either escaped or were turned loose, and subsequently bred and travelled up into North America via Mexico. As these wild herds increased in number they spread through many states and became favourite mounts for the Indian tribes. They were also used by the first settlers to mate with their imported horses to provide the foundation stock of various breeds. Formerly much used as cow ponies, they have now largely been replaced by better quality animals and their numbers have declined in recent years. The breed, however, is protected in some areas and is unlikely to die out entirely. It is a small, inelegant, lightweight horse, standing between 14 and 15 h.h. and possesses an intractable temperament. It is extremely hardy and its years of foraging for itself have made it an economical feeder. All colours are found.

▲ Pinto

Tennessee Walking Horse ▼

The Pinto

Like the Albino, the Pinto is a colour type which in America is selectively bred and is recognized as a distinct breed. It takes its name from the Spanish word meaning 'painted' and is sometimes referred to as the Paint Horse. It is an all-purpose saddle horse of varying size and conformation, distinguished by its coat colouring which is either piebald (broken patches of black and white) or skewbald (broken patches of white and any other colour except black). The terms Overo and Tobiano are used to describe the two different types within the breed: the former is basically a dark coat with white patches while the latter is a white coat with dark patches. The Overo is considered to be the result of the influence of a recessive gene and is found mostly in South America while the dominant Tobiano gene is responsible for the type found in North America. The Pinto was a favourite mount of the Indian tribes, since its broken coat patterns afforded good camouflage. It also finds much popularity with producers of cowboy movies. Today it makes a good all-round riding horse but as with the Albino there is no very definite stamp of Pinto since breeding is aimed primarily at producing the right colouring, rather than a uniform size and type of horse.

The Tennessee Walking Horse

One of America's most popular breeds this horse was developed by the plantation owners of the south to carry them on inspection tours of their land. It was formerly known as the 'Turn-Row' because of its ability to travel between the rows of crops without damaging them. Narragansett Pacer, Arab, Thoroughbred and Morgan blood have all gone into the making of the Tennessee Walking Horse, but its foundation sire is a Standardbred, called Black Allan, foaled in 1886. He evinced a preference for travelling at the peculiar four-beat gait that is half walk and half run and which has become the characteristic feature of the breed. It is an exceptionally comfortable pace for the rider and the Tennessee Walker is actually claimed to be the most comfortable ride in the world. It is a notably good-tempered horse, of good conformation, with particularly powerful shoulders and strong limbs. It stands around 15 to 15·2 h.h. and is usually black, bay or chestnut.

▼ Canadian Cutting Horse

Mexico

The Native Mexican Horse

This wiry saddle horse is much used for ranch work, for which its great agility and toughness make it ideally suited. Like most horses in this part of the world it is descended from Spanish stock and so contains Andalucian and Arab blood. It is also likely that the wild Mustang has played a part in the development of the Mexican Horse. It stands about 15 h.h., may be of any colour, and invariably has good bone and feet. It is sometimes used in the Mexican bullrings where its handiness and courage make it an ideal mount.

Canada

The Canadian Cutting Horse

This is the Canadian equivalent of the American Quarter Horse from which it was developed and which it closely resembles in appearance. It is an intelligent horse with an innate talent for working cattle and its prowess as a cutting horse has led to its being highly developed for competition work. It stands between 15·2 and 16·1 h.h. and may be of almost any colour.

SOUTH AMERICA
Peru

The Peruvian Paso
Also known as the Peruvian Stepping Horse, this breed of Criollo type, descended from the invading Spaniard's horses taken to South America in the sixteenth century. It has been systematically developed for its characteristic gait, in which the forelegs display extravagant action and the hind legs are driven powerfully forward with the quarters lowered. It can best be described as resembling the amble, and is a comfortable pace for the rider. Possessing great stamina, the Paso can achieve and maintain a steady speed of about 18 km/h (11 mph) over the roughest of country. Its height varies between 14 and 15·2 h.h. and the principal colours are bay and chestnut.

Puerto Rico

The Paso Fino
The Paso Fino is a small horse, standing a little under 15 h.h., resembling the Andalucian and undoubtedly descended from the sixteenth century Spanish horses which were taken to South America. It displays the gaits which used to be common in Europe and at which the Andalucian was particularly adept. Selective breeding has perpetuated these paces which are: the paso fino, a collected, highly-elevated, four-time gait; the paso corto, a similar, but uncollected, four-time gait which is used for travelling long distances; and the paso largo, the extended four-beat gait which can achieve speeds of up to 25 km/h (16 mph). These four-time gaits are inherited and do not have to be taught, and all are extremely comfortable for the rider. The Paso Fino is bred in Peru and Colombia as well as in Puerto Rico and is an intelligent little horse of good temperament.

ASIA
Iran

The Darashomi
The Darashomi or Slurazi is a horse of uncertain origin, but its appearance suggests oriental forebears. Bred in southern Iran, it is a spirited riding horse, with Arabian characteristics, standing about 15 h.h. It has a good temperament and is usually grey, chestnut, brown or bay in colour.

The Jaf
Like the Darashomi, the Jaf is an oriental-looking saddle horse. It is bred in Kurdistan and has all the characteristics of the desert horse, being tough, wiry and possessed of great stamina. It is particularly noted for its tough, hard feet. It is a spirited horse but has a gentle disposition. The average height is a little over 15 h.h. and the usual colours are bay, brown, chestnut and grey.

The Tchenarani
The Tchenarani, bred in the north of Iran where it has been known for over 2,000 years, was produced by crossing Plateau stallions with Turkmene mares. This is still the favoured

▲ Peruvian Paso

Peruvian Paso ▼

65

▲ Turkoman

Waler ▼

cross since stock tends to deteriorate if Tchenarani is mated to Tchenarani, and also if Turkmene stallions are mated with Plateau Persian mares. (The different strains of Arab-type horse that have for many centuries been bred on the plateaus of Iran, formerly Persia, are now collectively termed Plateau Persian. Today both the Darashomi and the Jaf come under this blanket heading.) Popular for a long time as a cavalry mount, the Tchenarani is a wiry little saddle horse, standing about 15 h.h., araby in appearance, with the characteristic toughness and stamina of horses of this region. Like the Jaf, it is a spirited horse, but nevertheless has a gentle disposition. All solid colours are permissible.

The Turkoman

The Turkoman is also a descendant of the ancient Turkmene and is bred in northern Iran where it is much prized as a racehorse. It is a slow-maturing horse, excelling particularly in long-distance races. The Turkoman is an oriental-looking horse of some distinction, and possesses great speed and exceptional endurance. It is noted for its fine skin and floating action. The average height is 15·2 h.h. and the predominant colour is bay.

Turkey

The Karacabey

This dual-purpose horse originated at the Karacabey Stud, which had been in existence for many years before coming under the control of the Turkish Government in recent times. The breed was based on local mares who were mated to imported Nonius stallions, and the modern Karacabey still shows its Nonius ancestry. It is a versatile horse, standing around 16 h.h., strong enough to undertake light farm and draught work as well as making a good saddle horse. Noted as being a very good cavalry mount it has a calm temperament and is a willing worker. All solid colours are permissible.

AUSTRALASIA

Australia

The Brumby

The Brumby is a wild horse descended from domestic horses which were turned loose on the ranges during the mid-nineteenth century gold rush. These horses became somewhat inbred and tended to deteriorate in quality. However they thrived numerically and in time became so numerous, they were deemed a pest, at which point organized culling became necessary. Consequently there are fewer Brumbies in existence today, but they are invariably intractable if caught. They vary considerably in appearance and colour and stand anything up to about 15 h.h. The origin of the term Brumby is not known, though it probably derives from an aboriginal word, *baroomby*, meaning wild.

The Waler

This saddle horse is named after its place of origin, New South Wales, which in the early days of settlement was the name given to all newly inhabited areas of Australia. Although in time these areas were divided into separate states with their own names, the overall term 'Waler' was retained. Horses were not indigenous to Australia and the first ones were imported by European settlers in the late eighteenth century. These initially came from South Africa and subse-

quently from Europe, with the English Thoroughbred and the Arab being much in demand by breeders. The Waler is the result of crossing hack mares with Arab, Thoroughbred and Anglo-Arab stallions, and the best specimens have many of the characteristics of the Thoroughbred. The average height is 16 h.h. and all solid colours are permissible. The Waler is a horse of equable disposition, with rather more stamina than the Thoroughbred. It makes a good, general-purpose saddle horse.

U.S.S.R.

The Akhal-Teké

The Akhal-Teké is a strain of the ancient Turkmene or Turkoman horse which traces back over 2,500 years and was much favoured by mounted warriors. It is notable for its outstanding powers of endurance and is an ideal horse in desert conditions. Akhal-Tekés took part in the famous trek from Ashkabad to Moscow in 1935, a distance of over 4,100 km (2,500 miles) which included 360 km (225 miles) of desert. The latter were covered in three days by these extra-ordinary horses travelling totally without water. The Akhal-Teké is a very distinctive small, wiry horse, giving an overall appearance of being long and lean. It has a long head and neck, set on to a long body and legs, with sloping quarters and low-set tail. Both mane and tail are sparse and very fine in texture and the predominant colour is a very striking gold which often has a metallic sheen. Greys and bays do also occur and the average height is 14·2 to 15·2 h.h. The one disadvantage of the Akhal-Teké is its uncertain temper which may, however, be the result of its environment. It can be extremely obstinate, but when co-operative, makes a good all-round saddle horse that has excelled at such diverse activities as racing and dressage.

The Budyonny

This quality riding horse developed in the early part of this century as a cavalry mount and was named after Marshal Budyonny, the Russian cavalry general who instigated the breed. The Marshal based his breeding programme on Don mares and Thoroughbred stallions and the best of the resultant progeny were interbred. Still bred in the Rostov region where it originated, the Budyonny, unlike the Akhal-Teké, is a calm, sensible sort of horse although it, too, is possessed of great stamina and endurance. Originally bred to serve the cavalry, its great versatility today is being exploited in the field of competitive sports. It excels at steeplechasing and Budyonnys have in the past won the taxing Pardubice, the marathon race held in Czechoslovakia. It is a horse of excellent conformation standing 15·2 to 16 h.h., with a strong body that is deep through the girth. The quarters and shoulders are good, the head attractive and carried on a long, elegant neck and the legs strong, with generous bone. The predominant colour is chestnut and the gold sheen so prevalent among Russian horses is often seen. Bays and greys are common.

The Don

The Don horse, which was the mount of the Don cossacks as long ago as the eighteenth century, contains the blood of Turkmene and Karabakh stallions which were turned loose on the steppes to mingle and breed with the native herds. English Thoroughbred and Strelets Arab blood were introduced during the nineteenth century, since when no new infusions have been made. Centuries of life on the steppes, foraging for food in the harsh winter climate, have produced an exceptionally tough horse that is well able to care for itself with the minimum of help from man. It is, in fact, still herded on the plains and its toughness makes it a very useful working horse. It also excels in long-distance races, despite the rather

▲ Akhal-Teké

▲ Budyonny

Don ▼

▲ Kabardin

▲ Karabair

Latvian ▼

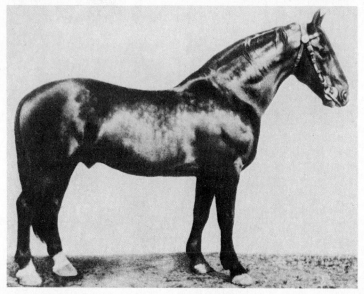

restricted action. Today the Don horse is both ridden and driven and makes an ideal mount for the herdsmen of the Kirghizskaya and Kazakhskaya regions of Russia. It is a wiry horse, rather long on the leg, standing 15·1 to 15·3 h.h. The usual colours are chestnut, bay and grey, and some horses have the characteristic Russian 'gold' sheen to the coat.

The Iomud

Like the Akhal-Teké, the Iomud is a strain of the ancient Turkmene horse though it shows an Arabian influence and has a much more tractable disposition. Also in common with the Akhal-Teké, it has great stamina and it, too, took part in the epic Ashkhabad to Moscow trek. Popular at one time as a cavalry mount, today it excels in long distance races. It is a sinewy little horse with longish legs and it is usually grey, although bays and chestnuts also occur. It is a little smaller than its relative, its maximum height being about 15 h.h.

The Kabardin

This mountain horse originated in the Caucasus some 400 years ago, when the indigenous mountain breed received infusions of Arab, Turkmene and Karabakh blood. The resultant progeny is a very strong little horse of equable temperament, with the sure-footedness and homing instinct that make it an ideal animal for tackling the tortuous mountain tracks of its native land. Like all mountain horses the Kabardin is exceptionally hardy and is particularly suited to making long-distance journeys. It is a popular sports horse in its local areas and is used for racing. It stands about 14·2 to 15 h.h. and is usually bay or black in colour. It has strong legs and good feet but the quarters are often of poor conformation and sickle hocks are very prevalent. The ears are distinctive in that they tend to turn inwards.

The Karabair

The region now called Uzbekskaya, the home of the Karabair, has been renowned for its good quality horses for 2,500 years. The exact origins of this breed have been lost in the annals of time but the distinctly Arabian appearance would suggest oriental influence. The Karabair is a spirited but tractable horse with the boundless endurance typical of the Russian mountain breeds. The heaviest animals make good agricultural workers while the lighter framed animals are suitable for being driven or ridden. The average height is about 15 h.h. and the breed resembles a rather stocky Arab but with rather less refinement. The usual colours are bay, chestnut and grey. The Karabair is an ideal mount for the popular and rather hair-raising Russian mounted games, such as 'Kok-par', a team game in which a stuffed goat carcass has to be carried through the opposite goal.

The Kirghiz

Also known as the Novokirghiz, the present-day Kirghiz is a relatively recent development of the native Kirghiz horse. In the last 100 years or so infusions of Don and Thoroughbred blood to the old Kirghiz stock have produced a small but immensely tough riding and pack horse, ideally suited to working at the high altitudes of its native Tien Shan mountains. It is a sure-footed horse with a longish back and straight shoulder, and short, strong legs with plenty of bone and good feet. It stands between 14·1 and 15·1 h.h. and may be of any solid colour, though bay is the most common. It is a good-tempered, active little horse that is used both for work and leisure.

The Latvian

This breed derives from the ancient forest horse of northern Europe which dates back to before the times of historical records. The modern Latvian, however, dates from the seventeenth century when warm-blood horses began to be crossed with the native stock. Several breeds were used, among them the Oldenburg. Cold-blood crosses were also made to add more substance and these included the Ardennes and Finnish Draught Horse. The result is an all-purpose draught horse which may, however, take its turn as a saddle or harness horse. It is strong and sensible and a willing worker with active paces and a kindly temperament. The conformation is good, with depth through the girth and good bone. The legs carry a little feather. The average height is 15·2 to 16 h.h. and the usual colours are bay, brown and chestnut.

The Lithuanian Heavy Draught
The Lithuanian Heavy Draught was evolved about 100 years ago by crossing Zhmud horses of the region, with imported Swedish Ardennes, the aim being to produce a good, strong agricultural horse. Selective breeding of the Zhmud/Ardennes progeny continued and the breed was finally registered as such in 1963. It is a massively built, medium sized horse, with short legs and good bone. The back is usually dipped and sickle hocks are prevalent, but the action is fast and free. It is a horse of extremely mild temperament with enormous powers of traction. The predominant colour is chestnut, with black, roan, bay and grey also occurring, and the average height is between 15 and 15·3 h.h.

The Metis Trotter
The Metis trotter is a breed of recent origin, dating from the early 1950s, when imported American Standardbreds began to be mated with the Orlov trotter. The result is a slightly less attractive horse than the Orlov, with the same upright shoulder. The Standardbred influence, however, has been beneficial for performance and the Metis is a faster horse on the racetrack than the Orlov. The usual colours are grey, black, chestnut and bay and the average height is the same as the Orlov, i.e. about 15·3 h.h.

The Orlov
The Orlov is named after Count Alexis Orlov who founded the Khrenov Stud in 1778, thereby laying the foundations of what was to become one of the world's best trotting breeds. The Orlov derives from Arab and Dutch blood and by the beginning of the nineteenth century was one of Russia's leading breeds. Trotting races were held in Moscow as far back as 1799 and as the sport developed during the nineteenth century so the Orlov prospered and became faster. As well as being used for racing the Orlov was a popular carriage horse, and before the development of the American Standardbred was probably the best trotter in the world. Over the years infusions of various other blood have been made, including Thoroughbred and Mecklenburg. Today the Orlov stands anywhere between 15·2 and 17 h.h., the average being a little under 16 h.h. It is a strong type of horse with powerful, if rather straight, shoulders, a long back but plenty of depth through the girth, strong legs with good bone and a rather heavy but attractive head. It is a long-lived, tough sort of horse and although it is bred for racing in harness, it is sometimes used under saddle in other sports. The predominant colours are grey and black.

The Russian Heavy Draught
Developed during the past 100 years or so, principally in the Ukraine, this is a small draught horse, with a distinctly 'cobby' appearance. Local draught mares were crossed with Ardennes, Percheron and Orlov stallions and the best of the progeny were inter-bred to create a fixed type. The Russian Heavy Draught is an active but very kind little horse and is noted for its great pulling power. It is a very compact animal, standing only about 14·2 h.h., with powerful shoulders, back and quarters set on fairly short, strong legs. The predominant colour is chestnut. It is a popular work horse on the farms of the Ukraine and in the Urals.

▲ Lithuanian Heavy Draught

▲ Orlov

Russian Heavy Draught ▼

▲ Tersky

The Tersky

The Tersky was evolved between 1921 and 1950 in an attempt to preserve the old Strelets Arab which had virtually died out during the First World War. The Strelets was an Anglo, not a pure-bred Arab, the result of crossing pure-breds with Anglos from the famous Orlov and Rastopchin studs. The Strelets thrived during the nineteenth century but by 1921 only two stallions remained, both having the characteristic silvery-grey colouring. Pure and part-bred Arabs were mated with these stallions and by a careful system of selection a new Strelets-type horse was developed. It was called the Tersky, after the Tersk Stud in the Caucasus which, along with the Stavropol Stud, was its birthplace. It is about 30 years since the breed was considered fixed and today the Tersky is very like a large Arabian, though with a little less refinement. The average height is 15 h.h. and the colour silver grey or white, often with a rosy tint caused by the pink skin. It is a good-natured, active horse, with plenty of stamina and makes a good all-round riding horse. It is also used for racing against Arabs and as a circus horse.

The Toric

This cobby type of work horse traces back to a Norfolk Roadster stallion called Hatman, who was imported into Estonia in 1894 and mated with the local mares, known as Kleppers. Initially the progeny were interbred to some extent but other blood has at various times been introduced, including Orlov Trotter. The Toric is an active, fast-moving, light

Vladimir Heavy Draught ▼

draught horse of good constitution and temperament, standing about 15 to 15·2 h.h. and usually bay or chestnut in colour. It takes its name from the Toric Stud where breeding first began and is still used in agriculture in Estonia.

The Vladimir Heavy Draught
This is a powerful draught horse which dates back to 1886 when a variety of heavy horses were brought into the Gavrilovo-Posadsk stables for crossing with local mares. Suffolks and Cleveland Bays were imported from England, and Percherons and Ardennais were also introduced. In the early twentieth century infusions of Clydesdale and Shire blood were added with the Shire taking precedence up until 1925. After that time a policy of interbreeding among the best progeny was followed and the breed was considered fixed some 25 years later. The Vladimir is not unlike the Shire in appearance although it is slightly smaller, averaging about 16 h.h. It is a well-built, powerful horse, a trifle long in the back but with good, sound limbs. It is bred in the Ivanovo and Vladimir regions and is used for agricultural and general heavy draught work. All solid colours are permissible.

AFRICA

Egypt

The Arab
The Arab is a horse of great antiquity and has had more influence on other breeds throughout the world than any other horse. Originating in Arabia, it is now bred throughout the world, and has over the years been crossed with all sorts of ponies and horses for up-grading purposes. Horses of recognizable Arab type can be seen on Egyptian antiquities going back some 3000 years and the Arab historian, El Kelbi, writing in the 8th century AD, traces the pedigrees of Arab horses back to the time of Baz, Noah's great-great grandson. The oldest and purest of breeds, the Arab is a horse of exceptional beauty and refinement and of quite distinctive appearance. Its lovely head with characteristically dished profile, broad forehead, large eyes and small muzzle, is carried high on an elegant neck. The body is compact and muscular, the legs slender but strong, and the coat, mane and tail are silky, the latter being carried very high. The overall impression is of a gay, spirited horse, who nevertheless has the gentlest of dispositions. The Arab is renowned for its powers of endurance and its ability to carry weight despite its relatively small size (14 to 15 h.h.). It is excellent for long-distance riding.

Libya, Algeria, Morocco

The Barb
Another horse of ancient origin, the Barb comes from the Barbary coast which has been noted for its horses for some 2000 years. Like the Arab, the Barb has had considerable influence on other breeds. It was used in the development of the Andalucian during the Moorish occupation of Spain, and through that breed has influenced many others, and it was imported into Europe, especially England, in large numbers during the seventeenth century. Standing about 14 to 15 h.h. it is the all-purpose riding horse of North Africa. Not the handsomest of horses, having a long head, and sloping quarters with a rather low-set tail, it is, however, immensely tough and combines considerable speed over short distances with great endurance over longer ones. It is an economical feeder and is usually bay, brown, chestnut, black or grey.

▲ Arab

Barb ▼

Principal Pony Breeds

Following *Eohippus* and his descendants, four main primitive types of horse survived the Ice Age. These were the Forest horse, a heavily built, solid type with a big, heavy head which lived in Northern Europe; the Steppe horse, a finer pony, light in build, which came from Asia and North Africa and stood about 12 h.h.; the Plateau horse, and the Tundra. Of these, the Forest horse is the basic founder of the cold-blooded breeds and the Steppe and Plateau horse are the joint founders of the warm-bloods – the Steppe being the ancestor of the Oriental breeds. The Plateau horse originated in Siberia and Northern Asia and Europe and is the less common of the two. The Tundra has had virtually no influence on any of the present-day breeds, with the possible exception of the Yakut horse which lives in the polar regions.

Przewalski ▼

The Przewalski (*Equus przewalskii przewalskii* Poliakoff) The Mongolian wild horse, called the Przewalski, is the last survivor of the Plateau horse and was discovered as late as 1881 by a Russian explorer from whom it takes its name. Colonel N. M. Przewalski found a small herd of these animals in the area of the Tachin Schara Nuru Mountains at the western edge of the Gobi desert, and they are the last truly wild horse or pony, on whom no attempts at domestication have been made. Known by native Mongolian herdsmen as the Taki, it is debatable whether any still exist today in their wild state, since the extensive hunting to which they have been subjected has driven them back into the desert and mountain regions and into China. Many are still preserved in zoos all over the world.

In its wild state, the Przewalski stands between 12 and 14 h.h. and is powerfully built, with a large, rather heavy, but short, head which has a straight or convex profile. The ears are long, the neck short, sometimes with a tendency towards a 'ewe' neck, the shoulder straight, the chest wide and the back short with virtually no wither. The quarters are generally weak and underdeveloped and the legs short and strong with large, shallow hooves composed of good horn. The mane, devoid of forelock, is short and erect and the tail hairs are long and coarse and sparse at the top. At birth, the coat is bright yellowish-brown and this changes to shades of dun – varying between reddish-bay and a pale grey or sandy colour – as the animal matures. There are mealy markings round the eyes and muzzle, the mane and tail are black and there is a pronounced black eel stripe down the centre of the back with zebra markings on the legs. The Przewalski has great powers of endurance and was able to exist on the very poorest of vegetation in the salty steppe and mountain regions of Mongolia, where it could withstand the severest of climatic conditions. The Mongolian, Chinese and Tibetan ponies are direct descendants of the Przewalski and are probably not unlike those used by Genghis Khan.

The Tarpan (*Equus przewalskii gmelini* Antonius)
This is the last survivor of the primitive Steppe horse, that lived on the Southern Russian steppes in Eastern Europe. It would appear that there are two strains of Tarpan, one living on the steppes and a forest type, but both were extensively hunted for meat and were finally killed off during the nineteenth century. The last herd, privately-owned of the forest type, lived on the Zemoyski estate in the Tauric Steppland of Poland, but the numbers of this gradually diminished. The last surviving mare finally escaped from the free-range herd, with her foal, who had been sired by a domestic stallion. She had such a disquieting effect on the local stallions, who pursued her into the steppes, that herdsmen organized a drive to capture her. However she died from shock after falling down a crevasse and breaking her leg, near Askania Nova in 1879. The last Tarpan in captivity is reported by the Russian zoologist, Heptner, to have died in 1919.

Polish peasants had been in the habit of catching the local wild ponies to use on their holdings and with the extermination of the wild Tarpan, the Polish authorities collected together all those that bore a marked resemblance to the Tarpan with the object of 'preserving' or 'restoring' the forest strain. They were put into the forest breeding reserves at Popielno and Bialowieza, where many still live in a semi-wild state. These ponies are around 13 h.h. and are brown or mouse dun in colour with a black eel stripe down the centre of the back. They have a black mane and tail, zebra markings on the legs, and occasionally, stripes on the body. In the winter the coat may turn white. They have a long, broad head, with a straight or convex profile and a bulge around the nostrils, longish ears, a short thick neck and good shoulder. The back tends to be long with high withers, the quarters are weak and sloping and the tail is set low. The legs are fine, long and hard.

Renownedly brave and independent animals, Tarpan stallions will attack other stallions who threaten their mares, often fighting to the death. They are very sturdy and hardy, never succumbing to the common diseases. Experiments at cross-breeding undertaken by Professor Lutz Heck at the zoo park at Hallabrunn, Munich, using Przewalski stallions and Polish Konik mares (to whom the Tarpan bears a likeness), have produced a horse that strongly resembles the steppe Tarpan.

▲ Tarpan

Connemara ▼

EUROPE

Great Britain

The Connemara
Originally a native of Ireland, the Connemara pony is now bred in England as well and has been exported to many parts of the world. It descended from the Celtic pony, but over the years has had infusions of Andalucian and, surprisingly, Clydesdale blood. Rather more recently, Arab stock has been introduced to add quality and refinement, and when put to a Thoroughbred a rather larger, very good all-round riding horse results which is suitable for almost any purpose. Standing 13 to 14·2 h.h., it is a sturdy, useful general-purpose riding pony, with good free action, a quality pony head, good length of neck, depth through the girth and a good sloping riding shoulder. The back is straight, the quarters well developed and the tail well set on, with good hard feet and legs with plenty of bone. It is a sure-footed and very agile pony, with a kindly, tractable nature, and it may be grey, bay, black, dun or brown.

▲ Dale

▲ Dartmoor

Exmoor ▼

The Dale

Very similar to the Fell pony, the Dale, together with the Highland, is the heaviest of Great Britain's native breeds and is bred on the eastern side of the Pennines in Northumberland, Co. Durham and Yorkshire. There is also a likeness to the Welsh Cob and in fact, all today's Dales can be traced back to Comet, a Welsh Cob stallion which competed in trotting matches and was used extensively on Dales mares about 100 years ago. The trotting aspect is present in the modern Dale, making it a good harness pony, capable of pulling great weights. It is also used as a trekking pony, being very sound, active and sure-footed, with a docile and sensible temperament. Standing 14·1 h.h., the Dale is black, dark brown or occasionally grey in colour with an abundance of mane, tail and feather on the legs, a quality 'pony' head and a deal of good hard bone.

The Dartmoor

A native of the Dartmoor area of Devonshire from where it gets its name, this tough little breed has inhabited the moorlands for thousands of years. The type has varied during the ages, infusions of Arab and Welsh blood having been introduced at the beginning of this century. It is ideal as a child's first pony, being small and narrow, but having a fairly high head carriage. It is also sensible and sure-footed, with an equable, kindly temperament. The Dartmoor has a reputation too, for being a naturally good jumper.

It has a fine, pretty, intelligent head which is held high, a large eye, small pricked ears and a good front and sloping shoulder. The short, compact body has strong quarters, a well set-on tail and good hard legs and feet. Black, bay and brown with only a small amount of white markings are the acceptable colours and the height limit is 12·2 h.h. This good-looking pony is also useful as a foundation stock from which to breed larger riding pony stock and is bred at many studs throughout Britain.

The Exmoor

A breed of great antiquity, the Exmoor, a native of the south-western area of Devon and Somerset is first recorded in the Domesday Book of 1085. In fact it is a much older breed probably being the last survivor of the Celtic ponies of the Pleistocene age. Comparative experiments conducted between the fossilized remains of the original Celtic ponies found in Alaska with those of the Exmoor, have revealed the same shaped jaw bones and beginnings of a seventh molar tooth which are found in no other breed of horse or pony. An exceptionally tough, strong and hardy pony with great powers of endurance, there are now only three principal herds actually running on the moor, and although a number are bred in studs throughout the country they tend to lose type and grow slightly larger when bred away from the moor. They are highly intelligent and independent and may be wilful if not correctly handled. The height limit is 12·2 h.h. for mares and 12·3 h.h. for stallions and colours may be bay, brown and a mousey dun, with no white markings permitted. The ponies are noted for their distinctive mealy muzzle and mealy coloured markings round the eyes, the underbelly and between the thighs. They have a short, thick head with a straight profile which is well set onto a neck with a good length of rein, good sloping shoulders, depth through the girth, a short back, powerful quarters, and short legs with plenty of bone and good hard feet. They have unique 'toad' eyes the heavy top lids of which give a hooded look, and short, pricked ears set wide apart. The tail too, is distinctive and is known as an 'ice' tail. It is very thick with a fan like growth at the top. The coat is short, close and springy and virtually waterproof. Although when properly trained the Exmoor makes a good, if strong, child's pony, its exceptional strength makes it quite capable of carrying a fully grown man. One of its principal assets, however, is its use as a foundation from which to breed larger animals. If put to a Thoroughbred a superb, useful quality little horse results.

74

The Fell

Slightly smaller and lighter than his close relation the Dale, the Fell is bred on the northern side of the Pennine range and in the Cumberland and Westmorland areas of the Lake District. It was extensively used in the eighteenth century as a pack pony for carting lead from the mines, for all kinds of farm work, and for the local sport of trotting. Having a much better riding shoulder than the Dale it produces a very good stamp of hunter when mated with a Thoroughbred mare, and being deep through the girth, compact and with plenty of bone it has a good head carriage and moves well from the shoulder. Sensible, very hardy and strong and sure-footed, it makes a good trekking pony. The height can vary between 13 to 14 h.h. and the colour may be black, dark brown, dark bay and occasionally grey. There are none, or very few white markings.

The Highland

A very old breed, the Highland is probably descended from the primeval Forest horse, and some of the ponies show the primitive markings. They are natives of the north of Scotland and the Western Isles, and would appear to comprise two distinct types – the bigger and rather heavier Mainland type, and the lighter, more active Western Isles pony. Both have had infusions of outside blood; French and Clydesdale in the Mainland type and Arab in the Island type. Although originally bred for working the crofts (they are very sure-footed and are still used to carry shot deer down from the hill), being very docile, strong, steady, hardy and up to weight they are also used in harness and for trekking and general riding. The Western Isles type in particular, produces very good hunters when crossed with Thoroughbreds. The height varies between 13 and 14·2 h.h., the Western Isles type being smaller and more refined. The usual colours are grey, black, bay, and various shades of dun from a mousey grey to a deep, rich chestnut with a flaxen mane and tail. They have fine silky hair on the legs, and almost all of them have a dark eel stripe down the centre of the back. Some have zebra markings on the legs.

The New Forest

Natives of the New Forest area of Hampshire, these ponies have had many infusions of outside blood. As far back as the thirteenth century, it is recorded that Welsh mares were turned out in the Forest and since then Dartmoor, Exmoor, Highland, Fell, Dale, Hackney, Clydesdales and Arabs have all been introduced in an effort to improve both the size and substance of the breed. Marske, the Thoroughbred sire of Eclipse, stood at stud in the Forest for a time, to serve selected mares as did three Arabians – Zorah, Abagan, and Yuresson. It is thought that these have had only a limited influence on the breed, however. These infusions of outside blood have made it difficult to define a fixed type of New Forest pony, but they average 12·2 to 14·2 h.h. and may be any colour except piebald and skewbald. Various shades of bay are the most usual. New Forest ponies are noted for their sure-footedness and adaptability, and they usually have good riding action, made possible by a nicely sloping shoulder with free straight movement. Most have plenty of bone, good feet, short backs and strong quarters and are deep through the girth. There is a tendency towards a somewhat large head and shortish neck. They are real family ponies being suitable for any member of the family to ride or drive, and their usually generous and docile temperament makes them easily handled by children. At present there are probably about 3,000 ponies running on the Forest, owned by those with 'commoners' grazing rights. They are rounded up regularly for branding, tail marking or selling at the regularly-held New Forest Beaulieu Road sales. Very popular ponies, they are bred at many studs throughout Great Britain and abroad, ponies having been exported since the early 1950s to the United States, Canada, Holland, Denmark, Norway, Sweden, France, Luxemborg, Germany and Australia.

▲ Fell

▲ Highland

New Forest ▼

75

▲ Shetland

▲ Welsh Mountain Pony

Welsh Pony ▼

The Shetland

The Shetland pony is the smallest of Britain's nine native pony breeds, coming originally from the Shetland Islands some 160 km (100 miles) off the north coast of Scotland. It is possible that the Shetland was introduced to these islands from Scandinavia before the lands were divided in around 8000 BC and that subsequently it crossed with ponies brought over to Scotland by the Celts. Be that as it may, the Shetland has been used by the island's crofters to work their land, as a pack pony to collect the peat from the moor and as a means of transport, both ridden and driven, for very many years. In the mid-1800s many Shetlands were exported to the mainland for use in the collieries of Co. Durham, and Londonderry. Being very strong and low to the ground, they proved ideal pit ponies and were soon bred selectively for this purpose. At the present time there are around 100 Shetland ponies on the islands but they are also bred extensively on the mainland as well as in Australia, North and South America, Scandinavia, Spain, Holland, France, Switzerland and most other countries of Europe. The Shetland varies in height from 95–106 cm (38–42 in) at the wither and is extremely strong and hardy, with a short, strong back, and considerable depth through the girth. The most favoured colour is black but ponies may be any colour including piebald and skewbald. All have an abundant supply of mane and tail hair. Mechanization has made them no longer in demand to work the islanders' crofts, and instead they have become very popular as small children's ponies – a task they admirably fulfil provided they are not allowed to get over fat.

The Welsh Mountain Pony

One of the most numerous as well as probably the most beautiful and popular of the native pony breeds, the Welsh Mountain pony (Section A in the Welsh Stud Book), has roamed the mountains and moorlands of Wales since Roman times, although over the years certain outcrosses have been introduced. Julius Caesar formed a stud in Merionethshire at Bala, and later introduced oriental blood to upgrade the stock. In the nineteenth century there were infusions of Arab blood as well as the now extinct predecessor of the Hackney, the Norfolk Roadster. At about the same time the Thoroughbred Merlin was introduced. For many years now, the Welsh Mountain has been free from outside influence. It is very intelligent and courageous as well as being kind and gentle. A splendid child's riding pony, its good free movement combined with a certain amount of knee action make it equally suitable for harness work. It has a fine, slightly dished head, very large wide spaced eyes and small pricked ears. The alert outlook shows the native Celtic 'fire' and it is very sound, tough and hardy with a true pony character. The shoulder is sloping, the body deep and compact, and the tail well set-on and carried high. Legs are short and hard with plenty of bone and substance and the feet are good and hard. Any colour, except piebald and skewbald, is permissible and the height limit is 12·2 h.h.

The Welsh Pony

The Welsh pony is known as the riding pony of the Welsh breeds, (Section B of the Welsh Stud Book) and is derived from the Welsh Mountain and the Welsh Section C Cob with an infusion of Thoroughbred blood. Formerly, it was used extensively for shepherding on the Welsh hills. Successful crosses with small Thoroughbreds or Arabs often produce the larger show pony type but care must be taken that hardiness and substance are not lost. The characteristics are similar to those of the Welsh Mountain, but the action is lower to the ground and there is not so much knee action. They are courageous and intelligent ponies with a small, neat head, a good length of rein, a good sloping riding shoulder, rounded, well-muscled quarters and a tail set high and carried gaily. Legs should be strong and hard with good flat joints and hard feet. The height limit is 13·2 h.h. and any colour except piebald and skewbald is permissible.

The Welsh Cob

The Welsh Cob, largest of the Welsh breeds (Section D in the Welsh Stud Book), again follows the conformation of the Welsh Mountain pony but is probably based on the old Welsh Pembrokeshire cart horse, although the Cob is mainly bred in Cardiganshire. The largest and strongest of the Welsh breeds, it is courageous with great powers of endurance and is famed for its trotting ability, and its performance in harness. It is just as good under saddle, however, and being very active and a good jumper makes a splendid hunter in all but the faster grass countries. Added size and speed is achieved by crossing with a Thoroughbred. As a general, all-round riding horse there is little to beat the notoriously sound and hardy Welsh Cob. It stands at 14·2 to 15·2 h.h. and may be any colour except piebald and skewbald.

The Welsh Pony of Cob Type

Also descended from the Welsh Mountain, the Welsh pony of Cob type (Section C in the Welsh Stud Book), has had infusions in the past of Andalucian, the now extinct Pembroke cart horse and Norfolk Roadster blood as well as more recently that of the Hackney. Originally used for shepherding and for general farm work, it is courageous, kind, intelligent and very sound and hardy. With a height limit of 13·2 h.h., it is the smaller edition of the Welsh Cob, and is very versatile, combining strength, with quality and common sense. Ideal as a child or small adult's hunter and for trekking purposes, its good, free trotting action also make it suitable for harness work. It should have an abundance of pony character, well laid back shoulder and a good length of rein with a compact, 'stuffy' body that is deep through the girth, powerful quarters, and good bone. Mane and tail hair should be silky and there should only be a small amount of feather on the heels. Any colour is permitted except piebald and skewbald.

The Palomino

The term Palomino refers to a colour type and not a breed. Indeed the colouring can be found in a number of different horse and pony breeds. To qualify for the description Palomino, the coat colour must be that of 'a newly minted gold coin' or three shades lighter or darker than this, with a pure white (*not* flaxen or silver), mane and tail. White markings on the legs and face are permissible. Foals tend to darken with age, the colour changing slightly according to the time of year, and the coat colour is not considered to have set until the animal is six years old. Breeding this correct colouring is a rather hit or miss affair, but the crosses most likely to produce Palomino colouring are two Palominos crossed, chestnut cross Palomino, chestnut cross albino and Palomino cross albino. The colouring is thought to have originated in Spain where such horses were termed Ysabellas after the Spanish queen (1451–1504) but there is evidence of golden horses many centuries before her time. Palominos are becoming increasingly popular for Western riding.

The Polo Pony

Polo is one of the world's oldest mounted games, and was played in Persia before 500 BC. Later it spread to China, India and Tibet and in the nineteenth century Army officers stationed in India brought the game back to England. Now it is played all over the world. Small hunter type ponies were once the favourite mounts – native pony crosses, particularly Connemara and New Forest, being used extensively until 1918 when the 14·2 h.h. height limit was abolished. This let in the larger, but still small Thoroughbred types of around 15·1 h.h. as well as the much sought after imported ponies from Argentina. The principal requirements for Polo Ponies are stamina, courage and balance, combined with speed, and the ability to 'turn on a sixpence'. In addition they must be obedient, handy and responsive. Those that have strong, short backs, powerful quarters and hard tough legs are likely to make the most successful Polo Ponies.

▲ Welsh Cob

▲ Welsh Pony of Cob Type   Palamino ▼

▲ Riding Pony

▲ Camargue

Haflinger ▼

The Riding Pony

The Riding Pony is of fairly recent development being derived for the show ring from small Thoroughbred or Polo Pony stallions and native pony – principally Welsh and Dartmoor – mares. Arabs, too, have been crossed successfully with these ponies and the ideal is probably a Welsh cross Thoroughbred with a dash of Arab blood at a previous or subsequent mating. The Riding Pony is essentially a quality animal with superb conformation, and free straight action from the shoulder (not the knee), and possessing that indefinable 'presence'. It should in fact be a smaller edition of the hack, with the same impeccable manner. The head should be full of quality, intelligent and fine with large, wide spaced eyes, and small ears. There should be a good length of rein, a sloping riding shoulder, a fairly wide chest, depth through the girth and a straight, medium length back, well muscled quarters and well set-on tail. Legs should be clean and hard with short cannons and flat, hard joints, and the feet, hard and of equal size. Action must be straight and true, the hind feet being planted in the prints of the fore feet. Three principal height limits are catered for in the show ring: up to 12·2 h.h., 12·3 to 13·2 h.h., and 13·3 to 14·2 h.h.

The Spotted Pony

Spotted refers to a type of coat pattern and is not therefore a breed. Three different types of markings are recognized, namely Leopard, Blanket and Snowflake. Leopard markings refer to spots of any colour on a white or light coloured background; blanket refers to spots of any colour on a white rump or back, and snowflake refers to white spots on a foundation of any colour. In addition, spotted horses or ponies have special characteristics such as white sclera round the eyes, hooves with yellowish-white and black or brown vertical stripes, mottled bare skin, and usually very sparse manes and tails.

France

The Camargue

The Camargue area of Southern France in the Rhone delta between the town of Aigues-Mortes and the sea, is the swampland home of the Camargue pony. Currently there are only about 30 herds or manades comprising some 45 stallions and 400 mares in the area. Known as the 'white horses of the sea' the white coat is the most striking point about this hardy breed which thrives on a diet of tough grass and salt water. Rarely exceeding 15 h.h., their conformation is generally poor, having a large square head, short neck and upright shoulder, but they are noted for their depth through the girth and short strong back. They have plenty of bone and good hard feet and long, thick manes and tails. Their action is principally noted for the high-stepping walk, their ability to twist and turn, and the gallop, the paces most used to work the famous black bulls of that area for the bullring, and the job for which these horses are so frequently used. The foals are born black, dark grey or brown, but their coat lightens with age.

Austria

The Haflinger

The Haflinger is a hardy mountain breed which originated in the Austrian Tyrol. Tough and thickset with plenty of bone and substance, its breeding can be traced back to the Arabian on one side and to the cold-blooded heavier breeds on the other. This combination makes it ideal for both draught and ridden work in its native land and its sure-footedness and placid temperament make it especially suitable for beginners to ride. The name was taken from the village of Hafling, the centre of an area in what is now Northern Italy, where the Haflinger was extensively bred. State studs were later established at Piber and Ossiach but the ponies are now widely bred throughout Austria although individual breeders are allowed only to keep mares. Stallions are all owned by the State and kept at the government stud farms. Colt foals are subjected to rigorous inspection by official inspectors and only a very few will be chosen as possible future stallions. Haflingers are also bred in some 20 other countries, of which Germany, Switzerland and Holland are the main ones. Rarely exceeding 14·2 h.h., the Haflinger is exceptionally strong for its small size. It is always chestnut in colour, ranging from shades of gold through to rust, and it frequently has white facial markings. The mane and tail are flaxen, varying from greyish-cream to reddish brown.

Germany

The Dülmen

Germany has only two native pony breeds, the Dülmen and the Senner and although the latter, once found in the Teutoburg Forest of Hanover, is virtually extinct, both of these breeds have had an influence on the rather better known horse breed, the Hanoverian. The Dülmen is now a rather mixed breed, having run in the Meerfelder Bruch in Westphalia in a semi-wild state since the early 1300s. It averages about 12·3 h.h. and may be any colour although brown, black and dun are the most usual. Not unlike the New Forest pony in overall appearance, the Dülmen tends to have an upright shoulder, short back and poor hindquarters with a neck a little on the short side. These ponies are privately owned by the Duke of Croy and they are rounded up to sell the surplus stock annually.

Poland

The Hucul

The Hucul is a native of the Carparthian region of Poland, where herds have wandered the mountain regions for thousands of years and where it is known locally as the Carparthian pony. It is probably a direct descendant of the primitive Tarpan, which it resembles more than any other breed. In fairly recent times, however, Arab blood has been introduced to improve the breed and selective breeding is now carried out at several studs throughout Poland, the principal one being at Siary near Gorlice. The Hucul makes an ideal pack and draught pony and being very hardy is used extensively on the mountainous farmlands of southern Poland. Sure-footed, docile, strong and willing, it averages 12·1 to 13·1 h.h. and has a characteristic 'primitive', short head, a rather poor back end and a low set tail. The principal colours are dun and bay but most colours may be seen.

The Konik

Similar to the Hucul and having a common ancestor in the Tarpan, the Konik is used to work the lowland farms in Poland, as well as Eastern Europe, where a number have been exported. It also has had infusions of Arab blood and although it stands only about 13·1 h.h., it has lost a degree of its 'pony' qualities, more resembling a little horse. It is bred selectively at the two state studs at Popielno and Jezewice as well as by numerous small farmers for use on their land. It is very tough and hardy, works willingly on a limited diet and is easily managed. It is always varying shades of dun in colour.

▲ Dülmen

▲ Hucul   Konik ▼

▲ Sorraia

Skyros ▼

Spain

The Sorraia

Spain's only native pony, the Sorraia, comes from the western area in the regions bordering the Sorraia river and its tributaries, on into Portugal. It is a true 'primitive' having characteristics of both the Tarpan and Przewalski and being extremely hardy it is able to survive on the very poor vegetation available, whilst withstanding the extreme climatic conditions. The Sorraia was at one time used for agricultural work but the numbers have now greatly decreased. Standing 12·2 to 13 h.h., it is usually dun in colour although it may also be grey or Palomino. It has the black eel stripe down the centre of the back and the zebra markings on the legs associated with the 'primitive' types. The head tends to be large with a straight or convex profile, the ears long with black tips and the eyes set a little high. The neck tends to be long and the shoulder is upright. The hindquarters are poor and underdeveloped with the tail set low and the legs tend to be rather long and lacking in bone.

Portugal

The Garrano

Also known as the Minho, this native of Portugal comes from the mountain valleys of the Garrano do Minho and Traz dos Montes areas. Arab blood has been introduced into the breed by the selective breeding of certain ponies and the result is a lightly built animal with good conformation and noticeable quality. It is very strong, hardy, and sure-footed and used extensively for hauling timber and light agricultural work. Garranos also make good riding ponies and are in demand as pack ponies. Standing 10 to 12 h.h., they are almost always dark chestnut in colour with a luxurious mane and tail. At one time very popular trotting races were run with these ponies, the pace being a collected trot, for which they were specially bred and trained. The horse fairs at Vila Real and Famalicao specialized in the sale of high quality Garranos.

Greece

The Peneia

Greece has only three breeds of native pony left, those such as the Thracian, Thessalian and Achean having long since disappeared. Of those remaining the Peneia is the local pony bred in the district of Eleia in the Peloponnese, and it is used for light agricultural work and as a pack pony. Usually bay, brown, chestnut or grey in colour, it is small, rarely exceeding 14 h.h., sturdy and very willing and can live on the meagrest of rations. A pony of 'oriental' type, the stallions are often used to breed hinnies.

The Pindos

Bred in the mountainous regions of Thessaly and Epirus, the Pindos pony is another of 'oriental' type and is used for light farm work, as well as for riding. Strong and hardy, this mountain pony can also live very frugally and is therefore popular with the farmers. Standing 12 to 13 h.h., the Pindos is usually dark grey but may also be brown, bay and black. The mares are frequently used for breeding mules.

The Skyros

The Skyros pony comes from the Island of Skyros in the Aegean sea and is the smallest, and probably the oldest, of the

Greek breeds. It stands no more than 11 h.h. and is of 'primitive' Tarpan type. It is used principally as a pack pony on the island, but on the Greek mainland it is widely used as a child's riding pony, being very quiet and amenable. A hardy breed, able to exist frugally, it is small and very light of bone with a weak neck, upright shoulder, poor quarters and a tendency towards cow hocks. It may be almost any colour but brown, grey and dun are the most usual.

Norway

The Døle Gudbrandsdal

The Døle Gudbrandsdal is not unlike the British Dales pony and the Friesian from Holland. It is also similar, although rather heavier, to the Døle Trotter, which was bred from the lighter of the Gudbrandsdals. Infusions of Thoroughbred stock from Odin, a stallion imported in to Norway in the nineteenth century, as well as infusions of heavy draught blood make it of mixed origin. The Døle Gudbrandsdal has now spread throughout Scandinavia, and is used as a general utility and a riding horse. Almost always black, brown or bay, he averages 14·2 to 15·2 h.h. and has a neat, pony head with a straight profile, a luxurious mane and tail, strong shoulders, wide chest and a long back. The quarters are powerful, the girth deep and the legs short with lots of feather.

▲ Døle Gudbrandsdal

The Fjord

The mount of the Vikings, and used by them for the 'sport' of horse fighting, the Fjord or Westlands pony originated in western Norway. It has since spread thoughout the whole of Scandinavia, as well as West Germany, and is particularly popular in Denmark, especially Jutland, where it was imported at the beginning of the century for light agricultural work. It is a 'primitive' type and has the characteristic dun colouring with a dark eel stripe down the centre of the back and zebra markings on the legs. The mane which, like the tail is composed of black hairs in the centre and silver around the outside, stands upright and is cut in a characteristic crescent shape. The head is small, neat and 'pony like' with widely spaced eyes, and the neck is muscled. The Fjord pony is very strong, hardy and sure-footed with short, strong legs and good feet. It stands 13 to 14·2 h.h., is a tireless worker and is used extensively in the mountain areas for farm work in the regions where to use a tractor would be impossible. It also performs well in harness or as a riding or pack pony.

▲ Fjord   Gotland ▼

Sweden

The Gotland

The oldest of the Scandinavian breeds, the Gotland or Skogsruss pony is now bred extensively on the mainland as well as on Gotland Island from where it originated in Stone Age times. It is probably a descendant of the Tarpan and a number run wild in the forest lands of Lojsta. About 100 years ago Oriental blood was introduced into the breed but they still retain their 'primitive' characteristics and are not unlike Poland's Hucul and Konik and the extinct Lofoten pony. They are now in demand as light agricultural workers and, with the interest in trotting races, are also selectively bred for that purpose. Standing 12 to 12·2 h.h. in height they may be brown, black, dun, chestnut, grey or Palomino in colour and are hardy and easily managed, although inclined to be obstinate. They are small, rather light and narrow, with a small head, straight profile and short neck, long back, sloping quarters, poor hind legs and a low set tail. Although light of bone, Gotland ponies are fast and also good jumpers.

Iceland

The Icelandic
Introduced into Iceland from Scandinavia (particularly Norway), this Celtic pony has since interbred with those imported later from Scotland, Ireland and the Isle of Man to form what is now known as the Icelandic pony. From subsequent selective breeding, two distinct types have emerged; one rather heavy sort used for draught and pack work, and a lighter type for riding. Both were used extensively until some 50 years ago, as up until then, they formed the only transport on the island, especially during the severe winter months when the few existing roads were impassable. Up to the turn of the century, ponies were exported from Iceland to work in the British coal mines where their extreme hardiness, strength, small size and great powers of endurance made them very popular. With the end of this export trade, the number of ponies kept on the island declined, but since local conditions do not favour cattle farming, herds of ponies are often bred for meat instead. Icelandic ponies are small and stocky, deep through the girth and with a rather large head set on to a short, thick neck. They have an abundance of mane and tail hair and feather on the heels, and although usually grey or dun, all other colours may be seen. The usual height is between 12 to 13 h.h. but occasionally larger ponies are found. One of the toughest of the pony breeds, they are extremely intelligent and docile and noted for their independence and homing instinct. The usual pace is a fast and comfortable ambling gait known as the tølt which covers a great deal of ground. Recently there have been attempts to improve the breed by introducing small Thoroughbred stallions but this has met with very little success.

Italy

The Avelignese
A native of central and northern Italy, the Avelignese is bred principally in the hill regions surrounding Venetia and Tuscany, where it is used extensively for light agricultural draught work. In the Alps and Apennines it is popular as a pack pony. Very similar to the Haflinger to whom it is related (they share a common ancestor in the now extinct Avellinum-Haflinger), the Avelignese is believed to contain a degree of Arabian blood having descended from an imported Arab, El Bedavi. It is extremely hardy and sure-footed and can pick its way over the mountain trails in the worst of winter conditions. Always chestnut in colour with a flaxen mane and tail and possibly white facial markings, it is very strong and tough, noted for its docile disposition and its longevity. It is deep through the girth with a wide chest, a well muscled neck and quarters, short legs, and a short broad head, with plenty of bone and good hard horn. It stands 13·3 to 14·3 h.h.

NORTH AMERICA

U.S.A.

The American Shetland
Developed in the United States by crossing imported Shetlands with Hackney ponies, the resultant American Shetland is a larger and finer edition of its British counterpart. It is bred throughout the United States and Puerto Rico, and in addition to being kept as a pet and as a child's pony, it is raced in trotting races hitched to a lightweight racing sulky, as well as being shown in halter and harness classes. If used in the latter

▲ Icelandic

American Shetland ▼

82

the ponies have their tails nicked to give an artificially high tail carriage, and their action, especially at the trot, is high and exaggerated. The American Shetland can be any colour and the height limit is 11·2 h.h.

The Chincoteague
Inhabitants of Chincoteague and Assateague, two small islands off the coast of Maryland and Virginia, it is uncertain how these ponies came to be living on the islands where their keep consists of whatever they can find on the sandy marshland, and where there is no shelter from the Atlantic storms. One theory is that they are descended from animals that survived shipwrecks during the English and Spanish colonial period, and that their size became stunted on account of the sparse vegetation. They are no more than about 12 h.h. and are more like small horses than ponies. Many are piebald and skewbald and the recent infusion of Arab blood has improved their quality. Currently there are about 150 living on Assateague, which, unlike Chincoteague is uninhabited. Consequently on the last Wednesday in July all these ponies are rounded up and swum across to Chincoteague for the annual grand round-up, sale and branding exercise. Those that are not sold are swum back to Assateague the next day.

The Pony of the Americas
A breed founded only 20 years ago by crossing a Shetland stallion and an Appaloosa mare, the Pony of the Americas has fulfilled a need throughout America for a small, useful, child's pony with plenty of substance. The height must be bewteen 11·2 to 13 h.h. and any of the six Appaloosa colours are acceptable for registration purposes. They are willing, active, versatile and easy to manage, with straight, free action. The head should be small and 'Araby' with a dished profile, large eyes and small ears, the shoulder sloping, the chest wide and the body deep, with well rounded quarters and tail set high, and short legs with plenty of bone. These ponies have competed successfully in jumping classes and trail rides and have also been used for racing.

▲ Chincoteague

Pony of the Americas ▼

Mexico

The Galiceno
Descended from the Garrano or Minho ponies of Portugal and the Spanish Sorraia, the Galiceno's ancestors are thought to have been those brought over to America by the Spaniards from Hispaniola. Although a native of Mexico, since 1959 it has spread throughout the United States, and in the better conditions elsewhere it has grown in stature. In these places it is used in harness and for ranch work as well as for ordinary riding. It may be bay, black, dun, grey or chestnut in colour and stands 12 to 13·2 h.h. A lightly built, compact pony, it has a fine head, large well spaced eyes, an upright shoulder and short back. The chest tends to be narrow but the limbs and feet are good and the pony moves with a characteristic natural gait of a fast comfortable running walk. It is hardy and intelligent and being of a tractable disposition, is used a great deal in competitions.

Canada

The Sable Island Pony
Descendants of the principally French stock which were taken to Canada by the French in the mid 1600s, the Sable Island pony is also supposed to have been introduced to Sable Island (a sandbank some 320 km (200 miles) or so off Nova

Scotia in the Atlantic Ocean), early in the eighteenth century. There are at present some 300 ponies, most of them scrub stock, running on the small 40 km (25 mile) long island, and they are extremely hardy, tough and wiry, living on the poor vegetation the island offers. Standing about 14 h.h., they may be chestnut, bay, brown, black or grey and having a tractable nature are used for both riding and light draught purposes.

SOUTH AMERICA

The Criollo
Descended from Spanish stock, a mixture of Arab, Barb and Andalucian, brought over to South America by the sixteenth century conquistadores, the Criollo has now spread all over South America acquiring slightly different characteristics according to its environment. Essentially it is sturdy, compact and very muscular with a short broad head, straight profile and wide set eyes. The neck and quarters are well developed, the chest wide, the back short and the shoulder fairly sloping. The legs are short with plenty of bone and the feet hard. It is a very willing and tough pony with great powers of endurance and an ability to carry weight. The favourite colour is dun with black points and an eel stripe down the centre of the back and zebra markings on the legs, but chestnut, grey, roan, Palomino, bay and black are also found. The height and type varies slightly throughout South America although all types are essentially the same. The ponies are used principally as stock horses by the gauchos and for general riding. In the Argentine they are known as Criollos; in Brazil as the Crioulo; in Chile – the Caballo Chileno; in Venezuela – the Llanero, and in Peru there are three types – the Costeno, the Morochuco and the Chola.

Criollo ▲

Burmese ▼

The Falabella
The Falabella is really a miniature horse rather than a pony, and standing at under 7 h.h., it is the smallest horse in the world. It was first bred by the Falabella family, from whom it gets its name, on their ranch near Buenos Aires in the Argentine, by crossing a small Thoroughbred with small Shetland ponies and thereafter inbreeding. It is not suitable for riding but is sometimes used in harness in the United States. Its principal purpose however is purely as a pet and being very friendly and intelligent it fulfills this object well. Small studs of these ponies are now established all over the world.

ASIA
Assam

The Manipuri
Bred in the hill state of Assam and the Himalayas, the Manipuri is a descendant of both the Mongolian wild horse and the Arab. It has been claimed as the original polo pony, as a result of the British tea planters using it to play the local game in 1850. (The game was reputed to have been introduced to the State of Manipur in the seventh century). A sturdy pony of between 11 and 13 h.h., it is tough, and sure-footed and can be any colour. It is deep through the girth with a good shoulder, short back and well developed quarters. The legs are short with plenty of bone and the feet are hard.

Burma

The Burmese
Also known as the Shan pony this breed is very similar to the
Manipur but is a native of Burma and the Shan states, where
it is bred by the hill tribes. A strong and active, but not very
fast pony, it was used by the British as a polo pony for want of
anything better. Now it is used as a pack and riding pony. The
height varies but averages about 13 h.h. and the pony can be
any colour. Generally bad tempered, although very hardy and
sure-footed, it is rather plain with a small head, longish back
and rather under developed quarters with a poor hind leg.

China

The Chinese
Found in most districts of the Chinese Republic, ponies of
this type exist throughout the Far East and cannot really be
considered a breed. As there has been no form of controlled
breeding, they have bred with the wild Mongolian horses
from early times. In consequence, they are similar to the wild
Mongolian pony and are frequently dun in colour with a
black eel stripe and black points, although other colours are
found. They are extremely hardy and sure-footed and their
speed over short distances has led to them being used for
racing as well as general riding. Conformation however, is
generally poor and underdeveloped with a large head and
weak neck. The height varies between 12 and 13·2 h.h.

▲ Chinese

▼ Kathiawari

India

The Bhutia
A thick-set pony from the Himalayan mountain area of India
the Bhutia is principally used as a pack pony on the mountain
passes. It is sure-footed, extremely hardy and intelligent with
plenty of stamina and the ability to live frugally. Usually grey
in colour, it is strong and sturdy with muscular quarters and
good bone, and stands 13 to 13·2 h.h.

The Kathiawari and Marwari
Although separate breeds, the Kathiawari and Marwari are
virtually identical, both having descended from the indigenous Indian country breeds crossed with Arab stock. They
tend to be generally bad tempered but extremely tough with
lots of stamina, and they thrive on little food. Varying in
height from 14 to 15 h.h. they are very light and narrow with
weak necks and quarters, low set tail and sickle hocks. Any
colour is found including piebald and skewbalds. The ears
curve inwards with the tips almost touching at the points,
thus indicating the Arab influence.

The Spiti
From the same Himalayan area of India as the Bhutia, and
very similar to it in type and conformation, although smaller,
the Spiti is bred principally by the Kanyat tribesmen who use
it to trade with neighbouring tribes. It is only about 12 h.h.,
but up to weight, as well as being hardy and tireless with
plenty of stamina. Well muscled with a short, thick neck,
straight shoulder, short back and strong limbs and feet, the
Spiti, like the Bhutia, tends to be temperamental. Both the
Spiti and Bhutia are closely related, and very similar, to the
all-purpose Tibetan Nanfan about whom very little is known.

Indonesia

The Bali

This native of the island of Bali is of primitive type, bearing a resemblance to the wild Mongolian pony. It is frequently dun in colour with a black eel stripe down the centre of its back and an upright mane. It stands 12 to 13 h.h. Very strong and economical to keep, it is a willing worker and is used primarily as a pack pony.

The Batak

The Batak is bred selectively on the island of Sumatra where Arabian imports have been introduced to the studs to upgrade the rather common native pony, and lend a little quality to the breed. The resultant young stock are then sent to the other Indonesian islands to improve the breeds there. It is a kindly, gentle pony, easy to manage and economical to keep, but the Arabian blood has added a touch of spirit and elegance which is not found in most of the other Indonesian breeds (the Sandalwood being an exception). It is a general purpose animal, can be any colour and stands 12 to 13 h.h.

The Java

Slightly larger than some of the other Indonesian ponies the Java, a native of that island, stands 12·2 h.h. Although lightly built it is tough, hardy, very willing and apparently tireless, capable of working all day in tropical conditions. Its principal function is to pull the heavily laden two-wheeled Sados which serve as a taxi service on the island. The Java is found in almost any colour and is generally of poor conformation with weak necks and quarters, long backs, rather long legs and frequently cow hocks.

The Sandalwood

A native of the islands of Sumba and Sumbawa, the Sandalwood is the quality pony of Indonesia being finer than the others and with an 'Araby' head. Named after the island's principal export, it is used mainly for bareback racing although it stands only 12·1 to 13·1 h.h. It has a small, well-shaped head, with a large eye and wide chest and is deep through the girth. Legs and feet are good and hard, and the coat, which may be any colour, is very fine.

The Sumba

Since the likeness of the Indonesian ponies to the wild Mongolian and Chinese ponies is very apparent, it is quite possible that the ancient Chinese may have brought the ponies to Indonesia in very early times. The native ponies of Sumba and Sumbawa, which are almost identical, are very tough and willing and again somewhat primitive in appearance, being dun with the black eel stripe and upright mane. They stand about 12·2 h.h. and are agile, and intelligent. They are used on the islands in lance-throwing, the competitive national sport of Indonesia, as well as in 'dancing' competitions, when they are ridden bareback in a bitless bridle by young boys, while a trainer on the other end of a lunge line directs the various movements. The ponies have bells attached to their knees and they dance in time to the beat of the tom-toms. Judging is on the elegance and lightness of performance.

The Timor

The native pony of the island of Timor, is the smallest of the Indonesian breeds and is used by the islanders as a cow pony. It is exceptionally agile and strong, although standing only 11 to 12 h.h., and has great powers of endurance coupled with a mass of common sense. Also very docile and sure-footed, it makes a good children's pony, and many have been imported to the Australian mainland for this purpose. It is usually black, brown or bay in colour and is finely made with a small head, short back, strong quarters and good hard legs and feet.

Iran

Caspian ▼

The Caspian

Until recently the Caspian pony, a native of the area around the Elburtz mountains and Caspian sea in Persia, was thought to be extinct, but in 1965 a number were found pulling carts in the coastal towns and wandering along the shores of the Caspian Sea in Northern Iran. The current theory is that the Caspian is the ancient miniature horse of Mesopotamia which, after being used by the Mesopotamians in the third millenium BC until the seventh century AD, was believed to have become extinct. Research into this theory is however still in progress. More like a small horse than a pony in appearance, it may be grey, brown, bay or chestnut in colour and stands between 10 to 12 h.h. It is sure-footed, intelligent and tractable, with a remarkable jumping ability – all of which makes it a useful mount for children. The Caspian has a small, fine, Arab-type head with wide set eyes, short back, poor hind legs, narrow chest and is light of bone.

AUSTRALASIA
Australia

The Australian Pony
The native pony of Australia has derived principally from imported Welsh Mountain with a mixture of Arab, Thoroughbred, Timor and Shetland ponies, and is thus not indigenous. The height varies from 12 to 14 h.h. and used as a child's riding pony, it is intelligent, hardy and sound with good, free movement. Principal colours are grey and chestnut but this compact, cobby sort of pony may be any whole colour.

U.S.S.R.

The Kazakh
An ancient breed originally bred in the region of Kazahstan, these ponies are exceptionally hardy and able to withstand the extremes of climatic conditions, being expected to forage for themselves equally in thick snow or in the desert. Some have recently had infusions of Don blood and crosses with the Don or Akhal-Teké have produced good cavalry mounts. Standing 12·2 to 13·2 h.h., their principal use, however, is as a 'cow pony' and they are strong, willing mounts with good hard limbs and feet. They are usually grey, bay, chestnut, or black. The mares are used to produce milk and many of the young stock are fattened for meat.

The Viatka
Bred mainly in the basins of the Viatka and Obva rivers, these ponies are used principally to pull the troika sledges – a job for which their peculiar trotting gait, makes them particularly suitable. They are also used for light agricultural work and are very useful all-round ponies. Possessed of great powers of endurance, the Viatka stands 13 to 14 h.h., has a full mane and tail and is usually grey in colour, sometimes with the primitive zebra markings on the legs. It has a rather plain head with a well muscled neck and quarters, a short back, depth through the girth and good strong limbs and feet. It is a fast and willing worker and its ability to live on the minimum of food makes it economical to keep.

AFRICA

Lesotho (Basutoland)

The Basuto
The Basuto pony is derived principally from the Arab and Barb horses which were imported to the Cape Province of South Africa from Java in 1653 and, by various crossings with Thoroughbreds, formed the Cape Horse. Following raids in the early nineteenth century the Cape Horse found its way into Basutoland where a combination of crossing with local scrub stock and the unfavourable climatic conditions, caused it to degenerate into what is now known as the Basuto pony. This exceptionally tough, hardy and enduring pony is not then an indigenous one, but being well up to weight was used extensively during the Boer War. It is 14·2 h.h. and proves its versatility by being used for polo and racing as well as for riding and as a pack pony. The usual colours are bay, brown, grey or chestnut and it is thickset, frequently with a quality head, long neck and back, and upright shoulder. It has very hard feet and is extremely sure-footed.

▲ Australian Pony

▲ Viatka   Basuto ▼

PART THREE

EQUESTRIAN SPORTS
AND
RECREATION

Dressage in the 20th Century

THE origin of training horses for the most classical form of riding, normally referred to as dressage, can be traced at least as far back as the fourth or fifth centuries BC when its value and basic principles were appreciated and established by the Greeks. The Greeks studied the systematic training of their horses both as an artistic and pleasurable accomplishment, as well as a means of improving the performance of their cavalry. Most notable among these early horsemasters was a cavalry general called Xenophon who embodied the principles in a book, parts of which exist and are valid today. It also mentions the existence at that time of another book or treatise on the same subject by one, Simon of Athens.

The name dressage, being French, did not come into use to describe this training and riding until the early eighteenth century. It is derived from the French verb *dresser*, which means to train, to adjust, to straighten-out. Like many other French words adopted by the Anglo-Saxons, it could hardly be more apt for its purpose. A *dresseur* is a man who practises dressage.

Dressage as we recognize it therefore, was developed in the first place for the essentially practical purpose of producing easily controlled horses, that would be battle-winning assets for army cavalries. Troopers who could not control their mounts with one hand in battle were then, as in much later times, no asset at all. Fortunately for the horses of all subsequent periods, the Greeks discovered that a quiet and civilized approach to obtain the cooperation of these beautiful, but powerful, animals invariably produced by far the best results.

Over the intervening centuries right up to the present day, dressage has developed in a sporadic fashion in different countries, in different degrees and at different times. It has always flourished however only in the more advanced civilizations and social cultures, for there has never been any place for activities requiring such patience, applied intelligence and aesthetic sensitivity in poor or primitive societies. There has to be a certain amount of leisure time to turn what is desirable, but perhaps inessential, into a practical proposition.

Revived after the dark and middle ages along with all other cultural activities in Renaissance Italy, dressage began to assume almost precisely the form in which we know it today in the late seventeenth and early eighteenth century. This was particulary true of the latter period when the Frenchman François de la Guérinière,

working at Versailles, elaborated and developed fully the original Greek principles, establishing conclusively that the rough and even brutal methods of training horses that had crept into practice during the Renaissance were unnecessary and unacceptable. De la Guérinière's concepts were codified in his great work 'l'Ecole de Cavalarie' which remains the source of all contemporary thinking. It also forms the basis of the work perpetuated at the great academy of the Spanish Riding School in Vienna which stands as the arbiter of true classical riding across the world.

One major distinction between the general practice of dressage and classical riding in the twentieth century and that of all previous times has been the introduction of competition riding. This is best expressed in the international contests that lead up to and include the Olympic Games. Previously, as we have seen, dressage had been primarily the concern of the military, through the teaching at their cavalry schools, and also of the wealthy civilian minorities focussed round royal courts and similar centres of culture. In the military, dressage was a professional requirement, whereas among the wealthy civilians, it was a gentlemanly accomplishment, highly regarded as an integral part of a complete education. No doubt the harsh necessities of military life precluded all but a small minority of the soldiers from following dressage to its highest levels but through them the spirit of Versailles and Vienna was kept fresh and was handed down and practised at many relatively small establishments. In the riding schools maintained at the royal courts, the dressage achievements may have reached higher levels.

By the beginning of this century, the courts were rapidly dwindling in number, and the improvement in communcations and travel facilities had radically changed the life in those that remained. The cavalry schools consequently became virtually the sole bearers of the dressage torch and they themselves were to last only for the next forty years or so. By the end of the Second World War they had all gone and the lead passed to civilians and to the few professional or retired soldiers who had received their training before the war. Interest became more widely spread and quickly found its expression in the expanding world of competitive sport of all kinds. Dressage was first included in an Olympic programme in the Stockholm Games of 1912.

This changing pattern resulted in some variation between what was taught and practised in the secluded academy in Vienna on the one hand and what was produced by the majority of riders in the wider, and mainly amateur, world of national and international competition on the other. The artistic element in dressage is all too easily sacrificed to the need to score points or to speed up the training programme in time for the next Olympic Games or other major event. On the other hand, the changes have not all been for the worse. The periodic gatherings of dedicated dres-

sage riders from all over the world provide an excellent and recurrent opportunity to compare standards, techniques and ideas. They also serve to bring dressage before a much larger audience than has experienced it since it was used in the sixteenth century in popular festivities. Above all they have resulted in the reintroduction of a degree of freedom of movement as an accepted standard that might have been lost for ever if twentieth century dressage had been restricted to indoor displays and academic institutions.

A very beneficial aspect of competition riding is that the riders have regularly to subject their performances to the comprehensive scrutiny of trained assessors. Their duty is to recognize and expose weak results or false techniques as well as to commend correct and admirable work. This continuous and worldwide process of technical assessment cannot fail to improve and maintain the purity of contemporary dressage to an extent that could hardly be possible without the stimulus provided by competitive events. A further

beneficial aspect of contemporary dressage is that in its lower echelons it has become a true leisure sport, giving pleasure to many thousands of the less ambitious riders. This is partly because of the widely felt urge to escape – even for short periods – from the stresses of modern day living, and partly because of the ever decreasing opportunities for long range or cross-country riding. Paradoxically though, in the higher competitive echelons, it is in danger of becoming very intense indeed, and very large sums of money are spent in the pursuit of fame and success in competitions.

Climatic conditions have always had a marked impact on the development and practice of dressage within different countries. Given the opportunity, mankind the world over shares the love of riding horses in some aspect, but much depends on the conditions available. In Great Britain for example, where the winters are mild and much of the terrain is agricultural or pastoral, it is possible and pleasant to ride outdoors the whole year round. Thus the

ardour of young men has often expressed itself in riding across country usually following a hunt. In other countries, particularly Germany and central Europe, the terrain and the climate combine to keep riders indoors for large portions of the year. This has produced an atmosphere that is conducive to an interest in the skills and science of pure horsemanship rather than the more immediate and simpler excitements of hunting. It followed therefore, that for the first forty years of this century the art of dressage riding in competitions was pursued throughout continental Europe but was hardly recognized as existing, much less understood, in Great Britain. The result is that the continental countries, with their 250-year unbroken tradition of skilled horsemanship, arrived in the present era of competitive dressage with a long start over Britain and the younger nations. This is particularly apparent when the results of major competitions are studied.

The twentieth century transition from a mainly military or aristocratic activity to the present status of dressage as an interna-

The dressage horse. Sun and Air, ridden by Miss Sheila Willcox, in an advanced dressage competition at Goodwood. The supple outline of the horse combined with the obedience to the rider's aids shown here are the product of the long hours of schooling required to bring a horse to this level.

tionally recognized and almost totally civilian sport has in practice been remarkably smooth. Although, since the mid-sixties, the sight of a military uniform in the arena has been rare and the titles rarer still, this change has not affected the sport adversely. The military establishments were superseded by riders from private domestic stables, many of whom had only modest financial backing. One significant innovation was the emergence of women riders at the highest levels. From a previous standpoint of non-participation in the sport, they were soon to show themselves well able to challenge the men on equal terms. The first woman to win an Olympic medal in dressage was Mme Liz Hartel of Denmark, a courageous lady who had been

severely handicapped by poliomyelitis. Riding her horse Jubilee, Mme Hartel won the silver medals at Helsinki and Stockholm, 1952 and 1956. Frau Liselott Linsenhoff of Germany won the Bronze medal in 1956 and the Gold Medal in 1968. In 1972 Mme Elena Petouschkova of the USSR, then the reigning World Champion, took the Silver on Pepel and in 1976 Christine Stuckelberger of Switzerland took the Gold at Montreal. In the World Championship competitions in Copenhagen in 1974, women riders out-numbered the men.

The influence of dressage on the general welfare of the horse must be recognized as being considerable. Taken up very widely as a sport, it has encouraged many thousands of riders all over the world to accept the challenge of improving their riding which is clearly of great benefit to their mounts. This challenge, coupled with the time and concentration needed to train a dressage horse, has resulted in dressage riding becoming almost a way of life for many people in which they find great interest, great pleasure and great relief from the pressures of contemporary, over-mechanized life. It also has the enormous advantage of being practicable for riders in the seventh or eighth decades of their lives, provided they have kept reasonably fit.

Apart from the private dressage riding practised and enjoyed by individuals solely for their own interest, there are two forms in which it is known and appreciated by the public. As already mentioned, one is in the world of competitive events which are governed by precise rules and conventions. The fact that the performance of each competitor has to be judged separately, means that most competitions tend to be too slow and prolonged to hold the attention of large audiences except at the highest level and where major championships are involved. In addition some basic knowledge of the principles of this somewhat esoteric sport is essential for a real appreciation of its finer points. The other and more popular form is that of special and relatively short displays given by one or more riders, usually as only one item in a programme of more varied entertainment. Such displays can be enjoyed by many thousands for their aesthetic value and for the sense of rhythmical movement and precision timing that they provoke. However, as with most other activities, really top class performers are required to ensure the full success of such a display.

Regular displays of very high quality and renown are given all over the world by the uniformed riders and white Lipizzaner horses of the Spanish Riding School, and by a very few great masters of classical

horsemanship such as Nuno Oliveira of Portugal. Some of the top competition riders also give displays. In all cases, the dressage performed conforms as closely as possible to pure classical concepts. It should not be confused with the type of exhibition normally seen in circuses which, although often of very high quality and demanding very fine horsemanship, is likely to accept a degree of license in the interest of entertaining a possibly less critical audience. Such an audience, however, will have no difficulty in appreciating a display of fine dressage for precisely the same reasons as would influence spectators watching dancing, skating, gymnastics or other form of physical prowess that combine skill and grace with strength and discipline.

Above The 'passage', an advanced dressage movement, performed here by Piaff and his German rider, Liselotte Linsenhoff, who won the gold medal at the 1972 Munich Olympics.
Opposite top Dressage on display: the white Lipizzaner stallions at the Spanish Riding School in Vienna entering their magnificent arena for the quadrille.
Opposite bottom left A quadrille can consist of four or more horses and riders and the group will perform dressage movements in unison.
Opposite bottom right Mrs. Lorna Johnstone, who rode in the Munich Olympics aged 70.

Competition dressage covers a very wide variety of standards from those of provincial riding-club events through to continental or world championships and the Olympic Games. The same basic principles and rules apply to all of these and competitions at all levels are controlled by the Dressage Bureau of the International Equestrian Federation founded in 1921, the headquarters of which are in Brussels. The Bureau lays down and keeps up-to-date the necessary rules to cover the standards of performance, the rules and guidelines for judges and competition organizers, the qualifications for judges and all other factors that directly affect the sport. Each federated nation maintains its own national dressage bureau to control its purely national affairs and through which contact is maintained worldwide on matters of principle and method. The highest priority is given throughout the organization to maintaining the purity of classical concept and to preventing the growth of potentially false methods of training that would lead to a lowering of standards.

There are various conventionally recognized grades of training in dressage and contests for all or some of the grades may be held at a normal competitive event. Competitors can enter for one or more contest, and in each case will be required to perform a preordained sequence of movements in exactly the order stipulated. In the United Kingdom the grades, and thus the contests, are referred to as Preliminary, Novice, Elementary, Medium and Advanced. Each grade is further subdivided into two or more degrees of difficulty. The advanced grades in all countries are clearly distinguished from the early grades by the inclusion of flying-changes of leg and pirouettes and, at the Grand Prix or highest level, the *haute école* airs of piaffe and passage. Airs above the ground, such as the levade, courbette and others, which are the ultimate achieve-

Above An example of the power and control needed to execute some of the testing movements in an advanced event. Granat, ridden by Christine Stuckelberger.
Below A Lipizzaner from the Spanish Riding School practises the 'ballotade'.

ment at such academies as the Spanish Riding School are never included in competitions.

The national federations are responsible for devising and publishing a set of tests for all levels of national competition. These are called National Tests. The International Federation further devises and publishes four standard International Tests, all at Advanced grade, the lowest being the Prix St Georges which is separated from the Grand Prix at the top by the Intermediate I and the Intermediate II. These four tests form the basis of all International Competitions. Five judges for each of the four tests are recommended, although this number has varied from time to time in different places. From one to three judges are normally required for national contests.

The precise content of each of the stan-

dard international tests is revized approximately every four years so as to prevent the horses from becoming too narrowly routined, but they always take from eight to twelve minutes to perform. The programme at an international competition also frequently includes a Free-Style contest or Kur, in which competitors devise their own display, the only proviso being that they include and show all the particular movements that the organizers may prescribe.

Dressage contests are always ridden in rectangular arenas, the standard size of which is either 20 × 40 or 20 × 60 m. The standard international tests invariably require the larger arena. All arenas use a conventional system of lettering to indicate to riders and judges where the movements to be performed should begin and end. The origins of this somewhat illogical lettering system are obscure.

Competition judges are required to allocate a mark out of a maximum of ten for each movement or combination of movements as set out on the published test sheet. To do this efficiently the judge has to criticize and evaluate the performance, and then voice his conclusions. He is always accompanied by a writer whose duty it is to record on the judging sheet provided for each competitor, the mark allotted together with a summary of the judge's comments. These sheets are later made available for perusal by the competitors. The marks allotted by each of the presiding judges are collected, checked and totalled by the secretariat and the competitor scoring the highest total is the winner.

It is obvious that a good judge must have a very thorough knowledge of the principles of dressage and of the problems involved in training a horse. It is a great advantage if he has had practical experience of those problems from the saddle. He also has to memorize the test he is judging, since he cannot afford to take his eyes off the competitor during the performance and he must know the correct point at which each mark has to be given. Quick thinking, good judgement, moral courage, integrity and experience are essential qualities for a good judge. In fact his task is almost as difficult to perform well as that of the rider!

The International Federation maintains its own panel of judges who may officiate at international competitions. Each nation maintains its own list of judges, graded according to the standard of dressage for which they are considered qualified. As a guide and aid for standardized judging, the International Federation has specified certain connotations for each of the marks from nought to ten. These are:

0	Not performed	6	Satisfactory
1	Very bad	7	Fairly good
2	Bad	8	Good
3	Fairly bad	9	Very good
4	Insufficient	10	Excellent
5	Sufficient		

Dressage for combined training or eventing is not so demanding as the advanced form. Horse and rider have to perform an easier test but must still be supple, active and obedient. The tests are designed to show these attributes and are marked accordingly by skilled and experienced judges.

To assist in maintaining a reasonably high standard of training and performance it is stipulated in the rules that no horse shall receive a prize unless he has earned at least 50% of the maximum marks available. As an indication of the standard actually achieved in this century, it is a fact that there is no record of a horse ever scoring as much as 80% of possible marks from all five judges. A scoring at an international Grand Prix of anything over 75% is exceptional. The record is 79·5% achieved by Switzerland's Christine Stuckelberger and her horse Granat at Salzburg in 1975.

In Olympic Games and in Continental and World Championships it is usual to award team prizes for teams of three from any one nation in addition to the individual awards.

The dressage contest at the Stockholm Olympic Games, 1912, staged in a 20 × 40 m arena, was in the form of a Free Style and the degree of difficulty was extremely modest by later standards. No lateral movements of any kind were required, no piaffe, no passage and no sequence changes of leg. A jumping section, comprising five jumps and an obedience section were included. Eight nations competed with a total of 21 competitors and Swedish riders were placed first, second, third, fifth, sixth and eighth.

By the next Games held in Antwerp in 1920, a much more comprehensive set test had been devised including counter-changes-of-hand in trot and canter and sequence changes of leg in four-, three-, two- and one-time. Various coefficients were used for what were considered the most important movements, the highest coefficient being 30 for canter circles incorporating changes of rein and without changes of leg. The coefficient of 20 was given for the counter-change-of-hand in trot and canter, the serpentine in canter and for the sequence changes of leg in two- and one-time.

The piaffe and passage were first introduced into the Olympic dressage test in Los Angeles and have remained thereafter, with the exception of the post-war Games held in London in 1948. Canter pirouettes were required for the first time in Berlin in 1936.

Despite the enormous expansion of interest in pleasure riding and the various forms of equestrian sports that are such a feature of the mid-twentieth century, the number of truly first class international horse/rider combinations from any country (with the single exception of West Germany), remains surprisingly small. It actually seldom exceeds four or five, and with such small numbers, it is hardly surprising that the representation of any one nation has been liable to fluctuate quickly and dramatically in quality. For a few years

a country may show great promise or achieve outstanding success, but then, as one, or perhaps two, of their good horses retire, there may be no replacement available. Thus their team may be of little account for some years. Fortunes can also be seriously affected by the availability or otherwise of really good trainers – invaluable assets who are always in short supply. On all these counts West Germany stands alone with an apparently inexhaustible supply of trainers, good horses and skilful riders. A few countries (some of them famous in other forms of horsemanship, notably Italy), have either shown little interest in dressage or have made no significant impact internationally. This is also true of countries with relatively small populations such as Australia, New Zealand and Norway.

When one considers the principles and aims of modern dressage, it is perhaps easier to understand why most countries can boast only a few top class horses at any one time. Firstly it is required that a horse should be active and free, but still display all the qualities of power and speed that are its inherent characteristics. It must be light in hand, allowing the rider to control and deploy its movements with no visible effort and no more than a light contact with the reins. It must be calm, but keen, so that it gives the impression of always wanting to go forwards when allowed and asked to do so. It must be supple and submissive, willing to adjust its paces without resistance or resentment according to the slightest and outwardly invisible indications from its rider.

Other requirements are that the horse should remain perfectly straight from its head to its tail when moving on a straight line, and bent slightly in the direction in which it is travelling when on a curved line, so that full use can be made of its natural impulsion. All paces must have perfect regularity of rhythm, with the correct natural sequence of footfall at the walk, trot and canter. The horse must

accept a light, but continuous, contact through the reins, remaining confident, attentive and diligent, so that in effect, it gives the impression of doing of its own accord what is required of it. Together horse and rider should create an impression of elegance and total harmony.

The type of horse likely to conform to these requirements and to work successfully in the gymnastic discipline of dressage and high school will always be one that combines mental alertness and muscular freedom with a thoroughly strong, robust and symmetrical conformation. In particular it must have the potential ability to carry much of its own weight and that of its rider, with the hindquarters. The quarters and the loins therefore have to be strongly constructed with hocks that naturally fall into place in a weight carrying position in relation to the quarters themselves.

There has always been a tendency for certain breeds of horse to be popularly credited with possessing the best qualities for high school or, in this century, for high level competition dressage. The Spanish breeds, especially the Andalucians, which were considered to be unusually intelligent, courageous and well balanced, were very popular in the sixteenth and seventeenth centuries. Horses of umistakably Andalucian type were frequently chosen for important equestrian statues or paintings, the mounted statue of King Charles I in Trafalgar Square in London being an example. For similar reasons horses of Spanish blood were chosen as the breeding stock for the great school in Vienna in the late sixteenth century. It is for that reason that the school originally became known as the Spanish Riding Stable and later as the Spanish Riding School.

It was a further three hundred years before Thoroughbred blood, which did not exist until the early part of the eighteenth century, began to be used to influence the conformation and mental aspects of other breeds throughout Europe and the world.

Horses from the two remaining classical centres of *haute école*. *top*: A rider from the French school of the Cadre Noire at Saumur. The horse is in 'passage', an advanced movement. *bottom*: A Lipizzaner stallion in 'piaffe' on the long rein, which forms another aspect of the training at the Spanish Riding School in Vienna. Long reining in its simplest form is one of the early training stages for a young horse.

Nowadays it is renowned for its special qualities of speed, lightness of action, and beauty. Currently the most popular and successful dressage horses appear to be the German and Swedish breeds, both of which are strongly modified by Thoroughbred blood although it has only been introduced into the German breeds in quite recent years. The Hanoverian, Trakehner, Westphalian and Holstein studs all produce fine horses of substance and quality, and the breeding is carefully controlled so as to eliminate lines that do not come up to the required standards of movement and temperament. Some of the popularity of these horses as dressage mounts no doubt stems from the fame and success of the German riders in this discipline, but it cannot be denied that their horses do have many excellent qualities. They have been bred for many years essentially as riding horses rather than for speed alone as has largely been the case with the Thoroughbred. Swedish horses have been almost as successful as their German counterparts and are mainly a mixture of German and Thoroughbred blood.

The Thoroughbred itself has not yet become widely accepted as ideal for dressage purposes although there have been a number of pure Thoroughbreds that have earned themselves great distinction in this sphere. There is little evidence to suggest that they are physically or mentally unsuitable or incapable of even the most demanding movements such as piaffe and passage. However their inherent intelligence and sensitiveness demands a higher degree of sympathetic handling than is essential in some coarser breeds. It is generally considered that horses of most, or at least many, breeds can become excellent dressage horses provided that they are well constructed, well handled and well ridden. Surprisingly it is also true that for competition purposes the Lipizzaner, for all his great ability and fame, is put at some disadvantage by his relatively small size combined with his naturally rather short action. Consequently the breed is not as popular as might be supposed among ambitious competition riders, though there have been one or two with distinguished careers. Notable among them was Conversano Caprice who represented England during the sixties when ridden by Mrs R. N. Hall and won a number of Grand Prix and other prizes in Europe.

With its seemingly endless supply of good horses, riders and talented professional trainers, West Germany leads the world in the field of dressage. Their impressive achievements at past Olympics show this to be a position they have enjoyed for some considerable time, and their overwhelming domination of the world dressage scene seems unlikely to change significantly during this century. The sport is undoubtedly helped by the immensely strong support given to it throughout the country and this is further upheld by the interest shown from the government. The state controlled school at Warendorf, for example, with its permanent establishment of school horses and trainers, acts as a controlling centre. Dressage has virtually assumed the status of a national sport in Germany, and although this is partly because of the restrictions on outdoor riding in winter, the interest is widely spread, with a high standard of connoisseurship among the population.

The very large number of competition horses that are regularly trained and ridden up to Grand Prix level throughout the country, has resulted in Germany becoming the main source of supply for other countries wishing to import top quality, at least partly-trained, dressage horses. These horses command very high prices, and indeed the German riders themselves are prepared to pay large sums of money for trained horses.

Elsewhere on the continent of Europe, dressage training in France has mainly been based at, and fostered by, the long-established, one-time cavalry school at Saumur. In recent years however, the school's output has dwindled and is now being overtaken by individual civilians.

Switzerland has ideal conditions for dressage which it owes to wartime neutrality and a severe winter climate. The leading riders have until recently all been soldiers based on the cavalry school at Berne, but as in other countries, the closure of this establishment has resulted in the balance tilting in favour of civilian riders. During the fifties and sixties, the Swiss developed a distinct style of dressage that owed more to the teaching and practice of Saumur than to that of Vienna or the more precise and forceful German style. More recently, the Swiss have tended to make use of their geographical link with Austria to liaise more closely with the Spanish Riding School.

The Swiss have always looked to other countries, Sweden in particular, for their best cavalry, and thus dressage, horses. However, one of their most successful and famous horses, Granat, owned and ridden by Christine Stuckelberger is a Holstein, who was trained with the help of the Austrian ex-Oberbereiter of the Spanish School, Georg Wahl. Granat is considered by many to be one of the finest dressage horses in living memory.

The Scandinavian countries, notably Sweden, have long been prominent on the dressage map, and Sweden in fact held a leading role in the development of modern dressage throughout the first half of the present century. Her inspiration came from the cavalry school at Stromsholm and her neutrality during both world wars helped to ensure a strong position when most other countries were struggling to

Below Bruce Davidson and Irish Cap preparing for the dressage phase of the Olympic Three-Day Event in Montreal where he was a member of the winning American team.
Below right HRH Princess Anne and Doublet. For an eventer, Doublet's dressage was excellent.

reestablish their postwar economies. Sweden's northern climate has always encouraged indoor riding during the winter, which inevitably led to a feeling for and an interest in dressage riding.

Swedish riders completely dominated the competition world dressage arenas during the first twenty-five years of the century and they have remained a strong force ever since. Possibly their most famous rider has been Major H. St Cyr who took the gold medals in 1952 and 1956 riding Master Rujus and Juli. The country's well controlled and intelligent breeding system has produced a very robust and handsome type of horse that has found popularity in many other countries.

In Denmark, dressage has always enjoyed a high degree of participation in relation to the population, although the main interest comes from the small private establishments. Denmark first came to prominence in 1952 when Mme Liz Hartel took the Olympic silver medal at Helsinki on Jubilee, a horse which she herself originally trained. Subsequent progress and success can be mainly attributed to the talent of trainer Gunnar Andersen.

Participation in international dressage in the United States has been sporadic both in quality and volume. In the past, many German horses, most of them at least partly trained in Germany, have been used but there are definite indications now of a swing in favour to the many high quality American Thoroughbreds. Much reliance has been placed on the frequent visits of top grade professional trainers, many of whom have taken up temporary residence, and as such, are in constant demand.

As we have seen previously, Great Britain lags far behind other nations in this sport, and virtually no interest was shown until just before the Second World War. The cavalry school at Weedon, which

might have provided a nucleus of skilled riders had been abolished by the end of the war and it was left to a very small number of civilian enthusiasts to establish this form of equestrianism in a country infinitely more interested in such sports as hunting. In spite of the fact that there was little in the way of knowledgeable or professional help available, this small number included two or three with considerable talent – all of them women – who quickly assumed a place in European circles. The general disinterest persisted, making overall progress slow, but by the sixties a substantial degree of achievement had been made, the highlight coming in 1963 when Mrs Brenda Williams and Little Model took the bronze position in the European championship. Britain has no Olympic medals for dressage to her credit.

Dressage in the USSR owes its origins to the work of the Englishman James Fillis, who was Ecuyer-en-chef at the cavalry school at St Petersburg from 1898 to 1910. Widely considered to be the greatest high school rider of his or any previous age, Fillis had previously been a pupil of the Frenchman Baucher, who had developed theories and techniques somewhat at variance with those of Gueriniere and the eighteenth century classicists. Fillis simplified and modified Baucher's teaching and set down his own ideas in his book *The Principles of Dressage and Equitation*.

The sport was inevitably eclipsed by the revolution and its after effects, but it gradually began to be practised again after the Second World War in the state riding schools of the bigger cities. The U.S.S.R. first achieved major international status in the Rome Olympics of 1960, since when they have been consistently to the fore in their annual excursions to the European championships and their participation in the Olympic Games.

The Hunting Horse

THE hunting horse is a type, not a breed, and there is no record of the first use of the horse as a means of transport in pursuing hounds. It is something that happened in the mists of pre-recorded history.

We must define hunting as the pursuit of a wild animal in its own environment by man employing a pack of hounds. The link between horse and hound is vital, since the speed and activity of the hound has always been the major influence in producing the hunting horse.

The ancient Chinese, Egyptian and Greek civilizations did much of their hunting on foot, although they used horses extensively in the Chase as well as on the battlefield. The great horse master, Xenophon, born in 430 BC in Athens, made it clear in his classic book on equitation that basically the same priorities in stamina, fitness and obedience were required in the hunting horse then, as are still sought by the hunting fraternity of today.

The Roman writer, Oppian, in the third century AD described the points he would look for in buying a hunter-charger as follows: 'He must have size and substance and well knit limbs; a small head carried high, with a neck arching like the plume on a helmet; forehead broad, thick curly forelock; eye clear and fiery, broad chest; and back with a double chine; a good full tail; muscular thighs; fine, clean legs, pastern sloping, hoof rising high, close

grained and strong. These are the qualities prominent in Tuscan, Armenian, Achaean, and the famous Cappadocian horses, and such are the horses for hunting wild beasts or for use as chargers in war.'

Oppian referred to the need in hunting for 'an active horse accustomed to leap over stone fences and dykes', but for many centuries – certainly throughout medieval times – the hunting horse was not required to possess the jumping ability expected from the modern top-class quality hunter.

To be relevant, it is inevitable that any discussion of the hunting horse must be centred almost exclusively on Britain and Ireland. In both these countries organized hunting (providing the pattern for that practised in America, Southern Africa, Australia, New Zealand, India and elsewhere) has been a major equestrian activity for some 300 years and has exerted, in consequence, a corresponding influence on horse-breeding. Indeed, before the growth of competitive riding to its present level, an extension belonging only to the last quarter of a century, hunting was the principal horse sport and today it is still the one attracting the largest number of participants. As a result, established hunter breeding industries exist in Britain and Ireland but are not found in other countries where less emphasis is given to the sport.

Stag, boar and fallow buck were the main quarry for hounds in Europe for centuries, and continued to be so long after William the Conqueror brought discipline to the Chase. To pursue these, the hunting horse needed stamina for the long days in the great royal hunting grounds, of which the New Forest in Hampshire is the last surviving example, but there was little requirement for a horse capable of jumping vertical obstacles at speed in the hunting field until the latter half of the seventeenth century at last saw the fox becoming a more popular quarry.

The clearance of the great forests coupled with changes in farming methods,

especially the enclosure of fields in the early eighteenth century, increased the emphasis on hunting the fox in the open, rather than pursuing the deer in the woodland. The great grazing grounds of Leicestershire allowed hounds to run fast in the open country, and the fox proved a worthy quarry in such a setting. In the late eighteenth century William Childe came to the Quorn country from Shropshire and is credited with introducing the art of riding 'to hounds' as opposed to 'after hounds'.

Now the hunting horse was required to gallop and jump fences and take ditches in his stride. He had to clear without hesitation the new 'oxer fence' – a hedge with a rail in front designed to keep young beef cattle from damaging the hedge. A double oxer, a hedge with timber rails standing on both sides, was a formidable obstacle indeed, and is still encountered in some areas in the hunting field, as well as in a more sophisticated form in show jumping courses.

As foxhunting gained strength, the hunting man in Leicestershire required far more quality in his horse and it became essential to use Thoroughbred sires in producing hunters. Not everyone approved of the trend. Hugo Meynell, Master of the Quorn, complained that after the young 'bloods' emulated 'Flying' Childe's methods 'he had not enjoyed a day's happiness'.

The rate at which Childe and his friends crossed country in pursuit of hounds was to be far exceeded in the nineteenth century when huntsmen of the Leicestershire packs developed the art of providing 'the quick thing'. This was a very fast burst across grass and fences with the mounted field riding as close to hounds as their nerves, and their horses' ability, would allow.

In the early days of the nineteenth century the conditioning of hunters frequently fell far short of the new demands imposed by the increasingly popular sport of fox-

hunting. Charles James Apperley, who was the most celebrated hunting correspondent of the period, writing under the nom de plume Nimrod, advised: 'Do not trespass too far on the willing powers of your horses. Rather than insist upon their coming home, when showing signs of distress, let them remain at some village for the night, leaving a whipper-in in attendance. Hundreds of good hunters have been destroyed by the neglect of this mere act of humanity towards exhausted nature in a noble and willing animal.'

The practice was growing of taking out two hunters for a day's sport, particularly in the grass countries of Leicestershire, Rutland and Northamptonshire. Frequently the hunting man would also use a 'covert hack' as well, riding this horse to the first covert to be drawn by hounds. There he would change to his first hunter which would have been taken on ahead by the groom so as to be fit and fresh for the first run of the day.

The growing demands for suitable horses were immense, and provided impetus for enormous growth in all the ancillary activities such as growing corn and hay, horse doctoring and dealing, and making saddlery.

Nimrod had grand ideas, but he was a good reporter, and he estimated that a Master hunting hounds would need 14 hunters to ride himself, and a further 12 for the use of whippers-in. Labour was cheap, but the price of really top-class hunters could be

Fig 1. The Standing Leap
Fig 2. The Flying Leap
Fig 3. The Back Jump
Fig 4. The Water Leap

Below Hunting – one of the great British traditions that has spread to other countries. The huntsman casts his pack of hounds for the first draw to pick up the scent of the quarry, in this case a fox.

Above Some older styles for hunting showing the more backward seat adopted in the 18th and 19th centuries.

Right An Ascot meet in 1858. Once a sport of the rich, hunting is now enjoyed by a wide spectrum of people.

extremely high as can be realized by translating several thousand guineas in the last century into today's money values.

Already Ireland was recognized as a source of superb hunters. The mild climate and abundant grass produced horses of bone and substance; as Nimrod said, 'It is owing to the practice of the young horses of Ireland scampering across the country in their colthood, that they are such good fencers as we find them, unless it be at timber, at which they have no practice.'

Ireland's importance as a producer of hunters is as strong now as then, but today the English hunting man finds it increasingly difficult to compete with buyers from the continent of Europe, the United States and even South Africa, who pay high prices for Irish horses as potential show jumpers and eventers.

At the top of the sport in the nineteenth century such colourful characters as Squire Osbaldeston and Thomas Assheton Smith were performing extraordinary feats of endurance and courage with their hunters. Yet the bottom of the hunter market was often appalling, both in the lack of quality of horses available, and the difficulty of finding a sound one. Robert Surtees wrote amusingly, yet scathingly, of the tricks employed by horse dealers who found a new market of 'mugs' in the influx of newly-rich, middle class merchants and businessmen benefiting from the industrial revolution and seeking to gain status in the hunting field. This was obviously a gullible and readily exploited market.

The new demand for riding horses in the hunting field was such that nearly £7 million was spent abroad on importing horses into Britain in the ten years up to 1882. In 1885 the Hunters' Improvement and National Light Horse Breeding Society was founded to encourage breeding in Britain, and it continues to perform an invaluable service today. The Society distributes thousands of pounds each year in the form of premiums, or subsidies, to the owners of about 60 stallions selected at the Society's annual stallion show, held each spring at Newmarket.

The owner of each stallion awarded a premium, receives a grant, and in addition there are a number of 'super premiums' receiving extra awards. Through these subsidies the stallions are made available to non-Thoroughbred brood mares at reduced fees. Fees for Thoroughbred mares are made by arrangement with the owner of the stallion concerned. The stallions, selected from regions throughout the country, are regularly and rigorously checked to ensure that they remain sound and therefore fit for their work.

Top The West Waterford foxhound pack in Ireland, arguably the best hunting country in the world and producer of some of the finest horses.
Bottom An English hunt going on to draw.

It is impossible, however, to consider the hunting horse in isolation for it was from the hunting field that steeplechasing, show jumping and horse trials evolved. The HIS scheme, therefore, has produced distinguished winners in National Hunt racing as well as other types of equestrian sports and its basic influence on the quality of horses in the hunting field has doubtless been immensely beneficial.

The HIS summer show for mares and youngstock, held at Shrewsbury, is a wonderful shop window, displaying much that is best in modern hunter breeding. Ireland's great exhibition of hunters is in August at the famous Dublin Horse Show. This event is as much a fair as a show, for nearly every exhibited animal is available for buyers, who come from all over the world. In England the great county shows, and the Royal International and Horse of the Year Shows at Wembley in London, provide the stage for the show hunter classes. Despite increasing costs and much lower prize money than is available in show jumping, these classes are keenly contested.

Judging the ridden hunter classes in the main ring at say, the Royal at Stoneleigh, requires considerable aplomb as well as skill and experience from the judges. Their own performance in the saddle as they ride and assess each entry in the ring is as keenly noted as the quality of the animals on show. The judges who officiate at the wealth of in-hand and ridden classes throughout the summer season shows provide an immense service in helping to maintain standards. But the greatest boon of all to the hunter type is that it is still a genuine working horse for which attested performance is the priority. It is never just a question of 'how does he look?'; the more important query in the mind of a hunter judge is 'how does he move?'. Many a good looking horse never gets into the front row of a hunter class because he does not gallop well.

The recent growth and popularity of the working hunter classes places the emphasis even more firmly on performance, and here the hunters are required to jump as well as work on the flat in front of the judges.

It is, however, the continuance of more

than 245 packs of foxhounds in Britain and Ireland, plus nearly 60 harrier packs, and half a dozen each of staghounds and draghounds, that ensures more work and demand than ever before for the hunting horse. Foxhunting, in particular, has seen an immense boom in the postwar years and there are over 30 more packs of foxhounds in existence in England and Wales now than at the turn of the century. Hunts are better supported and more people are following hounds on horseback than ever before, in spite of the fact that the quality of cross-country riding available to the hunting field has deteriorated considerably in many areas. This is mainly attributable to modern farming's increasing reliance on arable land instead of grass, and the enormous increase of barbed wire in the traditional beef, dairying and sheep farming areas has been another blow to the mounted field.

The biggest problem in terms of the hunting horse in recent years has been in finding a suitable mount for the heavyweight man. He requires a seven-eighths bred horse with quality and substance, but not only is this the hardest to come by, it is also the most expensive to purchase and maintain. Such a horse can fetch several thousand pounds nowadays as an untried youngster if it has real potential for show jumping or horse trials.

In the English and Irish hunting field clean bred horses are still in a minority, but those people who are of the right weight, and possess the skill to ride Thoroughbreds out hunting, claim that no better hunter exists. The threequarter-bred and half-bred hunter is still heavily relied upon for adults in the United Kingdom and Ireland.

There has been considerable disquiet and concern over the decrease in the Irish draught horse, which probably constitutes the best foundation stock of all for producing hunters of substance. The Irish draught is not a heavy horse of the ilk of the Shires used on the land in England. As a breed, it was traditionally used by the Irish farmer on the land, but when crossed with a Thoroughbred, the mare would provide a first rate hunter – no doubt a great help in augmenting the farmer's income when sent to the local horse fair, or up to Dublin. The Irish Horse Board, formed by the Government to safeguard and improve the breeding industry, has recently recognized the importance of the draught horse and current efforts to save this foundation stock deserve every encouragement.

The real weight-carrying cob is sadly a much rarer sight in the hunting field nowadays than at one time, but there is a considerable increase in middleweight riding horses which generally contain a large proportion of Thoroughbred blood. These are suitable mounts for many of the lady riders who nowadays often form the majority of the mounted followers in the hunting field, especially on weekdays.

The native pony breeds have had considerable influence on horses used in the English hunting field. Their inherent hardiness, toughness and agility are all traits required when following hounds in the extremely varied countries where hunting still flourishes. Galloping on the moors of

Top The winning line-up at a recent stallion show at Newmarket, England. The Hunters' Improvement Society scheme helps to make good quality stallions available all over the country for reasonable stud fees.
Above An Irish Draught horse which, when crossed with a Thoroughbred produces the renowned Irish hunter.

the West Country and the north, traversing hilly tracks in Wales and the Border countries, scrambling over banks, or negotiating stone walls, all call for physical and

Foxhunting originated in Great Britain but has spread with remarkably little change to other parts of the world. *top*: An Irish ditch in Tipperary. Many young Irish horses are 'made' in the hunting field, and are much sought after as show jumpers and event horses. *middle*: The Rallye Piqu'avant Nivernais hunt in Burgundy. Hunting in continental Europe is threatened by the spread of rabies. *bottom*: There are about a hundred packs of hounds recognized by the American Masters of Foxhounds Association. Both the indigenous grey and the imported red fox are hunted.

mental qualities which can be well supplied by horses containing Welsh pony or cob blood.

The Connemara is another highly favoured foundation stock for producing excellent hunters, and the native ponies themselves have successfully introduced many an aspiring Nimrod to the hunting field in his youth. The modern riding pony containing Thoroughbred blood, may perform brilliantly in the hunting field, but the native pony's sensible temperament, sure-footedness and instinctive knowledge of his own environment still make him the best choice for a child's first pony to be ridden after hounds. Indeed they are not exclusively for children – in Wales, and the West Country particularly, you will see many an adult enjoying his hunting on a

pony. The Exmoor shepherd, on his sturdy little mount, his legs dangling by its sides, will see more of the sport than most followers when the Devon and Somerset Staghounds are running.

In France, where deer, hare, and wild boar are still hunted, there are in general far fewer obstacles to be jumped in the hunting field than in the majority of English hunting countries. A blood horse, or nearly clean bred horse, would be appropriate to follow staghounds when the speed of the quarry and the stronger scent associated with deer, decree many long, fast points throughout the day.

Foxhunting enjoys popularity as a sport in the United States and the Thoroughbred horse is used far more widely in following hounds than in Britain. In Virginia and Maryland, particularly favoured for the sport, there is still plenty of grass, and the horses are mainly faced with timber fences, some of which are imposing in height and solidity. Americans who visit Britain usually find the hedges and ditches of the vale countries and High Leicestershire a most novel challenge.

Australians and New Zealanders often use Thoroughbreds in the hunting field, but again the nature of the terrain is a major factor. In New Zealand there are no foxes, and it is the harrier packs that are well supported. Visitors are frequently surprised and impressed by the ease with which New Zealand hunters habitually jump formidable barbed wire fences, five or six strands high.

Teaching horses to jump wire is a somewhat increasing trend in the English hunting field, but wire is still shunned by many riders. In Ireland the wide ditches of Co. Meath, and the banks and walls of such famous hunting countries as Limerick, Tipperary and Kilkenny offer a special challenge to the hunting horse and his intrepid rider.

It is still considered advisable to buy Irish horses young if they are to hunt in England or elsewhere. The experienced Irish hunter tends to take his fences slowly, often from a trot or a walk. He will usually jump on to an obstacle rather than over it, which works brilliantly over an Irish country, but woe betide the horse who takes off slowly and attempts to bank an English thorn hedge with a wide ditch on the landing side! Properly cut and laid hedges are rarer nowadays, and the modern hedge cutting machine makes a hedge an even broader and more difficult obstacle for the hunter. The Blackmore Vale in Dorset, the Berkeley country in Gloucestershire, parts of Buckinghamshire and Northamptonshire, and some areas of Leicestershire, are among the countries offering the stiffest fences still tackled by the modern hunter.

The hunting horse is a miracle of evolution and survival; he is much in demand, and still performs a tough job in an extraordinary diversity of environments. And because he remains a true working animal, he has avoided the destructive fads and fancies which have ruined so many breeds of pet dogs.

Show Jumping

ALTHOUGH men have been riding horses for more than 3,000 years, persuading them to jump over obstacles is a comparatively new idea. Show-jumping, which has grown out of this, is thus also a fairly recent innovation compared with other equestrian activities. Only in the second half of the eighteenth century did jumping on horses begin to achieve some recognition and then it was slow to gain ground. The first mention of it being included in any cavalry manual belongs to the French, in 1788 and although the British foxhunter thinks of his predecessors going across country from time immemorial, it was the Enclosure Acts of the eighteenth century, bringing about the considerable increase in the number of hedges and fences to enclose fields, that set them jumping.

It was something like another hundred years before jumping, as opposed to steeplechasing, was officially recorded, and then it sprang up in various parts of the world within a very short period. Ireland, in which country steeplechasing had its infancy, was again a front runner in show-jumping, and at the Royal Dublin Society's annual show in 1865 there were competitions for 'wide' and 'high' leaps. There were competitions in Russia at about the same time, and in Paris in 1866, although here, the competitors paraded at the show and then went out into the country to jump over mainly natural fences. Nine years later the famous French Cavalry School at Saumur included an exhibition of jumping in their display of *haute école*.

In England jumping was primarily a part of agricultural shows, and was first officially recorded at the five-day show at the Agricultural Hall, Islington, London, in 1876. Horses entered for the show classes were also eligible for the leaping, which was decided solely on style, and judged by Masters of Foxhounds. Even when a few rules concerning jumping ability were introduced, style was still an important factor. It enabled the judges to arrive at the most diplomatic result for it would never have done for the local squire to be beaten by one of his tenants!

In the United States the National Horse Show was started at Madison Square Garden, New York, in 1883. The 'Garden' has been moved twice since then but the show goes on as strongly as ever. By the turn of the century, the 'new' sport was very firmly established internationally; Germany held shows in towns all over the country and in the second of the Modern Olympic Games, at Paris in 1900, three jumping competitions were included, a High Jump, a Long Jump and Prize jumping. The following year in Turin, saw the first recorded official international show-jumping, with German Army Officers invited to pit their skill against their Italian counterparts.

In London the first International Horse Show (forerunner of the Royal International), was held at Olympia in 1907, as a result of a meeting held at The Hague two years earlier. The Earl of Lonsdale directed the International Horse Show, the board and directors of which, comprised

Top-class show jumping has become the major money sport in the equestrian world apart from racing. The German riders and horses are always hard to beat.

men from many European countries and the United States. High and wide jumps were included in the programme, and the prize money was quite considerable. Two Belgian riders – Haegemann and Van Langendonck – had won at the Paris Games, and the same country, and Holland, dominated that first International.

Tommy Glencross, who was to play an important part in the development of show-jumping in Britain, won a High Jump competition.

Speakeasy jumping at Hickstead, with Harvey Smith, one of the sport's great personalities and a big winner.

In 1906 the Swedish Count Clarence von Rosen had put a proposition to the Congress of the International Olympic Committee that equestrian sports should be included on a permanent basis in the Games – there had been none at all in St Louis in 1904 – and although the suggestion was not greeted with abundant enthusiasm, Baron Pierre de Coubertin, the founder of the Modern Games, asked von Rosen to present more detailed proposals to the 1907 Congress. These were for three events – dressage, an equestrian pentathlon and a game called Jeu de Rose.

The British members of the IOC agreed that these should be included in the 1908 Games, which were to be held in London, and the committee of the International Horse Show consented to organize them, provided there was a minimum of 24 entries from six different countries. In fact there were 88 entries from eight countries, which perhaps proved too much for the International Show, itself still in its infancy. At the last minute the equestrian events were dropped from the Olympic programme. Von Rosen did not lose heart, however. The next Olympics were to be held in Stockholm, and in 1909 a committee, with himself as secretary-general and Prince Carl of Sweden as president, produced three events for the 1912 Games. These were, dressage, a three-day event, otherwise known as the Military, and show-jumping.

International jumping was increasing. In 1909 the first Lucerne show was held, with Italians, Germans, French and Belgians in opposition to the Swiss. That same year the National Horse Show in New York introduced international jumping. A team of five British Army officers, captained by Major J. G. Beresford, took part, and won one of the events. Four years later, a Military Team competition, a forerunner of the Nations Cup, was held at the show.

Team jumping was held at the London International for the first time in 1909, when the French won the inaugural King Edward VII Cup. Before the show, in common with almost all others, was suspended for the First World War, and before

the Russian revolution, the Czarist cavalry came to London to complete a glorious hat-trick of wins of the Cup, in 1912–14, under the leadership of the Captain, Paul Rodzianko. He and his compatriots took the King Edward VII Cup, which they had then won outright, back to Russia, in 1914 and it was never seen again.

The 1912 Olympic show-jumping was run under a complicated set of rules. Ten marks were given for each fence, with deductions for faults, for example a first refusal cost two marks, a second, or fall of horse and rider, four, a third, or fall of rider only, six. Clearly it was considered more ignominious to fall off a horse than to cause him to fall too. There were marks for hitting a fence with hind or forelegs, for landing on or within the demarcation line of a spread fence, and altogether so many complications that judging must have been far from easy.

Perhaps one of the great appeals of show-jumping nowadays as a public spectacle is the ease of its judging. Every ringside spectator can see for himself whether or not a horse has hit a fence and lowered it, and only the water still produces disputed judgements. These are now being eliminated by the use of plastic strips on the landing edge. In the early days however, it was so complicated that at the London International for example, every fence had its own judge, who would send his marks back to the main judging box, all to be added up before the winner could be announced.

In the 1912 Games each country was allowed to enter six competitors for the individual jumping and four, with the best three scores counting, for the team. Eight countries – Belgium, Chile, France, Germany, Britain, Norway, Russia and Sweden – entered a total of 31 riders in the individual, which was won by Captain Cariou of France, also the winner of a bronze in the Three-Day Event. Sweden won the team gold medal, from France and Germany, followed, in order, by the United States, Russia and Belgium. The next year Germany founded their own Olympic Equestrian Committee, but of course the war brought the sport to a standstill in

Europe. In the United States in 1917 what was to become known as the American Horse Shows Association was founded, with representatives of 50 shows at its inaugural meeting. The AHSA was to be the official representative body for the United States in international affairs.

The effects of the famous Italian, Federico Caprilli's system of training was given dramatic emphasis at the first post-War Olympics held at Antwerp in 1920 when two Italians schooled under his methods, Lt Tommaso Lequio, and Major Valerio, won the gold and silver medals. The Italian team took the bronze, behind Sweden and Belgium. No British riders took part in the 1920 Games, because of a cattle-disease ban, but the London International was reopened that same year.

Although equestrian sports were now a recognized part of the Olympic movement, they had no ruling body of their own. But Baron de Coubertin, looking ahead, had encouraged the creation of World federations for each sport, so that they could standardize their rules and bring an overall uniformity and control into sports. Commandant Georges Hector, of France, drew up statutes for the Federation Equestre Internationale, which were adopted at a Congress in Paris in November 1921. Thus Sweden and France were the prime movers in the establishment of the FEI, and the other six founder-members were Belgium, Denmark, Italy, Japan, Norway and the United States. Germany became affiliated to the International Federation in the year of its creation, and Switzerland joined in 1922.

Canada began to take an active interest when the Toronto Winter Fair started in 1922, and the first Canadian Nations Cup was held five years later. Show-jumping was by no means confined to the Northern half of the American continent. The first international show in Buenos Aires was held in 1910, with riders from Italy, Spain and France as well as other South American countries. Two Chilean riders had also competed in London and the Olympics in 1912.

Britain's fairly chaotic show-jumping situation was gradually sorted out after the foundation of the British Show Jumping Association in 1923. Lord Lonsdale accepted the position of President of the Association, with Colonel V. D. S. Williams, father of television commentator Dorian Williams, as secretary. A mixture of military men and the top civilian riders helped to form the Association, which, by improving both judging and the courses they jumped, began to produce British riders and horses of international standard.

A record entry of 99 riders on 110 horses from 17 countries at the first Olympic events to be held under FEI rules, at Paris in 1924, showed that the sport was continuing to grow in popularity. Sweden again won the team event, but Lecquio, the individual winner four years earlier, was now beaten by the Swiss, Alphons Gemuseus.

Britain joined the FEI the following year and in 1926 the Royal Dublin Society, having helped to get the sport off the starting block some 60 years earlier, introduced international jumping.

Although successes for United States show-jumpers are no rarity nowadays, their rider Fred Bontecou was something of an exception when he won the coveted King George V Gold Cup at the London International in 1926.

Jack Talbot-Ponsonby, the first man to win the King George V Cup three times, and later to become one of Britain's finest course builders, had the first of his three victories in the 1930 show, at which Mike Ansell also had his first taste of international success. Both went with the successful British Army team to New York the following year, helping to foster in Ansell an enthusiasm for the sport which grew and in turn helped Britain develop into a World power in show-jumping.

Olympic equestrian events were held outside Europe for the first time, when the Games went to Los Angeles, but they were hardly a success. Only six countries and a total of 34 riders competed. International travel for horses in those days was a long, arduous and expensive business, and only

France, Holland, Sweden and Japan sent horses to take on the United States and Mexico. France and Holland did not enter show-jumpers, and no country had three finishers in the show jumping, so there were no team awards. Baron Takeichi Nishi won the gold for Japan, beating the American Harry Chamberlin, one of the most brilliant horsemen his country has ever produced.

The Berlin Games in 1936, proved a show case for German superiority, and their riders won the individual and team gold medals at show-jumping, dressage and the Three-Day Event.

During the war, while a prisoner, the now legendary figure of British and international show-jumping, Mike Ansell, started to work on his master-plan for bringing the sport in his home country up to the top international level. It was fortunate that Ansell, who had been partially blinded and was to end up completely without his sight, should have found himself in the same prisoner-of-war camp as two other show-jumping enthusiasts and old team mates of his, Nat Kindersley and Bede Cameron. From the ideas they tossed

Two leading figures in British show jumping. *above*: Col. Sir Michael Ansell, chief architect of modern show jumping in Britain even though blinded in World War II. *below*: Douglas Bunn, founder of Hickstead.

around grew the dream which, as soon as he was repatriated in 1944, Ansell started to make into a reality. In December of that year he was invited to become chairman of the British Show Jumping Association, a post he held for more than two decades.

He chose for his committee, men of like mind, intent on making show-jumping into the exciting, crowd-pulling sport it has become. They had a lot to do. In those days there was virtually no limit to the time a rider could take to complete his round, circling as often he wished to make his approach to a fence exactly right, unclipping his martingale as he came to the water jump. On each fence was a slat, a thin lath of wood which, if knocked off, cost half a fault. Thus accuracy was essential, no matter how long it might take. The courses were uninteresting, normally consisting of a few uprights along each side of the ring, before turning into a water jump or big spread in the middle.

Gradually these impediments to a slick show were weeded out. A grading system, on prize money won, was introduced, so that horses would compete against others of roughly similar ability and experience. Then Ansell and his men looked for a venue at which to put their new-look show-jumping to the public test. They chose the White City, London, and so began what was to be a long and successful association. The first show included the National Championship, won with that story-book touch which Ansell so often seemed to conjure out of thin air, by a repatriated Nat Kindersley. The following year, two shows were held at the White City, and the Victory Championship went to Colonel Harry Llewellyn, who in the jump-off beat the 18-year-old Douglas Bunn – two men who were to have incalculable influence on British show-jumping over the next few decades.

The National Show in New York

restarted in 1945; the FEI reopened its shop in 1946, and throughout Europe show-jumping, in common with other sports, was restarted. For the first time civilian riders took the International stage, including one of the greatest of all, the Frenchman Pierre Jonqueres d'Oriola, a mercurial man whose career has been a succession of ups and downs. The ups started with the 1946 Grand Prix in Zurich and took in two Olympic Individual Gold Medals – a feat no other rider has achieved – in 1952 and 1964. The International was re-born, at the White City, when d'Oriola won the King George V Cup. For the first time the show was televised, so beginning the build-up of a massive audience which, in turn, has had a considerable effect on the growth of the sport.

The Olympic Games restarted in 1948 when they were held in England. The Royal International Committee, under Mike Ansell, were given the job of preparing a combined team and individual competition, for the show-jumping which, was to be the last competitive event before the closing ceremony, in the vast Wembley Stadium. Getting the course built in time was a herculean task, for weeks of rain had left the ground a quagmire and work could only start after the Soccer final had finished the night before. All the fences had to be manhandled onto the ground, and the water jump dug by hand because of the state of the ground. Fifteen teams of three started, and the Individual Gold was won by the Mexican Humberto Mariles on

the one-eyed Arete. His team, too, emerged triumphant, beating Spain, with the British gaining their first Olympic show jumping medal, the team bronze.

The following week, the British team captain, Harry Llewellyn and Foxhunter won the first of their three King George V Gold Cups – Foxhunter is the only horse so far to have won this classic three times. And four years later in Helsinki, Foxhunter's final clear round clinched the team gold medal for Britain. Wilf White and Nizefela might well have taken the Individual gold too, but for a belated decision, by only one of the two judges, that he had gone in the water. In the end there was a five-sided jump-off for the medals, won by d'Oriola, with Chile's Oscar Christi winning the individual silver and ensuring that his team also finished second.

That year was notable also for the first of the official FEI Championships, for Juniors – those between 14 and 18 years – in which there were only two teams. The Italians, including Graziano Mancinelli, beat Belgium. Gradually the International Federation introduced other championships, for seniors also, beginning with the Men's World Championship, held for the first time in Paris in 1953. It was won by the popular Spaniard Francisco 'Paco' Goyoaga, an achievement made more remarkable by the fact he was riding a horse who had, or so it seemed beforehand, lost his enthusiasm for the game. They beat Germany's Thiedemann by just half a point. D'Oriola was third, followed by

Piero d'Inzeo, an auspicious cast indeed to the new championship.

Initially the World Championships were held every year and two years later Hans Gunter Winkler, won the first of two successive World titles on Halla. This horse was arguably the greatest show-jumping mare of all time, on whom Winkler also won the Individual Olympic gold in Stockholm, 1956, when she had practically to carry him round the second course after he had badly hurt a muscle. Winkler was also in the winning team, a feat he repeated in Rome, Tokyo and Munich, to give him five golds, more than any other rider in Olympic history.

Raimondo d'Inzeo, the more successful of the two classical Italian brothers, won the next two World titles – after going down to Winkler and Halla in a jump-off in 1955. By this time, the World Championship had settled down to a four-year cycle, interspersed by the European championships, which are now held every other year. Winkler won the first of the continental titles, in 1957, and Thiedemann the second. There was often a challenger from outside Europe for the title, and in 1966 Nelson Pessoa, the Brazilian who spends his summers in Europe, won from Frank Chapot of the United States, with Hugo Arrambide of Argentina third. Soon after this the FEI decreed that the European championship should be confined to the riders that its title suggested, a sensible enough move, for it makes the World Championships relatively more important.

There is a fundamental difference in the two championships. The European is decided on a basis of three rounds, with points from each accumulating to decide the champion, while the World Championship has three qualifying rounds. These produce the top four riders who, in the final, all ride each other's horses. This has been a somewhat controversial formula ever since its inception, and the opposition to it is still growing. It would therefore be no suprise if the event eventually falls in line with the European scheme.

A European championship for women was also introduced in 1957, going to Pat Smythe, who is conceivably the greatest woman rider the sport has produced. Britain has dominated this title over the years (until it was amalgamated with the men's title in 1975), but no-one more so than Pat, who achieved a hat-trick in 1961–63 on Flanagan. When women were first admitted to Olympic show jumping, Pat Smythe and Flanagan were in the team in Stockholm, 1956, together with Wilf White and Peter Robeson, and they took the bronze behind Germany and Italy.

Pat Smythe and Flanagan were back in the British squad four years later in Rome, together with another of their sex, Dawn Wofford, née Palethorpe. The brilliant young David Broome joined them in the Individual on Sunsalve, a horse he had ridden to victory in the King's Cup within two weeks of first trying him, and now took the bronze. It was Italy's day, however and

Four of the world's leading international show jumpers. *above far left*: Capt. Raimondo d'Inzeo and Talky. Capt. d'Inzeo won two world titles and with his brother Piero has formed the backbone of the Italian team for some twenty years. *above*: United States team captain Frank Chapot competing at the International Horse Show in London. He was a finalist in the World Championships held in 1974 at Hickstead. *above right*: Alwin Schockemöhle of Germany, gold medallist at the Montreal Olympics. Due to recurring back trouble this great competitor has now retired from the show jumping arena. *right*: David Broome of Great Britain, who won the World Championships in 1970 on Douglas Bunn's fine horse Beethoven. He is also joint master of his local fox hunt in Wales, the Curre, which occupies much of his time during winter months.

Raimondo d'Inzeo took the Gold and his brother, Piero, the silver. Their team could finish only third behind Germany, in which Winkler and Thiedemann were joined by another destined for the highest honours, Alwin Schockemöhle, who, having been reserve for both the show-jumping and Three-Day Event teams four years earlier, was making his debut.

Alwin, after winning this team gold, went through an aggravating series of individual near-misses for major titles, three times second and twice third for the European, and fourth for the World in 1970 behind David Broome. He finally broke his duck in 1975 in the first running

of the European Amateur Championship (until then Professionals and Amateurs alike were eligible for all FEI titles), and then went on to take the Olympic Gold in Montreal. He did not have a horse good enough to make his country's team in Tokyo, where Winkler was joined by Herman Schridde and Kurt Jarasinski, who collectively proved good enough to complete a German hat-trick of team golds. D'Oriola helped his team take the silver, but for himself it had to be the gold, riding a horse who had only made his international debut that same season.

With d'Oriola in the French team at the Tokyo Games, was a girl, only 18 years old, whose brilliance was on a par with his, Janou Lefèbvre (now Janou Tissot). She went on to take another team silver in Mexico, and holds two of the only three women's World championships to be held. The first of these was in 1965 at Hickstead, the ground that Douglas Bunn had founded in Sussex five years earlier. With its exciting permanent obstacles and gradually improved facilities, it has had a profound effect on show-jumping in England, introducing the sort of course that had previously only been found on the

Show jumping is one of the few sports where men and women compete on equal terms; and the women are just as successful as the men. *left*: Marion Mould and Dunlynne clearing the Hickstead water in immaculate style. She will always be remembered for her unique partnership with the great little pony Stroller on whom she won an Olympic silver medal in Mexico. *below far left*: American Bill Steinkraus descending the formidable Hickstead Derby Bank. He was a gold medal winner at the Mexico Olympics. *below middle*: Kathy Kusner, one of America's leading woman jumpers. She also has a keen interest in racing. *below right*: French rider Janou Tissot, former women's show jumping world champion, shown here competing in the 1968 Championships at Hickstead, Britain's only permanent outdoor show jumping arena.

Continent. Kathy Kusner, the American girl, with two victories in the Dublin Grand Prix to her credit, was confidently expected to take this first World title, but could finish only second to Marion Coakes (now Marion Mould) and her brilliant pony Stroller. This pair had just become the youngest rider and the smallest horse to win the Queen Elizabeth Cup.

Hickstead was to prove the happiest of hunting grounds for Marion and Stroller, where they also won the British Jumping Derby two years later. They also won the silver medal in Mexico in 1968 behind Bill Steinkraus, who climaxed a brilliant career by giving the United States their first ever individual show-jumping gold. The course for the team competition was generally condemned as one of the worst ever for an Olympic Games, primarily because of the awkward placing of fences, which produced some astronomical scores. It was finally won by the Canadians with 102¾ faults. By contrast Germany won in Tokyo with 68½ – itself a record – and in Munich with 32. The course in Munich was a much more sensible one, although still demanding enough. The Montreal course had to be reduced in size because of the torrential rain which nearly prevented the competition being run in the main Olympic stadium at all.

There has long been debate whether the Olympic course should be of a set pattern, rather than left to the local course-designer. As it is the supreme test there is a lot to be said in favour of such a proposition. The tracks for athletic races are, after all, uniform to a large degree, but this does not in the least detract from the excitement, nor make winning any easier. It would help eliminate the element of luck and make for a fairer result.

The tendency among course-builders to erect ever higher, more demanding courses for the major championships, gives an advantage to those, such as the Germans, with big, powerful horses, rather than giving scope for the skilful rider to compensate for any lack in his horse's make-up. This is a fashion which may, and one hopes will, swing the other way.

It was in 1975 that all equestrian competitions became open for men and women. This made sense, for in the Olympic Games the competitions were mixed, and the women, though numerically outnumbered, repeatedly showed their merit by taking a large percentage of the medals. It was in that same year also, that changes to the various championships separated amateurs from professionals. Thus the European championship, won by Alwin Schockemöhle, was for amateurs only, as a result of which, after some arguing, no British riders took part. The British federation was the only one which had taken Prince Philip's strictures to 'put their house in order' seriously, creaming off the top score or so, of their riders into professional status and putting the country at a great disadvantage in Olympic competition. The World Professional Championship that should have been held in 1975 was not, because the FEI refused to allow

the sponsors to append their name to it. It seems likely that the fluid situation will resolve itself again, into 'Open' competitions everywhere, save in the Olympic Games, over which the FEI does not have the final say. One day they too may be open but that is surely a long way off.

Although Schockemöhle's victory in the 1975 amateur championship was a fairly bloodless one, with his compatriots also filling the minor places, he undoubtedly gave a superlative performance to win the Gold Medal in Montreal. The Individual was held in the stadium at Bromont, some 70 km (43 miles) from Montreal, on a dirt surface which rode deep after a lot of rain. Over two big courses, there was only one clear round each time, both from Schockemöhle. His horse was thus first ever to win an Olympic gold with two clears.

Because of the unexpected rainfall before and during the Games, on ground which had not been drained because it was afterwards to have an artificial surface, there were doubts until the very last minute whether or not it would be possible to hold the team jumping there. Luckily the weather relented sufficiently just in time; the course was reduced in size, the final fence, which should have been a treble became a double, and the competition went on. At halfway, the French and German teams were level in the lead, the pendulum slightly tipped in favour of the consistent French quartet, and although a clear by Schockemöhle would have clinched another team gold for Germany, they hit two fences. Thus France achieved their first show-jumping team gold in Olympic history.

The British, labouring under the handicap of having most of their top riders ineligible because of their professional status, never got into the running. It is doubtful if anything is likely to be done, either to reinstate them, which the IOC have refused to countenance, or to equalize matters by making their main rivals also turn professional.

Show-jumping is essentially an individual sport, but to encourage team spirit the FEI introduced the President's Cup in 1965. It is based on each country's six best results in Nations Cups throughout the season. Five points are given if there are five teams or fewer (there have to be at least three for a Nations Cup), six for six teams, and seven for seven or more. By confining the number of competitions that count to six, the countries which have a long way to travel are not penalized too much compared with the central European nations who can get to many Official Internationals with little difficulty or expense. So far the President's Cup has been dominated by Britain, Germany and the United States.

Two of Britain's top international showjumpers. *top*: Ann Moore on April Love. *bottom*: Pat Smythe on Flanagan, with whom she made history, at the height of her long career, as the first woman rider to compete in the Olympic Games at Stockholm in 1956 when her team won the bronze medal.

The Three-Day Event

THE term 'Three-Day Event' is very inadequate for an exciting, exhilarating sport which calls on the full range of a horse's ability and his rider's skill. Though the name implies some form of threefold competition, it divulges nothing of the qualities to be tested.

The Three-Day Event was designed originally as a trial for military chargers, and was in fact known as the 'Military'. The requirements of a charger were that he should be fit to cover sometimes long distances at a good average speed, travel over open country jumping whatever obstacles stood in his path and be bold enough to tackle any unkown hazards at which his rider presented him. For his part, the rider had to be able to produce a really fit horse and keep him that way, to know just how much he could ask of his mount and judge exactly the right pace, or combination of paces, to reach his target safely and quickly – but without exhausting his horse, because a new day would bring fresh demands.

The hard core of the 'Military', therefore, was an endurance test at working pace, with a section across country negotiating natural obstacles, and generally some form of steeplechase course to be ridden at speed. Later, a dressage test was added to demonstrate the charger's physical development, his mastery of the basic paces and obedience to his rider's unspoken commands. Finally there was a simple show-jumping test, to represent the everyday life to which a charger must be fit to return, even after an exceptionally demanding exercise.

The arts of military equitation have long been practised and admired on the continent of Europe and for many years this was strictly a continental sport. France's military academy of equitation at Saumur still maintains the highest cavalry tradition, while the Spanish Riding School in Vienna is famous to this day for its cultivation of classical equitation, using the white Lipizzaner stallions they have used for generations.

The British – possibly because their native horses were the small, stocky, hardy, Mountain and Moorland breeds – had no such tradition of high-school equitation. With their temperate climate they could ride out-of-doors throughout the year and hunting was their national equestrian sport. When they did import Arabian horses to found the fleeter, more refined Thoroughbred strain, it was for the headier delights of racing, both on the flat and over fences.

For most sports, international competition got under way with the foundation of the modern Olympic movement by Baron de Coubertin in 1896, but equestrian events were not introduced to the Games until 1912, in Stockholm, largely at the instigation of Count von Rosen, Master of the Horse to the King of Sweden. He realized their tremendous value – that of the 'Military' in particular – in stimulating interest and improving standards of equitation and horsemastership, and he saw the Olympic Games as a means of spreading this improvement beyond army circles to all horsemen.

Entries for the Olympic equestrian events were exclusively from the military at first, but gradually civilians took part too. The Three-Day Event became known as the 'Concours Complet', or complete competition, and today hardly a military rank is to be found amongst the competitors.

The form of the Concours Complet was fairly fluid at first, but between the wars it settled down into more or less the form in which we know it now. The competitors, following each other in succession, must undertake three different tests on three separate days. These are:

(i) Dressage – a set programme of some 20 different movements of medium difficulty, to be performed at the walk, trot or canter, in an arena 60 × 20 m in area. Marks are awarded by a panel of three judges, who assess fluency and accuracy of performance, balance, impulsion, rhythm and suppleness in the horse, as well as the rider's seat and application of the aids (or directions).

(ii) Speed and endurance – a four-phase test consisting of: Phases A and C held over roads and tracks totalling 10–20 km (6–12 miles) to be ridden at the trot or slow canter; Phase B, a steeplechase course, roughly 2–4 km (1–2·5 miles) long with 8–12 fences, to be ridden at the gallop; Phase D, a cross-country course, between 5–8 km (3–5 miles), with 20–32 fixed obstacles, to be ridden at the gallop.

Penalties are incurred for falls or refusals at the obstacles and for exceeding the minimum time allowed for each phase.

(iii) Show-jumping – a course of 700–900 m (750–1000 yds) with 10–12 obstacles. Penalties are incurred for falls or refusals at the obstacles and for exceeding the time allowed.

Horses are submitted to a veterinary inspection before the start of the competition, another during the speed and endurance test and a final one before the show-jumping test on the last day. The same horse and rider have to complete all three tests and the competitor with the lowest total penalties is the winner. In a team competition, there may be three team members or four, and it is the three best final scores that count for the team's final placing.

The scale of marks weights the value of the three tests in the ratio of three for dressage, 12 for speed and endurance, and one for jumping. Whilst the rules lay down the speeds and distances, and the dimensions of the obstacles, the course and condtions should be so planned as to conform as closely as practicable to this ratio.

Although this is the basic task confronting a Three-Day Event competitor, it is really only the beginning. No two events are alike; the essence of the competition is the natural countryside in which it is set and this, of course, can vary enormously. Besides the type of terrain, there are always variations in the state of the going, the altitude, the climate, the weather – and that is all quite apart from the obstacles. The permutations are endless and the horse must be fit and bold to cope with them all, as he gallops and jumps over a course he has never seen before.

The rider has the advantage of being allowed to walk the course the day before, to assess the problems it poses and decide how to tackle them in the light of his

Eventing is a tough sport. Here the rider is about to take a bath in the water jump, one of the formidable obstacles on the cross-country course at Goodwood in Sussex.

horse's particular capabilities. He must work out the speed, the line of approach to an obstacle, and the angle and exact point at which to jump it (there is often a choice, with one alternative perhaps easier but more time-consuming than another). He must not be tempted to ride the steeple-chase faster than necessary, or he will take too much out of his horse too early in the day, and he must keep up a good steady pace on the cross-country, taking the jumps in his horse's stride without any waste of time, if he is to escape penalty. The horse may be tiring by then and it will take all the rider's strength and skill to get him safely round without undue effort.

Both horse and rider must be supremely fit, with steady nerves and considerable courage, and the greater the experience they can muster – preferably in partnership – and the greater their mutual understanding and confidence, the better.

There is a notable absence of personal rivalry amongst competitors. For them the challenge lies in the course rather than the other contestants, and it is with the course that each one must settle his own account. Furthermore, victory for the team is, in general, much more highly prized than individual success.

The roads and tracks for Phases A and C, which constitute the endurance element, are perfectly straightforward. So is the steeplechase course for Phase B, although the definition of a steeplechase fence may vary in different countries.

The crux comes in Phase D, the cross-country. For this the track may be flat or steep, and the obstacles are fixed, solid in appearance and built of the strongest materials. The stronger and more solid the obstacle, the more inviting and reassuring it will appear to the horse, and therefore the safer it will be to jump. Also, each obstacle must be able to withstand the assault of wind and weather, so that it is the same for the hundredth competitor as it was for the first.

The course-builder must contrive to test the rider's judgement and nerve, and the horse's scope, courage and obedience, but without making any unnatural demands or springing any unfair surprises. His course must produce a worthy winner, but must not destroy the losers and it is undoubtedly a job which calls for special skill and great experience. Like any other craft that is exposed to constant comparison and critical inspection, course building in general is improving all the time and the international standard is now very high indeed.

Certain obstacles have become bywords in the sport and will be found in more or less the same form on many courses. The Coffin, at Badminton, is one and comprises a narrow trough at the bottom of a wide ditch, with a post-and-rails on both banks, before and after. The Trout Hatchery, at Burghley, is another – a pool approached downhill, with a tree trunk or rails to be jumped on the way in or out, or both. The Normandy Bank, which is a jump up on to a flat bank with a rail on the edge of the drop on the far side, was unknown before the European Champion-

The Trout Hatchery at the Burghley Three-Day Event. The jump into the water is a good test of the horse's obedience and trust in his rider.

ships in Normandy in 1969. The Helsinki Steps – rails forming the outline of steps dropping down a hillside – first appeared in the 1952 Olympic Games, while the Trakehner – a tall post-and-rails set in the bottom of a ditch – is familiar in Germany. An Irish Bank – a high bank which is too big to fly at a single leap, so that the horse has to touch down fleetingly on the top, – can be very disconcerting to a horse that has never met one before. As can be seen, every country has its own style of obstacles and the more distinctive ones are sure to find a place, sooner or later, in the repertoire of other course-builders.

The first Olympic Three-Day Event, at Stockholm in 1912, started with speed and endurance tests, followed by the show-jumping. The dressage came last. Sweden won both the team and individual gold medals, as she did again at Antwerp, in 1920, when the dressage was replaced by a second endurance test.

For the 1924 Games in Paris, the Three-Day Event took shape as the competition we know today, with dressage first, speed and endurance second and show-jumping last. Holland managed to break Sweden's grip and won both team and individual competitions.

A record number of 20 nations took part at Amsterdam in 1928, including Japan, Argentine and the United States. Once again, Holland won both titles, the individual gold medal going to Lt. C. P. de Mortanges on Marcroix, who together set up a record never yet broken, by winning again in Los Angeles in 1932. On that occasion only six nations were represented, probably because of the enormous cost to European countries of transporting their teams halfway round the world. The United States took the gold in the team event.

At Berlin in 1936, the cross-country course was a particularly stiff one and the fourth obstacle, a pond, with sloping bed and swollen with rain, caused havoc amongst the competitors. Germany won both team and individual gold medals. For

the London Games, in 1948, the recently-formed British Horse Society was charged with the organization of the Three-Day Event at Aldershot – the first time Great Britain had ever held such an event. The United States won the team competition and Capt. Chevallier, of France, the individual, but this was a turning-point for Britain in the history of the sport.

Despite the complete absence of Three-Day Event background, Britain had got along well enough so far, recruiting and training army teams for each Games as they came along. But in 1948 the Duke of Beaufort, then Master of the Horse, came to the conclusion that this was a sport at which British horses and riders ought to excel. He was determined that at the next Games in Helsinki in 1952, Britain would put up a team which was not only properly trained, but had gained some experience at the game before being thrown into the international arena.

The park of the Duke of Beaufort's home at Badminton, in Gloucestershire, covered some of the finest open country in England, and as Vice-Patron of the British Horse Society, he invited the B.H.S. to hold a national Three-Day Event there in the spring of 1949. It was to be called the 'Olympic Horse Trials'. The event attracted a great deal of interest and quickly became popular, so much so in fact, that it turned into a highly successful annual fixture and soon gained a reputation as the foremost Three-Day Event in the world. As a result, Britain was to become a leading Olympic contender, with more international honours in Three-Day Events to her credit than any other country, and regarded as an authority both on course design and organization in general.

But back in 1952, a small band of British riders and horses who had shown up well in national events were sent for several months of concentrated training under the direction of Capt. Tony Collings (winner of the second Badminton), at his riding establishment at Porlock, in Somerset. Two years later, Capt. Collings was tragically killed when one of the early Comets, in which he was travelling on a lecturing and judging tour, crashed into the Mediterranean. In his lifetime, however, he had a tremendous influence on Three-Day Eventing in Great Britain and must take his place amongst the sport's founders.

The British team at Helsinki (Reg Hindley, Bertie Hill and Laurence Rook) put up a very good show, but Laurence Rook's horse unfortunately put his foot in a hole towards the end of the cross-country course and his rider was concussed in the fall. Rook remounted and completed the course, but passed the wrong side of the finishing post and was eliminated. In those days each country was allowed to enter only three competitors, so this put the whole team out of the running. Sweden regained both team and individual titles, their gold medallist being Baron Hans von Blixen-Finecke.

The suggestion was then put forward that a European Championship should be held in non-Olympic years and Badminton was asked to be the first to hold it, in 1953. Sadly, Badminton's April date proved too early in the year for most European countries to produce really fit horses, and only Switzerland and Ireland, apart from the hosts, were able to raise a team, so the championship was abandoned.

That autumn, the B.H.S. started up an autumn Three-Day Event at Harewood, in Yorkshire, by permission of the Princess Royal. Vivien Machin-Goodall won, to become the first lady winner of a Three-Day Event.

In 1954, Switzerland volunteered to hold the championships and put on an event of high standard at Basle. Britain's Bertie Hill was the winner and British riders filled four out of the next six places, so they took the team championship as well. Among them were the first lady riders to compete in an official international championship – Margaret Hough, who finished sixth, and Diana Mason riding for

the team, who finished seventh.

This was a red-letter year for Britain on several counts: their new-found success, proof that girls could hold their own in what had been regarded hitherto as too tough a game for them, and the emergence as a team of three riders, Bertie Hill, Frank Weldon and Laurence Rook, who, apart from their outstanding record of success, were all to play a leading part in the Three-Day Event world. Hill was to produce some superb horses and train many of the leading riders of future generations; Weldon was to captain the British team when he gave up competing and became a world authority on cross-country courses when he subsequently took over the direction of Badminton, and Rook was to become chairman of the sport's governing body in Britain and the technical delegate of the Fédération Equestre Internationale at many official championships and Olympic Games.

In 1955, the European Championships were held at Windsor, by invitation of HRH Queen Elizabeth II. Britain successfully defended her title with the same team and Weldon carried off the individual championship. In seventeenth place was a youngster from Lancashire who had won the Pony Club championships, Sheila Willcox on High And Mighty.

In the Olympic Games at Stockholm in 1956 Britain's hopes were high and they were represented by three very experienced and successful riders, mounted on proven, high-quality horses. They didn't have it all their own way (Bertie Hill's Countryman slipped in the heavy rain and got hung up on a trakehner fence, but was salvaged and went on to finish the course), but they established a clear lead which they retained to the end. So Britain won her first team gold medal, while Frank Weldon took the individual bronze. Sweden's Kastenman won the individual gold medal.

In 1957, Britain won the European Championship at Copenhagen, where Sheila Willcox on High And Mighty became the first lady champion. She made history again in 1958, with her third successive victory at Badminton.

In 1959 Harewood was the setting for

the European Championships, in which the U.S.S.R. entered for the first time. Britain's star had waned, and Germany won the team championship and Switzerland's Hans Schwarzenbach the individual, on a horse he had purchased from Frank Weldon. In the interim, Weldon had suffered the tragic loss of his great horse Kilbarry, who had broken his neck in falling at an innocent-looking fence in a one-day event at home.

In 1960, Australia sent a posse of horses and riders to train for six months in Britain before tackling the Olympic Games in Rome. They joined the circuit of national horse trials, as they had done in 1956, but this time with marked success. Bill Roycroft won at Badminton, and the team went on to capture the gold medal in Rome (Bill Roycroft was taken to hospital with a broken collar-bone after the cross-country, but defied doctors' orders to ride in the show-jumping next day). Australia's Laurie Morgan won the individual gold medal and his compatriot, Neal Lavis took the silver. The others went home to Australia afterwards, but Morgan returned to England, to ride in the Grand National and win at Badminton the following spring.

A new Three-Day Event was started up at Burghley, home of the Marquess of Exeter, in 1961, to take the place of the Harewood event, which had closed down. It was won by Anneli Drummond-Hay on Merely-A-Monarch, the great horse with which she went on to win at Badminton in 1962 and then to become a successful international show-jumper. In 1962, Burghley was the scene of the European Championships, which were won by the U.S.S.R., the individual champion being Britain's James Templer.

Below left The first stage of the Three-Day Event is the dressage test. Here Bruce Davidson and Irish Cap perform well at Bromont, Canada, for the 1976 Olympics. *Below* One of the greatest Three-Day Event horses, Merely-a-Monarch, with Anneli Drummond-Hay competing at Hickstead. After winning at Burghley and Badminton they turned to show jumping with some success.

At the 1964 Olympics, the only 'first' scored by the British horses was that of flying over the North Pole on the newly-opened route to Tokyo! Richard Meade, fresh from winning at Burghley, had led at the end of the speed and endurance test – only to jump a disastrous round on the final day. Italy won both team and individual titles.

It was fitting that Russia should win the European team championship at Moscow in 1965, while Poland's Marian Barbierecki on Volt won the individual, gaining this country's sole victory in the history of the sport.

The first World Championships were scheduled for Burghley in 1966, but an outbreak of African Horse Sickness prevented the movement of horses throughout Europe. Nevertheless, Ireland, the U.S.S.R. and the United States overcame the veterinary ban by flying their horses direct to England and a gallant band from Argentine made the mammoth journey by sea, their horses regaining health and vigour during a month's enforced quarantine. It proved worthwhile, since Argentine's Tokyo silver medallist, Carlos Moratorio, put up a performance worthy of the first World Champion. Ireland, always a dashing and joyous participant in Three-Day Events, achieved the team title at last, with their superb team of Eddie Boylan, Tom Brennan, Penny Moreton and Virginia Freeman-Jackson.

Ireland's first international event was the European Championships, held at Punchestown, in 1967. The organization was good and the hospitality generous, but the Argentinian technical delegate had thought it best to add an apron of gorse to the front of each steeplechase fence, with disastrous effect. Ireland's Eddie Boylan won the individual title with Durlas Eile, on which he had won Badminton two years earlier, and Britain carried away the team title.

Britain's star was in the ascendant once more and by 1968 she was again in a position to send a team of experienced, successful riders on top-quality horses to the Olympic Games. The course at unprecedented altitude in Mexico was not a difficult one and was approved as such by Britain's technical delegate Laurence Rook. Halfway through the speed and endurance test the rain started to fall heavily, turning the course into a quagmire and the water jumps into torrents. Derek Allhusen on Lochinvar was safely round, but Jane Bullen's Our Nobby (the little horse that had won at Badminton in the spring) slipped and fell twice. It was left to Ben Jones on The Poacher and Richard Meade on Cornishman V to perform epic feats of valour to bring the team out on top. They took the gold medal and Allhusen the individual silver, behind France's J. Guyon on Pitou.

Reunited with his owner, Mary Gordon-Watson, Cornishman won the European individual championship at Haras-du-Pin the following year and Britain the team title, with what amounted to her 'second eleven', although it included Ben Jones on The Poacher. These two great horses (who both have the distinction of contributing to the British team's victory in five successive international championships or Olympic Games) figured in the team again in 1970, for the World Championships at Punchestown, The Poacher ridden this time by Richard Meade.

An insubstantial fence constructed on the brink of a sharp drop caused a lot of trouble at Punchestown and collected much criticism, but the British team survived to win the team championship and Mary Gordon-Watson, on Cornishman, the individual.

Nobody was surprised when Britain won the European Championships at Burghley the following summer, but the individual title went to something of an outsider, Princess Anne on Doublet. This brilliant horse she was later to lose in most distressing circumstances, the horse breaking a hind leg during gentle exercise at home. Despite her success at Burghley, Princess Anne was considered insufficiently experienced for the Olympic Games at Munich in 1972. The British team, however, took the gold medal, and Richard Meade, at last, after many years' sterling service in the team, won a well-deserved (and Britain's first) individual gold.

This moment of triumph marked the end of Britain's second cycle of international success. Germany won the team, and Russia the individual European title at Kiev in 1973, and the United States took the World Championships by storm at Burghley in 1974. America's Bruce Davidson, on Irish Cap, won the individual title. Things perked up a bit for Britain at Luhmuhlen in 1975, when Lucinda Prior-Palmer won on Be Fair and Princess Anne was second on Goodwill, but the team championship slipped from the grasp of the first all-girl team, leaving the USSR to collect the laurels.

The various phases of the Three-Day Event. *below left*: Richard Meade and Maj. Derek Allhusen's Laurieston in the show jumping phase. *below middle*: The same horse and rider on the cross country course at the Munich Olympics where they won individual and team gold medals. *below right*: Here they both concentrate on their dressage phase. *right*: HRH Princess Anne and Doublet at Badminton in 1971. They were to win the European Championships at Burghley later the same year. Three-Day Eventing is the complete test for horse and rider, as it covers all aspects of horsemanship: obedience and calmness for the dressage on the first day; boldness and speed across country on the second day; and the ability to jump a small course on the third and final day.

Top American rider Mike Plumb and his horse Better and Better well through the water complex at Bromont near Montreal, 1976.
Above Capt. Mark Phillips on Favour in the Lake at Badminton.

Both these leading ladies were in the British team for the Montreal Olympics in 1976, but Be Fair slipped a ligament on completing the speed and endurance test, Princess Anne was concussed in a fall (though she remounted and completed the event most creditably) and Hugh Thomas's horse broke down. Only Richard Meade, riding an inexperienced horse and competing now in his fourth Olympic Games, was able to finish well up the line, in fourth place. The much-fancied United States team on the crest of the international wave, took a richly-deserved team gold medal, and also the individual gold and silver by Tad Coffin and Mike Plumb respectively.

For Britain then, Three-Day Eventing started with a bang in 1949. Badminton sparked off a succession of preparatory one-day events and these have grown steadily in number, efficiency and popular-

ity ever since. Controlled by the B.H.S.'s Combined Training Committee, the sport has taken firm root, with a packed programme of annual fixtures and a registry of hundreds of competitors, most of whom take part simply for fun, with no aspirations to ride for their country.

Popular though these events are with competitors, however, it is difficult for them to make enough money to be really self-sufficient, and commercial sponsors have provided invaluable support. Badminton and Burghley, both have their sponsors, and the prize money they contribute at least helps the winners towards the high cost of keeping a horse for these competitions. In 1969, the B.H.S. had the good fortune to find a sponsor for its official horse trials, in the Midland Bank, a partnership which has played an important part in consolidating the sport in Britain.

Britain is not the only country to have experienced a postwar boom in Three-Day Eventing. Ireland's progress has been similar, since Irish competitors have ridden at Badminton from the start. Interest spread to Australia and then to New Zealand, who received great stimulus from

Australia's gold medals in 1960.

The United States has had a very consistent Olympic record right from the start, and their programme of national fixtures has grown enormously in the last couple of decades. Canada is a keen participant too. Mexico and Argentina have always had a strong equestrian tradition and these four countries have been the mainstay of the Pan-American Three-Day Event, held at regular intervals since 1955. Japan, too, has adopted the sport, though it has less opportunity than most for international competition.

In Europe, the Three-Day Event tradition has continued to grow, notably in Sweden, Holland, Germany, Switzerland, Italy and France. There have been ups and downs (in Sweden, for instance, Three-Day Events disappeared altogether for almost a decade, following a fatal accident), but the general development has been maintained. Eastern European countries have followed suit – particularly the U.S.S.R., Poland, Bulgaria and Rumania.

Most countries have at least one international Three-Day Event a year, in addition to their domestic programme. These competitions, relieved of the importance and solemnity of an official championship, are extremely friendly, enjoyable affairs and do much to foster international goodwill. But the large-scale development of Three-Day Events as a whole has had another result – one which would have gladdened the heart of Count von Rosen – and that is a steady improvement in the standard of fitness and training of the horses taking part and the general state of preparation amongst competitors.

Of course there is still plenty of room for improvement, but it must be a source of considerable satisfaction that, by continual comparison with the best horses and most successful riders over the best-built courses in all countries, and constant striving for success, standards are being set which are improving the lot of horses the world over. Horses are no longer a necessity of life to most people, but a source of pleasure. It is fitting that they should reap the benefit of a sport in which they play such a vital and gallant rôle.

Racing and Racehorses

HE had a leg at each corner, a head at one end and a tail at the other. His back had never felt a saddle and he was only a little over 12 months old. So what made the chestnut yearling colt worth the $1,500,000 – a world-record price for any animal – that a syndicate of Canadians paid for him at the Keeneland Sales in Kentucky in the summer of 1976? The short answer is that he was, or would be when matured, a racehorse, and his pedigree indicated him to be a prime example of that swiftest of all the equine breeds, the Thoroughbred. This superb breed was established in seventeenth century Britain, perfected through a judicious programme of selective breeding in many of the countries to which it has spread and now, in the final quarter of the twentieth century, it is the basis of an international industry linking five continents.

This global connection becomes evident from an examination of the record-priced yearling's ancestors. His sire was Secretariat, one of the greatest American horses of recent years who, on retiring to stud in 1973, had won $1,316,808 in stakes. His dam was the top American race mare Charming Alibi, which makes him a half-brother to the champion filly Dahlia. Owned by an American but trained in France, Dahlia twice won Britain's richest race, the King George VI and Queen Elizabeth Stakes at Ascot. She also returned to the land of her birth to triumph in the important international invitation event run every November at Laurel Park, Maryland.

Dahlia was Charming Alibi's daughter by Vaguely Noble, a stallion who was a product of the best British Thoroughbred lines and won France's richest race, the Prix de l'Arc de Triomphe, before being sent to stud in the United States. One of Vaguely Noble's many successful sons, Empery, was shipped from America to France to learn the racing game and then, in 1976, crossed the English Channel to win Britain's premier classic race, the Derby at Epsom.

Empery, like Dahlia, ran in the ownership of an American, Mr Nelson Bunker Hunt, who controls a racing empire with representatives in Australia, New Zealand, Canada, France, England, and Ireland, as well as in his home country. Another person who operates on an international scale is an Englishman, Mr Robert Sangster, who at the most recent count had 95 mares spread around studs in Europe, America and Australia, in addition to owning or having shares in numerous stallions. Some of these are flown to Australia for the southern hemisphere covering season which runs from August to November, before returning to stand in Ireland for the season there from February to May.

The British racehorse Grundy, bred at the Overbury Stud in Gloucestershire, netted £188,375 with successes in the Derby and King George VI and Queen Elizabeth Stakes in 1975 for Dr Carlo Vittadini, an Italian whose horses compete all over Europe. But it is Japan that has shown the greatest increase in racing and breeding interests in the years since 1945. One leading Japanese owner, Mr Zenya Yosheda, has stud farms in Hokkaido and Kentucky maintaining some 250 brood mares and 25 stallions.

These, of course, are the men at the top. But racing's pyramid rests firmly on the countless enthusiasts whose pleasure is gained from owning perhaps just one racehorse; from seeing it carry their colours in some minor race at an unfashionable track, where the prize money – even assuming it managed to win – would go only a little way towards recouping the cost of keeping it in training. In Britain, where prize money lags far behind most other important racing countries, training fees can amount to as much as £2,500 a year, and calculations have fixed the 'average loss expectation' – a figure achieved by measuring annual costs against winning potential (assuming equal shares of the total) – at about £1,800 per annum.

That such a loss in fact represents payment for sport enjoyed might appear small consolation, yet the lure of the racetrack remains. A racehorse *can* provide the royal road to riches although the vast majority simply run up bills. But the glamour of the course, the tingling excitement of the race, and even the attraction of the additional social doors that ownership can open, means that there is no shortage of willing losers.

In its earliest days the cost of racing would have been of scant concern to participants. Not for nothing does it still carry the old tag 'the sport of kings'. It was a reigning monarch – King Charles II – who was responsible for its first major step forward in Britain, a country where racing in some form or another had been practised since the arrival of the Romans. The Romans had probably picked it up from the Greeks, for events involving mounted horses were recorded in the Olympic Games of 642 BC.

Records of horse racing in Britain prior to the sixteenth century are few. It was merely a knightly pastime, with one nobleman matching himself and his horse

The sport of kings and the king of sports. The arena for the Thoroughbred, swiftest of all equines, bred to race and possibly to net many thousands on the track.

against another, rather as they tested their prowess with lance and sword in the jousting tournaments. Royal studs were established under the later Tudors and early Stuarts, at Hampton Court, Tutbury and elsewhere, only to be dispersed after the Civil War had left Oliver Cromwell as the power in the land.

With the Restoration came King Charles II, a man of several passions – one of which was for horse racing. He developed the sport round the little town of Newmarket in Suffolk, where his grandfather, James I, had established a hunting lodge, and where his father, Charles I, had endowed the first cup race in 1634. Charles II was both competitor and organizer, using his royal authority to arrange races, establish rules and arbitrate in disputes. Until his time most races had been matches, that is just two horses racing to settle an argument of wager between their owners. The king encouraged the provision of special prizes – cups or cash – to be contested by larger fields, and the level heathlands around Newmarket were ideal for the stamina-testing 6·4 km (4 mile) gallops to which the horses were subjected. In fact, it was not just a matter of distance, most of the races were only decided after three or four heats, separated by about half-an-hour between each running.

Up to this time, horses used for racing were nearly all native-bred, and probably differed little from the animals which carried their owners on their everyday journeying. In the north there were fast ponies called Galloways; Ireland had its 'Hobby horses'. But from the reign of Queen Elizabeth I more and more horses began to be imported, initially from Italy and Spain, both for the royal studs and by prominent individuals. Among the latter was one of history's best-known horsemen, William Cavendish, Duke of Newcastle, who greatly favoured the Spanish animals.

These importations, together with those which arrived later from North Africa and the Eastern Mediterranean – the so-called Barbs (from the Barbary Coast), Turks and Arabians – achieved little actual racing success, but their blood, mixed with that of the native stock was to have a profound effect on the history of the horse. It led to nothing less than the establishment of the Thoroughbred as a breed in its own right.

All Thoroughbreds of today throughout the whole world descend from three famous eastern stallions – the Byerley Turk, the Darley Arabian and the Godolphin Arabian – who reached Britain as the sixteenth century was moving into the seventeenth. At the time their importers could have had precious little idea of the enormous consequences of their action.

First to arrive was the Byerley Turk. He got his name from his owner, a Colonel Byerley, who captured him from the Turks at the Battle of Buda. For several years the colonel used the horse as his charger, and later, when he retired from the Army in 1690, as a stallion. The Byerley Turk sired few horses of note himself, but became the great-great grandsire of the immensely successful racehorse King Herod, or Herod as he was more often called. One of the principal forefathers of the Thoroughbred, Herod himself sired the winners of 1,042 races collectively worth over £200,000 – an enormous sum in modern terms. One of his sons, Highflyer, was just as successful, producing the winners of 1,108 races valued at £170,000 and establishing the fortune of his owner, Richard Tattersall. This gentleman was the founder of the famous British firm of bloodstock auctioneers, responsible for running the sales at Newmarket which repeatedly draw buyers from the world over.

The Darley Arabian was described after he had been sent home to England in 1704 by Thomas Darley, British consul in Aleppo, as 'a horse of exquisite beauty'. He did make a mark with his first generation progeny, siring Flying Childers – the first truly great racehorse – and through the latter's brother, Bartlett's Childers (useless on the racecourse because of weak bloodvessels), he became the great-great grand-

sire of perhaps the most famous racehorse of all time, Eclipse:

Eclipse was bred in 1764 by the Duke of Cumberland, also the breeder, six years earlier, of the mighty Herod. Eclipse did not race until he was five years old, but thereafter he remained unbeaten. He retired with 26 races to his credit, including 11 King's Plates – races run in heats of 6·4 km (4 miles) in which runners had to carry 76 kg (12 st). One of the best-known phrases in the annals of the British Turf, 'Eclipse first, the rest nowhere', was coined by his owner, a somewhat disreputable Irishman named Dennis O'Kelly, when called upon to forecast the result of his first race. In those days any horse beaten by a distance – 220 m (240 yds) – was not officially placed, and when Eclipse came right away from his opponents three-quarters of the way home, O'Kelly's brash pronouncement was proved entirely correct.

At stud, Eclipse got 344 individual winners and established sire lines of paramount influence. One of his most celebrated descendants was St Simon, the 1884 Gold Cup winner at Ascot. Nothing could get near St Simon on the racecourse and his offspring won 571 races in Britain alone, where he headed the winning sire's list nine times, a feat never achieved before or since. From St Simon descends one of the greatest of modern racehorses, the Italian champion Ribot, also unbeaten through a lengthy career and twice successful in the Prix de l'Arc de Triomphe.

The origin of the third of the foundation sires, the Godolphin Arabian, is even more obscure than the other two. He was brought to England as a five-year-old in 1729 from France, where he is said to have been discovered pulling a coal cart through the streets of Paris by his importer, Edward Coke. Coke later sold him to Lord Godolphin and the horse became the grandsire of Matchem, who, like Eclipse and Herod was to be found an outstanding male line. One branch flourishes in the United States today thanks to the fabulously successful racehorse Man O' War, who, affectionately

named 'Big Red', was to American racegoers of the 1920s what Secretariat was to be 50 years later.

While Eclipse was enjoying his supremacy on the Turf and at stud, the Thoroughbred was still evolving. Considered in terms of Darwinian theory its development proceeded at an outstanding rate, for after less than 100 years it was fully established as an independent breed, whose abilities have remained largely unchanged ever since. The evidence that the racehorses of the 1970s can cover a given distance slightly faster than their nineteenth century counterparts, can

surely be laid at the door of improved courses and consequent better going, together with more enlightened and scientific training and management methods, and the modern riding styles which actively assist the horse's movement.

King Charles II won at least one race at Newmarket, where his favourite horse, Old Rowley, gave his name to racing's best known 1,600 m course, the Rowley Mile. In his day the aristocratic owners not infrequently rode their own horses, but as the sport progressed, so entered the age of the professional jockey, to be followed later by the professional trainer. Courses

Above George Stubbs' portrait of Eclipse, one of the outstanding racehorses of all time, foaled in 1764 and never beaten.
Below Early morning exercise for a trainer's string at Newmarket, one of the world's most famous racing centres.

began to spring up all over the country in the early eighteenth century but many of them were disreputable places. Except at Newmarket, where King Charles made and kept the rules, overall control was lax.

Charles was aided by a Dorset squire named Tregonwell Frampton, a sort of royal racing manager-cum-trainer who,

following his master's death, maintained his position of influence under four successive sovereigns. One was Queen Anne, who was responsible for the construction of the racecourse at Ascot in Berkshire, now the venue of what must be the most notable race meeting in the world – the four days of Royal Ascot every June.

The gap left when Frampton died was not filled for a couple of decades, but around 1750 came an event which was to have the utmost significance. This was the formation of the Jockey Club by a group of sportsmen at Newmarket. Its original aim was to regularize and control racing at its own centre, and this was eventually achieved over a fairly lengthy period by methodical acquisition of the freehold there of all lands on which the sport took place. With this process completed, the Jockey Club became the supreme authority over this small corner of Suffolk, and its right to 'warn off' any whom it considered undesirable was recognized by the courts in 1827.

Gradually the club's influence was extended until all racecourses in the country came under its aegis. It assumed responsibility for sanctioning tracks, approving programmes, licensing officials and framing the regulations. Its rule was absolute and it became the model on which similar authorities were set up in the many other countries to which the Thoroughbred was spreading.

The Jockey Club was, and still is, a self-elected body, with executive powers invested in its stewards. In the late eighteenth and nineteenth centuries, such power was often in the hands of one forceful personality. One of the first was a founder-member, Sir Charles Bunbury,

whose early claim to fame was as the breeder of Highflyer. Under his rule the Jockey Club was strong enough in 1791, to warn off the Prince of Wales, later George IV, after an inquiry into the suspicious circumstances concerning the running of a horse called Escape.

Bunbury owned Diomed, winner of the first running of a race at Epsom that was to become the world's premier 'classic', the Derby. This was in 1780 when the movement away from the 6·4 km (4 mile) races of old was gathering momentum and when the racing of younger horses was becoming more fashionable. Halfway through the seventeenth century few horses raced before they were five years old. In 1744, four-year-old racing was introduced, to be followed a dozen years later by races for three-year-olds. Subsequently races were brought in for two-year-olds and even, for a few seasons, for yearlings. The oldest two-year-old race in existence – the July Stakes, then of 50 guineas each – was first run over 1,000 m (five furlongs) in 1786 at Newmarket, where it has been held every year since.

But it was the three-year-olds which became the animals for the pattern of supreme tests – the classic races – designed to establish the ideal Thoroughbred capable of racing over 1,600 m (1 mile) in the spring through to 2,800 (1¾ miles) in the autumn. The series begins with the races at Newmarket in April over the Rowley Mile, the 2,000 Guineas for colts (established in 1809), and the fillies' equivalent, the 1,000 Guineas (1814). These are followed by the 2,400 m (1½ mile) tests on Epsom's downland circuit in May or June, the Derby and Oaks (for fillies, first run in 1779), and then the oldest of them all, the

An engraving captures unchanged excitement as the winners pass the post at the end of a race at Ascot Heath.

2,800 m (1¾ mile) St Leger (1778) at the Doncaster September meeting.

Sir Charles Bunbury's era – and it was only the toss of a coin that decided it would be Lord Derby's name and not his that would be perpetuated by the Epsom classic – also saw another significant development. This was the introduction of the handicap, a race in which the weights carried by the horses are allotted in accordance with their known ability so as to equalize their chances. In the first important handicap, the Oatlands Stakes at Ascot in 1791, the burdens imposed ranged from 57 kg (9 st) to 33 kg (5 st 3 lb). Handicaps greatly increased racing's hold on the public, as they became the most popular medium for betting. Betting remains the sport's principal attraction and, in the modern era, its main source of finance. Wagering between individuals had always existed, but as public interest grew so did public betting, their needs being catered for by men who offered varying odds against each horse. These men earned the name of bookmaker, through their habit of recording details of transactions in notebooks.

Sir Charles Bunbury was followed at the head of Jockey Club affairs by Lord George Bentinck. During his comparatively short reign, this gentleman was responsible for numerous innovations, among them the numbering of horses, the introduction of racecards and moderately efficient starting by means of a flag. He played an important part in exposing the Running Rein fraud, when the colt of that

The Flying Dutchman/Voltigeur race at York in 1851. The former horse won this great match, a triumph in handicapping.

name who won the 1834 Derby was later proved to have been a four-year-old named Maccabeus.

Lord George also earned a niche in racing history when the horse Elis was 'vanned' to Doncaster to win the 1836 St Leger. At that time horseboxes were virtually unknown and horses were required to walk to the racecourses. When it became known that Elis was still in his stable in the south of England a few days before the St Leger, the bookmakers, assuming a non-appearance on the day, extended the odds. Elis was placed in a specially-built van drawn by teams of horses and arrived in time to land a substantial gamble for his connections.

Third and last of the Turf 'dictators' was Admiral Rous. Though he was correctly described as the 'first great handicapper', and spending a great deal of his time calculating these weights, paradoxically he disapproved of handicaps, referring to them as 'boons to bad horses'. He is principally remembered for the scale of weight-for-age allowances he drew up to be used in non-handicap races. Rous's scale is basically the same as that still in use today, over 100 years later.

One of Rous's most famous handicapping achievements was for the Great Match of 1851 between The Flying Dutchman – the winner of the Derby and St Leger in 1849, and Voltigeur, who won the same two races the following year. The Admiral is said to have spent many hours deliberating, but finally decreed that the older horse should concede 4 kg (8½ lb), an amount identical to the allowance which his published scale indicated a five-year-old should give a four-year-old over 3·2 km (2 miles) in May. In the event The Flying Dutchman won the celebrated contest by what is quaintly described as 'a short length'.

Throughout this time racing had been developing in other lands. In North America, a continent devoid of horses until the arrival of the settlers from the eastern hemisphere, it existed in early colonial days. As such, however, it cannot have been of much account, since the first priority was to import horses suitable for agricultural work.

Quarter Horse racing – so called because it was practised on rough, quarter-mile strips cleared in the virgin forests – enjoyed brief popularity and the Quarter Horses of today are the fastest of all equines over a 400 m (2 furlongs) gallop. But the sport proper did not gain a real hold until after the revolutionary war, when among many influential horses imported from Britain was Sir Charles Bunbury's Derby winner Diomed. A failure at stud in England, he was 21 before arriving in North America where he soon began to produce offspring of fine quality. Another horse, Medley, who reached America in 1784, was also to have an enormous effect on the evolution of the American Thoroughbred, while two of the most successful sires in the history of racing in the New World were Leviathan, who arrived in 1830 and was five times leading sire, and Glencoe, who left an indelible mark on both sides of the ocean.

The greatest American-bred stallion of the nineteenth century was Lexington, champion sire on no fewer than 16 occasions, but stigmatized in Britain by being pronounced ineligible for the General Stud Book. The restrictive clauses which prevented the inclusion of any of his stock, principally introduced in 1913 by the then senior steward of the English Jockey Club, Lord Jersey (the measures were referred to as 'the Jersey Act') remained in existence until after the Second World War.

Lexington's career spanned the period of the Civil War, which shattered racing and breeding in the southern states. But development continued apace in the north – where New York became a major centre – together with the mid and far west, as well as the 'border' states of Maryland and Kentucky. The classic three-year-old races were all instituted in the decade following the Civil War. First came the Belmont Stakes in 1867, commemorating the name of a leading owner and breeder of the day, August Belmont. Since 1905 this race has been run at the famous New York course, Belmont Park, over 2,400 m (1½ miles). It was followed by the Preakness Stakes (1,900 m, 1 mile 1½ furlongs) established in 1873 on the Pimlico course near Baltimore, Maryland, and in 1875, by the Kentucky Derby (2,000 m, 1¼ miles) at Churchill Downs, Louisville, Kentucky. Thus the American 'Triple Crown' programme is of an overall lesser distance than its English and French counterparts, a trend continued throughout the United States calendar, which has relatively few important tests longer than 2,400 m (1½ miles).

The 40 years following the Civil War are sometimes termed the 'Golden Age' of racing in the United States (and during it American-bred horses began to come to Britain achieving no little success, notably Iroquois, winner of the Epsom Derby in

1881), but they also had a darker side. The sport's image was becoming increasingly tarnished through the malpractices of those concerned solely with 'making a fast buck'. Even the formation in 1894 of a Jockey Club on similar lines to the British organization failed to stem the rising tide of public indignation, which was sufficiently strong to lead to racing being banned or severely curtailed in state after state.

Only Maryland and Kentucky escaped and even in Kentucky the threat was but narrowly averted. Shortly before the 1908 Kentucky Derby, the Mayor of Louisville, bowing to pressure from reform groups, enforced an almost forgotten law prohibiting bookmakers. Without the draw of betting it seemed as if Churchill Downs would have to close its gates. However, Col Matt Winn, the man primarily responsible for raising the classic to its place of honour, overcame the problem by borrowing an idea from France and introducing pari-mutuel or totalizator wagering. In this system the odds – or dividends– are decided in direct relation to the amounts staked on each horse.

Facing no competition from bookmakers, this 'machine betting' proved an instant success – a success which soon attracted the attention of legislators, who saw in it a lucrative and easily workable form of tax gathering.

Now the pendulum began to swing, and racing slowly came back into favour, with the Jockey Club and its associated bodies exercising overall control and guidance. Each state, however, established racing commissions to licence tracks and supervise meetings within its boundaries. The only authorized form of gambling was through the totalizators, a percentage of the total stakes being creamed off for the state's coffers and another proportion being channelled back into the sport itself. Thus the more attractive the racing and the racecourses, the more money the public stakes – and the more money the various state governments were able to take out (and put back in). Now the states themselves had a vested interest in the success of the sport, but still its recovery was slow, for the almost total stoppage had been a virtual body blow. The bottom had dropped out of the bloodstock market during the period when there were so few racing opportunities and a great deal of the better stock had been sold, much of it at giveaway prices owing to the protective measures introduced by Britain and France.

However, with the money supply secure the resurgence of American racing, gradual though it may have been, was certain, and now the United States holds the premier position on the world racing stage. Prize money annually totals about $172,000,000 and foal production each year stands at about 26,000, more than three times the British figure and about six times greater than the other great bloodstock producing country, France.

The principal breeding area is in Kentucky, the world-renowned 'Blue Grass' country concentrated around the town of Lexington. The Keeneland Sales, where the record-priced Secretariat yearling referred to earlier was sold, offer the highest quality bloodstock anywhere in the world. Such is the concern for standards that the auctioneers refuse to accept any but the choicest for their catalogues, and in the July 1976 sale, they turned away nearly 700 from an entry of over 1,000.

American breeding is heavily inclined towards satisfying the needs of owners anxious for quick returns, and this has resulted in a high production of sprint-bred stock designed to win as two-year-olds. However, the superiority of its middle-distance horses in the 1960s and 1970s has been proven in European classic races. American owners and breeders have never been afraid to test their best animals to the limit and, because of the sheer volume of

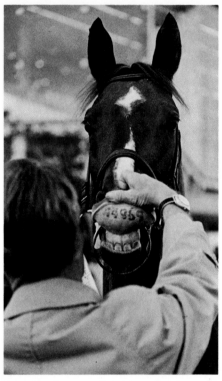

Tattooing the upper lip of American horses safeguards against fraudulent substitution in valuable races.

worthwhile opportunity, a champion may race as many as 30 times during his career. Defeat in a major handicap carrying a big weight is considered no blot on a record. Such a rigorous testing programme, plus a voracious acquisition of representatives of the world's best bloodlines, has brought the American-bred racehorse to an ascendancy well exemplified by the English Derby successes of such as Sir Ivor (1968), Mill Reef (1971) and Roberto (1972). In between came the victory of Canadian-bred Nijinsky in 1970.

Most recently there has been a resurgence of the French-bred. In 1976 success in four of the five English classics went to horses from across the Channel, and they also won numerous other big prizes, including the King George VI and Queen Elizabeth Stakes. France, in common with other European countries, was late to enter the racing scene. The sport

there did not begin to get under way in any recordable manner until more than 20 years after the English had their Jockey Club. Then what little organization there was disappeared in the holocaust of the Revolution and the ensuing ebb and flow of the Napoleonic Wars.

It was an Englishman, Lord Henry Seymour (slightly eccentric and Paris-born) who was largely instrumental in the renaissance of French racing in the second quarter of the nineteenth century. With his close friend the Duc d'Orléans, then heir to the throne, he founded the Jockey Club in 1833 and, when it became apparent that their fellow-members were more interested in the social aspect of the club than in racing, they led a breakaway group to form the Société d'Encouragement pour l'Amélioration des Races de Chevaux en France. Literally, this was the Society to encourage the betterment of horse racing in France and it was soon abbreviated everywhere to the Société d'Encouragement.

Once established and recognized by the Government, the Société moved rapidly. In 1836 a new racecourse was opened not far from Paris at Chantilly, and the training centre which has grown up around it now rivals that at Newmarket. The 2,400 m (1½ miles) Prix du Jockey Club, equivalent to the Epsom Derby, was founded there in 1836, and was followed within 10 years by the other classic races, the Poule d'Essai des Poulains and the Poule d'Essai des Pouliches (equivalent to the 2,000 and 1,000 Guineas), the Prix de Diane (French Oaks) and the Prix Royal Oak (St Leger).

Bloodstock in France was based entirely on imports from England – the French Thoroughbred was and still is named the *Pur Sang Anglais* – but the races were almost exclusively confined to horses foaled in France and this protective restriction was not totally removed for over 100 years. Paris soon had its own racecourse, Longchamp in the Bois de Boulogne, and the swift advance of the breeding industry was crowned in 1865 with the victory of Gladiateur – 'the avenger of Waterloo' – in the English Triple Crown. Two years earlier an extra 'classic', the 3,000-metre (1 mile 7 furlongs) Grand Prix de Paris, one of the few races open to foreign challengers, had been founded.

The First World War delivered an apparently shattering blow to racing in France, yet recovery was dramatically speedy, as it was to be again after the 1939–1945 conflict. The Prix de l'Arc de Triomphe, now the greatest of all the international races, was founded in 1920 at Longchamp. Racing is still on a more limited scale than in Britain and there are fewer major courses. Most meetings are confined to weekends, with Sunday the most important day. But prize money is larger, thanks to the huge cash intake from the percentage deduction from the pari-mutuel, the only legal form of betting. The most popular pool is the Tiercé, on which millions of francs are invested on, and off the course, by punters attempting to forecast the first three in the big race of the day.

Above Racing at Deauville, France. The French Thoroughbred is based entirely on its English counterpart and has always been bred for its stamina as well as speed.
Right A Thoroughbred stud in the fabled 'Blue Grass' region of Kentucky, where many of America's fastest horses have been bred.

French breeders are also happier than their cross-channel counterparts, since this money also allows for the provision of breeders' prizes.

The emphasis in France has always been on stamina as well as speed, and two-year-old racing is operated on a much lower scale than in Britain. Although up to the 1939–1945 war only three French horses had won the English Derby, this policy bore fruit thereafter, with seven French-bred winners from 1947 (Pearl Diver) to 1965 (Sea Bird II). Sea Bird was one of the outstanding Derby winners, and his unbeaten five-race three-year-old career ended with an astonishing six-length victory in the Prix de l'Arc de Triomphe from Reliance, the Prix du Jockey Club and Prix Royal Oak winner. A great horse himself, Reliance was made to look almost a second-rate handicapper.

The immediate post-war era will be forever remembered in Britain for the eminence of horses owned by M. Marcel Boussac, a leading owner-breeder since the 1920s. Thanks to his possession of two great stallions, Pharis II and Djebel, he attained an aura of invincibility, winning the Epsom Derby and Oaks in 1950 with Galcador and Asmena, and heading the list of winning owners in Britain. He was the first Frenchman to do so since Gladiateur's owner, Count de Lagrange, in 1865.

Italy is the most important of the other European racing countries, but again her start was late. Milan, now the principal centre, had regular meetings only from the 1840s, and racing in Rome did not begin until 1868. Although the Italian breeding industry is small, it has had a disproportionately large international influence, primarily due to the genius of one man, Federico Tesio. He founded what is now the Dormello-Olgiata Stud on the shores of Lake Maggiore in 1898. Between 1911 and his death in 1954 Tesio produced 20 winners of the Italian Derby, a dozen or more horses of top international class and two world-beaters, Nearco and Ribot, both undefeated throughout their careers. Nearco and another Tesio champion, Donatello II, both became leading sires in England, and Nearco's son Nasrullah and grandson Bold Ruler reigned supreme in the United States, where Ribot eventually held court.

The horse was unknown in Australia and New Zealand when the early English settlers landed there in the late eighteenth century. Now the Antipodes rank second only to North America in numerical terms, with more than 25,000 racehorses competing for prizes worth an annual A$25 million. The breeding industry is thriving, but imported stallions still constitute over 50 per cent of the leading 500 sires list.

In Australia the policy has always been to produce tough horses, with endurance and as much speed as possible. Each state has its individual classic programme, but these races are supplemented by valuable long-distance handicaps, like the 3,200 m (2 mile) Melbourne, Sydney and Brisbane Cups, which carry big prize money and offer attractive betting opportunities. Australia is one of the few countries outside Britain where bookmakers can operate freely on the courses.

It was from Australia that the first Thoroughbreds reached Japan in 1895. The public readily took to the new sport of racing, which had been introduced for native-bred horses at the instigation of English residents around Yokahama about 25 years earlier. Since the Second World War – and in 1945 only 542 mares remained – Japanese racing and breeding has made immense strides. Foal production is now running at 7,000 annually, but although Japanese buyers have patronized the world's best markets for their foundation stock, they have yet to show that they can produce animals of international class.

Racing as he does in about 50 countries, the Thoroughbred has undoubtedly proved himself to be an extremely adaptable animal. But his successful breeding to high standards demands an equable, temperate climate, such as that existing in parts

of Europe, North America, Argentina, Australia, New Zealand, Japan and, to a lesser extent, South Africa. Modern air transport facilities have led to the spread of international breeding, but international competition on a global basis is still prevented by insuperable differences in seasons, training methods, tracks, acclimitization and so on. The Washington International, run every November at Laurel Park in Maryland, is an exception, but this is an invitation event which owes its success in no small measure to the efforts of Laurel Park president John D. Shapiro, who scours the major racing centres of the world seeking possible contestants. Even so he does not always succeed in obtaining the best available representatives.

The grading of races in each country has greatly assisted the world's breeders to classify their horses. Usually such grading depends on prize money and the number of graded events for each country is in direct proportion to the total number of races run.

In Britain the Pattern of Racing Committee was set up in 1960 with the aim of providing a complete system of tests for the best horses of all ages over all distances. Other countries adopted similar policies. In Britain and Europe there were 297 Pattern races in 1976; North America had 273 Graded Stakes.

Prize money remains the incentive in all countries other than those where racing is totally state run. The money directly affects the quality of the horses, the level of entertainment offered to the public and the prosperity of the supporting breeding industry. Betting, through the percentage deducted from totalizators, provides a large, assured income where machine betting has a monopoly. In Britain this is not

so and bookmakers and totalizators exist side-by-side, but the former make their contribution in the sums extracted from them annually by the Levy Board. Most British wagering is off the course, either by credit or in cash through the 14,000 or so betting 'shops' of which only very few are run by the totalizator. The Levy Board is able to provide over £6 million annually from a total betting turnover of £2,000 million. Racecourses receive fixed amounts according to their grading, and also put up money themselves. Owners contribute to their own prizes by way of entry fees and stakes, and over a quarter of the total is provided through sponsors.

Although the basics remain the same, the racing scene has altered drastically since Admiral Rous's day. With increased public mobility, first via rail transport and later the motor car, the sport has become a major entertainment. Technical improvements have included the mechanical starting stalls to replace the rising tape 'gates' which even Rous never saw. At the other end the photo-finish has become an indispensible aid to judges, and indeed the whole race is recorded on film by means of patrol cameras mounted at vantage points. Such film is immediately available to the stewards at the end of the race to help them come to a decision if any inquiry should be necessary.

The Jockey Club remains in disciplinary control, with finance in the hands of the Levy Board, but day-to-day administration is still carried out by the family firm of Weatherby, founded by James Weatherby when he was appointed Keeper of the Match Book to the Jockey Club in 1773. Shortly afterwards he began publishing the *Racing Calendar* and then, 20 years

later, the first volume of the *General Stud Book*. This now appears every four years and registers the details of every Thoroughbred foaled in Great Britain or Ireland. The Weatherby firm has been transformed into a highly efficient modern business, with the quill pens and high stools of James's day replaced by a computer which stores the records of every horse and owner, tabulates the form, grades the horse for entry and even, with a little human assistance, produces the handicaps.

Racing on the world stage is *flat* racing. In the United States it operates all the year round, with meetings on regular, oval-shaped 'dirt' tracks lasting a month or more at a time. In Europe, the racing-on-grass season runs only from March to early November, but there is also the 'winter game'. This is National Hunt racing, staged over fences or hurdles and, in Britain and Ireland at least, attracting almost as large a following as 'the flat'.

National Hunt racing can never gain the international importance of its elder brother, mainly because it does not, by

Racing has become a huge industry round the world, with millions invested in breeding and betting. *opposite top*: Racing on a snowy course at St. Moritz, Switzerland. *opposite bottom*: A race in the Algarve region of Portugal – a far cry from Epsom, Longchamp or Laurel Park, but still hotly contested whatever the prize. *below left*: The paddock scene at Flemington Racecourse in Melbourne, Australia, with runners being escorted to the start. New Zealand and Australia have some 25,000 horses competing annually. *below right*: The start of a flat race in Frankfurt, Germany, using the starting stalls.

The world's greatest steeplechase, the Grand National, incorporates 30 fences in 4½ miles. Probably the most famous fence is the formidable Becher's Brook, which has to be negotiated twice on the course.

itself, support a large breeding industry. Some horses are bred with jump racing in mind and most of the leading performers stem from renowned Anglo-Irish jumping 'families', but the majority of the run-of-the-mill participants are horses who, for one reason or another, have either proved unsuitable for flat racing or have outlived their usefulness in that sphere.

The races, either over fences of birch or gorse (called steeplechases) or hurdles, are longer (the minimum is 3,200 m, (2 miles)) and contested by older animals. Most of the male horses taking part are geldings and, while the successful jump racing mare will frequently be used for breeding, she will have competed until much later in life than her flat racing sisters and so will not have as great an opportunity to produce offspring. In this sphere stallions often become known as begetters of 'jumping blood' only after they are dead, since steeplechasers usually do not achieve their best until the age of nine or ten.

Hunting is the direct ancestor of steeplechasing. Time was when man hunted to live; when this became no longer necessary, hunting continued as a sport, mainly indulged in by the aristrocracy of the day. Mounted on horseback, they pursued a variety of quarry; the stag, the boar, and later, the fox. Early hunting in much-forested Britain was a slow business, but, as the land became more open, so the speed increased. Hounds were bred to run faster, and horses had to be faster to keep up.

Jumping in the hunting field was still something of a rarity. On one occasion when the Duke of Devonshire was observed galloping headlong over a gate, his companions assumed his horse was bolting. The British Enclosure Acts of the seventeenth and eighteenth centuries, however, brought the spread of hedges, ditches, timber rails and other obstacles across the land and the followers of the chase found it essential to teach their horses to jump if they were to stay with the hunt to the end. Enthusiasts so much enjoyed this new and exciting development that a competitive element arose, which found expression in matches in which one young blood would test his horse and his ability against another across field, hedge and ditch, usually with a substantial sum wagered on the outcome.

These matches were over natural country, from one landmark to another, and what more obvious landmark in the eighteenth century British countryside than the steeple of the village church. Hence the name steeplechase. One of the earliest recorded matches, and certainly the most celebrated, took place in Co. Cork, Ireland, in 1752, when Cornelius O'Callaghan and Edmund Blake settled an argument as to the relative merits of their hunters by galloping the 6·4 km (4 miles) from Buttevant Church to St Leger Steeple. Blake won, and his prize was 'a hogshead of claret, a pipe of port and a quarter cask of old Jamaica rum'.

The first half of the nineteenth century brought a gradual division of the sport, one half retaining the essentially amateur, hunting-based element which was to become the foundation of point-to-pointing, and the other gathering round it an increasingly professional aura, with jumping races on regular public courses

over hurdles and fences. The first annual jumping meeting was inaugurated at St Albans in 1830, organized by the proprietor of the Turf Hotel, an ex-racehorse trainer named Tom Colman. The first St Albans' Steeplechase – 'a sweepstakes of 25 sov each' – drew 16 starters and was repeated each season, attracting the best horses and riders, until 1839. This was to be a year of considerable significance in steeplechasing history since it brought the first running of what has become the greatest steeplechase of them all, the Grand National at Aintree, near Liverpool. This race – 'a sweepstakes of 20 sov each, 5 forfeit, with 100 sov added' – was won by Lottery, a 16 hands bay horse, ridden by one of the leading professionals of the day, Jem Mason. Each horse carried 76 kg (12 st), and the 6·4 km (4 mile) course, most of it over plough, contained 29 obstacles. These varied from small banks to massive stone walls, and included two brooks to be jumped. One of them is still known today as Becher's Brook after the Captain Becher who came to grief there riding Conrad. Lottery's time was recorded as 14 min. 53 sec. – well over five minutes longer than is taken in present day Grand Nationals.

Until soon after the Second World War the Grand National continued to hold sway as the only worthwhile prize for the established 'chaser, being at least a dozen times more valuable than the Gold Cup which was established in 1924 as the principal level weight test for the staying 'chasers. Aintree's course was unique, and its big, upright hedges packed with gorse annually extracted a heavy toll. Although they have been modified in recent years they remain formidable obstacles. The names of some of them – Becher's Brook, the Canal Turn, Valentine's Brook, the Chair – are emblazoned in the history of the world's greatest steeplechase.

Some magnificent horses have won the Grand National. Golden Miller, claimed by many to have been the finest of them all and successful in five consecutive Cheltenham Gold Cups, won in 1934. Reynoldstown became a dual winner in 1935 and 1936, a feat not surpassed until the mighty Red Rum triumphed in 1973, 1974 and 1977. L'Escargot, who beat Red Rum in a memorable 1975 contest, had landed Gold Cup victories in 1970 and 1971 for his American owner, Raymond Guest. But it is thoroughly appropriate that the first name on the roll of honour should have been that of Lottery, for with the huge fields – often 30 or 40 strong – and with the handicap weights acting as the great leveller, there have been some remarkable upsets and dramas.

By the 1960s the Grand National was no longer out on its own in the prize money stakes. Thanks to the advent of commercial sponsorship there are now a series of rich prizes to be won by 'chasers and hurdlers, while the injection of Levy Board funds has lifted the value of established races like the Cheltenham Gold Cup and Champion Hurdle – both also partly-sponsored – to more respectable levels.

National Hunt racing now has a Pattern Committee of its own to plan the main events of the season and steeplechasers can carve out a worthwhile career without undergoing the gruelling test at Aintree. One who did so in the 1960s was the now legendary Irish 'chaser Arkle, who before his enforced retirement in 1966 with a cracked pedal bone, had won 27 races, including three Cheltenham Gold Cups, earning a total of £73,617 for his owner, Anne, Duchess of Westminster.

In operation in Britain today there are 62 racecourses, staging some 5,500 flat and National Hunt races annually. Newmarket remains exclusively a centre for flat racing; Cheltenham is the jumping counterpart. But many other courses promote both 'codes' and in the spring and autumn 'mixed' meetings are extremely popular.

The 'jumping game' has never really caught on other than in Britain and Ireland. Europe has one or two annual 'spectaculars', like the Grand Pardubice in Czechoslovakia (really more of a cross-country race). There are some winter opportunities for hurdlers and steeplechasers in Northern Italy, while the best-known centres in France are at Auteuil and Enghien.

Auteuil is the venue, every June, for the 6·4 km (4 mile) Grand Steeplechase de

A novice hurdle race at Kempton Park in England. Hurdling often forms the transition between flat racing and steeplechasing for the slightly slower-paced flat race horses.

Paris, often referred to as the French Grand National, though the obstacles are very different from Aintree. Some are little more than hurdles, others are big privet hedges, and there is the occasional bank with a small brush fence on top. It was in this race in 1962 that Fred Winter, perhaps the greatest English steeplechasing rider of all time, achieved undying fame by riding to victory on the gallant little French-bred but English-trained Mandarin, after its rubber bit had broken before the fourth fence. Three months earlier Mandarin had won the Cheltenham Gold Cup.

Though French steeplechasing is definitely the poor relation of the flat, some

of the prizes on offer are still mouth-watering by British standards. There is also good money to be won in French hurdle racing, the principal event of which is the Grande Course de Haies d'Auteuil. Again the obstacles are somewhat different from those found on British courses, where the hurdles are rather similar to those with which a farmer would pen his sheep, but laced with gorse and stuck into the ground so as to slope away from the approaching field. The height from top bar to ground is 106 cm (3 ft 6 ins). French hurdles are lower and fixed upright, and a horse can brush through the top half.

Early American jump racing was, like its British counterpart, based on the hunting which existed on the Eastern seaboard. But on regular tracks it had a later beginning and it was not until 1865 that the first American steeplechase was recorded. Thirty years later brought the formation of the National Steeplechase Association, but the sport never achieved the enormous public following accorded to flat racing and, as enthusiasm waned, races over obstacles at major centres gradually diminished. It is not entirely defunct, however, and the Maryland Hunt Cup is often likened to the Aintree Grand National, though in reality the two events are totally dissimilar. The Maryland meeting is more like an English point-to-point, with the crowds picnicking on a hillside overlooking the course. The big race is over 6·4 km (4 miles) of much more undulating country than Aintree. Fields are always smaller – sometimes as few as six starters – and all riders must be amateurs. The obstacles are fixed timber rails, with which no liberties can be taken.

Strangely, at a time of dwindling interest a new $100,000 race, the Colonial Cup

The legendary Red Rum at exercise on the sands at Southport, England, the setting for much of his training. Winner of three Grand Nationals and twice runner-up, he holds a unique place in racing history.

4·5 km (2 miles 6½ furlongs) over brush fences, was established in 1970 and has recently been attracting entries from across the Atlantic. The New Zealand-bred Grand Canyon, trained in Britain, won in November 1976.

Rubio (in 1908) and the 15 hands Battleship (1938) were American winners of the Aintree Grand National and in 1965 Jay Trump became the first horse to pull off the Maryland Hunt Cup/Grand National double. He was ridden in both his races by his owner, the then leading American amateur, Mr Tommy Crompton Smith.

The amateur has always been strongly represented in the jumping game. On the flat, jockeys and trainers are licensed professionals and although few races are set aside for both male and female amateurs, they can never compete against their paid counterparts. This is not the case in National Hunt racing, where the two sides literally rub shoulders in race and weighing-room. In Britain a National Hunt trainer holds a professional licence, but a whole army of men and women preparing their own horses, or those of their immediate family, are issued with 'permits' to train. Subject to certain restrictions these 'amateur' trainers can put their mounts against horses trained by professionals and, like them, can usually choose either amateur or professional jockeys.

In point-to-pointing, the third element of the racing scene in Britain and Ireland, the professional is prohibited. Prize money is restricted to artificially low levels and

the organization, subject to overall control by the National Hunt Committee, is decentralized and in amateur hands. It is, in fact, still based fairly and squarely on the same hunting field from which its senior partner sprang. Somewhere along the nineteenth century road of development a fork was reached; the infant National Hunt Committee, fully occupied with its efforts to regularize jumping meetings on established courses, was quite content to leave individual Hunts, which through their Masters exercised responsible authority, to run an annual fixture for their own enjoyment. Thus the private matches from which steeplechasing grew continued among hunting folk and became end-of-season 'jollies' where the sportsmen raced their hunters against one another across natural country. These were the real 'point-to-points', with the field despatched from one spot by the starter and ordered to gallop to another, perhaps 8 to 10 km away (5 to 6 miles), choosing their own route. Little attention was paid to the needs of spectators. The local country people would gather at vantage points en route, or more likely near the finish itself, where the breathless winner would receive his prize, which might be a small purse made up from a sweepstake, or a trophy presented by the Hunt.

Gradually the occasion became a focal point in the Hunt's calendar and the social aspect gained emphasis. A marquee or two would be erected near the finish and the opportunity seized to entertain the local farmers by way of thanks for their having allowed the Hunt over their land during the preceding season. These slightly bucolic farmers' lunches remained an important feature of the day for many years, but now have almost entirely disappeared.

The field streams over a fence at a point-to-point these originally began with wagers between hunting men on races run literally from 'point to point'. Now they are run on a more sophisticated and organized basis by hunts, like mini race meetings and attract a large following.

To add to the interest, the literal point-to-point aspect gave way to a start and finish sited at the same spot, so courses became round, oval, oblong, triangular or, occasionally 'there-and-back' with flags to mark turning points. The early point-to-points were solely for members of the Hunt, with a prize for the first heavyweight, the first serving officer, the first farmer and so on – a tradition maintained to this day in certain cross-country races like the Melton ride, which regularly draws fields 60 to 80 strong in Leicestershire each February. Later, programmes of four or five races were introduced, drawing contestants from neighbouring Hunts. Courses were still over natural country, although, to encourage faster racing, some of the hedges began to be a little 'improved'.

The horses were still the hunters that had carried their owners in pursuit of fox or stag from November to March, but the need for speed in the hunting field was leading to a greater use of the Thoroughbred, or at least the progeny of a Thoroughbred sire and a hunter mare. Even early in the nineteenth century, Dick Christian was proclaiming, 'I never heard of a great thing in the hunting field yet it was done by a Thoroughbred', and today the majority of horses competing are 'in the book'.

The evolution of point-to-pointing in the twentieth century was moulded by the economics of the countryside and the increased mobility of the urban population provided by the advent of the motor car. Hunt committees were finding it increasingly difficult to raise the money essential to maintain their usual level of sport and the annual race meeting changed from a local social occasion into a major money-making activity, with every effort made to draw the paying customers. The National Hunt Committee, jealous of the rival attraction offered to race meetings proper, has always set its face against permitting individual admission charges, but car-parking fees could not be ruled out. In consequence, these now make up the principal source of revenue for the nearly 200 meetings staged in the February to early June season. Venues are chosen with the visitor in mind, and car-parks, fees for which range from £1 to £5, are preferably sited on hillsides from which all the day's racing can be seen.

Natural country has given way to made fences, identical in structure, but slightly smaller than those on steeplechase courses. Indeed, some meetings are staged on defunct racecourses, like Tweseldown, Buckfastleigh and Bogside, where the permanent buildings and grandstands that remain can also be utilized. Frequently several Hunts will share the same course, which helps reduce financial outlay.

The normal programme comprises five or six races, all of them a minimum of 4·8 km (3 miles). One will be confined to members of the promoting Hunt (this is where one usually sees the genuine hunters), then there are a couple for horses from the half-a-dozen or so adjacent Hunts, and two so-called Open races, which, as their name implies, can be contested by horses qualified with any Hunt in the United Kingdom.

Since the advent of sex equality, ladies and men may compete against each other. Before the new legislation the ladies' Open race was often the most popular on the card and, with a minimum weight requirement of 70 kg (11 st) instead of 80 kg (12 st 7 lb), were run at a scorching pace throughout. Because of their popularity the division has been retained, with the other Open race confined to men.

There is not inconsiderable traffic between all the types of racing that have been discussed in this chapter. From flat racing to hurdling is a simple step. The hurdler can graduate with great difficulty to steeplechasing, and then end his days happily as a hunter/point-to-pointer.

Part of the fascination of horse racing has always been its 'glorious uncertainty'. Shining classic prospects at two can turn into bottom-weight failures in minor hurdle handicaps at four – and a point-to-point champion at seven. A sprint-bred two-year-old can end up a triple Grand National winner – as Red Rum proved. Breeding has always been an inexact science and 'paying for pedigree' has often resulted in badly burnt fingers. Those who bid the $1,500,000 for the Secretariat yearling mentioned at the outset will be hoping that this time they have got things right.

Long Distance and Endurance Riding

ENDURANCE riding and its related equestrian endeavours, competitive trail and long distance riding are comparatively recent additions to the great variety of sports in which man and horse participate together. Great effort and courage is required from the horse in this instance, as well as an application and dedication from the rider. As its name suggests it is a supreme test, for great distances are covered over all types of terrain, in sometimes diabolical climatic conditions. At the finish of a 120 km (75 mile) or 160 km (100 mile) ride, both parties must be in a fit state to turn around and go again – truly a feat of endurance.

Although the youngest of the equestrian sports, endurance riding has a large international following. In its present form it began little more than 20 years ago in the United States where it flourished for a decade before catching on in Australia. More recently, Great Britain, South Africa, New Zealand, and West Germany have become similarly involved.

Among its enthusiasts, may be found the widest range of riders mounted on the greatest variety of horses and ponies imaginable. Indeed it is one of the sport's main attractions that no specific type of horse is needed in order to participate and complete the course successfully. In endurance rides in America, I have come across the typical American breeds such as Appaloosa, Morgan, Quarter Horse, Moyle, Standardbred, Saddlebred and Walking Horse, as well as the Arabian, Thoroughbred, Connemara and Welsh. In Britain the range of breeds is not so great, but the Arabian and Thoroughbred and their crosses are a popular choice, as are hunters and a variety of cobby types. Larger native breeds are used, some crossed with Arabian or Thoroughbred, as well as many imported breeds. On Germany's 160 km (100 mile) ride from Hamburg to Hanover, representatives of such national breeds as Hanoverians, Trakheners, Westphalians, Holsteiners, German Trotters and Brandenburgs will be seen as well as such non-German breeds as Norwegian Fjords, Welsh Cobs, Arabs, Lipizzaners, Hungarian Halfbloods, Haflingers and Icelandic ponies.

From just these three participating countries it can be seen that the scope for the type of horse used is very wide indeed, although those people who really become involved, generally find the lean athletic type of horse is the most suitable and successful. Arabs and Arabian crosses are notable for enjoying markedly greater success

A group of competitors on a long-distance ride. This sport, although its origins date from long ago when horses were man's only form of transport, is one of the most recent of competitive events. Very popular in the US, it is a supreme test of a horse's stamina.

overall than any other breed. Horses are required to be five years of age or older before they can compete; there is no maximum or minimum age for riders and very young children often compete, accompanied by an adult.

The collective term 'long distance riding' covers the sport's three major aspects. In its lower echelons it offers an introduction to newcomers by participating in shorter-distanced pleasure rides, of between 23 km (15 miles) and 46 km (30 miles). These are ideal for novice riders, and/or horses and being non-competitive, provide an opportunity to learn to travel quietly and competently over a variety of terrain. Young horses become used to travelling in company, so that when a rider wants to turn to competitive riding, his mount will have achieved a fair amount of mental and physical stability on the trail and is thus able to cope with the stresses engendered by competition.

Competitive trail rides are the next step. These are judged rides in which there is a speed bracket which varies slightly in different countries. The prime judging factor however, is overall fitness of horses before, during, and after the competition. All CTRs have winning and placed horses, the criteria used being perfect time score and a veterinary assessment encompassing many aspects that indicate fitness. The major stress factors are those relating to pulse and respiration and the speed of

recovery to normal after heavy exertion. If a fit young horse has settled into the routine of travelling smoothly and efficiently and is unflustered by extraneous activity, he will register better recovery than one who is alarmed by all the unusual happenings of the ride.

CTRs range in distance from the lower limit of 40 km (25 miles) to the upward limit of 96 km (60 miles) in one day in Britain. America stages a great number, ranging from 40 km (25 miles) in one day up to 160 km (100 miles) run over three days. Germany has many rides run along similar, although not identical lines, with awards going to horses in the best condition and also to those completing the course in fit condition and approximating to ideal timing.

The top rung of the long distance riding ladder is endurance riding with courses ranging in Britain from 80 km (50 miles) to 160 km (100 miles) in one day, and in America from 40 km (25 miles) up to 163 km (102 miles). There is a strong move in America now to have a lower limit of 80 km (50 miles) to stop over-stressing horses at too high a speed, the feeling being that rides of this distance and above induce greater caution in competitors. Germany has rides of 80 km (50 miles) up to 160 km (100 miles); New Zealand has a lower limit of 72 km (45 miles) and a present upper limit of 120 km (75 miles), whilst Australia has the famous Quilty 160 km (100 mile) ride and a number of shorter 80 km (50 mile) rides. South Africa has a series of 80 km (50 mile) rides and a major 220 km (130 mile) ride each year.

An endurance ride winner is the fastest fit horse over the distance, and the times turned in on some of the endurance rides are a tribute to the stamina and courage of the horses taking part. Some of the 160 km (100 mile) rides held over really tough terrain are repeatedly won in riding times of under 12 hours. The 80 km (50 miles) rides consistently show winning times around the five-hour mark.

The leading country in this sport is undoubtedly still the United States, whose inauguration began in 1955 with the first running of the Tevis Cup. This 160 km (100 mile) ride was originally run from Lake Tahoe to Auburn, California over the Sierra Nevada and was mapped out along the old Western States Trail that carried hordes of hopeful miners during the California Gold Rush, as well as the equally acquisitive pioneers, heading for the Nevada Silver Lode.

Since then, endurance riding has gripped the enthusiasm of thousands of American horsemen so that this ride has blossomed into a fistful of similar distanced rides run nationwide, with more than 150 shorter, but demanding, events filling each year's long distance calendar. Associations exist solely to help run the sport's many aspects. Many of these are regional, as would be expected when such enormous territories are covered, but two in particular can be termed national. The American Endurance Rides Conference controls the endurance side and the North American Trail Ride Conference governs competitive trail riding. Other regional bodies are the Pacific Northwest Endurance System; the Midwest Endurance System; the East Coast Trail Ride Association which caters for both endurance and competitive trail rides, and the Eastern States Competitive Trail Ride Association. The Rocky Mountain Trail Ride System operates over Montana and Idaho, and there are many locally based groups that run unofficial rides prior to joining into the system best suited to their activity and locale.

Many of the breed associations are realizing that distance riding is the ideal testing ground for their horses, and many breeders are using the sport to prove their stock. The undoubted leader in this is the Appaloosa Horse Club Registry. There is also a considerable amount of veterinary research being done in America on distance rides, in an effort to determine what really makes a horse successful. From the results it is apparent that the lighter type of horse is more to the fore, and winners and placing horses consistently weigh about 430 kg (960 lbs) or less.

A real cross-country endurance test, run in the 1976 Bicentennial year, was the Great American Horse Race from New York to Sacramento, California. For the 4,800 km (3,000 miles) plus course each entrant was allowed two mounts – one led while the other was ridden. It began over the Memorial Day weekend in May and the scheduled finish was Labour Day in September, thus keeping horses en route for a little over three months. Veterinary supervision was drawn from top veterinarians on the Tevis and other endurance rides. The winner from 100 entries was Verl Norton riding a mule!

Above   The Appaloosa gained its name from the Palouse river in the lands of the Nez Percé Indians; the breed descends from Spanish stock. The Appaloosa Horse Club Registry was founded in 1937 to look after the interests of the breed, and is one of the breed associations testing and promoting horses by entering them in endurance rides.

Below   A scene at a veterinary checkpoint on the San Antonio 50-mile ride. The health and well-being of the equine competitors is rigorously scrutinised on all rides by veterinary specialists; the fitness of the horse is an important part of winning in competitive riding. It is not enough just to reach the finishing post first.

One of the most gruelling – and the most famous – of the American rides is the Tevis Cup, so named after a president of the Wells Fargo Company, Lloyd Tevis. The ride follows the route of the Company's express riders and stage coaches, and takes you over the Sierra Nevada range, from snowy mountain climbs to valleys in sweltering heat. 100 miles must be covered in one day, and only the fittest possible horses complete the ride. *opposite bottom*: The approach to Cougar Rock, one of the landmarks of the ride and a stiff climb, *top left*: At Cougar Rock itself. *top right*: A cooling moment for both horse and rider in the San Antonio 50-mile ride. Variety of terrain is part of the challenge of endurance riding.

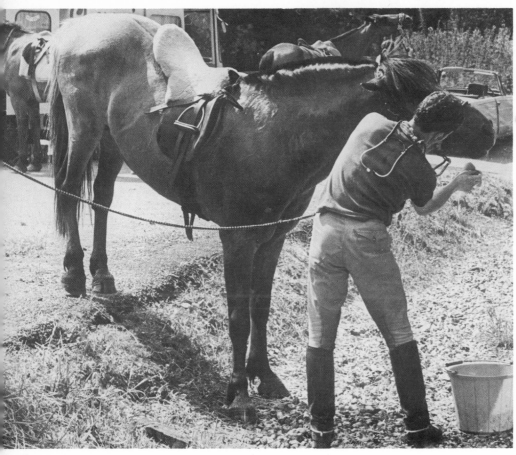

A German competitor sponges down his dun Norwegian Fjord stallion at the half-way checkpoint and veterinary inspection on the Summer Solstice ride.

Three notable endurance riders in the United States are Dr. Richard Barsaleau, DVM, also one of the nation's leading endurance judges, and as a regular and successful competitor in the Tevis and other endurance rides, he sees both sides of the coin; Appaloosa breeder Sharon Saare, a very experienced and constantly successful competitor who rides a variety of horses, and Jan Worthington, who has the outstanding record in the Eastern States of having won every three-day 160 km (100 mile) ride at some time with her crossbred Appaloosian/Arabian mare, Blanc Seurat.

Other countries have drawn heavily on the tried and proved format used in the United States both for endurance and competitive trail rides, with Australia being one of the first to tackle a 160 km (100 mile) ride in one day patterned on the Tevis Cup. This was the Tom Quilty Endurance Ride first run in 1966 and won in its inaugural year by Gabriel Stecher on his purebred Arab stallion, Shalawi, in a time of 11 hours 24 minutes. The achievement was even more remarkable as he rode the whole distance bareback! Staged annually ever since, the winning time has become increasingly faster with winners now coming in not much over the 10-hour mark. The ride was named after Tom Quilty, a famous horseman who was persuaded by Reg Williams, the Editor of Australia's premier equestrian magazine *Hoofs and Horns*, to sponsor the ride. It is

run in climatic conditions where temperatures and humidity soar, and over a tough course in the Blue Mountains of New South Wales.

Since 1966, the Australian endurance scene has grown, with new rides constantly being included and also with a National Association being formed to guide the sport along the right lines. As with all endurance ride systems the help of veterinary surgeons is essential and the Australians have been able to call on the experience of a team from the Sydney Veterinary School at Camden.

New Zealand also has a very thriving, although young, endurance riding structure and almost all the rides are in the endurance category. Only one or two are run along competitive trail ride lines. Up until recently, there have been eight major established endurance rides, five in the South Island and three in the North Island, but there are definite plans to include more in the annual calendar. Rules are drawn from the Tevis and Quilty rides and the varied terrain includes many steeply climbing sections. Weather conditions often turn the ground in some areas into bogland overnight, making an additional hazard. The longest ride is the Rocklands 80 km (50 miles) and 120 km (75 miles), run in January each year. Winning times for 80 km (50 mile) rides range around the five-hour mark with some competitors finishing in an appreciably shorter time. Leading combinations in New Zealand over the past few years, are Alastair Fleming riding Joe Pittam's Waimeha Whirlwind, a pure Arab gelding; Pat Hansen and Silver King, a pure Arab stallion, and Jocelyn Allen on Royal Blue, an

Anglo-Arab gelding. An up-and-coming partnership is Laurie Bethune and Flicka, a partbred Arab palomino mare, and Phil Proctor with Fella are noticeable for breaking the Arab dominance, Fella being a bay gelding of mixed Standardbred and Hack blood.

Plans for New Zealand's future are to work towards the 160 km (100 mile) ride in one day. As in other countries where the sport has not long emerged as a major horse activity, many riders are joined in a dedicated group which keeps enthusiasm growing by active participation.

Currently in Britain there are two bodies involved with long distance riding. One is under the aegis of the British Horse Society which operates a section for long distance riding. It runs a series of local Golden Horseshoe Qualifying Rides of 64 km (40 miles) and a final competition of 120 km (75 miles) run over two days on Exmoor, in Somerset. There are also plans for expanding the scope of rides.

The other body is the Endurance Horse and Pony Society (EHPS), a national body whose sole concern is the management of rides and the dissemination of ideas and practical information gained from veterinary research and actual ride data. The EHPS was founded in 1973 and has a network of rides throughout the country, the endurance rides following the Tevis Cup format, the competitive trail rides following along very similar lines to those used by the North American Trail Ride Conference. In 1975 the EHPS ran its first 160 km (100 mile) ride in the New Forest in Hampshire with a team of veterinary surgeons headed by the Society's veterinary advisors, Messrs R. G. Orton, MRCVS, John Hartley-Sampson, B.V. Sc., MRCVS, and Peter Hall-Patch, B.V. Sc., MRCVS. The winner of this, in a riding time of 12 hours, one minute was Nizzolan, a purebred Arab stallion. Winner of the best condition prize was Miss Margaret Montgomerie's black gelding Tarquin, also placed third in the ride. It was this pair who journeyed to Hamburg in 1976 to tackle the German 160 km (100 mile) ride. As a result of this EHPS ride, veterinary research into haemotology pertaining to endurance horses has been started, and other areas of research are under way.

Similar to the American judging procedure, the EHPS also has a points system where horses accumulating points throughout the year campaign for High Points Trophies. The overall trophies are the Manar Trophy for the Leading Senior Horse of the Year, and the Zarpa Trophy for the Leading Junior Rider.

The South African Long Distance Riding Association has been operative since 1972 and was initiated by McFee Morgan, an Arab horse breeder in the Transvaal. Another Arab horse breeder from the Transvaal, Dick de Voss, joined him as secretary, and the group owes a lot to its Veterinary Advisor and founder member Professor Sandy Littlejohn. Active participation is reported to be growing, with indications that the sport is soon to enjoy a tremendous upsurge. The South African

National Championships are held over a three-day 220 km (130 mile) ride held at Fauresmith in the Orange Free State. This ride is sponsored jointly, with trophies donated by the Farmers Weekly Trail at Fauresmith for the winner, and the Arabian Horse Society, for the leading Arab. The ride is run over varied terrain and rules are drawn from the Tevis Cup. Although run over three days, it is judged on endurance lines.

Prior to the championships, there are four 80 km (50 mile) pre-rides from which the committees decide the horses capable of tackling the longer course at Fauresmith. The pre-rides are held in Natal, Orange Free State, Transvaal and Cape Province. Minimum weights of 73 kgs (160 lbs) are mandatory except in the junior division, where riders up to 16 years of age ride at catch weight. Juniors must be accompanied by an adult rider. Results from the past three years indicate again that the ability of the Arab is prominent, and indeed most horses used in South African distance riding are of Arab blood. In 1974, Anglo-Arabs filled five out of ten of the highest places in the National Championships, and in following years, the winners have consistently been purebred Arabs.

South African distance horses are generally of the lean athletic type, that is becoming universally known for its ability to endure as it is not hampered by excess bone and flesh. It is indicative of the success of this type that throughout the endurance riding world, horses that are repeatedly successful fall into this category. Endurance riding is certainly one of the equine spheres where athletic ability and lean fitness are definitely a major plus.

West Germany is one of the European countries with a major involvement in the sport and a national body was formed in November 1976 to assist the running of distance riding. Distance riders in Germany have long been well catered for in a variety of rides but up until the formation of the national body there had been no standard guideline for the management of rides. Each organizer thus had to learn by trial and error. It says a lot for their ingenuity that the sport has flourished in the way it has. It is apparent that the majority of Germany's enthusiasts wish for cohesion amongst organizers, so competitors will know what to expect throughout the whole country. Regular correspondence has been held with the EHPS of Great Britain, in efforts to achieve an international set of rulings with only slight national and regional differences – itself a definite help in the furthering of endurance riding.

Most current German rides fall into the endurance category and range from 80 km (50 miles) to 160 km (100 miles) in length. Several shorter rides are held throughout the year, but the major rides at present are the Laichingen 100 km (60 mile) ride held near Ulm in Southern Germany over demanding territory, and the Hamburg to Hanover 160 km (100 mile) ride held each autumn.

Part of the training for endurance riding is to accustom the horse to any strange encounters or feats he may be asked to undertake – such as pulling his rider uphill.

Conditions on the Hamburg to Hanover ride as I experienced them in 1976 tended to be vastly different from similar distance rides held in other countries. Basically an endurance ride with the fastest horse pronounced the winner (except in a tie when the horse's condition was the deciding factor), it also had a series of penalty points and bonus points. Deviating from the course incurred penalties for so doing, as well as loss of time. Other penalties could be incurred for overtaking unless prior permission from leaders had been given and also for failure to negotiate hazards at first try. A curious feature of the ride was an 11 km (7 mile) section that had to be ridden in a specific time, riders not knowing how long or where the 'time trial' was to take place until they arrived at the venue. Penalties were incurred if horses went outside the time limits, a one minute leeway being allowed. The ride itself was well vetted and there were no casualties, and the awards for first four places were filled by completely different types of horse, namely an Irish heavyweight gelding, an Arabian stallion, a 16-year-old mare of mixed Hackney type (judging from her action) and a Trakhener gelding. A 13 h.h. Norwegian pony, with a ten-year-old rider won the class for Klein Pferde (Small Horses), proving that ponies and young children can readily tackle rides of this distance.

One other country in Europe that is showing signs of joining the endurance merry-go-round is Denmark. Discussions have been held with the EHPS Committee and advice sought on the founding of a long distance group. It would seem to be from amongst the Arab breeders and enthusiasts in Denmark that the beginnings of organized distance riding are likely to come. At present all long distance riding is on a purely informal friendly basis, the same way it has started in all other countries.

It can be seen from this overall picture that endurance riding is a major growth sport internationally. There is furthermore a tremendous rapport between interested and involved countries as evidenced by competitors who travel abroad to compete. The Germans have sent a team to Britain and in 1976 the EHPS reciprocated. Sharon Saare of the Appaloosa Horse Club of America has competed in British rides. The interflow between Australia and America for the Quilty and Tevis Cups is now commonplace; Switzerland sends horses to the German rides, and South Africa has both hosted overseas riders as well as sending representatives to compete elsewhere.

Each country has its own minor differences in rules and regulations but it is reassuring that the basic structure is similar so that riders travelling from one country to another know what to expect. This also gives a universal basis on which to work towards gathering information and relevant statistics from rides so that research and veterinary knowledge of the stresses involved can be furthered. This of course can only be generally beneficial, especially to the courageous horses that constantly give of their best throughout even the toughest of endurance rides.

Polo

POLO, a stick and ball game played on horseback by opposing teams of four a side, is a very ancient game which originated in the Orient well over 2000 years ago. The earliest references to it are made in conjunction with Alexander the Great and Darius, King of Persia, from which country the game is believed to have originated, although it was certainly played in one form or another throughout the East, from China and Mongolia to Japan.

The Moslem invaders from the North-West and the Chinese from the North-East, took the game into India. In the middle of the last century, English planters discovered it in Assam and brought it back to England. In Assam it was played on the local Manipuri ponies, some of them barely 12 h.h., and called *kangjai*. In Persia it was known as *chaugan* (a mallet – by which name the polo stick is known in the United States today) and its present name is a derivative of the Tibetan word *pulu*, meaning a root, from which the wooden polo ball is made.

It did not take the British very long to organize the sport in typical English military fashion. Silchar, capital of the Cachar district, was soon to become the birthplace of modern polo, and the Silchar Club is the oldest polo club in the world. It was founded in 1859, and the rules drawn up then are those on which the present rules are based. Teams originally had nine riders, but this was later reduced to seven and eventually to four, as the ponies became

Polo, one of the oldest games on horseback known to man, originated in China and then moved on to the Indian continent. In Assam it was played on these Manipuri ponies, some of which were scarcely 12 hands in height.

bigger and faster. In 1876 the height limit in India was set at 13·2 h.h., and in England at 14 h.h. Twenty years later it was increased to 14·2 h.h., and in 1919 the height limit was abolished. Nowadays, the average height is about 15·1 h.h.

In 1869 the game was introduced into England by some army officers from the 9th Lancers, 19th Hussars, 1st Life Guards and Royal Horse Guards. They played polo, with eight aside, on Hounslow Heath, near London and those who watched dubbed it 'hockey on horseback'. It immediately caught on and the Hurlingham Club became the headquarters of English polo, issuing the first English rules in 1875. At about the same time the Indian Polo Association was formed. It framed its own rules until the Second World War.

1878 saw the first Inter-Regimental Tournament, and in 1893 the National Pony Society was founded, with the purpose of promoting the breeding of polo ponies. The game soon spread across to other parts of the world, particularly the British Empire, the United States and Argentina. In the last-mentioned country it was an immediate success, as it still is today. Indeed, Argentina became the biggest breeders and exporters of polo ponies, owing to the scale on which horse breeding is carried out there on the estancias, the number of natural horsemen available for schooling ponies on a low wage, and the toughness of the native breed, which enabled ponies to be produced extremely economically. A number of English dealers have had contacts and connections in Argentina for many years; others went out there to live, so as to exploit a lucrative market, and make frequent shipments back to England.

Polo was introduced into the United States in 1876 by James Gordon Bennett, who brought Western horses East to be trained for the game. The 'Golden Age' of U.S. polo was during the 1920s and '30s when Tommy Hitchcock, Cecil Smith and others competed in national and international matches and tournaments. Now polo is mainly played on a club level under the aegis of the U.S. Polo Association.

International polo matches started in 1886 with teams from Britain and the

Above and opposite The essential handiness and conscious participation of top-class polo ponies. A good pony will not just be obedient but will follow the game on his own account, with experience almost anticipating what the rider will ask him to do. Polo has not become especially popular as a spectator sport in spite of the speed and excitement of the game, perhaps because it can be hard to follow progress in the melée – even though the referee is wearing a striped shirt to distinguish him from the players.

United States competing for the Westchester Cup. Between the wars, skilled teams from India – where most of the polo was still conducted on a regimental basis – were frequent visitors to England. Teams also came from Australia, but it was from the United States that the most successful players came – that is until Argentina overtook them. After 1945 the Argentinians reigned supreme and were unbeaten in the Cup of the Americas, the only international championship which remained in existence. Argentina by then had some 3000 active players to 1000 Americans and about 500 British.

After the war, Hurlingham, Ranelagh and Roehampton were no longer the headquarters of the game and it nearly became moribund. But there was a renaissance in 1950, largely thanks to the efforts of Lord Cowdray – who was a pre-war player as the Hon John Pearson – along with a handful of other pre-war players. The patronage of H.R.H. Prince Philip, Duke of Edinburgh – whose uncle, Admiral of the Fleet Earl Mountbatten, was a distinguished writer on the game under the pen-name of Marco – was another strong contributory factor in the general upsurge of interest.

The late Sir Humphrey de Trafford's small Thoroughbred, Rosewater, is generally considered to be the foundation of the modern polo pony which is bred in England. He was used on numerous pony

on a dummy horse in a polo pit. The strokes are: off side forward, offside backhand, offside under the neck of the pony, nearside forward, nearside backhand, nearside under the neck, and offside and nearside back shots under the tail. Other strokes which may be used to good effect are the push, an offside stroke to anticipate the action of an incoming player, and the lateral, that is underneath the pony's body and between his legs. For a forward shot, the ball is struck when it is in front of the withers, and a rear shot is taken when it is about level with the quarters.

The novice then, having mastered the strokes and proved able to hit the ball with accuracy in the pit, progresses to mounted work and then to slow chukkas in practice games. The game itself is played in chukkas of 7½ minutes each. There may be four, six, seven or eight, although now there are usually between four and six. There are 3 minutes between chukkas, and a 5-minute break at half time. Every time a goal is scored the teams change ends.

The number 3 player is the one who initiates attacks and covers number 4 in defence. Thus it is essential that he is well mounted, and is a long and accurate hitter. Numbers 1 and 2 follow up the attacking moves made by number 3, and in defence mark the opposing numbers 3 and 4. Number 4 defends his side's half of the territory, and is at the same time ready to support number 3.

Most games are played on a handicap basis, with all players rated at their value in goals or minus-goals, from minus-two to ten. In handicap tournaments the total individual handicaps are added together and then one is subtracted from the other, in order to assess the number of goals start given to the team with the lower handicap.

The rules are principally concerned with safety, and thus are mainly concerned to clarify right of possession of the ball. They lay down penalties for infringing this right and causing danger – for example by crossing the line of the ball in front of a player who has right of way, riding into a player at a dangerous angle, zig-zagging across a rider at full gallop, intimidation or sandwiching a player between two opponents. Penalties vary according to the offence and its gravity, while a deliberate foul to save a goal incurs the award of a penalty goal. Dangerous fouling carries 27 or 36 m (30 or 40 yd) free hits at an open, undefended goal. The game is stopped if a pony falls or is lame, if a player is injured, if there is a potentially dangerous accident to the pony's gear, if a player loses his helmet, and finally, if the ball goes out of play.

Polo is not a poor man's game, for ponies are expensive and at least three ponies are needed to play in a match. A pony can only play two chukkas, and there must be a reserve in case of injury or lameness. But although the old days of mounted cavalry being able to use troop horses and enthusiastic young officers being mounted

mares who had been selected for their performance on the polo ground. His three most famous sons were: Sandiway, out of Cuddington; Lord Polo, out of Lady Florence; and Hurlingham, out of Esmeralda.

The performance of any polo pony is the acid test of perfection, for in this very fast game he must be able to gallop flat out, stop in his own length, 'turn on a sixpence', swing round in a pirouette, and start off from a standstill at top speed in any direction. When riding off other ponies he must do two-track work at a gallop, and flying changes of leg must be second nature to him. Courage is a prime essential, and so are a long neck, good shoulders, a short, strong back, depth of girth, exceptionally strong quarters and hocks that are well let down.

The quick stop, and the turn at 180 degrees are the most important of all manoeuvres on the polo ground. It is also essential that the pony, ridden as he is with only one hand, should have been taught to neck rein. The mouth is unavoidably subjected to considerable strain from the hasty checks and turns. Likewise, the legs also come under great stress, for which reason supporting bandages are very necessary.

A polo ground may not exceed 274 m (300 yds) in length and the goals, 7.3 m (8 yds) wide, must not be less than 227 m (250 yds) apart. The goal posts are at least 3 m (10 ft) high. The ball is made of willow or bamboo root, is not more than 8 cm

Above A polo pony at speed displaying the need for agility and perfect obedience to the rider's aids.

(3¼ ins) in diameter and weighs 120–130 gms (4¼–4½ oz). The polo stick (mallet in America) is a cane of some 120–137 cm (48–54 ins) in length with a head set at right angles. This forms the hitting surface, and is 21–23 cm (8½–9½ ins) long. The stick is made of sycamore, ash or bamboo and the whippiness of the cane varies; a more whippy cane allows length of drive with a minimum of effort, but it is less easy to manoeuvre in close work. A stiffer cane is more accurate but requires more strength, and more accurate timing. The grip can be bound in leather, rubber, lampwick or towelling, and a wrist sling prevents the stick from being dropped.

The aim of the game, of course, is to get the ball into the opposing side's goal, to which purpose, because polo is essentially a team game, the four players – the forwards, numbers 1 and 2; the centre-half, number 3 and the back, number 4– connive and manoeuvre to attack the enemy's goal. Not all top-class polo players are outstanding horsemen, although basic horsemanship, good balance and a secure seat are all necessary attributes. More important still, however, is a good natural eye for a moving ball, while courage and judgement, plus a sense of timing, are equally essential.

Players are taught how to strike the ball

Protection for the legs of both horse and rider is essential to guard against tendon strain and injury from hooves and sticks.

through the regiment have gone, there are numerous polo clubs which enable the young man to play the game. Most have a pool of club ponies, which they hire out for a specified fee per chukka. A certain number of young players come up through the Pony Club, which encourages the game increasingly, and this has led to a number of girls becoming active players.

The governing body of polo in England is the Hurlingham Polo Association, but sadly the international effort is curtailed by lack of funds. Argentina and the United States head the world league from Australia, Mexico and other South American countries. Polo is also played regularly in Ireland, India and Pakistan, France, Germany, Italy, New Zealand, Rhodesia, South Africa, Kenya, Nigeria, Ghana, Malaysia and Jamaica.

The centres in England now are Cirencester, Cowdray Park and Windsor. There are some 49 polo clubs in existence in the United Kingdom, with some 400 players, and there are another 100 or so players within the British army in West Germany. Sponsorship has been of great benefit to English polo, as it has to all other equestrian sports, and so has the interest evinced by the Prince of Wales, who has followed in the footsteps of his father as a keen and gifted player.

A shortage of well-schooled ponies can only be regarded as inevitable in view of the current shortage of high-class trainers of horses. Apparently it takes two years to train a polo pony from the time of his initial breaking until he can play fast chukkas. Argentina ponies have nearly all been worked on the estancias before starting their specialized training, but their trainers still like to give them a further two years, to avoid a high wastage rate caused by unsoundness or problems of temperament. Some English racehorses have begun playing fast polo in just one season, but they have usually had a season or two in training and are physically mature.

The late John Board, a great expert on polo, said that there are three games of polo – Indian, English and American. He thought the Indian game the most attractive, the English the most difficult and the American infinitely best! He attributed the fact that England last won the Westchester Cup as long ago as 1921 to the fact that the Americans have adopted the forward position, ride a couple of holes shorter, keep well forward on their feet and seldom get left behind. In addition their balanced forward position enables them to hit more accurately and get enormous length on the ball. He once saw Raymond Guest hit a ball on a drizzly day, against a light breeze, which would have travelled at least 155 m (170 yds) had it not struck a pony.

The Indian is a natural horseman and a formidable opponent, particularly as he is usually superbly mounted on first-class ponies. These are the stock of English and Argentine Thoroughbreds, imported by the English, as well as some top-class Australian stock. There is also a theory that the native athlete can see a ball, whether cricket or polo, a full metre sooner

than the white man.

A variation of polo known as polo-crosse, which was played in Japan a thousand years earlier and is now popular in Australia, had a brief vogue in England, particularly in the West Country. The clumsy instrument with which the ball is scooped up and thrown made the vogue a short one, however, much to the relief of those who were dedicated to the revival of polo in post-war England and resented this distraction to potential followers.

Polo in three very different settings. *top*: A game in progress in West Pakistan on the Gigi Karakoram Range. *middle*: Swift action on the field at the Lahore Race Club. In India the game was at its height during the period of the British Raj, and used imported Thoroughbred ponies from the best stock. The Indians showed themselves to be formidable players. *bottom*: HRH The Prince of Wales, who has an obviously enthusiastic talent for the game, warming up before playing for his team, the Guards' Club, at Windsor.

Mounted Games

Mounted games constitute the oldest of equestrian skills and are not, as many believe, purely pursuits for the young. The Book of Job tells of mounted ostrich chases; jousting was a popular entertainment during the Middle Ages, and polo has its origins way back in history. As early as 600 AD the Chinese practised a form of polo with a light ball, while the Himalayan people of Hunza claimed the sport originated with their early ancestors. Modern polo is also similar to a game that was very popular with the Arabs and Persians, who used headless sticks.

During the 1860s, the British in Asia adopted polo and other mounted games in an effort to relieve the tedium of army life for officers, as well as to improve their horsemanship and to keep fit.

These exercises became known as 'gymkhana' games, a word of Anglo-Indian derivation meaning 'a field day on horseback'. By the 1880s and 1890s, mounted games, and in particular polo, had become a major source of entertainment in the United Kingdom. Fashionable London society spent summer afternoons at smart clubs with gymkhana games a feature. The events were great fun for all concerned, competitors and spectators alike, although the essence of a successful day was always organization and discipline.

In the United States of America, a favourite (if rather gruesome) mounted game of Red Indian tribes was to tether a live chicken to a stake, then, galloping at full speed, the rider would lean from his horse in an attempt to pluck the fluttering bird from the ground. It was no mean feat, for the Indians seldom rode with a saddle. The only aid employed to stay with the horse was a strip of hide plaited into the animal's mane through which the rider could secure a grip.

So, through the ages, mounted games have played an important part in the equestrian world and today, as a result of the enormously increased interest in horse riding as a sport and hobby, local horse shows and gymkhanas are numerous during the summer months, with mounted games a most important feature.

In 1957, H.R.H. Prince Philip instigated the Pony Club Mounted Games Championship in Britain for members of the movement. After area and zone finals, the Championship final is competed for annually at the Horse of the Year Show in London during October. As a result of the British Broadcasting Corporation's previous decision in 1949 to televise major

horse shows, the general public were introduced to the finer arts of such races as the sack race and the egg-and-spoon!

Limited to riders under the age of 15 on 1st May during the year of competition, all competitors' ponies must be at least four years old and under 14.2 h.h. to compete in the Prince Philip Cup. There are 18 to 20 area meetings, from which 36 teams are picked to go forward to the zone finals. Then there are a further six zone finals to select the six teams to fight it out at the Horse of the Year Show. The organizer has the final say in choosing six games from a total of 15 previously selected, his criteria being to ensure they are taxing enough to make for an exciting competition between the riders, and variable enough to interest the audience.

One of the most successful squads to have competed in the Mounted Games Championship are from the Strathblane and District branch of the Pony Club in Scotland. They won the Cup two years running in 1972 and 1973. The branch then split, the new branch being known as Kirkintilloch and Campsie and, with many of the previous winning team members, won again in 1974.

The inauguration of this event in the 1950s provided a great boost to the British

native breed societies whose handy, agile ponies were ideal for gymkhana games. The event also gave younger members of the Pony Club something to strive for, as any inexpensive, cross-bred, grass-fed pony can, with practice and patience, become every bit as good as its beautiful and often very expensive better-bred counterpart. Nowadays however, these mounted games – in keeping with other horse sports – have moved into the international league and a good, proven pony with experience can demand an extremely high price.

Teams also get 'professional', sometimes at the expense of their good name, and the will to win occasionally overshadows the simple good fun element. The fact remains, however, that this is one area where it does not matter what the breeding is – all an amateur needs is a good mount, good sportsmanship, a good sense of humour and a knowledge of the game.

The games as we know them today, are principally a pursuit of the English-speaking nations – British servicemen and their families no doubt having had a certain amount of influence. The British Pony Club is affiliated to clubs in more than 20 other countries worldwide, including Botswana, Ethiopia, Japan, Saudi

Arabia and Zambia, although this does not mean to say that they are all familiar with the skills of apple ducking and Gretna Green racing! In the United States, Canada and Australia, games on horseback such as the cowhide race (when horse and rider drag a team member lying on a sheet of hide down the arena) and barrel racing (explained later in the section) have long been popular and are closely connected to the work of the cowboy; consequently, they are generally performed by horse and rider in western saddle and dress. More anglicized games are a relatively new innovation though, and it is only in the last few years that the North Americans have taken part in International Competition.

In Europe the story is quite different. If the games were a pastime of the young in the confines of the paddock or back yard, until comparatively recently they were certainly not considered suitable entertainment for the masses. Then in 1974, the four leading teams competing in the Prince Philip Cup at The Horse of the Year Show travelled to Amsterdam to compete against each other once more in a demonstration to show what mounted games are all about. The following year, 1975, the top four branches once again packed their bags for a display abroad, this

time at the Paris Horse Show. In both cases, the local audiences responded magnificently, catching on very quickly to cheering a chosen team home, howling their dismay when a rider dropped an egg, or was just pipped at the post by an opposing team. All in all, the visits proved a great success.

In 1976, gymkhana teams from Canada and the United States visited Britain for a most successful international competition. It was tremendously exciting, with everything in the balance until the eighteenth and final game. This was the evergreen-favourite, the bending race, when Great Britain just held their lead – by one point only – to emerge winners over the Canadian visitors.

As previously mentioned, most horse shows include mounted games events and many gymkhanas consist of nothing else with open classes in which adult competitors can demonstrate their expertise.

Britain undoubtedly owes much of her interest and success in gymkhana games to her small native pony breeds which are generally nippy. In the United States and Australia, it is a different story. In both these places, horses are more generally ridden by both children and adults. However the cutting and quarter horses, which

Two different approaches to mounted equestrian games, both devised to test the pony's ability and rider's skill as well as to provide fun. *left*: English gymkhanas are fairly formal, as this neatly turned out competitor shows. *above*: In North America games can be strenuous – in the cow hide race, teams are pulled along on hides.

are bred for their quick reflexes and agility necessary in cattle and sheep herding, are actually ideal mounts for the gymkhana ring.

No matter how agile a horse is, training and obedience must be taught and practised beforehand. The animal should be taught to neck rein (move away from the pressure of the rein on the opposite side of the neck), stop instantly at the slightest touch, be ridden one-handed and go forward on command of the legs and seat (neither whips nor spurs are permitted under British rules). It must also be able to be relied upon to stand quite still when asked – no matter what the pressure of excitement.

Another important point for a good games horse or pony is that it be ready and willing to move away from its team-mates. Many is the time one sees competitors trying in vain to persuade their mounts to

Barrel racing in Canada; it is also a popular sport in the U.S. and Australia.

leave a line of other horses, even to get over the starting line. You can be sure such combinations are not destined for success!

Basic facilities necessary for training a gymkhana horse or pony are simple and within everyone's reach. All that is needed are some poles, old motor tyres, barrels or oil drums, buckets and perhaps some plastic cones of the type used by police and highway maintenance services. All will benefit from a good coat of paint so they can be easily seen by horse and rider and also accustom the horse to bright colours. Collect together a few such incidentals as sacks, stakes and flags and you can begin.

The schooling of the horse or pony is mostly commonsense and a case of practice makes perfect. Watch any gymkhana events at the local horse show or riding school and you will see that it is necessary for transitions into halt, walk, trot and canter to be fast and easy; bending and leading the pony should be practised; and riders should be able to open gates and move through obstacles with the minimum of fuss. A rider must learn to mount quickly (ideally to vault on) and to dismount, also at speed; to carry objects while in the saddle; to ride perfectly balanced without reins, stirrups or saddle, and to think clearly and calmly, and act accordingly. An excited, muddled rider makes for an excited, muddled pony.

Training and ability are as important for mounted games as they are for other equestrian sports. A rider does not enter for a show-jumping event if the horse does not like jumping, or for combined training if either he or his horse are not up to completing the required tests. So it is with mounted games. Events should be chosen in the light of such factors as whether the pony is better at racing in a straight line or at making rapid manoeuvres and turns – either way there is a wealth of choice.

As always when dealing with horses and ponies the preparation and training of anything new should not be hurried. Start slowly with strange exercises, perfecting the action at each pace before advancing to a faster gait. And *never* over-practise. A horse or pony will quickly become stale

and bored if it is asked to do the same movements time and again. It is always better to run through a game twice and finish on a happy note, than to try just once more and end up badly. Another important point is for the horse to be properly balanced at all times, always leading with the correct leg, otherwise time may be lost and even a fall incurred. Finally, learn to understand the pony, never ask too much and always reward it when it does well.

At most horse shows or gymkhanas, mounted games are staged in heats, the winner of each heat, or those placed first and second, competing in a final. As different countries favour a number of different games, rules tend to vary. Generally, however, riders will be eliminated if they:

(i) receive outside help from anyone other than stewards or horseholders
(ii) break a post or marker or knock it to the ground
(iii) fall off and not re-mount in the same place
(iv) fall off and lose the pony
(v) fail to dismount to pick up any dropped articles connected with the race
(vi) ride dangerously or interfere with any other competitors
(vii) do not cross the finishing line or pass the wrong side of a post or marker without correcting their mistake

It would be a mammoth and almost impossible task to give an account of all the mounted or gymkhana games on record, particularly as many have been altered or adapted to suit local conditions. However, it is worthwhile mentioning a few of the more popular or unusual races. In the Barrel Race, three barrels are set to form a triangular course which the competitors must complete at canter, doing a 360-degree turn at each barrel before crossing the finishing line. Each contestant rides separately and is timed – the fastest being the winner. This race is particularly popular in the United States and Australia where it is often included in rodeos. One of the most popular gymkhana events in Bri-

tain is the Bending Race. This is a race of between four and six contestants, each of whom must ride through a line of poles, bending between each, before returning along the same course. Musical chairs is a greatly-liked gymkhana game in the United States, in which riders go around the ring, then when the music stops, hasten to the nearest chair or bale of hay, dismount, and sit on it. There is always one less 'seat' than rider. The 'seatless' rider is eliminated after each round, until only one person – the winner – remains.

The Apple Ducking Race is always a favourite with spectators. Here, competitors race towards a bucket of water, in which an apple is floating. They have to dismount and pick the apple out of the water with their teeth, before remounting and racing back to the finishing line. In the Polo Race, the riders equipped with a polo stick and ball, race down to a post, hitting the ball as they go. Then they have to turn around the post and race back to the finish, still hitting the ball. The first ball over the finishing line heralds the winner.

Team races usually consist of the riders racing between given points, handing over a baton to the next team member as they arrive. An amusing variation is the Banana Relay Race, in which a banana is used instead of a baton. Speed is of the essence, but so is cautious handling, for the team is rated on time and the condition of the banana! If it breaks during the race the receiving rider has to dismount, retrieve all the pieces which he then has to pass on to the next person. At the end of the race, each broken section constitutes a two-second penalty, and each lost section a five-second penalty.

Finally, one of the most famous mounted games also happens to be an excellent introduction to hunting and in some island countries, such as Cyprus and Malta, is the only form of hunting practised. This is, of course, the mock hunt, the key to which lies in good planning beforehand and the atmosphere created by the 'hunt staff' on the day.

The principal players are the Fox, Huntsman and Field Master who beforehand survey the country over which they intend to hunt, plan the jumps, with a way round each obstacle so that no-one is over-faced, and decide on where the 'kill' is to be. The Fox lays the trail of wood shavings or sawdust which is hunted by the Hounds, Huntsman and Whippers-in who are followed by the field. Checks should last for up to ten minutes to give any stragglers time to join the rest of the field. At the end of the trail, the Fox is 'caught'.

Opposite A selection of events popular at gymkhanas held in the U.K. *top left*: The sack race requires an obedient pony which will readily follow its rider. *top right*: Apple bobbing or ducking is usually held at the end of the day, as the riders get very wet. *middle*: Musical poles, a variant of musical chairs. *bottom left*: Bending between poles is a good test of schooling. *bottom right*: Potato and spoon race – an understandable adaptation of the egg and spoon version.

Skill-at-Arms

BOTH animals and humans play in order to exercise mind and body in preparation for the other demands of life. For early man, the demands were mainly to hunt for food and to make war, and the mounted man had especial need to practise his skill. Sport was not only a necessity but recreation as well, albeit in preparation for wars in which unexpected situations often arose. Long use of specific exercises in one place resulted in boredom of horse and man, so that over the centuries a variety of contests were devised to provide excitement and maintain fitness and skill.

For the horseman, skill-at-arms required the training, and the co-operation of the horse so that he acted as one unit with his rider, man dominating mentally and dictating the strategies, but making use of the physically stronger partner, the horse, by using its exceptional memory. No man can obtain obedience from an animal far stronger than himself unless its training has been patient and kind, for cruel methods could backfire with disastrous results.

From earliest times mounted games of 'catch-as-catch can' were played. The Mongolian *baz-kiri*, for example, lasts for several hours, with horses and riders at full stretch as the riders try to wrest from each other, the carcase of a goat and carry it off to a 'goal'. It is often played over rough ground, where hardy and active ponies negotiate rocks, gullies, and brush.

A form of polo was played in the East from very early times and was adopted by Europe and later by America. The Tibetan name was *pulu*; the Persians called it *changar*, 'a mallet', and in the reign of King Chosroes II it was played by women. Nur-el-Din who fought the Crusaders, claimed it was more than a pastime. If men and horses were waiting in the prescience of the enemy, they must be ready at all times to take up arms. Horses hobbled in the lines would get fat and soft and not be nimble enough for close combat. Polo was even played by artificial light, and this and other ball games were excellent practice to keep horse and man fit and the horse handy and obedient. Modern polo is not played on horses required for war, but has long been a favourite game for cavalry officers, and thereafter for civilians. Polo-crosse is also popular and is a development of *tskhenburti*, a national game in the USSR.

The maidans and racecourses from Japan to Turkey were used for archery and javelin throwing from the saddle, and for team contests, when contestants were armed with wooden javelins. Teams took turns to ride between the opposing ranks who replied with a volley, and points were given. The individual winner was the one who scored most direct hits, but points were also awarded to those who caught or carried the greatest number. Other traditional games are *tchigan*, 'kiss the girl' and 'grab the hat' in the east; Ireland had its 'wild goose chase', forerunner of the steeplechase, although it is more of a mock hunt of one rider by others across open country and obstacles.

The most famous contests were the tournaments and jousts, popular in the days of chivalry. At first, riders engaged in

Mounted games Mongolian style, with a goat carcase as the objective for the horsemen in this game of *baz-kiri*.

The medieval tourney, where the knight and his mount showed their skill at jousting, was a relatively light-hearted preliminary to the rigours and possible disasters to be met on the battlefield.

wrestling, or tilting at the ring, (threading a ring suspended on a gallows through a lance at full gallop). The quintain was piercing or beheading an effigy at top speed. After this came duels with the lance, called *jeux de table ronde* or jousting, described as 'naked spectacles that banished the virgin and the matron', but later the lists or arenas, were decorated and 'crowned with the presence of chaste and high born beauty from whose hands the conqueror received the prize'. French chivalry decided that only the lance should be used, either blunted or with a crown of small points at the head.

Laws governing the tourney (medieval tournament) were codified by Geoffri de Preuilly at the end of the eleventh century, and the knights of England, Germany and France organized themselves into jousting associations. Only knights who could prove four ancestors of equestrian rank could be entered in the index and compete, although the sovereign could confer a right. Courts of marshals, heralds and arbitrators were in control. The lists were oval with raised seats for spectators and a barrier down the centre to prevent collision. Knights and their squires entered to a flourish of trumpets, the knight taking his place on the left of the barrier. The object was to unhorse his opponent, to what Shakespeare had called 'the grating shock of wrathful iron' as metal-encased horse and rider charged at 'full tilt'. The horse was hauled on to its haunches at the end of the charge by forceful use of a brutal bit.

Knights had to be hoisted into a saddle where they were wedged between high supports. Crown and Church both tried to suppress tourneys because of the loss of life. One strict rule was that no wound

Some mounted games, still known as skill-at-arms, were devised to improve the accuracy of the rider in battle: tilting at a small ring helped to perfect the aim and required considerable control.

must ever be given to the horse. Philip III held a great tournament to celebrate the knighting of his youngest brother Robert, who became so stifled by the heat, the weight of armour and clouds of dust, as well as heavy blows, that we are told 'he fell into idiocy for the rest of his life'. After Henry II was killed when a lance shivered on his cuirass, or breast plate, lifted his visor and pierced his eye, knights no longer fought in earnest as a show. There were combats with lance, sword, pistol, mace, dart, pike and battleaxe, so that spectators saw 'an exact picture of war' but no one was hurt. Each duke or prince who led a squadron of knights had to exhibit a device painted on a canvas curtain and 'an invention mobile' such as an allegorical chariot. Assailant and tenant broke three lances and performed with various different kinds of weapons.

Feats of horsemanship impressed rulers and their subjects, and those who performed them were the 'pop' heroes of our time. When Totola faced Western forces under Narses in 552 he gained time for reinforcements by casting his lance in the air, catching it with one hand and shifting it to the other and then throwing himself backwards and regaining his seat whilst at the same time riding his fiery steed in daring leaps and bounds.

The Emperor Basil started life as a slave boy whose equestrian circus tricks gained him recognition and then power. Equestrian acts in the circus, indeed may be part-entertainment and part-bravado, but they are never far from the superb horsemanship required to excel with arms. In the nineteenth century, Baucher trained his horses to perform in such a way that many European military leaders and

instructors studied his methods and became his pupils. Another such rider was James Fillis who became chief Instructor to the Imperial Cavalry School in Leningrad.

De Pluvinel, Riding Master to Louis XIII, devised mounted games to occupy and entertain the Court, and on one occasion the King won a prize of a gold watch. Competitions in which riders needed no armour and rode handy, light horses which the new Italian system (based on the School of Naples initiated by Grisone in the previous century) required were held at the Royal stables, and de Pluvinel said 'the

Officers of the Cadre Noir in full dress echoing the military origins of the school. The early European Schools were originally to provide training in mounted warfare.

favours of ladies have at all times done wonders for horsemen'.

From the tourney and these sports came the carousel which became very popular in seventeenth century Vienna. A ballet on horses was performed at the Imperial Palace in 1667, for the Hapsburg family who were all accomplished horsemen. When the great Spanish Riding School was completed its main purpose was to train riders, and the famous Lipizzaner horses for skill-at-arms and for war but many performances took place there such as quadrilles accompanied by an orchestra, and a 'kind of dance' performed by two parties of 12 accompanied by their pages. (These pages were permitted to be instructed in the School.)

There was also a contest for beheading the effigy of a Turk at full gallop, and others where a dummy was pierced with lance and sword. In the time of the Empress Marie Thérèse, a carousel was held in which ladies took part, dressed as legendary Amazons. One quadrille was on horseback and another in carriages. The Empress won a prize for skill with her lance, and pieces of jewellery were offered as prizes for skill with the sword and dagger. So famous were these competitions that a Sultan of Constantinople requested he should be allowed to see the performances.

The Riding Schools of Europe, which grew up around the royal courts from the Renaissance period onwards, were intended to provide training in the art of mounted warfare. The intricate movements of the horse, performed without any visible aids from its rider, were designed to perplex the enemy infantry, who by now were equipped with firearms. They also taught the rider to manoeuvre and turn his mount using only one hand and the pressure of his legs, so that he could use his weapons to the best advantage. The classical training pillars, the invention of de

ravines. For cavalry operating in the age of modern weapons, such skill and ability were a matter of life and death.

Other sports to exercise these skills were pig sticking (an extension of spearing lions and wild boar which called for courage as well as skill), hunting foxes, deer and hares and the paperchase. Horses did not always benefit as much as it was believed, particularly when they were in the hands of inexpert riders, but the competitive element in hot blood across country provided at least a civilian source of able men if needed.

Musical drives by artillery teams are reminders of ancient times when the chariot was the significant weapon of war. Chariot races were in fact often more dangerous than war itself and such contests at the early Olympiads were made deliberately more hazardous by the introduction of all sorts of distractions, designed to frighten the horses. All equestrian games and contests, however, were designed to keep skill and interest alive by competition, and also to demonstrate in public the might of mounted men.

One interesting test in mass defence, originating in Russia but sometimes included in Pony Club Games, is pushball, which entails two teams attempting to push a huge ball over their opponents' goal line. Combined weight is needed to push it, and an unbroken line of defence required to stop it once it starts to roll. Tetrathlon and Pentathlon contests, for children and for the services are other tests of the all-round competitor in use of arms, riding and swimming.

In Britain's Royal Tournament, held annually in London, the British cavalryman is put to severe test by a competition involving the use of sword, pistol and lance, over a course which has many sharp turns, he starts holding his sword at the slope, canters over a jump and immediately has to pierce a disc and then jump another fence. Increased momentum is needed to pierce the disc which is on a spring. He then swings to a line of targets, having left his sword in the disc, to test his marksmanship with a revolver. The first target is a balloon to the right of and above a fence; the next a block of wood on the ground, and the third a balloon on the left of a fence. Turning once more he seizes his lance, which has been placed in the ground point uppermost, and still at the gallop must take two rings suspended from a gallows, then lowering the lance to 'take' a tentpeg which has been driven into the ground leaving a few inches protruding. All three trophies have to be carried on the weapon to the finishing line. Points are given for performing all stages correctly and also for 'style'. The same tests of skill-at-arms are included in the training of mounted police.

Musical rides and drives call for supreme judgement and timing to avoid accident, and although the tank, armoured car and the aeroplane, as well as nuclear power, have made the horse redundant in warfare, the perpetuation of these military skills is still an incentive to good horsemanship.

Pluvinel, were used to teach the airs above the ground, as they still are today at the Spanish Riding School. These 'airs' were essential for cavalry leaders, and horses were trained to be completely obedient whether they were in a body or alone, within the manège or in the open.

The French Cavalry school, the famous Cadre Noir, transferred from Paris to the small town of Saumur, and employed N.C.O.s for the 'sauter' horses who were trained in the capriole, the levade and the courbette. As well as the art of classical dressage, the officers of the Cadre Noir also included cross-country work and jumping in their curriculum. The Spanish Riding School alone preserved classical riding exclusively, and a tablet there had an inscription ending 'for the instruction and training of young noblemen and their horses for school riding and combat'. Both schools allowed spectators at various times, and to watch morning exercise when the Archdukes were riding was a favourite pastime. The Hour of the Cavaliers, from noon to 3 p.m., was a time when any rider could use the school.

As land became enclosed, it became necessary for horses to jump. The Duke of Newcastle (1592–1676), described as 'the best riding master and the worst cavalry leader of the entire seventeenth century', insisted that horses must perform both in the manège and in the open. As a result, one of his pupils, Prince Rupert – the dashing, but somewhat inept commander of the Royalist cavalry in the Civil War – once escaped his pursuers by putting his horse at a hedge and clearing it so that his enemies could not follow.

The Tilting Yard had allowed the knights of a former age to test their horses

Tent pegging, or the use of the lance at speed, is still practised by both military and police riders in Britain. It figures in a three-part competition, involving the use of pistol, sword and lance, in which points are given for the skill with which they are used.

and their skill, and to appreciate obedient and supple horses. In actual battle, if neither side had won, more charges were made until the horses tired. At that point broken spears were thrown away and those still left fought with hacking swords and maces. Such warfare demanded a horse accustomed to trumpets and shouts; one which would stand when held by the squire, and even if demented with pain from arrows, might be restrained from creating havoc. The new warfare with firearms required the manoeuvrable, supple, lighter horse capable of speed, and therefore unhampered by the weight of heavy armour.

New demands were made by obstacles and roads, so, in the nineteenth and early twentieth centuries, the Military Versatility Test was devised from which came the Event. The dressage phase had 36 movements in nine sections, entry into the arena being at a 'gallop' (in fact probably a canter). The second day consisted of five sections ridden without pause; comprising 22 km (13 miles) of roads and tracks, 8 km (5 miles) cross-country over 35 obstacles, and 2 km (1 mile) on the flat. Those who survived – usually about half who had begun – competed in a show-jumping event on the third day. Cross-country fences included jumping into girth-deep water with a muddy bottom, streams and ditches at the bottom of banks on steep slopes, and fences set on either side of

Western Sports

The event that to most people is synonymous with Western sports is that of the rodeo. The roots of rodeo lie in the work and leisure activities of nineteenth-century cowboys in the American West. In the decades preceding the Civil War of 1860–65, great numbers of Americans went to the south-western region of the United States to work on ranches. Later, such postwar industrialization as railroading, opened lands west of the Mississippi River and huge ranches were carved out from Texas to Montana.

Ranch life was demanding and hard. Herds of cattle had to be brought each spring from winter pastures, so that calves could be branded, and altered into steers. Then the herd had to be tended until the autumn trail drives to the railroad depots. Each cowboy required a string of horses for this work, and no one could afford the time for the niceties and refinements of training. Green horses would be roped, saddles thrown on their backs, cowboys would climb aboard, and the education process went on until the animals – or the riders' bones – were broken.

One of the few respites from this existence came at the end of annual trail drives, when everybody got together in the saloons and gambling halls. Conversations soon turned to prowess with lariat or horse, and proof of alleged expertise would soon be demanded. The town's main street or stockyard became the scene of these impromptu riding and roping contests, with part or all of the year's wages bet on the outcome. Competitions of this sort quickly caught on. Called a 'rodeo' (from the Spanish word for 'round-up'), a more formal event was staged in Wyoming and another in Kansas during the 1870s. In 1883 the town of Pecos in Texas offered prize money for a steer-roping contest, and five years later, when a Denver, Colorado rodeo charged admission to spectators, rodeoing became a fully fledged business.

Two of the five 'classic' or standard events staged at rodeos today have their origins in actual ranch work. Calf-roping is one, and it demands dexterity with a lasso as well as a well-trained horse. The idea is to rope, then tie a calf, as if to prepare it for branding. A calf is given several seconds' head start down the arena, before horse and rider gallop in headlong pursuit. Then the cowboy tosses his lasso over the animal's head, and almost in one motion, he secures the other end of the rope around

Calf roping in Western rodeos is a basic test of a cowboy's skill.

his saddle horn, throws himself from the saddle and runs towards the calf. The horse has been trained to step back to keep the rope taut. The calf is thus restrained, and becomes fair game for the approaching cowboy, who flips it onto its side and ties three of its four legs together with a short length of rope (called a piggin' string) which he has been holding in his teeth. Time is the deciding factor, although a cowboy will be automatically disqualified from the competition if the calf slips out of the tie within five seconds.

The other event is saddle bronc riding which evokes memories of the method used by cowboys to 'break' their mounts for riding. The saddle in this instance is a modified stock saddle, smaller and without a horn, while the rein is merely a rope attached to the horse's halter. A bucking strap is tightened around the animal's flank to encourage its action. Horses and the order of going are selected by lottery. Before the ride begins, the cowboy lowers himself into the starting chute and onto the back of the horse he has drawn. When he has securely wrapped the rope around one hand, he signals for the gate to be opened, at which point the horse bucks wildly out into the ring. The rider is required to place his spurs on the horse's shoulders at the start and to use them on the first jump out of the chute. The actual ride, which must last ten seconds, calls for extraordinary balance and timing to achieve maximum scores.

Scoring for bronc riding follows a recognized procedure. Two judges each award from zero to 25 points for the rider's performance and the same range of points for the horse's, which explains the reason why cowboys hope to draw difficult mounts. The aggregate is the rider's score for that round. Disqualification results from a rider changing hands on the rein, touching the horse with his free hand, or being thrown before the ten-second buzzer sounds.

The three remaining 'classic' events that form part of every rodeo arose out of Westerners' bragging, along such lines as 'I'm so tough I can ride a bronc bareback, stay aboard a brahma bull, or wrestle a steer to

All the various aspects of rodeos stem from the days of the ranch cowboy, though the events now have an importance of their own. Even today, cattle have to be herded over enormous acreages, and horses must still be broken in from the wild state to become useful, willing partners. The events in rodeos are all based, though some loosely, on work traditionally done on cattle ranches in North America or Australia. *above left*: Bronc riding imitates the difficulties of breaking in wild horses and shows the cowboy's skill on an unbroken horse. *above*: Using only one hand, the intrepid cowboy attempts to cling on while an angry bull twists and turns in his efforts to be rid of his rider – this is one of the classic rodeo events. *below*: The end of the ride for a bronc buster as he hits the dust of the arena. *opposite top*: Calf roping is an important feature of work on the range. *below left*: In this contest the rider has to throw the steer to the ground by the tail before reaching a specified part of the arena. *below right*: The Toronto Winter Fair combines pageantry with traditional cowboy sports and a display by the famous Canadian Mounties.

the ground'. Naturally enough, from this, sprang the contests of bareback bronc riding, bull riding, and steer wrestling, which is also known as bull-dogging.

Although bareback bronc riding certainly requires brute strength, the rider can use only one hand to hold the grip, which is attached to a strap around the horse's girth. Rules and scoring are similar to saddle bronc competition, except that eight, not ten, seconds is the time limit. Bull riding is particularly perilous, since a bull will chase and gore an unseated cowboy. Riders are permitted to use both hands on

the girth grip, and again they must try to last until the eight-second buzzer sounds. Steer wrestling or bull-dogging, begins when a steer is released from a pen and made to run the length of the arena. The cowboy gallops after it, with another rider (called a hazer) racing on the other side to keep the animal running straight. When the cowboy draws level with the steer's head, he flings himself from the saddle, and grabs the animal's horns as he plants his boots in the dirt to get a firm grip. His arms tightly wrapped in a deadlock on the animal, the cowboy then wrestles the steer

onto its side. The deciding factor in this event is time.

Barrel racing is an event for cowgirls. Three large oil drums are placed to form a triangular course, around which horse and rider gallop in a cloverleaf pattern. The fastest time of all contestants wins.

Larger rodeos feature other events, beside the five standard ones. One popular competition is for cutting horses, trained to separate a calf or steer from a herd, then to interpose itself to prevent the animal from returning to the group. Another is team roping which involves two cowboys.

One of them lassoes a calf around the head while his partner ropes the animal's hind legs. Colourful and wild affairs are the chuck wagon races, which are reminiscent of something out of *Ben Hur*. Teams of four or six horses pull Connestoga wagons around a track at a madcap speed.

A rodeo is also a great display of pageantry, from the opening grand entry of all participants to the crowning of a rodeo queen and her court of attendants. Exhibitions put on for general amusement and as part of the day's proceedings may include trick riding, fancy roping, or a musical

ride. One group of rodeo employees whose function may appear to be primarily entertainment, although they actually fulfil a vital purpose, are the clowns. They divert the bulls and wild broncs from fallen riders. More than a few cowboys owe their lives to the quick reflexes and courage of rodeo clowns. Equally essential to the contestants, are the mounted pick-up men, who help bronc and bull riders dismount at the conclusion of their rounds.

Dedication, as well as ability, is a prerequisite for professional rodeo cowboys. The 'suicide circuit', as the tour is wryly known, goes on all year and involves travelling around very great distances. Unlike most other athletes, rodeo riders pay their own way throughout, and that includes entry fees, room and board, and stabling fees for their horses. As may be imagined, injuries are commonplace, yet still everyone will strive for the 'pot of gold' at the end of this rainbow. It contains prize money, which will help realize a profit for the season, but more important it means the gain of the title of All-Around Champion. Based on the amount of prize money won over the year, the Championship also opens the door to additional income from sponsoring clothing manufacturers, free beer, and other products which are somehow equestrian-related. Among the best known All-Around Champions are Casey Tibbs, Jim Shoulders, and Larry Mahan. In 1974, Tom Ferguson set the all-time money mark of $120,000. A year later he tied with Leo Camarillo for the title, each having won exactly $90,240.

There are more than 1,000 rodeos held annually in the United States and Canada. The 'big leagues' include the Cheyenne Frontier Days in Wyoming, Pendleton Round Up in Oregon, Denver Stock Show in Colorado, and the Oklahoma City All-American Finals. Small cities and towns have their own fixtures, many of which are sponsored by civic or charitable organizations. On a younger, but certainly not small, scale, university and high school

A rodeo queen on parade, dressed in traditional Indian costume.

students throughout the West, engage in the sport as part of intercollegiate, varsity, and club atheltics.

Less dangerous and perhaps spectacular than rodeos, but equally as enjoyable in their way are the four sections of Western-style riding found at horse shows around the United States. These four sections comprise stock seat equitation classes, stock horse classes, trail horse classes and pleasure horse classes. Riders wear the traditional and colourful gear of broad-brimmed hats, high-heeled boots, and chaps or Western pants. In some instances, a rain slicker is worn or secured to the saddle. Horses are shown in stock saddles and bridles, with curb bits and split reins. The technique of Western riding requires that riders hold the reins in only one hand, and sit with their legs hanging straight and slightly forward to the stirrups. They must not post to the jog trot.

Contestants in stock seat equitation classes are judged on their riding skills, although the performance of their horses contributes immeasurably to the final scores. Riders and their mounts are asked to walk, jog, and lope (the Western term for canter) in both directions, and the horses should be in perfect balance at all times, working off their haunches. Some classes involve a variety of tests, such as figures-of-eight at the jog and/or lope, riding without stirrups, flying changes of lead at the lope, 360° turns, and the impressive sliding stops.

The stock horse section demonstrates the kind of qualities and techniques

needed for ranch work. Each entry goes through the Western equivalent of a dressage test, which comprises figures-of-eight at the jog and lope, turns on the forehand and haunches, and halts. Particular qualities of stock horses are good manners, handiness, response to light rein contact, and the ability to work at reasonable speed whilst remaining completely under the rider's control. Hesitations, anticipations, and disobediences are deemed faults.

Trail horses are asked to negotiate obstacles which might be found on a cross-country ride. A course set up around the arena would probably include a gate (which has to be opened, passed through, and then closed), logs, a ditch, a bridge, an expanse of water (simulating a stream to be forded), and bales of straw through which the horse is made to back. Performance and manners are the criteria for judging.

Pleasure horse classes place great emphasis on suitability and manners to be a good Western hack. Horses are shown at the walk, jog, and lope on a reasonably loose rein. In some classes, conformation, as well as equipment may be taken into account.

In addition, certain breeds, such as Appaloosas, Arabians, Morgans, Palominos, Pintos, and Quarter Horses, are eligible to be shown in Western sections of their divisions.

Dude ranching or pack tripping has long been an integral part of Western riding. However, as it really comprises more of a vacational activity than a sport, it is included in 'Holidays with Horses'.

Australian Riding

Horses have made an enormous contribution to life in Australia. With unflagging energy and unfailing loyalty, they helped map out the vast areas of arid deserts, grassy plains and rugged mountains, and could well be described as pioneers in their own right. Although not indigenous to the country they settled happily and remain today in universal high esteem.

Governor Phillip brought the first horses to Australia in 1788 when he arrived with the First Fleet. Landing at the Cape of Good Hope to take on supplies, he took aboard a stallion, three mares and two yearling fillies. Unfortunately, on landing, all but the stallion and one mare escaped the lax eye of their convict groom, and fled into the bushland. More horses were imported over the next ten years from the same source, along with some English Thoroughbreds and Arabs from India and Persia, and although these first imports were not first class breeding stock, they progressively improved with each successive generation.

By 1798, there were 117 horses in the new colony, 73 of them mares. The first serious step to improve the stock came with the importation of the English bred horse Rockingham. By the early 1820s there were 5,000 horses, although Rockingham cannot be credited with siring all of them! During the 1899–1902 Boer War, 16,375 horses were gathered from all over Australia to mount the regiments.

It was from the mixed breeding lines of the early imports, that the famous Australian Waler was founded. Standing between 15 and 16 h.h. he was of 'dense bone' and capable of carrying up to 108 kg (17 stone) all day. The Waler proved himself to be a courageous mount and is on record as having out-lasted and out-paced the camel in the desert campaigns.

During the First World War, Australian horses, by now famous for their courage and stamina, were exported to India and Europe. In fact, more than 121,324 went to war. But the end of the war and the decline of the cavalry saw the end of the Waler. Now he is virtually extinct and no longer recorded in the stud books. If the early explorers were grateful for this toughly bred colonial horse, which proved himself indispensable to them, the fact is not recorded.

Robert O'Hara Burke, travelled across the continent and half way back again on his horse Billy before starvation made him shoot it. The diaries record that the; 'flesh was healthy and tender, without a trace of fat'. It seems the meat from his old friend did not stick in Burke's throat as one might have imagined.

As the colony became more settled and mail and coach routes were established, the bandit or bushranger made his appearance. Often excellent horsemen from Ireland, these escaped convicts or 'easy-living men' were fearless riders. The price on their heads made them particular about their mounts and they stole only the best – well-blooded horses in fact, which continue to prove their worth today as stockhorses.

In a country with an ever-expanding beef and wool industry, horses play a major part. Motor bikes, trucks, even light aircraft and hovercraft have failed to prove as efficient in the management of stock. Now larger properties carry several hundred head of horses which are bred (usually from the property's Thoroughbred stallion), born, work and die on the same station. They run often virtually wild in large paddocks, so that the overseas visitor travelling in the outback, may, on seeing a large mob, assume they are 'brumbies' or wild, unowned horses. This is seldom the case and closer inspection would show the property's brand mark.

The wild brumbies are still to be found in the desert or mountain areas, however, especially in the Northern Territory. Graziers resent sharing their grasslands, so wild horses in the Territory are classified as vermin and shot, or fenced off from water, so they perish. The same fate awaits the wild donkeys who roam the grassy plains in mobs of a hundred or so,

Australian stockmen at work rounding up cattle on one of the vast ranches in the Australian outback. The horse is still an essential part of the everyday life of Australian farms and is renowned for its stamina.

although the popularity of this little animal has reached the city and many are finding good homes or being used as foundation stock by newly formed donkey studs.

Years ago professional horsebreakers travelled from station to station breaking in mobs of horses, at the rate of dozens a day. Today the property's animals are broken by the stockmen as part of the station routine. The horses are mustered and brought to the station's yards, from where mares with foals at foot are returned to the paddocks, yearlings are branded and also returned, while those required for breaking are retained. Today most stockmen use the 'Jeffery' method of breaking which relies on gaining the horse's confidence and in nearly all cases this method succeeds. The horse is driven by himself into a small yard and caught with a loop of rope or greenhide carried on the end of a long pole. Once secured around the neck, he is gently encouraged to move closer to the breaker. Then he is tied up, handled, and the bridle and saddle put on him. This part of his breaking usually takes about three hours, after which he is turned loose in the yard to get the 'feel' of the saddle. Caught again he will be mounted. Some are led around the yards from a reliable breaking horse; others are required to walk around with the rider neck-reining them as they approach the corners of the yard. They are then taken to a larger yard and walked around that for sometime longer. The whole operation clearly requires a good deal of patience.

The stock saddle has a high pommel and knee pads and is fastened by canvas girths that are laced to rings or buckled in the conventional manner. The stockman rides in a loose, completely 'fluid' manner. His hands are featherlight on the long reins, his legs hang almost straight and slightly forward in long stirrups.

After a period of work – maybe many months – the horses are turned out, or 'spelled' and a new lot brought in for work.

In every mob of horses there is nearly always the 'rogue' that doesn't take kindly to working with or for man. He is the sort that will buck with real determination until the day he dies. These were the 'unrideables' that were talked about round bush fires in drovers' camps years ago, and men who had succeeded in riding them became legends, held in high esteem. The challenge to prove themselves as horsemen was great among the drovers and bets were wagered as to whether, and for how long, a man could ride a particular outlaw horse. This was the early beginning of rodeos – a real Australian sporting event that carries big prizes and attracts the toughest riders in the country. The sport is now organized and controlled by the Australian Rough Riders Association.

Saddle bronco riding is one of the foundation events of the sport, and one that requires skill, balance, timing and experience. As in the similar event in American rodeos the contestant literally climbs aboard the horse which is confined between high wooden rails with a gate at either end. As the horse bucks and plunges in this 'chute', mounting can be a hazard in itself! Once mounted, the rider takes the rope of the headcollar in one hand and positions his legs forward onto the horse's shoulder points. The gate is opened and he leaves the chutes for his ten-second ride, throughout which he must leave one hand free of all equipment, the horse and his own body. Staying on is not the only judging criteria though. Two judges, one either side, note how well he rides the bucks, how wide the sweep of his spurs and with what style the horse bucks.

The standard saddle for these events has two girths, one positioned further back than usual to prevent it being bucked over the horse's head. A headcollar with a rope from the central dee is the only means the rider has to guide his mount – if indeed there is any guiding to be done!

Bareback riding is another crowd pleaser at rodeos. In this instance the horse is unhaltered and wears only a surcingle to which is attached a leather loop for the rider to hold. Again it is a one-handed ride, lasting this time for eight seconds and judged on the competitor's style and the horse's ability to shift him.

Another event which has been handed down from the everyday work of the stockman is calf roping and here, a clever fast horse that can anticipate his rider's needs is invaluable. A rope is attached to the saddle horn and on a given signal the rider sets out after a calf which is released from the chutes. He ropes the calf around its neck, and exactly at the moment the rope touches the beast's neck, the horse skids to a halt on its haunches, thus pulling the rope taut. The competitor ties the calf's legs as quickly as possible and remounts. The fastest time wins.

Perfectly trained horses are used for steer wrestling too. A steer is let loose from the chutes and the rider gallops alongside it waiting for an opportune moment to leap from his horse and grab it by the horns, unbalance it and bring it to the ground. The whole process usually only takes between 2½–11 seconds, and is ridden at a speed of 50–65 km (30–40 mph).

The horses used for rodeo work are sometimes supplied by local farmers who have unrideable stock, or they may be the property of one person who travels the rodeo circuit with them. The horses that appear regularly have quite a reputation and are often promoted as 'killers'. Animal protection societies have for some years been trying to have all rodeos stopped on the grounds of cruelty to horses and cattle, but such is their popularity, that all attempts have so far been unsuccessful.

No such move has been made against camp-drafting events which are often staged at rodeos, major shows and as competitive attractions in their own right. This stockman's sport carries high prizes and has led to some specialized breeding of horses. Good drafting horses seldom change hands for under four figures. The ideal horse stands about 15 h.h. (any larger and they find it difficult to execute the acute turns necessary) and is up to carrying a fairly large man while pushing a beast around at the same time. He has to be fast, and for this reason many good drafters have Thoroughbred blood in them, although recent years have seen Quarter Horse lines introduced with success. Camp-drafting takes place in natural bush surroundings, and the rider selects a beast from the mob or camp, and drives it to another spot known as the yards. In competition camp-drafting, a course is marked out by pegs or oil drums, and the number of cattle in the herd kept small. The fewer false moves made along the route, the faster the course is completed, and the higher the score. A good horse never takes his eye off the chosen beast and any guiding becomes unnecessary. He will lean into the beast with his shoulder at the most frightening angles to prevent it from turning. Executed at great speeds, camp-drafting is a thrilling spectator sport.

Camp-drafting is not restricted only to adults. Pony Club members learn the rudiments during novelty races staged at their rallies through such competitions as bending in and out of oil drums at a gallop. Of course some country members get first hand experience at their home farms, but the Pony Club in Australia has given all young riders an opportunity to learn this and other techniques.

In the past horsemanship skills were handed down from one generation to the next. For country children there were always ponies to ride and adults to learn from, but new generations growing up in the cities and suburbs had parents, who themselves had no knowledge of horses. To them the Pony Club has been a boon, and the interest it has fostered is evident at the surburban rallies where sometimes more than 200 children attend. Formed in the 1950s, the Pony Club in Australia follows the same instructional lines as its parent body in England. Regular working rallies make up a major part of the meetings which are staged at local show grounds, race courses or individual's properties. All branches – from the tiny country branch with a membership of maybe 50 to the larger inner-suburban ones – hold courses.

Camps are run during the holidays and the climate and open spaces make Australian children luckier than many others. Informal barbecue meals under the shade of gum trees and sing-songs or horsey quizzes and competitions around the camp fire at night add to the fun.

Each State runs its own affairs, but is governed by the Australian Pony Club Council. Inter-State competitions are stages of the biggest event in the annual calendar – the Pony Club Championships.

In recent years the Inter-Pacific Exchange Scheme has been in operation. Every two years, members visit a 'host' country and, as guests are supplied with mounts and equipment, and taken on various tours. Countries participating in the

Left Highly trained horses are essential for successful steer wrestling, as the horse must gallop alongside the steer until the rider chooses his moment to leap, grabbing the steer by the horns in his attempt to bring it to the ground.

Below The Grand Parade at the Sydney Royal Easter Show marks the beginning of the Australian show season.

Bottom right The indomitable Australian Three-Day Event rider, Bill Roycroft, who competed in the Montreal Olympics at the age of 61 and helped to win the team bronze medal. He was also a member of the team at Rome in 1960, when they won the gold.

Exchange Scheme are America, Canada, New Zealand and Australia. It has been said that, per capita, Australia has the most enthusiastic members in the world and the interest and enthusiasm is certainly very evident at horse shows held around the country.

Every town, however small, holds an annual show and some of the larger town-

mounted police branches are great crowd pleasers. The jumping events are keenly contested for it is from the 'Royals' that future Olympic riders will be picked. At Sydney's Royal Easter show, a regular Three-Day Event is staged, which is closely watched by the Olympic selectors. The hack, hunter and other ridden classes attract so many entries that judges never ride – it would take too long. The breed classes with the heavy horse breeds, Arabs, British native breeds, palominos, harness and Australian ponies take hours to judge and the number of entries goes up every year.

Most States hold their Royal Show in such high regard that a public holiday is declared during its running, to give workers and school children a chance to attend. It is interesting to note, that unlike many Australian public holidays, show day is actually spent at the show, instead of on the beach, or at home. It demonstrates how interested city dwellers are in all things from and of the country.

For those competitors following the circuit of shows, Easter and the Sydney Royal marks the beginning of the season. The Brisbane (Queensland) Exhibition follows in August with Melbourne, Adelaide and Perth in September and Tasmania in October. The enormous distances between each State capitol make showing an expensive hobby, but, the prestige attached to winning a Royal championship makes many competitors travel the circuit. Obviously a hack that has won five or six State championships in one season is a very valuable animal.

One of the highest awards in the Australian showring, and one contested by riders from all States, is the Garryowen event staged at the Melbourne show. This riding event is for lady riders over 18 years of age and the winner receives the Perpetual Garryowen Trophy. The cup was named after a top hack who died in a fire more than 38 years ago. The horse's mistress, Violet Murrell died too, trying to save him from the flames. The winner of the event also receives a sash (sashes are used instead of rosettes in Australia) with a portrait of Mrs. Murrell on a brooch.

Nine Olympic Games passed before Australia competed with an equestrian team. In 1956 when the Games were held in Melbourne, they felt morally obliged to enter, even though the equestrian events were in Stockholm. Their first three-day event team consisted of Ern Barker, Bert Jacobs, John Winchester, Brian Crago and Wyatt Thomson and they finished a very creditable fourth. The Stockholm adventure fired the Australian's enthusiasm and thenceforth, three-day events became regular events in the country. In Rome, four years later, the team really triumphed, with Bill Roycroft making his heroic effort in the final phase and jumping a clear round even though he had a broken collar bone. As well as winning the team gold, Laurie Morgan won the individual gold. Australia was well and truly on the equestrian map. The 1964 Tokyo games saw Australia's first show jumping team and Bill Roycroft's son Barry was included, while 'Dad' was once again in the three day event team.

ships may stage more than one. Novelty races, jumping and riding events and displays by the local branch of the Pony Club are usually featured at these 'family affairs', but it is at each State's Royal Show that the country really comes to the city.

Amid an atmosphere, bustling with fair-ground sideshows and stalls, country life is well exhibited. The latest in agricultural equipment is on view; sheep shearing competitions, butter making demonstrations and wood chopping races are held; while cattle, sheep, poultry, pigs, caged birds, cats, dogs, goats and even fashions are judged, sold, viewed and (in the case of butter) tasted, during the show. Grand parades of the winning animals are held each day.

Horses remain one of the favourite exhibits amongst all the competition. The permanent stables are crowded with admirers and the evening jumping competitions, or displays of tent pegging by the

Mexico saw another Roycroft enter the ranks of Olympic horsemen, when Wayne joined the team. Clarke was to follow years later, and all the time Bill rode for his country.

The performances by the Australians, and in particular the veteran Roycroft, demonstrate the great talent of Australian riders and the ability of their horses. In the cross-country phase, both are in their element and recent years has seen much improvement in the dressage which is now an integral part of all major shows. It has developed quickly from beginners' classes to Prix St George standards.

If it was Bill Roycroft who put Australia on the international eventing map, that big red galloper, Phar Lap can claim the country's racing fame. Although he has been dead for more than 40 years, the nation remembers him with great affection, heightened maybe, by his mysterious death in the United States in 1932. Phar Lap died after a racing career of only three years in which he amassed more stake money than any other Australian horse before him, winning 37 times from 51 starts. Such was the affection of his fans

that his body was flown back to Australia, dissected and divided. His heart is now in the capital, Canberra, his skin in Melbourne and his skeleton in New Zealand – the country where he was bred.

The first race to be run in Australia was in 1810 at Sydney and the sport soon proved popular. The first Melbourne Cup – probably Australia's most famous race – was staged at Flemington, near Melbourne in 1861. It was won by Archer, a big horse who galloped along with his tongue lolling out, his long stride earning him the nick-

Australians in sport. *top left*: Kevin Bacon, a member of the Australian show jumping team in action at the Montreal Olympics. *top right*: Polocrosse is a uniquely Australian sport which has developed since the introduction of real polo. *below left*: A panoramic view of Melbourne's famous Flemington Racecourse, showing the Lawns and the various tracks. In Australia many races are held over dirt tracks rather than turf. *inset*: One of the renowned two-time winners of the Melbourne Cup, Rain Lover. *below right*: Another horse which has won the Melbourne Cup twice, the formidable Think Big.

name, the Bull. He won it the following year too, a record only repeated twice (at the time of going to print) – by Rain Lover in 1968/9, and Think Big in 1974/5. Thousands of eager racing enthusiasts, from all parts of the country, flock to Flemington each year for this popular race which is traditionally held on the first Tuesday in November.

However, such is the nation's interest in the sport of racing, that even the small bush track (which also serves as an airstrip) can attract a mighty crowd. Many false starts may be made and the horses lost from view in the dust, but the enjoyment amongst the heat and the flies is as real as the pleasure for those on the well kept lawns of Randwick racecourse in Sydney or that in Flemington.

A few years after the introduction of racing, fox hunting took on a popularity. Englishmen, bored with chasing kangaroo and dingo, imported a few foxes to brighten up their sport. In Tasmania natural, indigenous, quarry is still hunted, although the hunts do not last long. The largest hunting fraternity now is in Adelaide, South Australia, which has 11 Hunt Clubs. The Adelaide Hunt Club Cup is run in July each year for $1,700, the highest stake in the country for a Hunt Cup.

The oldest hunt in Australia, The Melbourne Hunt Club, meets on Saturdays and only hunts the fox. It gathers a relatively small field, usually of about 60. The season is from May to September, and during these months, the aim is to kill the fox, for from those few early imports, the bushy-tailed predator has multiplied. Hare and fox are hunted by another old established club while some use a drag, in which case hunts usually last no more than three to four hours, and are over strategically placed jumps. As in Great Britain, there are a few demonstrations every year to have foxhunting banned.

The introduction of polo came not long after racing and hunting, but it was since the end of the First World War that the game really went ahead. In 1925 the Australasian Gold Cup was introduced and was competed for between the different Australian States and New Zealand. Because station-bred ponies are readily adapted to polo, the game is much played in the country areas and Queensland has produced a number of top class players. All matches are well attended by spectators during the season. Polo crosse is also popular and is played by Pony Club and Riding Club members.

Australia's links with the horse are as strong today as they were at the birth of the nation and there exists a deep love and respect for the animal. Office workers on their way to work will stop and pat the police horse on point duty; the gambler will talk affectionately of 'his horse', even though he might lose; and school children are still held spellbound by the skill and daring of 'Clancy' and the 'Man From Snowy River', who chased the 'colt from old Regret'. To Australians, the horse is part of their heritage.

The Show Ring

SHOWING one animal against others of the same species and breed started some 200 years ago. It sprang from the natural desire of breeders of horses to prove to others, that they had used their skill and knowledge to produce an animal that was bigger, better made for the job in life to which it was to be put, and possessed of more strength, stamina, workmanlike qualities and classical conformation than those produced by other breeders. Its movement, quality, symmetrical proportions and general beauty of outline were, and still are, the yardsticks by which it was assessed.

In addition, by producing their products in the show ring, to win over those of their fellow-breeders when judged by experts, they were able to command the top market price for their young stock. Alternatively other breeders would be attracted to send mares to their stallions. Shows have always been convivial meeting places for those of similar interests and enthusiasms, bound together – albeit in friendly rivalry – by the same concern for good husbandry and the improvement of the breed towards the ideal: the perfect horse. Although this individual has probably yet to be foaled, just as the perfect human being has yet to be born, there is endless fascination in pursuing a quest to achieve it.

Probably the purest form of showing is that of showing the young horse in-hand. Showmanship, which is a considerable art must always play its part in showing an animal to its best advantage, and a real artist is able to disguise failings of movement, or even lameness, by the way he leads a horse, or runs him out in hand. There are tricks in every trade, and they comprise every professional showman's stock-in-trade, but there is less opportunity for artifice in the classes in which the exhibits are led in-hand than in those where they are ridden. Then an exaggerated throwing of the toe in the trot, or a flashy display at the gallop, can be used to disguise, or to divert the attention from, such failings as faulty action or some other shortcoming.

The aim of the showman is to produce a horse that will 'fill the eye', as the saying goes, and no horse wins many championships without the ultimate blessing of a hard-to-define quality known as *presence*. This is the quality which bestows upon its fortunate possessor the ability to command the attention of whoever beholds it – a quality which not only says, but demands: "Look at me – I'm the greatest!" A horse may be better made and a better mover than others, but if he lacks presence he will get no further in the world than the man who is denied the benefit of self-confidence.

The hunter classes are the most important of all the classes in the show ring, for they set the standard of the best sort of horse to breed and therefore wield a wide influence upon breeders and buyers alike. The youngstock classes, for brood mares and for foals, yearlings, two-year-olds and three-year-olds are largely patronized by people who breed horses for a hobby, or by farmers who breed them as a lucrative sideline, to their serious farm work. The ridden classes, on the other hand, although they too contain many people who show horses for the sheer fun of it, are also the happy hunting ground for the professional showmen who produce horses for other people – and in so doing, ensure that the standards of training, riding, production and presentation are maintained at a consistently high level.

The basic procedure for the led hunter classes never varies. The youngsters are led into the ring, circle around the judge at a walk (occasionally at a trot for a short spell, a valuable innovation borrowed from the Welsh pony classes – movement from the side being just as important as movement from the back or the front) until they are called in by the judge or his steward to stand in a straight line, in preliminary order of merit. The judge then walks down the line scrutinizing each animal, before pulling each out in turn to inspect it again as its leader 'stands it up' (i.e., makes it stand four-square). Then the judge sees it run out in hand; 'Walk away, and trot back' is the usual request, but if he is dubious about some small point – *does* it swing a leg, or throw a foot? – he will ask it to go again to confirm or allay his earlier suspicions.

In the last analysis, he has the line of horses circle around him once more before calling in his winner and then the lower-placed horses. In almost every class, he will only have succeeded in pleasing one person, although there can ever only be one winner! Those less fortunate will tell themselves and certain selected friends that the judge is a fool; tell themselves and one or two others, in strictest confidence, that the judge is a knave; or tell themselves that this is only one man's opinion, and there is always another day. A fourth category of exhibitor goes and attacks the judge, but this person is very rare, and indeed gets increasingly more rare as he has his entries refused by other shows for his reputation will quickly get around. There is an old and true show-ring saying, to the effect that: 'If you can't take defeat, don't show'.

The ridden hunter class may have either one or two judges, who are called upon in England and Ireland (though not in the United States or Canada) to ride the horses. This they do having seen them walk, trot, canter and gallop round the ring, whereupon the same system of calling the horses into a line prevails.

If there are two judges they then start riding, very often, from opposite ends; if there is only one he starts at the top and works his way down. It is desirable for every horse to be ridden, even if those at the bottom of the line stand no chance whatsoever of being placed. After all, the exhibitors have all paid the same entry fee,

Two aspects of the show ring: showing in-hand and the ridden pony. Pony stallions at the Ascot stallion show, where they are judged on their suitability for breeding good native ponies and children's riding ponies. *inset*: Showing can begin at a very early age, especially in leading rein classes where the pony is judged on its suitability for a child.

most have gone to the same trouble and expense to produce their horses and bring them to the show, and it is discouraging, to say the least, to be dismissed with a curt nod. Even if time does not permit the judges to ride every horse, (and judges are all too often not given sufficient time to do their job, being constantly hurried along by a steward who is himself being chivvied from higher up, very often because of the demands of the television people, impatient for the show-jumping to begin on time!) the better judges are punctilious about having a final look and a cheery word with the poor man or woman who is unfortunate to stand at the very end of the line. A pat of the horse's neck, and an admiring: 'I bet he's a super hunter!' goes a very long way towards mollifying an exhibitor who is about to be sent out of the ring with 'the rubbish'.

The bigger shows will put on classes not only for the conventional three weight divisions – lightweight, middleweight and heavyweight – but also for four-year-olds, novices, small hunters, and ladies' hunters to be ridden side-saddle (and judged, of course, by a lady judge who is proficient in the art of riding side-saddle). Lady judges are among the most long-suffering of all, for they often have to climb up into side-saddles of extreme discomfort which came out of some dank attic and are almost prehistoric in design! Happily, many of such older side-saddles have been sold abroad as antiques to hang on the walls of the home of some tycoon in the New World. Sufficient remain in use, however, to cast a cloud over the most stout hearted of lady judges.

The winning side-saddle horse does not qualify for the overall show championship, and nor do the four-year-old or the small hunter, but the first and second in the weight classes meet again to compete for the award of the championship and reserve – the final accolade in the life of the show hunter.

Working hunters have to jump a small, comparatively natural course of some six show jumps before being judged for conformation. Jumping performance counts for some 40 per cent of the whole assessment.

Weight-carrying cobs with show quality are, alas, a vanishing breed as the small demand for them makes them uneconomic to breed. The hack classes are quite well filled and the big shows stage classes for novices, and for ladies' hacks to be ridden side-saddle, in addition to the usual classes divided by height (not exceeding 15 h.h. and not exceeding 15·3 h.h.).

A hack is an elegant, well-trained animal. In days gone by, they were a common

Judging for three very different classes at a horse show. *top*: After giving a ridden display and also being ridden by the judge, a lady's hack is then 'stood up' for the judge to assess its conformation. *middle*: A riding pony mare and foal come forward for judging in hand – the mare will not be ridden in this class. *bottom*: A beautiful Arab is here being shown under saddle.

sight in Hyde Park when ridden by ladies and gentlemen for an hour or so on a sunny morning – partly, no doubt, to attract the admiring attention of some member of the opposite sex. Nowadays they are very largely confined to the show ring. A really good hack, of true 'hack' type, is lighter built and more graceful than a hunter, with a beautiful head and outlook. It is indeed a thing of beauty and, like it, a joy for as long as it lasts. Few modern hacks however seem to be schooled with that lightness in hand which, with its free and flowing movement, was so very characteristic of the champions of 30 years ago.

The British show pony, a miniature Thoroughbred, is a remarkable phenomenon which is found nowehere else in the world and is greatly admired in other countries although seldom coveted, except perhaps in the United States. A fair number of British show ponies have been exported to America, but on the Continent the buyers seem to feel, with some justification, that these ponies are altogether too light, too finely-bred and too precious to be suitable for the average child, who will have a great deal more fun riding a native pony, or one only a generation removed from foundation stock.

Even in England, the showing classes today are largely the hunting ground of the professional children on professionally-produced ponies, and few parents want their children to get involved in this sort of rat-race. I was at Windsor show one day when I heard a professional producer musing to himself: 'There are *five* people riding this pony!' – and so there were! There was the child herself, him, the pony's owner, and the child's mother and grandmother, all calling out instructions to the poor unfortunate jockey every time she came past. Small wonder that child now hates showing and far prefers working pony classes and Pony Club hunter trials and one day events – *anything*, in fact, which avoids swanning around the show ring looking pretty on a pretty pony which is not capable of doing anything else, and often has to be ridden-in by an adult for an hour or two at the show before it is safe for a child to ride.

It is the working ponies, I am quite convinced, that are the ponies of the future, and these classes, where the ponies are required to jump, are filled to capacity. They keep both child and pony in a happy frame of mind and in their comparatively natural state.

The in-hand riding pony classes are on the whole a great deal more sporting, than the ridden show pony classes, with the professional studs well balanced by private breeders who keep the odd mare or two as a hobby. Yet perhaps there is still too much money in these classes, despite the economic situation, for their own good. The dealers are always on the look-out for a top three-year-old to sell on to some deep-pocketed parent and the whole thing starts again, with the pony being sent on to a professional to produce for the show ring. Huge prices are involved and large sums of money change hands.

The native pony classes are far less professional, largely because there is much less money at stake, and the atmosphere is generally far more friendly. This is particularly noticeable among the breeders of Connemara and Welsh ponies, both of whom have a deep love for their protégé. Being sensible, down-to-earth folk, who know ponies, they are also very keen on the performance side. The hardy, sure-footed ponies, reared on the Welsh hills for generations and used as shepherding ponies by the hill farmers, produce offspring that are able to do any job that is required of them, from hunting and jumping to Pony Club events and driving competitions.

The Arab enthusiasts are a law unto themselves, for their breed is a breed apart which has little appeal for the foxhunter or for those who require a horse to enter in three-day events or show-jumping competitions. Most people regard the Arab mainly in the light of an outcross of blood, and many consider that it should ideally be found quite a long way back in the pedigree. But the true Arab lover considers his breed to be a 'pearl beyond price'. As an example, I have a friend who, having acquired an Arab stallion some years ago, sold it to someone in the United States, and was able to build a swimming pool and lay out an extensive shrubbery on the proceeds!

A scene at the Dublin Horse Show, one of the greatest displays of horseflesh in the world, and a spectacular occasion.

Pride of place at the classic shows, however and at all the major agricultural meetings such as the Royal, the Bath and West, Peterborough and the Great Yorkshire, and of course at the annual show of the Royal Dublin Society held each August, at Ballsbridge, is given to the hunters mentioned earlier. Perhaps Dublin is the most interesting of all, for whereas the English shows tend, towards the end of the showing season, to be simply a different permutation of the same horses, meeting at show after show, all the Dublin horses are new

each year. It is the exception, rather than the rule, for a horse to be shown there more than once, for if he is any good he is usually sold. The only reason a horse may appear there for two years is that he is someone's favourite and is not for sale.

There is an endless fascination in watching these horses, the crop of the current season, as they cascade into the ring on the first two days at Ballsbridge – lightweights, middleweights, and finally heavyweights. The last are the richest and rarest, and really what the Irish half-bred breeding industry is all about. Each year they appear to improve in quality, but is this really so or is it simply the inevitable grading-up process, when Thoroughbred sires are used exclusively on the Irish Draught mare? And will Ireland eventually come to the English *impasse*, when almost every horse is practically clean-bred, because of the prevailing shortage of heavyweight foundation stock?

Personally, I doubt it, because even the Irish Horse Board seems to realize that it is imperative to return to the *status quo* by means of the Irish Draught mare, the supreme sheet-anchor of the Irish half-bred breeding industry. Ireland is unique in the world in having this clean-limbed breed on which to draw and it has been the foundation stock of many famous show-jumpers. Many, indeed sadly most, of the Irish Draught foundation mares were sent to Belgium and eaten during the years immediately following the Second World War. Enough mares and stallions however were left to provide a nucleus, which hopefully is being cherished and nurtured, to ensure a foundation stone. Crossed once or twice, or even more often with Thoroughbred stallions, it will assure the retention of a breed sufficiently unique that the Italian dealers will continue to maintain stud farms, or at least depots, in Ireland to supply at least their international teams with Olympic-medal winning horses, while other nations turn to the cold-blooded riding horse of Germany.

Britain has no such foundation stock to put to Thoroughbred stallions in the hope of breeding a viable competition horse. The carthorse breeds – Clydesdale, Shire and Suffolk, – have all been tried and found wanting. The Cleveland Bay, with its long barrel, can throw up the odd freak of breeding, such as William Barker's North Flight, who was reserve for the 1964 British Olympic show jumping team in Tokyo, but by and large this is not the most successful foundation stock for the top-class international competition horse.

Since the end of the Second World War, no fewer than ten Olympic champions (i.e. the winner of a team or individual gold medal) have been bred in Ireland from Irish Draught foundation stock, while seven have been bred in England. Ireland has to her credit Colonel Harry Llewellyn's Aherlow, Colonel Frank Weldon's Kilbarry, Ted Marsh's Wild Venture, H.M. The Queen's Countryman III, Captain Martin Whiteley's The Poacher, Major Derek Allhusen's Lochinvar, Italy's Sunbeam (a double gold medallist in

157

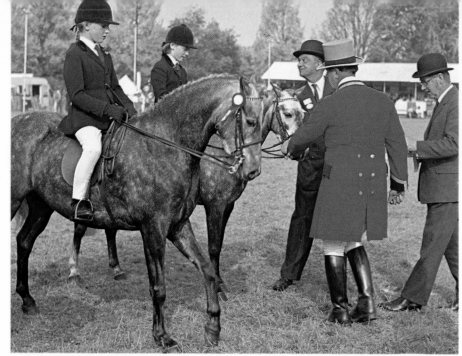

Tokyo), King and Royal Love, and Graziano Mancinelli's Ambassador. England's home-bred champions are Wilf White's Nizefela, Colonel Harry Llewellyn's Foxhunter, Mary Gordon-Watson's Cornishman V, Jane Bullen's Our Nobby, Bridget Parker's Cornish Gold, Major Derek Allhusen's Laurieston and Captain Mark Phillips's Great Ovation.

This concentration of success in one small corner of the globe is not simply a fortuitous coincidence – the result of a happy chance. The fact that only West Germany has 13 champions, all in the field of show-jumping, proves that the powerful German horses are the best performers over really big artificial fences in the world. But it also proves that for going across country, with safety, at speed, jumping whatever fate or the course designer elect to put in the way, there is nothing to touch the Irish hunter, although the English bred one runs him very close.

Nor is it a coincidence that England and Ireland are the only countries where show classes for hunters exist as they do, without the necessity to bring fences into the ring to find the winner. Conformation is extremely important to any horse. However good a performer, however brave his heart, he will never last unless he has the sound constitution and the correct conformation to stand up to the strains and stresses of work in holding going. For 200 years and more, foxhunting has imposed these strains and stresses, and out of it all has come a tough breed of horse, as well as a number of human beings who understand conformation, fortunately for the continuation of the hunter-type horse.

Luckily there is absolutely no sign that hunter showing is on the decline. It will always be a part, and an important one, of the Irish scene because Irish horses are nearly all for sale, and a horse who has won in the show ring must inevitably command a higher price than one which has not. But in England, too, showing is enjoying a vastly increased support. Sponsorship, once the prerogative of the show-jumpers, has now been extended to the hunters too, thanks initially, to the support of the British and Irish Steam Packet Company, and later to the Waterford Crystal Company – both Irish companies, not slow to realize the value of showing.

There could be said to be a decline in the ranks of the professional nagsmen who abounded in the show ring between the wars, but there are still young men coming on to follow in the footsteps of the Harry Bonners of this world. There is of course a vast number of amateurs who have all the keenness and enthusiasm for acquiring and riding a good horse in the show ring, even if they do not reach quite the same heights of expertize of men whose lives are spent seeking out, schooling and producing the champions.

Judging, too, is going through an interregnum, and for much the same reason. With the cavalry regiments mechanized, and the Army Equitation School at Weedon a thing of the past, young men are forced to look beyond the horse to make a

living. The fortunate few to whom this does not apply are denied the opportunity of learning in quite the same school. Their experience cannot extend to riding as many different horses as their predecessors were lucky enough to enjoy, and their knowledge is inevitably more limited. But the realm of the three-day event is a natural recruiting ground for young judges, and so are the ranks of young Masters of Foxhounds, who are very well placed to know what is required of a horse.

One often hears it said, although I do not believe it, that horses are no longer as sound as once they were, and that inherent weaknesses are being bred into English and Irish horses. The myth could have been given credence by the fact that in the old days, unsound horses just disappeared from the public eye, and vast numbers were simply put down, or else fell upon hard times. Now, thanks to the ever-increasing stores of veterinary knowledge and experience, palliative measures and techniques are being improved every year. Thus many horses which would once have been regarded as chronically unsound can now be restored to sound working.

All this must be to the ultimate good of the horse, which is surely the most important consideration, even though various governing bodies connected with showing both hunters and hacks have decreed that certain categories of operation render the subject ineligible for the show ring. The rights and wrongs of the matter are endlessly debatable, and I do not propose to enter into them here, save only to regret that this does sometimes lead to horses having their show careers cut short to very little purpose.

Although fashions change in the show ring, as everywhere else the hunter classes are ultra-conservative; any innovation is rightly regarded with suspicion and frowned upon by the more conservative exhibitors. Such practices as bringing a horse into the show ring with countless tiny plaits up his neck, secured by rubber bands, rather than with the traditional one in front and seven up the crest, neatly sewn in place, is to be deplored.

There is considerable prestige attached to being asked to judge at a leading show,

Prize-giving for beautifully turned out ponies at the Royal Windsor Horse Show.

and particularly to being invited to judge in Ireland. The Irish have always asked Englishmen to judge at their major shows, such as Dublin, Cork and Clonmel. This is partly because an English judge should have a good idea what sort of horse would win in England, and therefore will select the type of horse that could probably be sold to an English buyer. It is also felt that an English judge is more likely to be completely impartial, as he probably does not know the horses or many of the exhibitors.

It was the late Nat Galway-Greer, the wizard of Dunboyne, a world-famous and delightful horse dealer who won ten supreme championships at Dublin in the years following the Second World War who first hit upon the brilliant notion of bringing English riders over to ride his horses at Ballsbridge. There was ostensibly a very good reason for this; the English showmen are a great deal more experienced in showing a horse than their Irish counterparts, and with their meticulous attention to detail they are able to show a horse off to far better advantage. But there was also a more subtle benefit, and this was that the English riders would be known to, and recognized by the English judges, and the horses that they rode would at least be sure to get a second look.

Although some of the other exhibitors were known to resent the presence of the English riders (believing they gave Nat Greer an unfair advantage), the authorities recognized that it gave added interest to the proceedings and raised the standard of the green Irish horses.

There is considerable variety in the standard of horsemanship of the various hunter judges. The criterion is that every horse should go well for a judge, and so certain idiosyncrasies are overlooked as long as this principal requirement is met. Perhaps the worst failing in a judge is bad hands, which must upset any horse unless he happens to have a worse mouth. Once a judge acquires the reputation for being 'mutton-fisted' he will not remain long in ignorance of his failing! There will be several horses produced for him to ride with their curb chains wrapped in chamois leather, lest he hang on to their heads.

There is also the other side of the coin, when exhibitors produce horses in the ring which are quite insufficiently prepared and trained and expect the poor, unsuspecting judges to ride them, sometimes at great personal risk. A certain well known Major General, when faced with one of these animals – and a woman's horse, to boot, notorious for being allowed to do whatever it wishes – brought it straight back to its owner and declined to ride it any more, thundering: 'Madam, I have not come 200 miles to nag other people's horses!'

The judge who bases his decisions on the form which has prevailed at other shows is either unsure of himself, and thus prefers to play it safe by taking the line of least resistance, or has very little knowledge. The form judge soon becomes known for what he is, and of course he is all at sea at the first shows of the season, before the form book has been 'written'. It is one of the worst breaches of etiquette for any judge to be seen with a catalogue in his hands until he has finished his work in the ring. Of course, judges who are in demand, and are constantly on the circuit, can hardly remain in ignorance of the horses who have been winning at earlier shows, even if they have never actually judged them before. Luckily, there are many judges whose integrity is so well known, and whose reputations are so well established, that they are above criticism.

It must be remembered that judging is bound to be a personal matter of opinion, and few people think absolutely alike about a horse. A big, heavy man is likely to lean towards the big, weight-carrying type of horse that he would choose to ride himself. The slim, lightweight judge on the other hand prefers a Thoroughbred type.

Dublin's green horses, too, are great levellers, for riding green Irish horses is a peculiar art, especially where they have done most of their work in a snaffle and are but newly introduced to a double bridle.

In an age when every hunter is so much infused with Thoroughbred blood, Harry Bonner has said that years ago the back row of a hunter class was more impressive than the front row is today. Apart from the fact that the stamp of horse is often not so good as it used to be, he feels that the standard of production has suffered even more. It is impossible, he is sure, to spend too long in riding and making before the actual nagging begins. Most people indulge in far too much of the latter, plus an inordinate reliance on tack and similar contrivances which are sometimes wrongly regarded as a short-cut to success. Declining standards are also manifested by the spectacle of horses – particularly young horses – being forced beyond their natural paces. 'They learn to cut their corners and become ring-crafty quickly enough, without actually showing them the way.'

Looking at photographs of some of the great hunter champions of the past, with their abundance of bone and their great depth, one must concede that such specimens are becoming increasingly rare today. Bad hocks, weak hind legs and long cannon bones were not so prevalent in the old days, perhaps because the stallions of the time were bigger and stronger, with more bone and more substance.

The stallions that are shown at the National Stallion Show of the Hunter's Improvement and National Light Horse Breeding Society at Newmarket each March, for the award of the Society's premiums, are judged by a hunting man and a racehorse trainer, working together. This is an unusual alliance, as the hunting man requires qualities in a horse that will enable it to stay all day, while the racing man – particularly the flat race trainer – looks for the type of horse that will stay for no more than 1·5 km (1 mile) or so at top speed. Yet strangely enough, they usually seem to see eye to eye.

The really knowledgeable judge of every

American ridden show classes cater for three distinct riding styles as well as the many different breeds.

horse and pony looks for good limbs, a well-sloped shoulder going obliquely back into the body, depth in the girth and the loin, a nice front with generous outlook, and strong quarters and second thighs – in this order. Conversely, bad limbs, shortage of bone, bad walkers, straight shoulders, a shelly, shallow body, and weak hind legs are an anathema to all.

Many of the horses which are bred behind the Iron Curtain have many of these faults, which leads one to suppose that breeding is not as selective as it might be on the State Studs, or else that the priorities are different in parts of the world where foxhunting is not endemic. It may also be that whatever the breed, if all the emphasis is placed upon performance, rather than at least half of it being on conformation, there must inevitably be a decline.

Thus the show ring is of very real value to any breed of horse or pony, and while there are still people who care about a breed, as there always will be, there will be shows at which breeders and owners can exhibit their stock in competition with others. A champion obviously commands a higher price than the run-of-the-mill horse or pony, and great sums of money lie between the successful show horse and his full brother who has never proved himself in the show ring.

In discussing the show ring it is inevitable that much emphasis will be placed on the well-established British and Irish pattern which has provided the standard for shows held in other English-speaking countries, particularly in Australia and Southern Africa. Indeed, both these countries frequently invite British judges to officiate at their major shows and the classes held approximate, with local variations, very closely to those held in Britain.

America, deriving its tradition from the same source, has, however developed its own classes and established a system of judging that inclines strongly towards performance in the ring and, in many instances, takes particular account of style.

Holidays with Horses

HOLIDAY riding is a romantic notion. It holds out hopes of carefree canters along the seashore, or sauntering through new and superb scenery, where the sun shines continually from a clear, blue sky. Certainly this is the way it can be, but be warned – reality does not always match such high expectations. Horses kept at holiday riding centres are often listless, their mouths hard and their backs displaying tell-tale signs of saddle sores. Tack, too, is sometimes sadly neglected, and sometimes downright dangerous.

A thoughtful approach to your holiday needs can often divert disaster, however. If you simply want sun and sand with a little riding, then the casual hacking organized by the local stables at your chosen resort may be sufficient. The essence is to do a bit of research beforehand, so that you are more or less assured of a decent ride. It may mean limiting your choice of resorts, especially in the Mediterranean, or even going slightly inland, but it is well worthwhile, for nothing does surpass the joy of experiencing the sights of a foreign country from the back of a well-cared for and capable horse.

This pre-planning requisite applies to all kinds of holiday riding – be it trekking, trail riding (which varies in definition from country to country), or simply a few hours hacking.

Often you will have to make your own riding arrangements on arrival, but if given notice, some travel firms, especially those specializing in a set area, will create a special equestrian package deal. Thus, you can still benefit from charter flights, special inclusive fares available to travel companies, block bookings of hotels and so on.

Increasingly, however, actual horse-riding holidays are being offered all over the world.

Some countries see riding as an activity to promote – such as the British Isles, where the range of riding activities is enormous. Others, like Italy, will happily find you a seaside nag but tend to have their best horses at the riding clubs. Almost anywhere, however, a good many doors will open once people are aware you have a genuine interest in horse riding and not just a passing holiday interest. Language barriers quickly break down, too, as a mutual love of horses forms an inevitable bond.

There are two other vital factors, which must be considered – your riding experience and the weather. Nothing is worse than being caught in either extreme heat or cold after some eight hours, or maybe less, in the saddle when you are used to weekend riding in more equable conditions. Alternatively, as a more experienced and proficient rider, you may be expected to fall in line with a large group and keep to the pace of the slowest or novice rider.

Left Holidays with horses include pony trekking, which offers quiet riding to those with little experience who like to explore the countryside. Here riders from one of the many trekking centres based in the U.K. wind their way over the Devon hills.

This can often happen on trekking holidays, so find a centre which makes special arrangements for those with ability. Remember, though, that trekking, by definition, really means walking. Anything faster could be more readily classed as hacking.

Trail riding may be considered an advanced form of trekking, although the distinction is a little blurred depending in which country you are located. The Welsh Tourist Board sum it up as being for those 'able to ride at sustained speeds for long distances over tough country'.

Clothes must also be carefully selected, too. Prancing through the waves on a horse, in a bikini or a pair of shorts might seem pretty on a poster, but is scarcely practical if you are going any further than the beach – and decidedly uncomfortable after an hour or so. Conversely, in cold weather, do make sure you are warm. Such under garments as long johns, while inelegant, help to keep down the bulky items you might otherwise need. Oil wool sweaters and lightweight windcheaters can be a boon, as can plastic coats and leggings, but this is no time for flapping cycle capes!

The standard of riding holidays and horses used in the British Isles is generally high. You can ride virtually anywhere, according to local private property restrictions and the dictates of the terrain. Scotland is admirably suited both to trail riding – or post trekking – as well as simple trekking. Either way there is little road work involved and tough Highland ponies are widely used. Many centres are approved by the Scottish Sports Council and a list of these, along with others, are available from the Scottish Tourist Board.

Dropping south into England, there is fine riding in Northumbria, Cumbria and Yorkshire, with much admirable scenery. These regions are generally uncommercialized, so stables have to be sought out. The reward tends to be smaller groups, probably comprised of more experienced riders.

In the warmer English West Country, there is unlimited riding country among the high tors of Devon, or the wild moors of Cornwall. The more gentle countryside of the New Forest in the South of England, along with its wild ponies and deer, provides a good holiday setting, as also does the South Downs Way in Sussex.

One of the biggest booms in trekking has been in Wales and the Pony Trekking Society of Wales has produced a book on approved centres. Some of the bigger ones, such as Rhayader and Tregaron, can be a bit overwhelming with the sheer number of ponies and riders, a high percentage of the latter being beginners. This applies to some Scottish centres, too, so decide on one that suits your ability and temperament.

The British Horse Society handbook, or that of the Association of British Riding Schools are useful publications to consult for instructional holidays. Also invaluable, is the list of trekking and riding holiday centres approved by the Ponies of Britain.

Ireland has always been synonymous with the horse, and the scope for holiday riding is considerable. In the Republic there are centres close to Shannon, Cork, Galway and Dublin, and with roads virtually traffic-free outside of towns, it is easy

Right An introduction to the pony for a group of children on an adventure holiday in the Black Mountains of Wales. The children's somewhat unorthodox headgear protects them in all their other activities, as well as adopting the role of riding hat.

to switch from one area to another. Counties Wicklow and Wexford in the east and Connemara in the west offer picturesque possibilities for many riding holidays, while County Cork offers horse-drawn caravans, often based on traditional Romany lines.

In Northern Ireland there are numerous hunts, as well as trekking and riding around Rostrevor in the mountains of Mourne in County Down. Sea, forest and mountain views form the attraction.

Basically British, but with a strong French influence, the Channel Islands offer a novel experience for the holiday rider. Jersey, keenly aware of family holiday needs, has good riding at St Ouen's Bay. Neighbouring Guernsey, an island with a glut of good countryside, has four stables, one near St Peter Port providing some good hacks and pleasant riding on L'Ancresse Common close to the beach.

France vies strongly with Great Britain in the range of equestrian holidays offered, as can be seen by a glance at the handbook of the Association Nationale pour le Tourisme Equestre at l'Equitation de Loisirs (A.N.T.E.). Emphasis is often placed on dressage, and instructional holidays are numerous. The Etampes Riding Society, for instance, in the Ile de France, 55 km (34 miles) south-west of Paris, has both Portuguese and Lipizzaner horses for amateur dressage riders. For those keen on driving, the Equestrian Centre at Valençay in the South Loire has ten carriages for one, two or four in hand.

Brittany has long been popular and suitable for family holidays, especially campers and caravanners. There are a number of riding centres, including one halfway between Rennes and Saint Malo, at La Bourbansais (Ile et Vilaine) in the shadow

of a castle. The Dordogne region offers many opportunities to riding enthusiasts too.

Special holidays for young people are held in the Poursaudes Estate in the Ardennes and the Gunkel Stables, Granjalna in Alsace – a land of vineyards, storks, pine forests and pastures. Far more casual is riding in the Rhône delta area known as the Camargue, famed for its white horses. The main centre is at Mejanes, but you can find places to hire horses along the road to Saint-Maries-de-la-Mer. But do make sure you choose carefully because some hirers offer you little more than a chance to sit on a horse's back.

Horse-drawn caravans are available at Assier in the Lot Valley where rides are also given in a stage-coach. The Club Méditerranée runs the equestrian village of Pompadour near Limoges. Facilities include five indoor and five outdoor rings, two cross-country courses and stables for two hundred horses.

Corsica, the French island in the Mediterranean has some impressive mountain and coastal scenery and is quiet and virtually uncommercialized. Some of the best riding is in the *maquis* bushland and the main centre is at Venaco.

Belgium, with its collection of coastal dunes, fertile plains and forested hillsides is eager to promote riding. Hippotour, a non-profit making organization, include seven-day riding tours in the Ardennes (a region also ideal for boating, climbing, fishing and pot-holing), while another five-day tour takes in the historic and artistic sites in the woodlands and parks of the Brabant province, the capital of which is Brussels. You sleep overnight, incidentally, in haylofts! The Belgian coast features riding in the pine forests behind the vast

The native white horses of the Camargue, still used by the gardiens to herd the local bulls, now also take exploring holidaymakers through this marshy part of southern France.

sand dunes, particularly at Knokke-le-Zoute.

The Grand Duchy of Luxembourg makes up for what it lacks in size with a variety of scenery. It is well endowed with numerous bridle paths which have been put to good use by the fast growing and vigorous Luxembourg Federation of Equestrian Sports who run a week-long ride for the experienced covering 32 to 40 kms (20 to 25 miles) a day.

The fact that there are 16 riding schools in West Berlin alone, indicates the interest shown in the sport throughout West Germany. While general holiday prices can be high, hacking is still reasonably priced. The standard, too, is generally high whether you ride in a town or in the rural regions which range from the vast Luneburg Heath in the north to the Bavarian villages in the south. Resorts with riding establishments in the latter include Munich, Oberammergau, Bayreuth, Berchtesgaden and Mittenwald.

The Black Forest, offers many riding holidays, notably in the seventeenth century Schloss Weitenburg above the Neckar Valley. A heavy concentration on equestrian activities can be found in the Rhineland which touristically covers such well-known centres as Aachen, Heidelberg, Koblenz, Konigswinter and Rudesheim. Pony schools are popular, with a large one at Havixbeck near Munster. In the same area, at Warendorf, is the famous Deutsche Reitschule where the top German riders train, and prices for riding are correspondingly high.

Unfortunately holiday prices in the Alpine areas of Austria and Switzerland have soared dramatically, which is a pity, for there is much in the way of riding opportunities. Possible solutions are to stay in private rooms, rent a chalet or make use of the good camping facilities or youth hostels. The special holiday tickets, too, give a healthy discount on all forms of transport.

There are said to be around 150 Austrian towns where you can hire horses, but bad weather and rising costs are continually forcing some smaller establishments out of business, so check first or select a well-known centre. The most famous of all must be Vienna, where you can also see the Lipizzaners in action at the Spanish Riding School. Details of a 'book ahead' scheme are available from Austrian state tourist offices or from the Vienna Tourist Board, and many travel firms have special tours to the school.

Scenery throughout Austria varies considerably, with Lower Austria, for example, having both high mountains and subtropical meadows. Thirty-four riding establishments are listed in this area and, in common with other provinces, there are treks lasting several days. Ampflwang in Upper Austria is known as the Horseman's Village, and Burgenland, with its Hungarian influence, is strongly recommended for riding.

Equestrian activities in Switzerland are not all centred on riding alone; you can spend eight days in a horse-drawn caravan in the Jura or join a mule safari in the little-known province of Valais. Most major resorts offer riding though, and at Davos there is year round hacking, as well as instructional courses and moonlight rides. Fashionable St Moritz has a centre for dressage and jumping and stages ski-joring, or horse-racing across the ice with a skier in tow.

In Central Switzerland, Lake Lucerne is more geared to the young, with riding stables in Lucerne and others at Brunnen and Vitznau. The region of Berne and the Bernese Oberland, Interlaken, has marked trails as well as an indoor school offering instruction. Kandersteg and Grindelwald are two other popular resorts with riding available.

Thinly populated, with diverse scenery and a high standard of living, Scandinavia has a unique affinity with outdoor activities such as riding. One of the main centres in Denmark is in Jutland where the riding institute at Vejle runs a so-called Wild West camp for children near Billund. A stage coach also runs from the institute with overnight stops at village inns. Children are welcome too, at Højmarken, one of the many Danish farmhouses used as holiday homes, near Rabjerg, close to Skagen, the furthest point north on the Jutland Peninsula. Among the Danish islands, the ideal choice is probably Sealand, with Copenhagen on its eastern coast, while in Slagelse horse-drawn land-aus are available for hire.

Norway has impressive scenery with its fjords and mountains, and riding tours are held from late June to early August in the Hallingdal mountains inland from Oslo. There is also riding at Lillehammer, divided by a river and surrounded by spruce and pine forests.

For the least known of the Scandinavian countries, Finland has a fine selection of riding centres. In the capital, Helsinki, there is excellent riding in the wooded outskirts as there is further east at the old town of Eriknas near Porvoo. One of the best lakeland settings is the Hotel Aulanko, the stables of which offer a 40-minute ride round the huge Karlberg Estate. Other good centres with riding available are Lahti, with the Messila stables nearby, Tampere and also in Finnish Lapland, the administrative capital of which is Rovaniemi.

Sweden has around 90 riding centres, but with a wise emphasis on the West Coast which, north of Gothenburg, is rocky and interspersed with woods, coves and fishing villages. Along the more sandy beaches of the south, riding is featured at both Varberg and Falkenberg.

No horse has been imported into Iceland for over 800 years, so the tough, little Icelandic pony is essentially the same as that relied upon by the Viking hordes for their escapades. A particular advantage of this breed is the ability to use five distinct gaits – including pace and *tølt*, or running walk. With the long distances to be covered in a country consisting largely of rocks, stones, deserts and sandy wastes, this is a major asset.

On riding holidays jeans, a windcheater and gumboots are the order of the day and stamina is more important than style.

Inclusive pony trekking tours are available at Geldingaholt farm, two hours by bus from Reykjavik, and there is riding, too, at Lake Laugarvatn, Gullfoss, Geysir and Thingvellir. A word of warning though – cut down spending as much as possible in Iceland; the inflation rate is horrendous.

The USSR offers great satisfaction in riding more unusual breeds such as Tersky, Donsky or Anglo-Karbardin, especially in the vast indoor school at the Moscow Equestrian Centre. You will have to seek permission first from Intourist, the state tourist body, but visitors can be shown around the centre and riding is very cheap compared with Western prices, although it must be arranged in advance.

Elsewhere in Eastern Europe, restrictions have been increasingly relaxed, although riding is often regarded as a cultural rather than a vacational pursuit. One country with a high percentage of horses is Hungary with six- to eight-day tours at Hortobagy, Lake Balaton, the Danube Bend and Trans-Danubia. It is also possible to have horseback holidays at stud farms and clubs, but arrangements must be made well in advance. A similar situation exists in Poland, and the state tourist organization runs visits to stud farms at

Lakeside riding for holidaymakers in Poland. The state tourist organisation runs various types of holiday on horseback as well as visits to stud farms.

places such as Lack, near Warsaw, and Twno, Posadowo and Sierakow in the Poznan region.

If you want somewhere sunnier, riding is advertized at Slunchev Bryag on the Bulgarian Black Sea coast, and also at the new resort of Albena.

Yugoslavia is the location for the Lipice Stud Farm near Trieste, which is the true birthplace of the beautiful Lipizzaner breed of white horses. The best way to appreciate the history, which goes back to 1580, is to stay at the Hotel Maestoso in the grounds and ride there as well. Various travel firms feature riding holidays, or alternatively stay at a coastal resort, such as Porec where there is riding anyway.

'The horses were poor, half-starved beasts, given to stumbling . . .' Sadly such authentic comments as these can be applied to some of the holiday hacks which may be found in the sunspots of the Mediterranean, but good riding is available. The Horse Club of Rapallo, for instance, on the Italian Eastern Riviera, is superbly equipped with both an indoor school and two outdoor practice rings.

In the Rome area, riding is available at Le Palazze Country Club, Spoleto, where you can climb to the Tolfa Mountains, and at Sacrofano. Towards the Swiss border in the Biella region, off the Milan/Turin autostrada is the horse riding centre 'Citta di Biella' in the Andio Estate, Candelo. Further riding is offered in the Abruzzo National Park, in the Montefreddi residential park near Florence and at the officially backed horseback holiday centre at Soleschiano di Manzano, a town in the Udine in the Po Valley.

Spain, like Italy, suffers from a split attitude to riding – that either it is provided for the average tourist or it is enjoyed by the wealthy or the nobility. There are, of course, exceptions with some good establishments in the major resorts – although many stables run by hotels are often no more than a collection of half a dozen or so somewhat tired nags. It seems sensible generally to head inland – to Alondra, for instance. Much more rugged, but adventurous, are the 15-day expeditions using well-trained Andalucian horses in the Sierra Nevada Mountains, organized by an English company and approved by Ponies of Britain.

With Portugal's somewhat unsettled, political climate, tourist facilities, including riding, have been subjected to sudden changes. However it is safe to say that the Algarve, with its rolling Atlantic beaches, despite the growth in villas, is true riding country. Many small outfits are English run, such as that at the Quinta do Lago.

Others are situated at Quarteira and Tavira. There is a magnificently decorated indoor school at Vilamoura although the horses have waxed and waned in reputation over the years. The best idea is to judge for yourself; the whole coastline is quickly covered by car, provided you look out for the numerous donkeys and carts!

Riding in Greece is basically restricted to two riding clubs in the Athens area near the package deal resorts of Glyfada, Cavouri and Lagonissi. In Northern Greece there is riding at Thessaloniki.

In the United States and North America the Hollywood image of the cowboy and his faithful horse is as strong now, if not stronger, than before, thanks in part at least to the travel trade. This is particularly true in the Canadian Rockies, and more especially Alberta where the climate and scenery are idyllic for those wishing to relive the pioneer days from the back of a pony. Unique to Alberta is the Stoney Indian Wilderness Centre where you not only go

Riding holidays in North America. *below*: Trail riding high up in the mountains, one of the best ways to see the countryside, even when the snow is still lying. *opposite top*: Pack tripping is offered by dude ranches. *opposite bottom*: a dude camp, where riders rough it as cowboys once did.

horse-riding but learn Indian ways, including how to survive on berries, plants and roots. Both the Jasper and Banff national parks provide absorbing rides, some lasting six days or more. Although there is no actual equestrian body, the main trail rides are organized through the Trail Riders of the Canadian Rockies based in Calgary, the scene of the famous stampede.

There is similar sort of riding elsewhere in Canada, more especially British Columbia, and also in certain parts of the United States. In the Yellowstone National Park, Wyoming, stagecoach rides, with four-in-hand, fall in line with the traditional trail riding activities. It is similar with other Old West states such as Dakota where you can join an authentic cattle round-up. In Colorado there are numerous dude ranches and guest-houses, common in fact to vast tracts of America, especially west of the Mississippi.

The word 'dude' was originally applied to Eastern visitors whose cultivated manners and unfamiliarity with local customs made them the butts of snide remarks and practical jokes. When an increasing number of them, however, sought to spend their holidays on ranches, owners created facilities and activities for paying guests. There are now thousands of Western-style resorts throughout the United States and Canada, giving vacationers the opportunity to become as much a part of the Old West as the Twentieth century allows.

Almost all activities involve riding. Days are spent on cross-country expeditions to savour the area's scenery, 'helping' ranch hands tend herds of cattle, or polishing tack in the barn while listening to the staff tell tales of the 'good old days'. Evening events consist of barbecues, hayrides, and square dances, and there may be a weekly rodeo in which ranch employees – and daring guests – compete against people from nearby resorts and local cowboys and cowgirls.

Many dude ranches offer pack trips as part of their programme, but pack tripping can also be done as a vacation by itself. A weekend or weeklong excursion on horseback is a delightful way to see unspoiled parts of the country and to live the way frontiersmen did years ago. Happily for today's holiday-maker, pack tripping does not require living off the land. Travellers stay at camp sites, cabins, or farm houses along the way. Meals are served at these places or they are prepared along the trail by 'wranglers', who also look after the horses. In addition to riding, there might be stops for hunting, fishing, or photography, visits to scenic and historic sites, or for a day or two's respite at a resort.

Many states, such as Oklahoma and Wyoming hold rodeos which are popular spectator sport for those on holiday. This applies also to the Tennessee Walking Horse celebrations. Tours and riding are available in the famous Bluegrass region of Kentucky, and indeed horse farm tours extend from Florida to the Piedmont region of north and central Virginia. The New England states offer all that is best in riding country, particularly in autumn.

There are also English style riding centres situated throughout the United States with instruction available at them. Summer riding camps are popular for youngsters, and all major cities have riding academies serving urban parks. There is riding for instance, in New York's famous Central Park and in Washington D.C.'s Rock Creek Park.

Australia experienced a lull in riding, when the horse, revered as a working animal, gave way to mechanization. As everywhere, interest in riding as a sport soon grew, and now there is greater emphasis on style, than the loping gait of the old time bushwackers. Trail riding has intensified, with one of the most attractive areas being the Blue Mountains behind Sydney. Other centres are in the Lamington National Park, and the mountainous parts of the Gold Coast. 73 kms (48 miles) out of Alice Springs, the heart of the Red Centre of the Great Outback, the Ross River resort offers riding – plus a chance to become a boomerang thrower. Sheep stations too often take paying guests, allowing a touch of gracious living with the riding activities.

New Zealand is one of the world's largest farming countries, and holidays in a pastoral setting are increasingly popular. Many farms offer other opportunities such as fishing, tennis and sailing as well as horse-riding. Trail riding is not overlooked: the Wanderlust trekking centre at Hanmer Springs in the South Island have 14 teams for both experienced and amateur riders. Camping trips are arranged for up to a week or more.

Although vast areas have not been covered fully by this survey, holiday riding in some other place of your choice need not be ruled out. Decent horses can be found in North Africa; there is trekking in the Upper Galilee, Israel, and most towns and resorts offer riding in South Africa.

A New Yorker runs, and arranges holidays at, the Escuela Ecuestre at San Miguel de Allende in Mexico, two ex-English army officers run mountain treks in tiny Andorra, and Argentina ranch-house holidays with horses are available through another English concern.

In Jamaica try riding at the Good Hope estate or at the Upton Country Club, Ocho Rios, in Malaysia – the country club on Langkawi island offers riding among its other sports and a Himalayan pony trek is operated by a leading travel concern.

No doubt other countries have equally as attractive riding. Some might even spring some worthwhile suprises. If so share your secret with others. Or, on second thoughts, keep it to yourself!

PART FOUR

HORSE CARE
AND
MANAGEMENT

The Body of the Horse

THE horse's body is a fine example of nature's ability to relate structure to function, expressed elsewhere in the sharp carnassial teeth of the dog accustomed to tearing at flesh and using its 'bite' for defence, or in the fins of a fish developed for the purpose of propulsion through water. The horse's body is adapted for speed and size. Other animals are as fast as the horse, but not as big, and it is this combination that gives the clue to much of the horse's body structure. It accounts for the highly specialized limbs in which the number of bones has been reduced to a minimum, so that the horse stands on the tips of four fingers and toes, compared with sixteen in the dog and eight in cattle. The loss of muscle below the 'knee' and 'hock' has accompanied the reduction in the number of bones, for it is these muscles, together with the extra bones, that provide the human or animal ability to grasp and manipulate with the extremity of its limbs. Through the course of evolution, the horse

has lost this ability and can move its limbs only either forwards or backwards. This provides it with the optimum method of propulsion. The force is provided by the highly developed muscles attached to the bones of the forearm, thigh and body, the surfaces bone having been broadened to meet this increased commitment.

Evolution

We know from fossil records how the horse's skeleton has become adapted in the course of some 40 million years, from the fox-like creature *Eohippus*, or Dawn Horse, to *Equus caballus*, the modern horse. From these records we can follow, not only the elongation and simplification of the extremities of the limbs, but also such changes as the lengthening of the neck and skull, associated with the alteration from browsing habits (ie eating soft, succulent fruits above ground level) to grazing habits (ie cropping hard, fibrous grass at ground level).

The first fossil record is of the Dawn Horse but the horse presumably evolved from stock having the mammalian prototype appendages of five fingers and toes, which human beings have retained. The

The modern horse *Equus caballus* has evolved from the now extinct form *Eohippus* which is first recorded from the Eocene period about 40 million years ago. The coat colour and pattern of the tiny *Eohippus* are conjectural as it is known only from fossil bones.

sequence of development of the limb extremities and those which took place in the skull and teeth have been well researched. The teeth mirror the change in feeding habits; the modern horse has front teeth for cropping grass and back teeth with flat surfaces so that the upper and lower molars can grind the hard, fibrous content of its diet.

The horse's body is structured to meet the needs of the equine species; and purposes imposed by man are only incidental. This must be recognized so as to understand the best methods of caring for the horse, in order to gain maximum advantage from its prowess while interfering minimally with its natural functions.

Evolutionary changes help in understanding the horse of today, but it has also to be accepted that the structure of the body of the horse is unalterable, in the sense that within the relatively minor family differences, a horse is a horse; and no amount of artificial or man-inspired influences can change it. It is true that by selection it is possible to breed a miniature Shetland pony or an enormous Thoroughbred or draught horse, but these are still just different breeds of the domestic horse, belonging to the species *Equus caballus*. They all possess 64 chromosomes (ie inherited material in the cell nuclei). Near relatives such as the zebra, Przewalski's horse and wild ass have different numbers of chromosomes, but are nonetheless identifiable in their body structure as belonging to the Equidae.

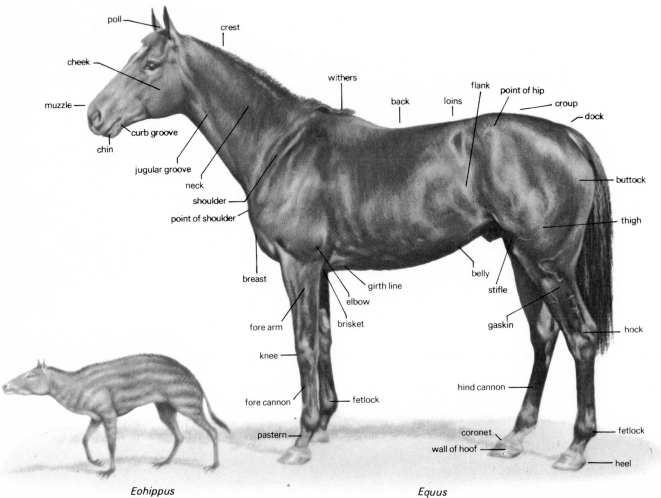

Eohippus

Equus

Tissues

The horse, in common with other mammalian species, is made up of four basic tissues known as muscle, nerve, connective and epithelium, each with its own special characteristics which contribute to the function of the whole body.

Epithelial Tissue

Epithelial tissue includes the covering and lining of the outside of the body (the skin), and the inner tubes and hollow organs such as the gut, bile duct, bladder and uterus. The glands which produce hormones and other substances are formed of epithelial tissue.

Connective Tissue

Connective tissue is that which contributes special functions such as the bony structures (the skeleton) which support and give form to the body and its softer structures. Blood is a very special form of connective tissue, while more simple forms include tendons, ligaments and sheets of fibrous material which bind or protect various organs or muscles.

Muscular Tissue

Muscular tissue is that which has the property of movement (contraction and relaxation) and is thus responsible for the work performed by the body, as in galloping or, in standing, by resisting the pull of gravity. Body functions are also performed by other types of muscle, such as that in the

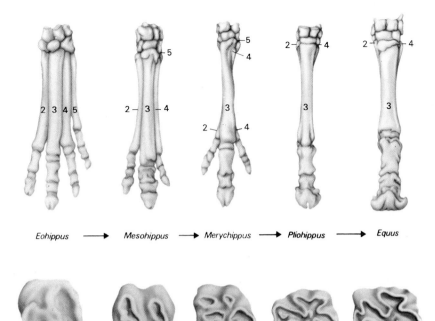

Eohippus ⟶ Mesohippus ⟶ Merychippus ⟶ Pliohippus ⟶ Equus

Above As the horse evolved from a cryptic forest browser to a conspicuous plains-dwelling grazer, and the need for speed to escape predators increased, the body size enlarged and the number of toes was reduced. The change of diet from easily chewed soft fruits to tough grass which needed grinding resulted in the development of hard enamel ridges on the teeth (drawings not to scale). *Below* The skeleton is made up of some 210 bones to form a supporting framework; a knowledge of the relationships and functions of the bones is always useful.

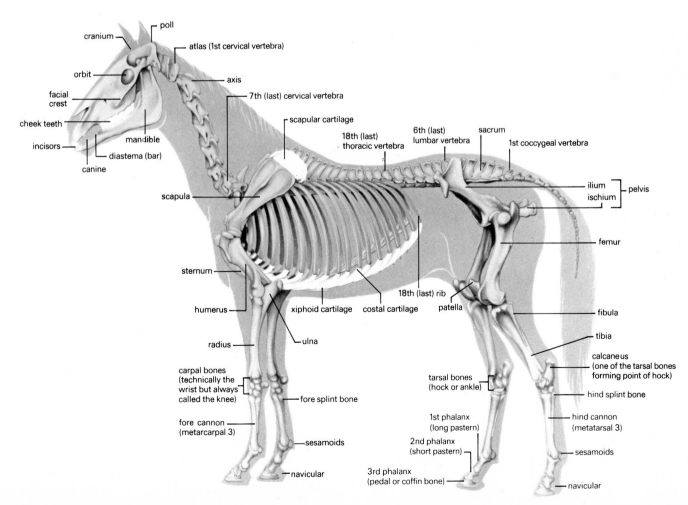

169

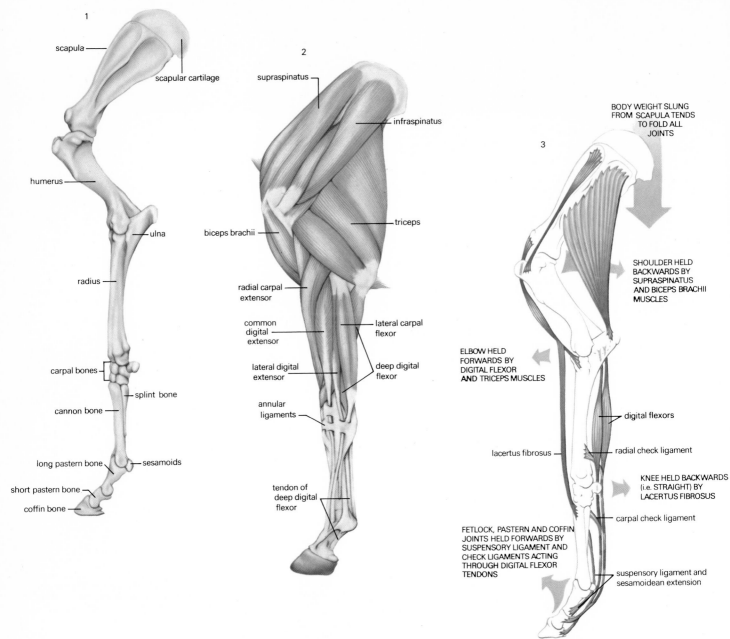

1
- scapula
- scapular cartilage
- humerus
- ulna
- radius
- carpal bones
- splint bone
- cannon bone
- long pastern bone
- sesamoids
- short pastern bone
- coffin bone

2
- supraspinatus
- infraspinatus
- triceps
- biceps brachii
- radial carpal extensor
- common digital extensor
- lateral carpal flexor
- lateral digital extensor
- deep digital flexor
- annular ligaments
- tendon of deep digital flexor

3
- BODY WEIGHT SLUNG FROM SCAPULA TENDS TO FOLD ALL JOINTS
- SHOULDER HELD BACKWARDS BY SUPRASPINATUS AND BICEPS BRACHII MUSCLES
- ELBOW HELD FORWARDS BY DIGITAL FLEXOR AND TRICEPS MUSCLES
- digital flexors
- lacertus fibrosus
- radial check ligament
- KNEE HELD BACKWARDS (i.e. STRAIGHT) BY LACERTUS FIBROSUS
- carpal check ligament
- suspensory ligament and sesamoidean extension
- FETLOCK, PASTERN AND COFFIN JOINTS HELD FORWARDS BY SUSPENSORY LIGAMENT AND CHECK LIGAMENTS ACTING THROUGH DIGITAL FLEXOR TENDONS

lining of the gut which produces the peristaltic movement propelling food from one end of the alimentary tract (gut) to the other. The heart too consists mostly of muscle doing the work of a pump.

Nervous Tissue
Nervous tissue has the capacity to transmit messages over long distances, and forms the brain, spinal cord and nerve pathways which control most of the body functions.

The Skeleton and Muscles

The horse's skeleton is composed of approximately 210 individual bones (excluding those of the tail). The skeleton gives support for the muscles, protection for the internal organs, and possesses the necessary mobility of its parts for the horse to move at various speeds or lie down or graze.

Varying degrees of mobility are provided by differing types of joints; for example, that between the femur and tibia, forming the 'stifle', gives great mobility, while those between two vertebrae in the backbone allow restricted movement only. The

bones forming all joints are capped with cartilage, which is softer than bone and can make good the effects of wear and tear at the surface. The joint is completed by a capsule which produces synovia (joint oil) to lubricate the joint surfaces, and it is strengthened by ligaments, ie fibrous bands connecting the bones on either side of the joint.

The way in which a joint can move is controlled by the shape of the joint surface and the position of the ligaments and other supporting structures which pass over it. The fetlock for example can be flexed further than it can be extended; the 'knee' can only be flexed whereas the stifle joint can be moved, to some extent, in several directions.

The skeleton has several examples of nature's way of adapting structure to meet particular requirements or function. The broad flat surface of the scapula or shoulder blade and the transverse processes of the lumbar vertebrae, provide ample space for the attachment of the powerful muscles required to move the fore and hind limbs. The special features of the skull are the relatively elongated face providing space

Three aspects of the horse's left foreleg seen from the left side. *1*: The skeleton is made up of 20 bones; there are no collar bones linking the shoulder blades in the horse. *2*: The deep muscles; the bones below the knee are moved by tendons arising from muscles much higher up the leg. *3*: A special system of muscles, tendons and ligaments forms the stay apparatus which prevents the leg from buckling and enables the horse to relax and even doze in the standing position; a similar system exists in the hindleg.

for the teeth and their roots; and the orbits housing the eyes which are placed well above ground level when the horse is grazing. These provide it with a greater area of vision to look out for impending danger.

The parts of the skeleton which have particular practical importance for horse owners are:
(i) the splint bones, on either side of the cannon bones, which are remnants of the digits lost during evolution. These bones are bound to the cannon bone by ligaments. It is a fracture of the shaft of this bone, or inflammation of the liga-

ment which binds it to the cannon bone, that causes the painful enlargements known as 'splints'.

(ii) other small bones which are sometimes troublesome, the sesamoids. These are two small bones forming the back of the fetlock joint, and the navicular bone below the pedal bone.

The Foot

The horse's foot is completely surrounded by a substance similar to a human's finger nail to protect it against having to sustain the wear and tear of carrying one quarter of the horse's weight in action over any terrain. A horse's foot consists of an outer layer of horn (hoof) inside which is contained the pedal and navicular bones, part of the second phalanx and the deep digital flexor tendon, the end of which is attached to the pedal bone. The foot also contains the digital pad, lateral cartilages, coronopedal joint, blood vessels and nerves.

The outer layer consists of the walls, sole, bars and frog. The hoof is an inert substance composed largely of keratin which is secreted by the coronary corium. The hoof grows at a rate of approximately 0·5 cm (0·2 in) per month and it receives nourishment from the sensitive laminae leaf-like structures which line the pedal bone and which bind the hoof to the bone as they interlock with comparable leaves from the insensitive laminae of the hoof. The foot as a whole absorbs concussion and by its continuous growth it is able to replace the surface as this is lost by everyday wear and tear.

Muscles

The muscles that enable the horse to move consist of muscle masses attached to bone at one end and to their respective tendons at the other. For example, the superficial digital flexor of the forelimb is attached to the humerus bone and the posterior aspect of the radius bone. At its lower end it forms the tendon which runs behind the knee and fetlock joints to become inserted on the lower end of the first and upper end of the second phalanx. Its action is to flex the toe and knee and to extend the elbow joint.

The tendon is encased in a synovial sheath as it runs behind the knee and fetlock joints. The thin fibrous sheet that composes this produces tendon oil or synovia which has similar lubricating properties to joint oil. Similar sheaths enclose tendons wherever there is likely to be friction between the tendon and bone, or other structures. A bursa is a similar structure except that it does not surround a tendon, but acts more like a cushion between parts that suffer friction.

Most muscles have tendons of varying lengths and not all are as long as those which run below the knee or hock joints. Ligaments, too, vary in length. Most are relatively short, such as those already mentioned which strengthen joints. The check and suspensory ligaments of the forelimb deserve special mention. The check ligament is attached to the ligament at the back of the knee joint and, at its lower end, it joins the deep digital flexor tendon in the region of the back of the cannon bone. It forms part of the stay apparatus which prevents over extension of the toe. The suspensory ligament is also concerned in this action and is attached above, to the back of the cannon bone and lower row of knee (carpal) bones, and below to the sesamoid bones behind the fetlock joint. From here it sends two branches around the front of the first phalangeal (pastern) bone on each side to join the common digital extensor tendon, through which they are inserted into the front of the second phalangeal and pedal bones. There is a similar arrangement in the hind limb.

Digestive System

The horse's digestive system consists of those organs concerned with digestion, or the turning of complex food material such as hay, grass and corn, into simple substances such as carbohydrate, protein (amino acids), fatty acids, etc, which can be used by the body for energy, storage or body building processes. The organs consist of the alimentary tract which is the tube extending from the mouth to the anus and known also as the gut, intestines or alimentary canal, and the accessory organs such as the teeth, tongue, salivary glands, liver and pancreas.

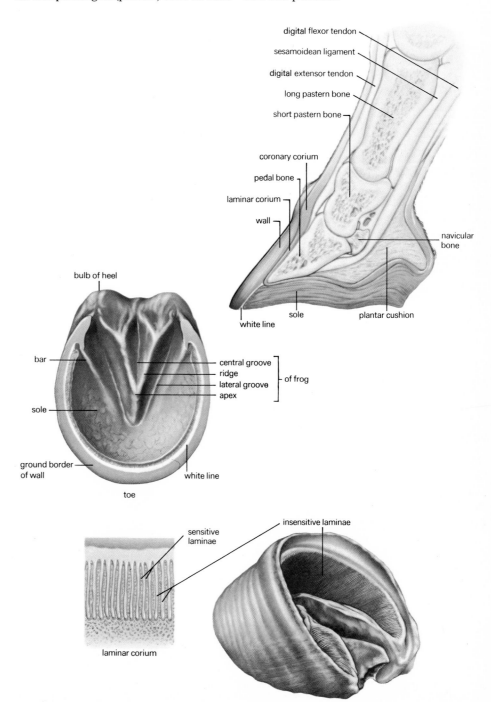

The structure of the foot. *top*: a section down the mid-line. *middle*: The sole surface of an unshod hoof. *bottom right*: The hoof detached from the foot shows the insensitive laminae on the inside face of the wall and heels. *bottom left*: a magnified cross section of the insensitive/sensitive laminar junction; the sensitive laminae have little room to expand if injured or inflamed and can thus be a source of extreme pain to the horse.

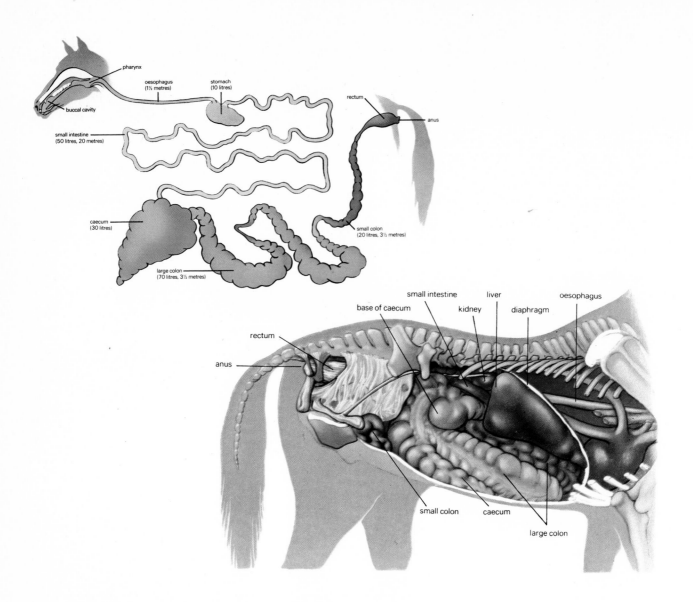

The special characteristics of the horse's mouth are the highly prehensile lips for gathering food which work in conjunction with the sharp front teeth when cropping grass, and the labile tongue which conveys the food to the back teeth. These have table-like surfaces crossed by ridges that form an ideal grinding surface between the upper and lower jaws.

An adult horse has 40 teeth arranged as follows: in each left and right, upper and lower jaw there are three incisors, one

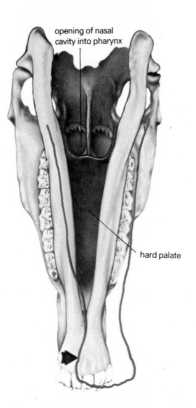

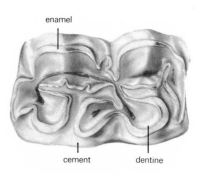

The mouth and teeth are specially adapted for grazing. *far left*: The large mobile lips can enfold bunches of grass which are torn free by the chisel-like incisor teeth. *left*: the skull viewed from below; the soft palate – an extension of the mouth lining – covers part of the nasal cavity opening; the lower jaw is narrower than the upper jaw and moves sideways as well as up and down to grind the tough food between the cheek teeth (molars). *above*: the molar surface is flat and formed of sharp enamel ridges; opposing teeth move across each other with a shearing action. *right*: the milk teeth are replaced by the time the horse is five years old; here a permanent incisor is erupting through the gum to replace the milk tooth in front.

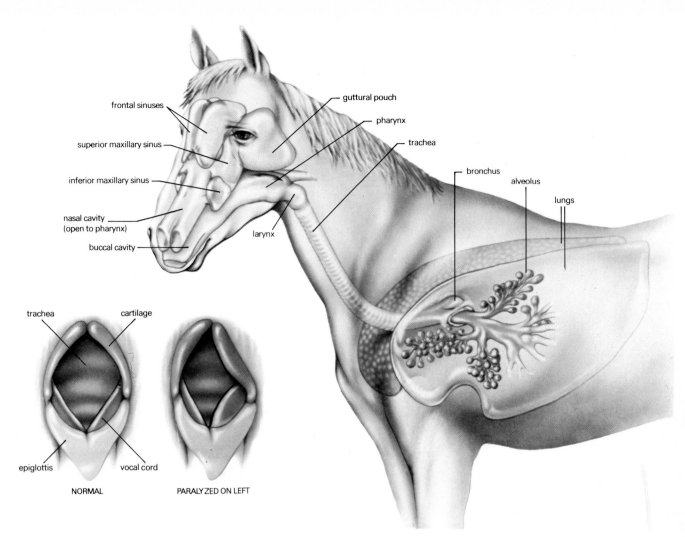

frontal sinuses

superior maxillary sinus

inferior maxillary sinus

nasal cavity
(open to pharynx)

buccal cavity

guttural pouch

pharynx

trachea

bronchus

alveolus

lungs

larynx

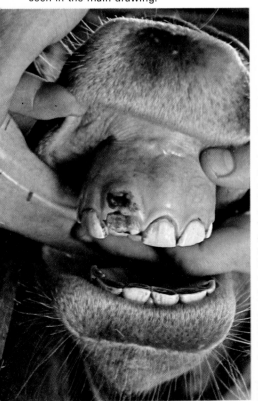

trachea

cartilage

epiglottis

vocal cord

NORMAL

PARALYZED ON LEFT

Left above The alimentary tract, showing its disposition in the abdomen (here in the mare), and the sequence of its parts. The small size of the stomach restricts the amount which can be ingested and the intake must be small but frequent. The stomach and most of the small intestine are chiefly in the left side and cannot be seen in the main drawing.

canine (present only in colts and geldings), and six cheek teeth (three premolars and three molars). A young horse has temporary teeth, which are replaced by the permanent teeth by the time it is five years old.

Ducts which discharge digestive juices from the parotid mandibular and sublingual salivary glands open into the mouth. The roof of the mouth is formed by the hard palate in front, which continues into the soft palate behind. The soft palate forms part of the pharynx where the air passages and digestive tract cross one another.

As a horse swallows, the food crosses the pharynx and enters the gullet or oesophagus, from where it is conveyed to the stomach and thence to the small intestines, large colon, small colon and rectum.

The alimentary tract, from the stomach to the rectum, together with the pancreas and liver (glands which contribute more digestive juices and bile) are contained in the abdominal cavity. This can be described as a large 'box', the sides of which are the diaphragm in front, the muscles below the spine forming the top, and the muscles of the 'belly', the bottom. The back part of the 'box' is closed by the pelvic outlet through which the rectum, urinary and reproductive tract reach the outside. The abdominal cavity also contains, in the female, the ovaries and the uterus; and in both male and female, the urinary organs, comprising the kidney, ureters and bladder.

The abdominal cavity is lined by the peritoneum and all the organs are suspended by reflections (mesenteries and lig-

The respiratory system. A large volume in the head is occupied by chambers which do not seem to have a respiratory function but do connect with the nasal cavity and are filled with air. The drawings on the left show the opening of the larynx into the pharynx; the nerve to the vocal cord on either side (usually the left) may become damaged due to overstretching or injury, resulting in the condition known as roaring or whistling, caused by vibration of the paralyzed vocal cord when the horse breathes in.

aments) of the peritoneum. A special free fold of the peritoneum is known as the omentum.

The anatomical peculiarities of the horse's digestive system compared with other mammals are:
(i) that the greatest volume of the tract is in the hind end, namely the caecum, and colon, where the major process of digesting fibre occurs by bacterial fermentation
(ii) the relatively small stomach
(iii) the absence of a gall bladder (probably associated with the need for a continual supply of bile in an animal which is a continuous feeder)

The Respiratory System

The respiratory system consists of the air passages of the head (nostrils to pharynx), the pharynx, larynx, trachea or windpipe, bronchi and lungs. The lungs are the two organs in which oxygen and carbon dioxide are exchanged between the blood and

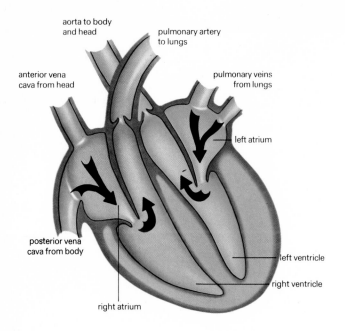

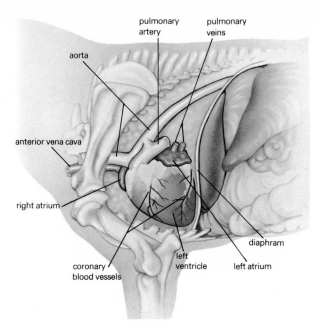

air. They are situated in the chest cavity known as the thorax, the walls (ribs and diaphragm) of which can expand or contract, thus allowing the lungs to enlarge or compress. The movements of the chest alternately draw in and expel air into and out of the lungs.

The anatomical features of the equine respiratory system which are of particular interest to horsemen are:

(i) the air sinuses of the head and the guttural pouches, which are large blind sacs connecting with the eustachian tubes of the ear and which may be the site of infection or bleeding.

(ii) the larynx, one side of which may become paralyzed and cause an obstruction to the inflow of air, thus resulting in whistling or roaring.

(iii) the minute endings of the airways in tubes, known as bronchioles, which connect with the air sacs (alveoli) in the lung. It is these structures which are involved in the condition of 'broken wind'.

The Heart and Vascular System

As in other mammals, the horse's heart consists of four chambers with four sets of valves. Racehorses, as might be expected, have hearts which are rather larger than the average; that of Eclipse weighed about 6·5 kg (14 lbs).

Blood is pumped by the heart into arteries which extend to all parts of the body, before returning to the heart in veins. Few people need to know the horse's vascular system in detail, but the following arteries and veins are worthy of note:

(i) The jugular vein that lies on either side of the neck, carries the blood from

The heart is situated between the lungs in the thoracic cavity. It is effectively a double muscular pump; the right side receives deoxygenated blood through the vena cavae from the body and pumps it to the lungs; the more muscular left side receives blood from the lungs (where the blood is oxygenated) and pumps it out through the aorta to begin its long circulation through the body.

the head and neck back to the heart. It is easily 'raised' by pressure in the lower part of the neck and may be used therefore for collecting blood samples or in the course of administering intravenous fluid therapy.

(ii) The aorta is the main artery leaving the heart, and it carries blood to all parts posterior to the chest. It runs along the roof of the chest and abdominal cavity, and in the latter it distributes a branch to the intestines, called the anterior mesenteric artery. It is this branch which may become blocked as a result of the activity of the parasite *Strongylus vulgaris*. This is one of the causes of colic.

Lymphatic System

The lymph system consists of a series of minute channels and venules which carry a relatively colourless fluid known as lymph, from the extremities and other parts of the body, back towards the heart where they discharge it into the blood stream. Along these channels are special glands or lymph nodes which filter bacteria and other matter from the lymph stream, thus purifying it. The lymph system is not noticeable except in such diseases as lymphangitis, or when the lymph

nodes become enlarged, as in strangles or other infectious conditions.

The Uro-Genital System

The horse, in common with other mammals, has two kidneys, whose function is to filter the blood and form urine. This passes to the bladder through the ureters and from there, the urine passes to the outside through the urethra. The urethra has a common exit from the body with the sexual tract, namely the vagina in the mare and the penis in the stallion. The genital organs of the mare consist of two ovaries and oviducts or fallopian tubes, the uterus, cervix, vagina and vulva.

The ovaries are responsible for producing the female sex cell, ie the egg or ovum. A filly is born with many thousands of eggs in her ovaries and no more form during her lifetime. However during times of sexual activity oestrus fluid follicles develop round one or more eggs and rupture to shed the egg into the fallopian tube. This is known as ovulation. The lining of the follicle bleeds and a 'yellow-body' is formed. The follicle, while it is developing, produces the hormone oestrogen, and the 'yellow-body', the hormone progesterone. If the ovary of a sexually mature filly is cut in half it will contain follicles and 'yellow bodies' in varying stages of development.

Right The urogenital system of the mare (top) and the stallion (bottom). In the mare the vagina, body of the uterus and bladder are shown here in section through the mid-line. The uterus and ovaries are suspended from the roof of the abdominal cavity on two folds of its lining (peritoneum) called the broad ligaments (not depicted here).

A stallion's sexual organs consist of two testes in which the spermatozoa are produced; collecting ducts (including the epididymis) which connect with the urethra after travelling in the spermatic cord with arteries and veins; the accessory glands comprising the prostate, vesicular seminales and bulbo-urethral, and the penis. The penis is housed in the prepuce or 'sheath', and the testes in the scrotum.

The Nervous System

The nervous system is composed of the central nervous system (CNS) and the peripheral nervous system (PNS). The CNS consists of the brain and spinal cord.

The PNS comprises the nerve trunks that leave the brain and others, which emerge from the spinal cord, together with those belonging to the special sympathetic nervous system.

The features of the equine nervous system are the relatively highly developed cerebellum, that part responsible for the control of movement; the long course of the spinal cord through the cervical region which makes this part susceptible to injury and to such nervous conditions as 'wobbler' disease; and the routes taken by the nerves running to the extremities of the fore and hind limbs. A knowledge of the latter can be used in the diagnosis of lameness, since they can be 'blocked' at various points by injecting a local anaesthetic around them, so as to desensitize the areas they supply.

The nervous system is something like a telephone exchange, in that it depends on the input and output of messages, to and from the centre. In using this analogy, the brain and spinal cord represent the exchange and its substations, and the nerve trunks are of two sorts, a) sensory, that is carrying messages to the CNS and b) motor, carrying messages from the CNS to the muscles and other endpoints where they produce activity or movement. The sensory nerves depend on endings which are sensitive to pain, pressure, heat, cold, etc, and which, when stimulated, convey these impressions to the brain where they are interpreted by reflex or voluntary action. The special sensory endings are those of smell, sight and hearing, mediated through the nose, eyes and ears.

The Endocrine (Hormonal) System

The endocrine system consists of a number of glands which secrete hormones. A hormone is a substance produced by a gland and transported in blood or lymph streams, to exert an action or cause an effect on another part or parts. For example, the pituitary gland, which is situated below the brain, produces a hormone known as follicle-stimulating hormone (FSH) the action of which is to stimulate follicles to develop in the ovary. Insulin is produced by cells in the pancreatic gland and is responsible for regulating the level of sugar in the blood. Cortisone is secreted by the adrenal cortex and has widespread effects on many metabolic functions of the body. The endocrine glands (and the hormones they produce) are as follows:

(a) anterior pituitary – follicle stimulating hormone (FSH), luteinizing hormone (LH), prolactin, growth, thyroid stimulating hormone
(b) posterior pituitary – oxytocin, vasopressin
(c) thyroid – thyroxine
(d) pancreas – insulin
(e) adrenal cortex – cortisone
(f) adrenal medulla – adrenalin
(g) ovary – oestrogen, progesterone
(h) testes – testosterone
(i) uterus – prostaglandin

The Skin

The skin is composed of three layers, an outer cellular or epithelial layer which is capable of replacing itself as wear and tear erode the outer surface; a sub-epithelial layer which nourishes the outer layer and in which pain endings and other sensitive structures are found; and the sub-dermal layer which is continuous with the sub-epithelial layer and binds the skin to the underlying bone or muscle. The hair follicles occur in the sub-dermal layer. The skin contains sweat glands and other glands which secrete an oil substance known as sebum.

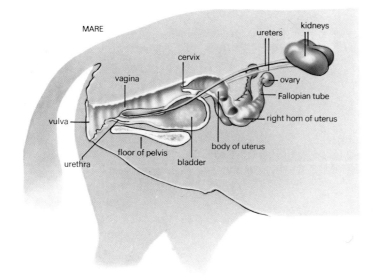

MARE

kidneys
ureters
cervix
vagina
ovary
Fallopian tube
vulva
right horn of uterus
body of uterus
floor of pelvis
bladder
urethra

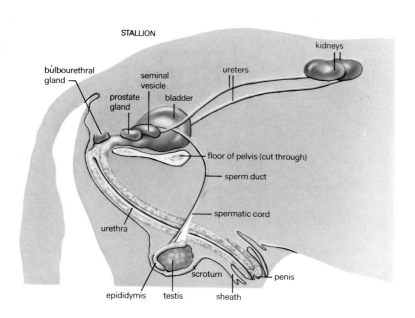

STALLION

kidneys
bulbourethral gland
seminal vesicle
ureters
prostate gland
bladder
floor of pelvis (cut through)
sperm duct
spermatic cord
urethra
epididymis   testis
scrotum   penis
sheath

The Mind of the Horse

A COMMON failing among animal-lovers is the tendency to regard the animal species in human terms of intelligence, motivation and similar matters. The dog, possibly the earliest of the animals domesticated by man, is the extreme example of 'humanization' being regarded by a large number of owners in the same light as a human child and endowed by them with human intelligence and imagination which it cannot possibly possess. Many of the arguments advanced by anti-hunting factions are based on a similarly false premise – the reactions of the quarry being related to those of the human in the unlikely eventuality of the latter being placed in the same situation.

The horse may not suffer 'humanization' to quite the same degree but without doubt he is popularly, and quite wrongly, thought to be an animal of high intelligence. The performances of which he is capable are all too often considered as manifestations of that quality rather than as products of a training system based on repetition, which results in a variety of conditioned reflexes. Much of the argument may depend upon the interpretation of the word 'intelligence', but what is certainly beyond doubt is that animal intelligence cannot be equated with the human quality.

In fact, the brain of the horse is very small in relation to his size, smaller indeed – although the point is hardly relevant – than that of the turtle. In general terms and at the risk of over-simplification, it can be said that the horse is a creature of instinct, not of reason, which is a human attribute, since its mentality is based upon instincts

When trying to understand a horse don't fall into the trap of interpreting its behaviour in human terms. It would be anthropomorphic, and wrong, to guess that because this horse looks to be laughing it is showing amusement.

developed in the wild state as a means of survival against the natural hazards of the environment and the activities of predatory carnivores, foremost of which has been man himself.

The horse is an herbivorous animal and his defensive mechanisms – that is the physical ability to move swiftly away from the threat of attack and the possession of highly-developed senses – are in the main directed towards flight as a means of preservation. Any study of the horse personality, relevant to the animal's training, must take these factors into account, whilst discounting the fact that in the domestic state the original stimuli have long been absent.

The existence of a flight-orientated defence explains the highly-strung and excitable nature of the horse, although the degree of excitability and nervousness displayed naturally varies according to the individual. In most cases the common, 'cold-blood' horse, slower in his reactions, will be a notably less excitable subject than the highly-bred 'warm-blood' typified by the Thoroughbred and the Arabian. In all cases, however, the feeding of the horse exerts an important influence. A high protein diet will have the effect of making him more prone to becoming excited and more likely to indulge in defiance of his trainer's or rider's wishes. For this reason much attention has to be paid to the horse's diet, the consumption of heating, or energizing, foods being balanced by a corresponding expenditure of energy through physical exercise.

The prime considerations of the horse trainer, apart from the natural tendency in his pupil to be nervous and excitable as a result of the instinctive, self-preservative, flight reaction, will be concerned with the horse's deeply-rooted herd instinct in which the provision of security is implicit and which involves, also, an acceptance of discipline and a degree of submission.

The herd instinct is continually present in the horse, who will always seek to return to or to remain with companions of his own kind. In a domestic state, horses are frequently kept singly out of necessity, but it is noticeable that such horses, lacking the security which membership of a group provides, will often develop peculiar and sometimes neurotic traits of behaviour which do not occur where a number of horses live together, such as in a military troop, a riding school or a racing stable. It is not impossible to keep a horse on its own but, like an only child, it will be more inclined to pose problems. The child can make friends with others of his own age at school and is able to invite them to his own home or to go and play with them at theirs. No such possibilities are open to the horse. A dog is quite content with human companionship and it would be possible for a horse to be similarly conditioned – but only if his owner was able to share his stable or devote most of the day to romping in the field with him, proceedings which are beyond the capacity of the most dedicated of horse-owners. The company of other horses, simulating the herd condition, causes excitement in most horses but in

Underlying many aspects of the behaviour of the horse are two basic characteristics on which its survival in the wild depends – a powerful herd instinct and the ability to run quickly from trouble. *above*: Alerted by potential danger, these horses are ready to run; any apprehension quickly spreads through the herd. *below right*: The herd instinct; there is safety in numbers, and the tendency for one horse to follow another keeps the group together. *above right*: Racing is just one of the activities which takes advantage of the herd instinct; even loose horses will stay with the field because it represents, if only temporarily, their herd.

the case of the 'only' horse, the reaction may well be accentuated to an unacceptable level.

It is possible for the herd instinct to be exploited in a variety of ways, the most obvious being in the sport of racing which, in a sense, is a simulation of the herd in flight. It is exploited when the young horse is introduced to the hunting field. In order to remain with or return to the herd the youngster will frequently jump fences which would not have been countenanced in cold blood. In this last instance the element of excitement caused by the presence of other animals galloping and jumping is also, of course, a contributory factor. Early jumping lessons similarly take advantage of the instinct. A young horse will usually jump a fence going towards his companions when he might very well refuse if asked to jump in the opposite direction.

On the other hand the natural instinct can be subdued by training, as is shown when a horse leaves the collecting ring – and thus his temporary herd – to jump the fences in a show-jumping arena on his own. But even in this instance, courses are frequently planned to take account of the 'gravitational pull' of the collecting ring. A wise course-builder begins his course with one or two comparatively easy fences, siting the big, difficult ones in such a position that the horse jumps towards the collecting ring.

The stable exerts a profound influence on the horse, to whom it represents security and a source of food.

Very closely connected with the herd instinct is the sense of security which the horse finds in being a member of a herd. This is a factor not always sufficiently appreciated but it is a very relevant one.

In the domestic state it is not possible to simulate the wild herd condition, nor indeed is it necessary, but it is advisable, for reasons already given, to keep horses in company with their own kind. For the domestic horse the centre of his security is his stable and immediate surroundings and, ideally, the presence of another horse. It is not really so much different in the human condition where security is found in the home.

The influence of the stable is a very strong one, largely because of its association with food, one of the horse's major preoccupations. Because of its influence it would be unwise, for instance, to site a training area in close proximity to the horse's box. Such an arrangement would ensure a lack of concentration on the work in hand, as the horse would be more concerned with returning to his stable and the prospect of food. In consequence, he would continually veer towards it.

Although stallions may occasionally fight, horses are basically non-aggressive and are probably relatively intolerant of pain.

Like the herd aspect, the stable can be used to advantage. Every horseman knows how a horse perks up and quickens the stride when turned for home after a morning's exercise. His mind is then occupied with thoughts of food and in that state he is less likely to take notice of road hazards or other obstacles which might have worried him on the way out. In introducing young horses to traffic the wise horseman will, therefore, choose a quiet route away from the stable, returning to it by a busier one when the horse's attention is distracted from the vehicles by the thought of home and food.

If a horse is to be a calm and therefore receptive individual, security is an essential factor in his life. Loss of security, as can happen when a horse is sold on to a new home, can produce a variety of reactions. Uneasy and unsure of his new surroundings, a formerly well-mannered horse may make difficulties about leaving his new stable, or, once he has been persuaded to make a move, may nap persistently in his efforts to return home.

A recent incident highlights the effects that can be caused by a loss of security. A horse was bought from a town environment and moved by his new owner to the country. In the town the stable-yard and exercise ring were surrounded by high-rise buildings and, on one side, a railway station. When the horse was ridden out, the route to the nearest park was on a main road in a built-up area with a heavy traffic density. Frequently, the exercise was carried out on such roads without going to the park. The horse had grown to accept this environment and the traffic and the noise held no fears for him.

His new home was deep in the country. A place of tranquillity with wide, open skies, broad fields and little-used country lanes. It was all too much for the town-boy who developed a fairly violent form of equine *agoraphobia*. Put out for an hour or two in a paddock with an old, steady horse he galloped about wildly, injured himself and then, dripping with sweat and wild-eyed, jumped the gate and returned to his stable (a port of temporary security in the storm) standing outside, shivering with fear. Ridden out on lanes encompassed by hedges instead of tall buildings, he shied violently at every rustling leaf, whilst the approach of a bicycle reduced him to a point of near-hysteria. On one occasion he reacted so violently to a twig lying on the road that he lost his footing and came down. His new owner, by the exercise of much patient understanding, finally won his trust and solved the problem, but it took nearly two months to do so.

The mention of trust leads to another factor arising directly from the herd condition. In the wild state the herd was controlled and led by a dominant stallion who exerted discipline over the members of the herd and upon whose sagacity their safety depended.

In the domestic state the need for leadership still remains. Horses at grass very soon establish a pecking order and geldings will frequently cut out one or two

mares from the group, protecting them in just the same way as a stallion – even displaying such 'entire' characteristics as marking out a territory by droppings and urination. Fortunately horses appear to accept the dominance of man in substitution for the herd leader and properly handled will come to repose a great trust in their two-legged leader, on whom their well-being depends. Nonetheless, they will, as they would have done in the herd condition, test the authority of the leader. Resistances made by the horse in training are prime examples of this testing and quite natural. Met with quiet firmness they are usually easily enough overcome, but if the horse is once allowed to succeed in a resistance, he will quickly enough take advantage of the situation, thereafter attempting to reverse the roles of leader and follower.

Those other problems, of nervousness and excitement, are forever with the horse trainer. The highly-strung nature of the horse arises from the flight instinct and a common manifestation of it is the tendency towards shying at seemingly insignificant objects, while smells and sudden noises will give rise to similar reactions. A shy may, indeed, go so far as a buck or two, which is just another defensive reaction. Shying, if it can never be entirely eradicated, can be reduced to a minimum by common-sense treatment – that is as long as it is not the result of defective eyesight. If the horse can draw confidence from his rider's firm seat and encouraging voice, or if he can be persuaded to smell or touch the offending article, his fear will be removed, and if these practices are carried out continually the incidence of shying will decrease. On the other hand punishment given for such natural lapses only confirms the fear in the horse's mind and makes him even more nervous.

Accepting the premise of the horse as a non-aggressive animal, it is reasonable to assume a greater sensitivity to pain and a lower pain tolerance than animals of an opposite nature, like the dog. Stallions, will, of course, fight each other to establish their ascendancy, but very few horses, whether stallions or not, will attack a man. Instinctively the horse flees from pain or the threat of it. Indeed, without this innate sensitivity, it would be difficult for the human to control and train so large and powerful an animal. As an example, a tap with a long whip on the horse's flank will cause him to move his quarters away; later, when a single leg is applied, the quarters will be shifted in the same manner. The reaction to the bit, however, when it is applied in moments of excitement is somewhat different, if just as logical. Horsemen, quite incorrectly, talk of horses 'fighting' the bit. In fact, they do just the opposite. As usual they are running away from the discomfort imposed and the harder the rider pulls, the more urgent becomes the need to escape from the pain.

Overt resistance, apart from the early 'testing' of the leader's authority which, as explained, is easily enough eliminated, is rare in horses unless they become confused or excited, or when the fear of greater discomfort assumes the ascendancy. Occasionally, a horse may seem to act contrary to his nature, particularly at feed times, when he may show signs of aggression by laying back his ears and even kicking out behind. It is possible that the horse at these moments is suffering from what may be termed a 'reversion'.

Not comprehending that the human bringing the food has no interest in it, he behaves as he would if being fed outside in company with others. There he would threaten another horse to keep it away from his food bowl. More often the horse is expressing anxiety and impatience by kicking, since food is both of great importance and a source of excitement to him.

The senses of the horse, highly developed in accord with the basic instincts, are integral to the personality and relevant to the behavioural pattern. The sense of taste acts in much the same way as in all sensate beings, but those of sight and, to a degree, of hearing are peculiar to the species.

The eyes, set more or less on either side of the head, do not, in general, focus together on objects directly to the front, but they do allow very considerable lateral vision. Furthermore, when the head is raised vision to the rear is made possible. This all-round vision is part of the protective equipment but is not particularly helpful when jumping – an exercise that may seem entirely natural to the human, but is actually unnatural to the horse. Given sufficient freedom of the head, both eyes are able to see a fence at about a distance of 13·5 m (15 yds). 1·2 m (4 ft) from the fence, the lower part of the head makes the simultaneous use of two eyes impossible and necessitates a tilting of the whole head for one eye alone to see the fence. It is quite possible, therefore, for a horse to be forced to jump virtually blind unless the rider allows adequate freedom to the head and neck.

Hearing in the horse is acute, since the head is rather like a sound-box. The ears, which are exceptionally mobile, can be erected and directed at will towards a sound. Indeed, the horse is very responsive to sound, particularly to the tones employed by the human voice. The sense of smell is equally acute and there was much good sense in the old horseman's practice of rubbing the hands with an aromatic fluid. Without doubt the horse easily perceives the smell of fear given off by the nervous human and reacts accordingly. Similarly the smell of blood and death is quickly picked up and there are numerous instances of horses displaying extreme agitation when in the vicinity of an abattoir.

Touch would seem to have some significance also. Horses will gain assurance from touching objects laid on the ground with a hoof and they will frequently when smelling an object, touch it with the nose.

Lastly, there is sufficient evidence to assume the existence of a sixth animal sense. Horses are certainly sensitive to atmosphere and are able to assess the mood of the rider, becoming to some extent the mirror of the men or women who sit on

Only by understanding how the working of the horse's mind dictates its actions and influences its responses can the trainer achieve such peaks of performance as this.

them. Certainly, the horse has the ability to perceive instantly such factors as timidity or hesitation in the human, as well as confidence and courage. With a skilled trainer it is possible for a very close rapport to be achieved that may nearly approach telepathy.

In training much use is made of the prodigiously retentive memory of the horse. In fact this is a two-edged sword in the hands of the trainer, since the horse remembers both good and bad experiences, preserving forever in the memory bank the trainer's mistakes as well as his correct actions.

The horse is not able to connect related happenings separated by a period of time, but he does have the power to associate cause and effect not so separated. If something is done well and he is immediately rewarded, the action is associated in his mind with a pleasurable experience which he remembers when called on to repeat the action at a later date. Conversely, should he kick and receive immediate retribution for his sin, he associates the action of kicking with an unpleasant and possibly painful experience and is likely to desist from repeating the experiment thereafter. But the horse cannot understand delayed punishment or reward. If he is hit five minutes after a disobedience, it is impossible for him to relate the punishment to the crime and he will only become resentful at unjust treatment that he cannot understand.

In studies of the horse instances are often quoted implying a perception and ability that is out of the ordinary. Cases of circus horses trained to count or to perform various movements without the trainer seeming to give any sort of command are cases in point. There is, of course, nothing out of the ordinary or in any sense mystical about such performances; they are merely the products of skilful training. It is true that not all horses are suitable subjects for this type of work, some being less receptive than others, but many are quite capable of producing performances at this level, so long as the trainer is sufficiently patient and skilled. The horse is taught by the usual system of repetition and reward and gradually it is possible to reduce the strength of the command until the horse will obey barely perceptible movements on the part of the trainer. The same thing occurs in the training of the riding horse. In the early stages the rider had to exaggerate his aids in order to give his message clearly to the horse. As the training progresses the aids become less noticeable until in the schooled horse they may amount to no more than a flexing of the calf muscle or a minute tensioning of a finger on the rein.

In training horses much emphasis is very properly given to the physical development, involving the build-up and suppling of the muscles. The mental development is, however, just as important; the small mind, with all its limitations, is developed in terms of the limited periods of concentration of which it is capable in just the same gradual way as the body.

Principles of Feeding

THERE are three basic rules governing the correct feeding of horses:

    (i) feed in small quantities and often
    (ii) do not work hard immediately after a full meal
    (iii) provide plenty of water

These are founded on the principle of following as closely as possible, the feeding habits of the horse in its natural state, which, obviously, will be those most suited to its digestive system.

(i) Feed in small quantities and often

The horse is a herbivore or grazing animal, and when out at pasture, grazes more or less all the time. Apart from occasional slops the digestive apparatus will be having small quantities of food passed through to it from the stomach fairly continuously.

It is this kind of leisurely feeding to which the horse's digestion is adapted. Unlike carnivores, the horse has a small stomach not designed for coping with big meals spaced at long intervals. It has, however, capacious bowels which accommodate its food during the process of slow digestion.

When a horse eats, as soon as its stomach is about two-thirds full (which is when it is working best), the food begins to pass through into the bowels, and thereafter continues to do so at the same rate it is being taken in at the mouth.

Horses that are in work, as well as their bulk food – hay or grass – need regular, palatable short, or 'concentrate' feeds. If these are too large, they will distend the stomach, upset the natural balance of digestion and eventually cause acute indigestion, or colic. Colic is not only very painful, but can also be dangerous if not dealt with knowledgeably.

Between 1·3 and 1·8 kg (3 and 4 lbs) of concentrates, such as oats, mixed with a small amount of bran or chaff, is as much as the horse can digest properly in one feed. If one of the many brands of cubes are being fed, rather more can be given: up to 2·7 kg (6 lbs), because the cubes have a high fibre content and are generally eaten more slowly. Therefore when horses need to be given extra concentrates, they should be given as an extra feed, not by enlarging the established regular ones.

Hay and grass are 'bulk' foods, and are always eaten slowly, so they do not overload the stomach. The only exception to this is when horses are first turned out on to lush spring grass, when they may eat too much, too quickly.

(ii) Do not work hard immediately after a full meal

The physical reason for this rule is that when a horse has just eaten a concentrate feed, its stomach and bowels are actually bigger than before. This means they are taking up more room, distending the belly not only outwards and sideways, but also forwards on to the diaphragm, which in turn presses on the lungs. Any pressure on the lungs means that they cannot expand and contract properly, and therefore hard work when the belly is still distended will cause distress and laboured breathing. A horse should have its concentrate feed one hour before it is asked to do any serious work such as galloping, jumping, schooling, etc. The operative words of this rule are 'hard work' – it will not harm a horse to be taken out for a quiet hack half-an-hour

Grass, the natural food of all horses and ponies in the wild state, will need to be supplemented, especially during the winter, bearing in mind his type, his state of health and what work he does.

after its feed; but the longer it can be given for digestion, the better.

(iii) Always provide plenty of clean water

The old saying 'water before feeding' is quite correct, but it does not mean that this is the only time horses should be allowed to drink. If water is always available, a horse will never drink too much, although naturally it is sensible, when coming in from work, to give it the opportunity to drink before putting a feed in the manger. It does not harm a horse to take an occasional sip from the bucket while feeding, nor will it harm to let it have short drinks at streams or rivers when out on a long ride. Too much water before very hard work, such as a race, or a cross-country course, will slow a horse down, but if a horse is never kept short of water, it will seldom develop the kind of thirst that forces it to drink too much.

A hot, tired horse will naturally want to drink a lot, and should be allowed to do so, but give it a hay-net to pull at, and a rest,

before giving a short feed.

In ordinary weather, water is seldom too cold, but in frosty weather, it is as well to take the chill off it before offering it to horses coming in hot from work. Standing the full buckets in a warm tack room will do this satisfactorily.

Horses are fastidious drinkers. They do not relish water which has become contaminated by dirt; stale water; or water from buckets that have become slimy. They also prefer, and it is better for them, genuinely fresh water to the chlorinated type prevalent in towns and cities. Rainwater collected in water butts or tanks, from down-pipes, is much appreciated.

Of the three feeding rules, 'feed in small quantities and often' needs to be considered in more detail.

How Much to Feed

The exact ration to give a particular horse doing particular work can only be learnt from experience. As a guide, however, it can be taken that the total amount of food given to the domesticated horse per day should approximate in weight to the amount it would get through in 24 hours if it were at liberty.

Taking a horse of 15 h.h. as an example, that weight would be 11·5 kg (26 lbs). For larger or smaller animals, add or subtract 1 kg (2 lbs) for every 5 cm (2 in) of height. A horse at pasture would eat this total weight in grass alone, but with the working horse it must be divided between bulk, and concentrates, or energy producing foods. Concentrates are fed according to the work expected. The difference in weight must be made up in bulk – hay, or, if partly out at grass, hay and grass.

If a 15 h.h. horse in full work is getting 5·5 kg (12 lbs) of concentrates, it will need 6·5 kg (14 lbs) of bulk. If doing lighter work and therefore getting less concentrates, perhaps 3·5 kg (8 lbs), it will need 8·5 kg (18 lbs) of hay. If doing no work, so concentrates have been cut down, or right out, hay can be given almost ad lib.

Because horses are individuals, variations from the strict weight-for-height guide will sometimes be necessary: overfat horses need to diet, while those in poor condition need as much bulk as they will eat. It is, however, a sound working hypothesis.

When to Feed

Horses that are stabled and working need feeds at 7–7.30 am, mid-day, 4–4.30 pm and in the evening. Once times have been established, they should be consistently adhered to so far as is possible, particularly for the early morning and the evening feeds. There will obviously be days when a horse is working through its usual feeding time, (see 'Management of the Stabled Horse' for making necessary changes) but they are creatures of habit and will soon learn when to expect their feeds.

The quantity of each feed, both of concentrate and bulk, should increase towards the end of the day, with the most concen-

Above Horses at grass must have access to plenty of fresh water, although baths do not make ideal containers.
Below Every animal differs in the amount of food it needs, so each horse requires individual feeding. Careful measuring of concentrates, like these nuts, is necessary to avoid over- or under-feeding.

trates given in the last feed, and the biggest hay-net at night. A horse does not sleep for six to eight consecutive hours as we do, but rests and feeds intermittently. If it runs out of hay too early in the night, it will probably start eating its bed, and may also, through boredom, acquire a few stable vices such as wind-sucking or crib-biting. Unless a horse is grossly overfat, it does no harm to fill the last hay-net extra full.

What to Feed

So as to maintain the energy and physical well-being necessary for a horse to carry out the work expected of it, its diet should supply a correct balance of:

Protein: essential to the body's need. A diet without protein would cause wastage and death.

Fats, starches, and sugars: energy and heat producing
Salts: a dietary necessity
Water: contained in all foods, even those thought of as 'dry', varying from 10 per cent in most grains to 90 per cent in roots
Fibrous or woody substances: give bulk and help digestion; found in all foods, but particularly in hay
Vitamins: essential to horses

The concentrate food providing the best dietary balance for the horse is oats.

Oats

Oats contain all the necessary dietary elements in such balance that a horse can consume a large quantity without upsetting its digestion. Oats should be fed bruised rather than whole, and the amount fed must always depend on the work done or asked for – the energy to be expended, and replaced. With the riding horse, the amount should also relate to temperament, and the capabilities of its rider, as oats can have an alarmingly exhilarating effect on some horses. For this reason children's ponies should be fed no oats, or fed them very judiciously.

Barley

Although universally not so generally used as it might be, barley falls very little short in nutritional value and dietary balance, to oats. It actually contains a slightly higher proportion of fats and starches and nitrogenous elements, but a little less salts and fibre. Horses do not tend to 'hot up' so much on barley as on oats. It should be fed bruised, or 'flaked' when used as a staple feed; but it can also be fed boiled, when whole kernels should be used. Barley is an excellent feed for young stock, outwintered horses, and horses needing to put on condition.

Maize

Maize is a much less fibrous grain than oats, or barley, and is somewhat lacking in salts; but it does contain a high proportion of starches, fats and sugars. If fed with other grains, or with cubes, it makes a good 'heating' food for winter. It is also palatable, and is useful added to feeds to encourage shy feeders.

Wheat

As wheat is generally in such demand for human consumption, the only form in which it is fed to horses nowadays is as bran.

Bran

Bran is a by-product of wheat after the flour has been taken out by milling. It has little nutritive value of its own, as scientific milling removes most of the nutritious part, i.e. flour, although good bran still contains vitamins B and E. Bran is nevertheless a useful dietary additive; it makes the horse eat more slowly and chew properly; it increases bulk, and it helps regulate the bowels. Fed damp, it is a mild laxative; if the droppings become too loose, bran fed dry will help to bring them back to normal. It is also much used as a mash and as such, is palatable and easy to digest, and excellent for horses coming in tired after a hard day's work. Molasses (black treacle) added to a bran mash make it extra palatable, as well as being good for the digestion.

Peas and beans

Both are very nutritious, containing a high proportion of flesh producing elements; but they should be fed in small quantities, as they are very 'heating'. Because of this, they should only be given to horses in very hard work, or outwintering in severe conditions.

A mare is fed concentrates in a carefully placed portable manger. Care must be taken to avoid wasting expensive food and ensure that each horse receives its proper ration.

Linseed

Linseed contains a large proportion of fat-forming elements and is much used in preparing horses for show, and 'putting a bloom' on their coats. It is fed by boiling the seeds, and then simmering until a jelly-like substance is formed, which is best done in the slow oven of a cooker, overnight. This linseed jelly, mixed with bran and cereal, makes an excellent feed for a horse that needs fattening, but has to be fed daily for about a fortnight before its benefits will become apparent. If rather a lot of water is used, there will be some over when the jelly has formed; this is also very nutritious and can be used to make a bran mash.

Sugar beet pulp nuts

These must be soaked before feeding as they absorb a lot of water. They are good fed as a 'change', or mixed with usual rations, but not as a staple diet on their own.

Horse cubes

There are many brands of horse and pony cubes available on the market today. The best are very good and comprise a compound of all the ingredients necessary for a balanced diet. They include vitamins and minerals, many of which are nowadays lacking in grains and hay grown on land that is artificially fertilized. If the content analysis (which should be printed on the outside of the cube bags) is satisfactory, and horses are fed according to the manufacturers' instructions, there are many advantages in feeding a cube diet. The

product is guaranteed to be always the same; they are easily handled; feeds need no mixing, and it should not be necessary to feed vitamin or mineral additives. It is however best to mix a little bran with the cubes, as an aid to digestion. Cubes are considerably dehydrated and swell when wet, so horses fed on them will drink more. Because cubes all have a fairly high fibre content, horses tend to eat them more slowly than grains, and so slightly less hay is needed.

Many cubes are available in different grades; from ordinary cubes for horses and ponies doing light work or general hacking, to high protein cubes for racehorses and bloodstock, and specially nutritious ones for brood mares and youngsters.

Carrots, swedes and turnips

All horses enjoy carrots, which should be given sliced, mixed with a feed. Swedes and turnips should be fed whole; in the manger, or thrown out into the field. Cut-up apples or apple peelings, also make an appetizing addition to a feed.

Gruel

Very tired horses can be given gruel on first coming in to the stable. It is made by putting a double handful of oatmeal into a bucket, pouring on boiling water and stirring well. It is fed when cool, and should be thin enough for a horse to drink easily.

Hay

There are four main kinds of hay: timothy, clover, mixed and meadow.

The stalks of timothy hay are fairly coarse and woody, but it is very nutritious. Old horses however may find softer hays easier to chew. Clover hay is excellent when well-made, but if not, can be heavy, and quickly go mouldy. Mixed hay is that taken off specially seeded pasture, and contains many mixed grasses and clovers. It is the most usual hay, and if well-made, is probably the best for horses of all ages. Meadow hay is hay taken from permanent pastures. It can be very good, as many old pastures contain herbs and flowers not normally found in new leys; but it can be less good, if taken from rough land or water meadows liable to flood. It is usually lighter and softer than timothy or mixed hay; if taken from good upland pasture it should smell particularly sweet.

Mouldy or musty hay should never be fed. A bale of good hay should fall apart when the string is cut (swathes of hay will stay together in 'slices'), and it should not emit a cloud of dust, nor show dark, moist patches, nor smell musty.

Oat straw

Oat straw, as well as hay, can be used as 'chaff', or 'chop', which is excellent to add to concentrate feeds to ensure proper mastication and to add bulk. In itself, it is quite appetizing to horses, which is one of the disadvantages of using it for bedding.

It is important to remember that any basic change in a horse's diet, such as changing from grains to cube feeding, or vice-versa, must be done gradually.

Management of the Stabled Horse

Implements hang tidily on the wall in this well-appointed stable yard. All the horses can readily see what is going on, an important factor in preventing boredom.

STABLED horses spend the greater proportion of their lives in stables.

This obvious fact is nevertheless one which everyone concerned with the management of stabled horses should keep constantly in mind. Horses are by nature free-roaming, gregarious animals and it is basically unnatural for them to live perpetually in a state of semi-confinement. To keep stabled horses in good heart, as well as good health, therefore, it is not quite enough just to know how, when and with what to feed them. If they are to adjust satisfactorily to an artificial, man-imposed environment, they must do so mentally as well as physically and whatever opinion we have of the horse's intelligence, it cannot be denied that he has a mind as well as a body. From this it follows that what he needs from his human master is not only physical care, but also a good deal of understanding of the character needs of horses in general.

Horses, like ourselves, can suffer from boredom, and this is particularly true of stabled horses, cut off from the free companionship of the herd. Also like ourselves, horses are individuals; some are highly-strung, some are placid; some are more, or less, intelligent. Unlike ourselves, however, all horses are by nature nervous and suspicious of anything new or strange, of sudden movements, and of loud harsh voices. In the wild, their reaction to fear and suspicion is flight, but stabled horses that are made nervous by rough grooms shouting at them, bullying them, or hitting them with pitchfork handles to move them over, have no escape. Instead they are forced into the reaction of trying to defend themselves, which, if the rough handler is not speedily replaced, will result in them becoming permanently nervous, frightened, and difficult to handle. All horses, but perhaps stabled ones in particular, should be handled with what can best be summarized as firm kindliness.

The Stable

The stabled horse needs space, air, and light. A loose box or stable should be big enough for him to move around it freely; to lie down, roll and get up again without danger of casting himself (getting so close to a wall that he cannot roll himself free). 3·5 m × 3·5 m (12 ft × 12 ft) is ideal; 3·5 m × 3 m (12 ft × 10 ft) is sufficient, 3 m × 3 m (10 ft × 10 ft) is enough for a pony. Anything bigger is unnecessary (except for a foaling box), but a nice bonus for the horse.

A horse needs air; those kept in stuffy stables are more liable to colds and bronchial troubles. And he needs light, for it is not good for the eyes of any diurnal outdoor animal to be too long in unnatural darkness; that is darkness other than that of night.

In the past, stables were often as elaborately built as the houses of the horses' owners. They would have intricately laid brick flooring sloping gently to a centre drain grating; tiles round the mangers; solid wooden doors and partitions with, often, decorative ironwork above them; a warm tack room at one end of the stable block; a feed room at the other, and a loft above with a trap door through which the hay could be dropped. Nowadays, unless one has been fortunate enough to inherit such a horse-palace, stables mostly consist of one or two, or a series, of wooden loose boxes sited conveniently to the owner's or the groom's house. In some countries, the custom is to build individual boxes inside a big barn or shed; the boxes running on either side of a centre passageway which has a door, usually, at either end. In cold climates, this method has many advantages and it could surely be adopted more generally, for there must be many existing big barns which lend themselves to this sort of conversion.

Whether a loose-box is free-standing or within a stable building or barn, it will need a manger for concentrate feeds, a hay-rack, or a ring to which to attach a hay-net, and a tie ring (which could be the same one as used for the hay-net), for tying the horse when grooming. Water can be supplied through automatic drinking bowls, which horses soon learn the trick of working, or in buckets. If buckets are used they should be a heavy type that are not easy to tip over, and should be placed in a corner, held in position with a cross-piece of wood. Buckets must be kept clean. With constant drinking during which the horse's saliva mixes with the water, a slime will form on the inside of the buckets if they are not regularly scrubbed out.

Ideally the bottom of the manger should not be less than 60 cm (2 ft) from the ground, although the actual height will depend on the animals. Small ponies will clearly not be able to reach into mangers set high for big horses. Some people like to have mangers at ground level, to comply with the theory that a horse normally eats with its head down. There is nothing against this, except that the mangers are liable to get dirty as bedding and droppings get pushed into them. The easiest type to keep clean are removable ones, set into corner holders. They can be simply taken out and washed after each feed. It is important to keep mangers clean – just as we do not like eating off dirty dishes, a horse finds his meal more appetizing if it is not thrown into a manger where clotted bits of stale food are sticking to the sides and bottom. It is also better for him to eat from a clean manger: stale food can ferment and become unwholesome. If a horse does not eat the whole of a feed, it should be taken out of the manger before the next one.

The easiest hay-racks both for the horse and the handler are curving triangular ones set in a corner. The base of the rack should be about 120 cm (4 ft) from the ground, so there is no danger of the horse getting caught under it as he gets up. If racks are placed too high, however, any dust or loose seeds in the hay tend to fall into the horse's eyes as he eats. Hay-net and tie rings should be bolted through a wall batten, at about the height of a man's shoulder from the ground. If they are higher, short people will find it difficult to reach up to them with a heavy hay-net. Hay-nets should always be tied with a slip-knot, the draw-string of the net either threaded back through itself, pulled tight and then slip-knotted, or threaded through one of the loops of the net. This is to prevent the net dropping too low as the hay is eaten, at which point the horse could get his foot caught in it.

Boxes in stable buildings or barns will be ventilated by the windows and doors of the building, so that the doors to the individual boxes can be in one piece. Free-standing boxes should have doors in two halves, the bottom half having two bolts, on the outside, at the top and bottom. For the groom or handler, who is nearly always carrying something, it is a help if the bottom bolt slips easily and can be opened with the foot. The top half of the door should be kept hooked back, and only closed on the rare occasions when there may be a hurricane, or a blizzard, or sleet driving directly into the box. This is not only because horses need the fresh air; just as important, they need to be able to look out, to see their neighbours and to watch what's going on in the yard. What are called stable vices – crib-biting, wind-sucking and weaving – are neurotic in origin, and generally start because a horse has nothing to do, or to look at and is bored. Solitary confinement will produce neuroses in both man and beast, particularly in such naturally gregarious animals as horses.

Boxes should have windows, part of which can open, although this is not necessary if the boxes are made with roof ventilation. The windows should have bars or netting on the inside, so that they cannot be broken by the horse or by carelessly handled tools when mucking out the stable. Light switches should be situated either outside the box, or concealed and inset so that only a finger can reach in and operate them; horses learn quite quickly how to work switches!

The flooring of boxes should not be too smooth. Special 'stable bricks' are ideal but expensive, and roughened concrete is quite satisfactory. The floor should slope slightly towards the front of the box, preferably towards the corner away from the door, where a small hole can lead out into a draining gully. Covered drains inside boxes are difficult to keep clean.

On free-standing boxes, the roof should have an overhang; that is, it should slope out at least 1 m (3 ft) beyond the front of the box, so that in rainy weather horses can look out and grooms can go from box to box without getting wet.

Bedding

It is not good for a horse to stand for any length of time on bare concrete or bricks. A stabled horse needs bedding in the box both by night and by day, although with straw bedding there is a difference between

The stabled horse must be mucked out thoroughly at least once a day and the bed kept neat and clean.

the night and day bed.

Wheat straw is the best bedding, but it is often the most difficult to get and the most expensive. Oat straw can be too palatable, and many horses will eat it. Barley straw tends to be prickly and so irritates a horse's skin, although if it is combined straw, the prickly awns are usually missing, and it makes good bedding.

A straw bed must be deep. It is false economy to lay a thin bed, as it absorbs much less moisture, and much more has to be removed. That apart, the point of a deep night bed is to encourage the horse to lie down. If the bed is too thin, parts of his body may be resting on the bare flooring, which can soon lead to capped hocks and elbows. Moreover, he may find it difficult to get up if the floor has become slippery and has not sufficient cover on which to get a grip. Straw should be tossed well as it is put down, and banked up round the sides of the box and at the inside of the door. The day bed is made by sweeping and airing the floor and replacing what clean straw is left after mucking out. Fresh straw is then added in the evening for the deep, banked up, night bed.

Sawdust makes a comfortable bed, and if there is a local sawmill, a cheap one as well. It needs to be laid thickly. Wet patches and droppings should be lifted and removed frequently, and the whole bed raked over daily. It can be combined with shavings, in which case the sawdust should form the bottom layer of the bed.

Peat moss can also be used as bedding, but again it must be laid thickly, wet and soiled patches removed frequently, and the bed raked over daily. With both sawdust and peat moss bedding, it is particulary important to keep a horse's feet picked out and clean, as both will heat and soften the feet, if they are allowed to become clogged.

Routine

Whatever precise times any individual horse-owner or stable manager decides upon as being the most suitable for the feeding of his horse or horses, they should be adhered to thereafter, so far as possible. This is particularly important with the first and the last feed. During the day there will

obviously be occasions when times have to be adjusted according to the work the horse is doing.

The management routine for stabled horses can be divided as given below. The exact times of each division can be varied to suit individual stables, but once established, they should be maintained.

Early morning (not later than 7.30 am)
Give first feed, a small hay-net and fresh water. Tie up horse, and muck out, brushing floor clean, banking up retained bedding, and leaving centre of floor to air. Release the horse when this is completed. It is best to remove the water bucket while mucking out, to keep it clean, and then replace before releasing the horse.

9 o'clock
Tie up horse, and remove any droppings from the floor. Give first grooming; if the horse is rugged, this is called 'quartering', and is done by throwing the rug back and brushing the front, then throwing it forwards, and brushing the quarters. Pick out the feet. If the horse is to be exercised straight away, take off rugs after quartering, put on saddle, throw rug back over the saddle, before taking down hay-net and re-filling it ready for re-use. Then put on bridle, take off rug, and take horse out for exercise. The rug should be shaken out, and left airing, inside out, over a rack in the tack room.

On return from exercise
Water the horse. Remove saddle and bridle, tie up horse and give small hay-net. Groom thoroughly; this should take at least three-quarters of an hour. Thorough grooming is always best done after exercise, unless the horse has become very hot, when a sweat rug should be put on until he is cool; then he can be groomed. After grooming, put on day-rug, set day-bed, give fresh water and release horse. *Give second feed* at about 12.30. Tidy the yard, if there has been no one to do this already.

Afternoon
Riding School horses will often have to work again in the afternoon. If the morning's exercise, or work, has been delayed so that there has been no time for thorough grooming on return, this should be done before the second outing. Horses not working in the afternoon can be:

(i) left to lie down and rest. This is important for young horses, and those which have had a concentrated morning of schooling work.

(ii) led out for a short time, in fine weather, in their headcollars, to have a pick of grass.

(iii) if possible, in fine weather in spring and summer, turned out for a short time in a convenient paddock. All stabled horses with the exception of racehorses in training (whose management is highly specialized) benefit from a period of freedom.

4.30 pm (or on return from work)

Tie-up horse, un-tack and pick out feet. Give small hay-net and fresh water. Put on night rug. Lay bed for the night, having removed droppings and taken out any bedding made wet during the day. *Give third feed*, release horse.

Clean tack. Tidy tack room, and yard.

Evening (not earlier than 7 pm)

Re-fill water bucket. Remove droppings. Give a full net of hay, and the *fourth feed*.

Many horse owners like to go round their stables last thing at night. Until you have done this, it is hard to realize how satisfying it can be to hear soft whickers greeting you and to see horses lying down so relaxed they do not immediately jump on hearing your footsteps. Only horses with complete confidence in their surroundings, and their handlers, will stay lying down in human company.

Apart from the pleasurable aspect a late visit to the stables can help to avert a number of possible mishaps. A horse may have caught its foot in a hay-net, or tipped over its water bucket so it would remain thirsty all through the night. A rug may not have been put on properly and have slipped down out of position (remember to check in the morning with whoever put it on); or, fortunately more rarely, a horse may be showing signs of internal discomfort indicating colic. If this is left till morning it will be harder to alleviate as well as having caused the horse a night's pain. Veterinary surgeons are used to being called at night and if you are in any doubt, telephone yours. Describe what seem to you to be the horse's symptoms and the vet may be able to tell you what to do on the telephone. If not, he will come to your help right away.

Grooming, Clipping and Rugs

Stabled horses should be groomed thoroughly every day, not simply to make them look smart, but to keep their coats and their skins in healthy condition. Horses at liberty, although they cannot groom themselves, can do a lot for their coats and skins. They can roll if they feel itchy or are sweaty; they can rub themselves against trees to help them shed their coats in spring and autumn; they can scratch each other when they feel like it, and if they have itchy places under their bellies or between their thighs, they can find handy shrubs or bushes to rub against.

Grooming does not constitute a gentle going over with a brush. On the contrary, it is a strenuous exercise for the groom, who even in cold weather, should get quite hot in the process.

Grooming kit consists of a dandy brush, body brush, water brush, curry comb, mane comb, hoof pick, hoof oil and brush, stable rubber, small sponges, a rubber curry comb and a sweat scraper.

The dandy brush is used only for removing surface mud and dirt, and never on the horse's more sensitive parts such as the under belly, between the thighs, and the face. Nor should it be used on the mane or

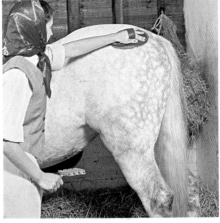

The body brush both cleans the coat and promotes circulation; the curry comb is used to clean the brush every few strokes.

tail as it breaks the hairs, producing a fringe effect on the mane and breaking the flow of the tail. The body brush is the main grease remover, and should be used with firm pressure (which does not mean banging it down on the coat). The grease is removed from the brush constantly by scraping it with the curry comb. This is the curry comb's sole purpose. The water brush is used dampened, for laying the

The basic grooming kit: 1. dandy brush 2. body brush 3. water brush 4. curry comb 5. mane comb 6. hoof pick 7. hoof oil and brush 8. stable rubber 9. sponge 10. rubber curry comb 11 sweat scraper

mane after brushing, or before plaiting and also for laying the tail before bandaging or plaiting. The hoof pick's use is obvious and very important. Hoof oil helps to prevent brittleness especially in light-coloured hooves. The stable rubber is folded into a pad and used to give the horse a final polish but it can be used also to dry the horse's ears if he comes in wet and cold. The small sponges are for the eyes and nostrils, and for the dock. A rubber curry comb can be helpful when a horse is casting his coat and, used with a circular movement, it will remove a lot of loose hair. The massaging effect is also appreciated by the horse. The sweat scraper has a squeegee action and is used to remove excess sweat or water from the coat.

Grooming, particularly of the body with the body brush, should be done without gloves, so that the sensitive tips of the fingers can be used to feel for any lumps or scratches or irregularities in the skin. Always run your hands down the legs. They should feel cool, almost cold, and the tendons should be firm. If you feel little nodules of mud or dirt work these out gently with the fingers, and then use the brush afterwards. If mud or dirt are left on the legs, they will eventually clog the pores, and may produce a condition known as mud fever. Feel for mud also on the inside of the pasterns, between the coronet and the fetlock joint.

When grooming the head, the head-collar should be undone and buckled round the neck. Care should be taken not

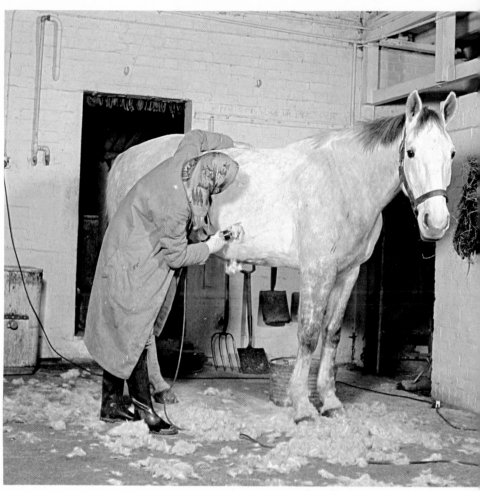

Proper care of the stabled horse requires a good deal of attention and can take up a lot of time. *above*: The first job in any grooming routine is to pick out the feet to remove any dirt and foreign objects. *right*: The process of clipping the coat should be attempted only by an experienced person, as it is highly skilled work. Three types of clip are *below*: a trace clip, useful for a horse or pony that will be turned out part of the time during the winter; *right top*: a blanket clip, which keeps the back area warm; *right bottom*: a hunter clip, with saddle patch and leg hair left on for protection against soreness and scratches.

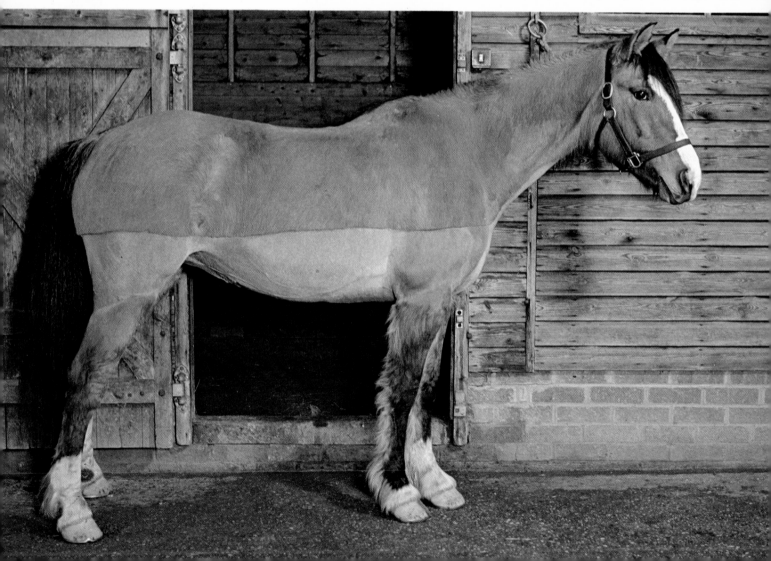

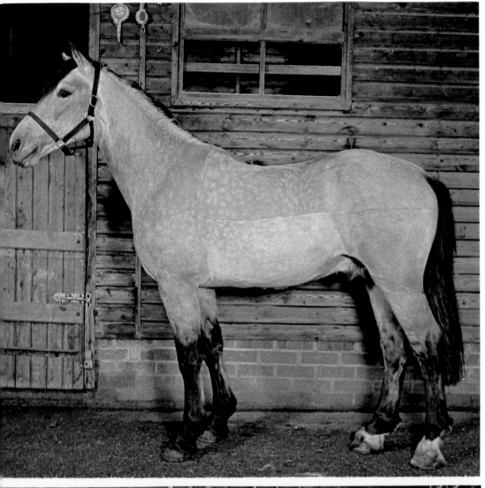

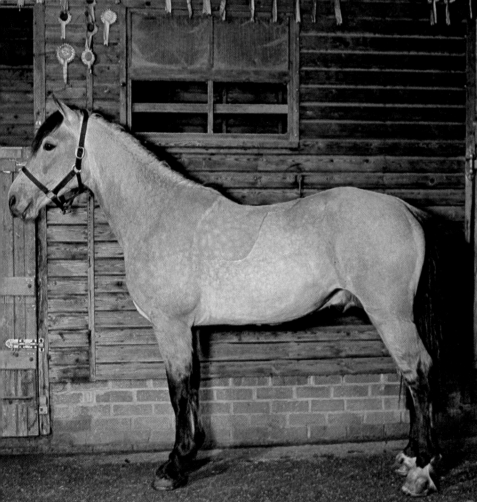

to bump the horse's face with the back of the brush, or get it into his eyes. Eyes and nostrils and the dock should be sponged with tepid water. Mares' udders should be kept clean, and with geldings, the sheath should be washed periodically. Not everyone realizes this to be a necessity, but if the sheath becomes too clogged with grease and dirt, the animal can eventually find it difficult, even painful, to stale.

Feet should be picked out at least twice a day, during the first grooming and on return from work. Hoof oil should be brushed on, not simply to give a smart appearance but because it is good for the hoof. It should be applied right up to the coronet, which is where the growth of the hoof starts.

A 'wisp' of straw can be made for strapping, a particularly energetic form of grooming which helps to build up the muscle especially on the neck and quarters, as well as toning up the skin. The stable rubber made into a firm pad can be used to achieve the same result.

Horses change, or 'cast', their coats twice a year at roughly six month intervals, in spring and autumn. The summer coat is much less dense, and finer, than the winter coat. Few horses except racehorses and those being prepared for showing need rugging in summer, although a cotton day sheet put on after grooming will help keep the coat sleek and clean, and is particularly advantageous when travelling. A horse should also have a sweat rug put on if it is brought in very hot after work or if it has to stand about while it is hot after any kind of long ride or competition. Sweat rugs are made of cotton and are similar to men's string vests.

Winter is a different matter. Horses in work will need to be clipped, as in their heavier winter coats, they are likely to sweat unduly every time they go out, and consequently will lose condition.

There are three principal types of clip known as a full clip, a hunter clip, and a trace clip.

In a full clip, the coat is removed from the entire body. In a hunter clip, the hair is left on the legs as far up as the elbows and the thighs, and on the saddle patch. The theory is that the hair left on the legs offers protection against cold, injury from thorns or other hazards that might cause slight tears and scratches, and wet, muddy conditions that could lead to mud fever and cracked heels. The saddle patch can help prevent a sore or scalded back resulting from a long day's riding.

In a trace clip, the hair is removed from the belly, between the thighs and the forearms, across the chest and up the underside of the neck. It is used mostly on horses or ponies that are kept out, rather than those that are stabled. Sometimes the hair is further clipped off the neck and head, leaving a blanket shape of hair over the back and quarters. This is known as a blanket clip.

Horses that have had a full, or a hunter, clip will need rugging all the time. As the first clipping is usually done in October, they will probably initially need only

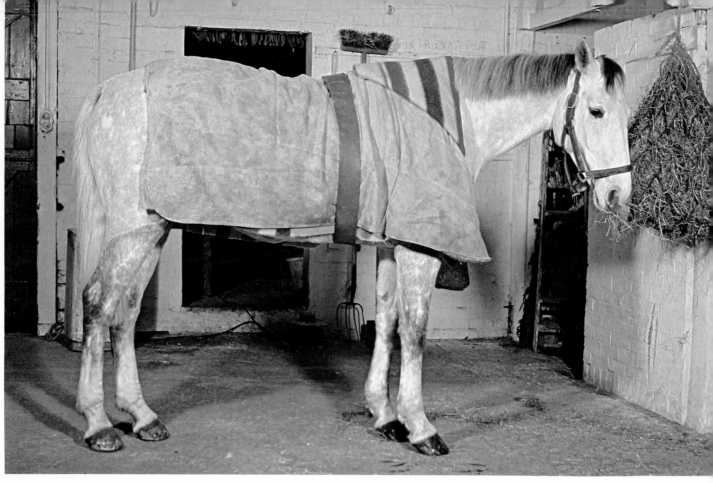

single rugs, that is a wool-lined jute night rug, and a woollen day rug. Nowadays several patent variations of the traditional forms of rug are available. These are more expensive to buy, but have many advantages. They are much lighter than the old type, but just as warm. The same rug can be worn during the night and day, although it is better to have two, as night rugs invariably get dirty. However the new rugs are both easy to wash and quick to dry, so a dirty night rug can be washed in the morning, and be dry by the evening.

As the weather gets colder, the horse will need extra warmth, which is provided by putting on one, sometimes even two, soft woollen blankets under the top rug. These must be large, as about a quarter of the blanket should come right over the neck when it is put on, so that it can be folded back over the top rug and caught in place under the roller. Once a horse has started wearing a rug, or rugs, he must continue to do so until the weather gets warmer in spring. If he is wearing under blankets, these can be discarded in succession until finally it is warm enough to discard the top rug as well. If the days are considerably warmer than the nights, as often happens in winter, the horse may not need his under blankets in daytime – this is where commonsense must be used. Some horses, like some people, feel the cold more than others. During the winter if a stabled horse is led out for a walk, or turned out for a short time, he should wear a New Zealand rug, which is made of waterproofed canvas, and lined with wool. Alternatively one of the new patented rugs which are also made in waterproof versions can be used. All rugs in use should be aired and shaken out daily. After clipping, the coat will continue to grow, although not so fully as before. Nevertheless, the

During the winter clipped horses need a jute night rug, and also a warm woollen under-blanket in cold weather. They are secured with a webbing or leather surcingle or roller.

horse will need a second clip before winter is out, and some horses even need a third. The last clip should be done by the end of January.

Bandages

Tail bandages should be in daily use for stabled horses, and are put on after grooming to lay and smarten the line of the tail. Two other types of bandages are necessary – stable bandages and exercise bandages.

Stable bandages are made of flannel, and are fairly wide. They are used to provide warmth if a horse is chilled or has a cold; to dry off the legs if he comes in wet and muddy so that the mud can be brushed off later; on top of cotton wool or gamgee-tissue soaked in cold water as cold water bandages, and for travelling when they are put on over dry cotton wool or gamgee. There are nowadays many patent leg protectors available for travelling that are quicker to put on and, unless bandaging is skilfully done, probably more reliable.

Stable bandages should run from the knee down to, and over the fetlock joint, at which point the bandage should be rolled upwards again, to finish just below the knee. Bandages should never be put on too tightly; it should be possible to insert a finger between the bandage and the leg, both top and bottom. The tapes should not be tied tighter than the bandage itself and they should be tied on the outside of the leg, in a bow, with the ends tucked in.

Exercise bandages are made of stockinette or crepe, and are used to support the

tendons and to protect the leg from thorns or prickly undergrowth in rough country. They are put on with cotton wool or gamgee underneath, a small part of which should protrude above and below the bandage itself. It takes a lot of practice to put these on so that they will stay in place during work. It is often better for example, if a horse is going to be asked to go fast across country, perhaps in heavy going, and it is felt he needs extra support, to use special tendon boots. Young horses should wear exercise bandages or boots during lungeing, and early schooling, when they can be awkward with their legs. This will prevent unnecessary bumps and bruises. Exercise bandages are also useful for putting on over a poultice, or a liniment which is relieving a sprained tendon. Again, they should never be put on too tightly, or the bandaging will defeat its own ends by stopping the circulation. After taking off any bandage, the leg should be given a brisk rub with the hands. Bandages should be kept clean, which means washing them after use, drying them, and putting them away re-rolled. They should be rolled with the sewn part of the tapes inwards, so that when the bandage is put on the leg, the tapes will be on the outside of the bandage.

Medicine

It is not a good idea to indulge in a lot of amateur doctoring with horses, but basic necessities should be kept in every stable.

DISINFECTANT: The horse has a very sensitive skin, and only the mildest disinfectants should be used to clean out or bathe any cut or injury. Dettol, or similar, is acceptable provided it is used heavily diluted. If there is none to hand when it is wanted, salt and water is an efficient emergency disinfectant. A stronger, domestic disinfectant should be used to keep the stable clean and sweet smelling.

LINIMENT: There are many excellent brands on the market, some stronger than others. Take your pick, and use according to the manufacturer's instructions for the relief of sprains and strains.

ANTISEPTIC POWDER: Very important, as small cuts and scratches, once clean, heal better if they are kept dry and protected by dusting with antiseptic powder. Use the one recommended by your veterinary surgeon.

ANTISEPTIC OINTMENT: Any good, soft, zinc-based ointment will help to prevent scar tissue forming once a wound has healed. It also encourages the hair to grow again.

KAOLIN POULTICE: This has many uses: put on hot, as a poultice under a bandage, it relieves sprains and strains; put on a cut or, more particularly a puncture wound which is not easy to clean, it will draw out dirt and poison, which will be seen as pus or discoloration when the pad with the kaolin is removed. Being a natural substance and not a drug, kaolin can never do any harm, and in fact often does a great deal of good.

GOLDEN EYE OINTMENT: Horses may get particles of dust etc. in their eyes; have

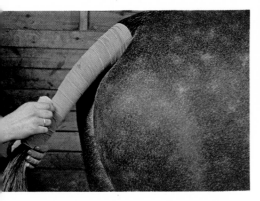

runny eyes caused by a cold, or scratch an eye against a sharp object. The eye should be bathed with a very weak solution of Dettol and water, and some eye ointment squeezed into the corner to help give relief.

COUGH ELECTUARY: This should be supplied by the veterinary surgeon, but it is a good thing to have it always in stock. Sometimes a cough can be simply the result of eating hay too quickly, but it never hurts to give the horse some electuary straight away.

COLIC DRENCH: In most cases of colic, all but the most experienced people would telephone their vet. It is quite likely, however, that unless he can come at once, he will suggest giving a drench, so it is useful to keep it against such an emergency.

EPSOM SALTS: These are good for horses that may have been on too heating a diet; but all will benefit from a small handful in their weekly bran mash.

SALT AND WATER: This is cooling, refreshing and helps to harden the skin. Sponged over a horse's back, and behind and under the elbows where the girth lies, it will help prevent galls and sores.

WORM DOSING DRUGS: Horses should be wormed regularly. All horses harbour

worms, and it is only by regular worming that a dangerous infestation can be prevented. For a horse in healthy condition, dosing every three months should keep him relatively worm-free. Every year, new drugs are discovered and put on the market, all reputed to be more lethal to the worms, and less harmful to the horse. The best solution to this ever-present problem is to ask the veterinary surgeon which he considers most suitable and then, if possible, get him to make up a number of individual doses which can be kept in the stable and given when necessary. New horses coming into a stable should be wormed on arrival.

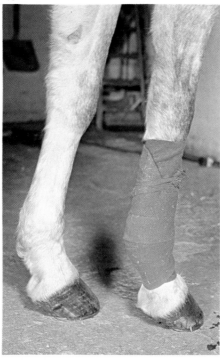

Bandages and boots are for veterinary use and to give the horse support, protection and warmth. *left*: The elastic tail bandage will keep the tail neat and tidy and protect the upper part when travelling. It should not be left on overnight. *Above*: Woollen leg bandages warm and protect the legs, and are used when travelling or after a long day's hunting, to help the horse dry off; they may also be used to keep a veterinary dressing in place on an injured leg. Although usually of wool, they are available in other materials as well. *right*: Brushing boots are padded to prevent injury should the horse strike itself, or 'brush', while at work or exercise.

SCISSORS: A sharp but blunt-ended pair should be kept for cutting away the hair from the edges of wounds or cuts that need dressing.

In addition to all these items it is a good idea to keep some pieces of linen as dressings, or poultice pads, together with some long strips of linen for under-bandaging wounds – a large pack of cotton wool, several packs of gamgee tissue and one or two ordinary crepe bandages. The experienced stable manager will also keep a hypodermic syringe and a supply of needles; but only those who really know what they are doing should attempt to give injections. It

is not that this is in itself difficult, but it must be known just where to put the needle, and how to use the syringe skilfully and quickly.

Stalls

A last word.

It has become so established a custom to keep stabled horses in loose boxes that it is forgotten how many thousands of horses, in the real hey-day of the horse, were stabled perfectly competently, and comfortably, in stalls. It is certainly not an impossibility to keep a stabled horse in a stall, provided it is wide enough for the horse to lie down in comfort. Stalls should be bedded deeply, the straw banked up well towards the back and sides. The halter rope, after going through the tie-ring, should be passed through a solid wooden block, which should be at floor level when the horse's head is in its normal position. This block keeps the rope taut and prevents the horse's legs getting entangled in it when lying down, or getting up.

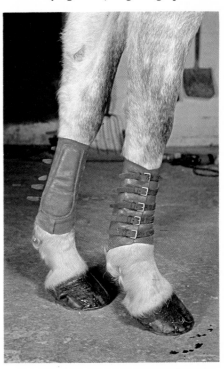

Divisions between stalls should be high enough to stop horses nipping at each other over the top; in fact bars are best, at the top, so the horses can see one another without being able to become too maliciously personal. Water buckets should be placed on the side away from the hay rack or net, so they are not constantly filling up with dust and bits of hay. Particular care must be taken to pick out the hind feet of stalled horses, as obviously all the dung will be at the back. If the hind feet are not kept clean, they will become hot and clogged, and the horse may develop thrush. Where horses are stabled in stalls, it is often the custom, when the horses are tacked up, to turn them round and stand them facing outwards attached to 'pillar reins'. These are short leather straps or chains attached to each side pillar and clipped on to the bridle.

Management of the Grass-kept Horse

T HE term 'grass-kept' does not altogether accurately describe the condition of horses and ponies that live mostly out-of-doors instead of in stables. Unless the climate is so idyllic that the temperature never drops to freezing point, the snow never falls and the grass is always not only green but luscious, at certain times of year even the toughest of Mountain and Moorland ponies need food extra to that which they can find for themselves, even when they're not working. A horse that has to work must have more than a plain grass diet if he is to have energy and keep his condition.

When horses are kept out, and required to work, there should be some kind of shed, shelter or stable into which they can be brought for feeding, grooming, and tacking up. For working horses, the system of living out and being brought in before riding is best termed the 'Combined System'. It is an excellent one; the horse is living a comparatively natural life, keeping fit and healthy without the absolute necessity of daily ridden exercise, and needs less care and attention. It will also give an easier

Good quality grazing. Do not assume that horses will know the harmful plants.

ride, for horses that live mostly out-of-doors work off much of their surplus energy on their own and are seldom so ebullient as those that are permanently stabled.

There are certain rules of management for horses kept according to this system. It is not quite good enough to leave them out and unattended for days, and then suddenly catch them for a ride. Ideally, horses living out should be brought in each morning, given a feed, quickly brushed over, generally checked for cuts, scratches, bumps or lameness, and then, if not needed for work, turned out again. In summer, they will need no further attention until next morning. In winter, most horses, except the very highly bred, can live out all the time, although most, except Mountains and Moorlands, will need to wear a rug. If they are to be worked, however, it's best to reverse the summer plan; that is to bring them in at night, and turn them out during all or whatever part of the day they are not being used. This system works well for all horses other than those in training, hunt and show horses and ponies, and those used for competitive events. It's also certainly the easiest for most owner-riders.

There are of course times when horses can be left out entirely, without the benefit of stables – hunters turned out for the summer; children's ponies when the children are away at school; horses and ponies used chiefly for summer, or holiday, riding, which can out-winter. All will still need a certain amount of care and attention. They should be in suitable fields, properly fenced and gated, with a constant source of water, and suitable amenities for when they need extra feeding – necessities in fact, common to all horses living out, whether working or not.

All fields should be carefully inspected and cleared of poisonous plants, such as this yellow-flowered ragwort which is highly toxic to horses.

Fields, Fences and Gates

Horses living out do best if they have plenty of space, and a variety of terrain, and therefore, of herbage. In many parts of the country however, only small areas are available; sometimes only one not very large field. It then becomes particularly important to conserve the quality of the grazing by not allowing the horses to eat all of it, all the time. Horses are wasteful grazers, trampling down a lot of perfectly good feeding grasses in their perpetual search for the tastiest.

The most economical way of conserving a pasture is to divide it into three parts, so that two parts can be rested while one is eaten. In spring, one can be shut off for a cut of hay; the horses can be turned out in

it a couple of weeks or so after the hay is taken. In small fields it is wise to remove the droppings regularly, or they will eventually foul up so much of the grazing that little that is palatable remains. In larger fields this is often impractical, but these can be harrowed occasionally.

The quality of pasture can only be assessed by an expert; the greenest and most lush looking grass is not always the best. Even the best pasture, however, will not keep its quality indefinitely and to keep it in heart it will need periodic applications of fertilizer, lime, or slag. Exactly what it needs and in what proportion is determined by soil analysis; representatives of Colleges of Agriculture will generally perform this service free. Fields, or divisions of fields, should be fertilized, limed or slagged in annual succession, not all at once, and horses should not graze a fertilized field for at least three weeks.

If possible there should be some natural

Below A pony in a New Zealand rug shelters from the winter cold, and will probably make use of the field shelter in summer as well to avoid the heat and buzzing insects.

shelter in the field – hedges, a belt of trees, stone walls, or maybe some banks or hollows to take the edge off the wind. Failing these, a field shelter should be provided. It should be three-sided, set with its back to the prevailing wind and with a wide opening so that horses can get in and out easily. There should be a long rack for hay against the back wall; and in winter, it's an encouragement for horses to use it if straw is laid on the ground inside. Mucking-out is not necessary; just the droppings removed and more straw added when needed.

The ideal field water supply is a running stream. A stagnant pool is worse than useless for the water is unappetizing, and the pond will breed flies and mosquitoes. Where there is no running water, a long, solid but not too deep, galvanized iron trough, with no sharp edges, serves well. It can be supplied by water piped to the field, and operated on a ball-cock system, or it will have to be filled manually from buckets or a hose. Troughs should have a plugged hole in the bottom so they can be emptied and cleaned out and they should be set very firmly on bricks, or concrete blocks, so that the base of the trough is 15–30 cm (6–12 ins) from the ground.

In winter, horses will always manage to

Above This well-designed trough, serving two fields, has rounded edges, stands well off the ground, and has fresh water piped in.
Below The best type of fencing for all equines is solid posts and rails. The field on the left is being rested on rotation to provide fresh pasture.

break the ice on running water for themselves. In troughs, it will have to be broken for them as it freezes more solidly.

Troughs must be kept clean, and positioned clear of trees, and away from gateways where the ground will probably become muddied in wet weather.

A field can be divided with electric fencing, which is easy to put up and move, and horses, after one small shock, will not go near it again. Some ponies, however, have been known to work out the connection between the ticking of the battery, and the shock from the fence, and if they hear no ticking, they ignore the fence!

All main and boundary fences should be strong and safe. The best and most expensive, is post and rails. Hedges, where they are customary, and are kept in good order, have the added advantage of providing shelter. Wire fencing is probably the most universal; to be satisfactory, it must be properly erected, with good posts, preferably creosoted, with the wires strung as tightly as possible between them. Three strands are enough for horses, except for foals and small ponies who could push through the wide spaces between each. The bottom wire should be 30 cm (1 ft) from the ground; if lower, horses can catch their feet in it. On no account should barbed wire be used for either the top or the bottom strand. The only possible permissible use for barbed wire is if horses are confirmed fence-leaners, when one strand can be run along the inside of the fence

about 15 cm (6 ins) below the top strand. This discourages leaning. Fences should be checked regularly, and kept in constant good repair.

Gates should swing easily on hinges, and have proper fastenings, ideally a patent hook, the hinged tongue of which prevents it being lifted by horses. It is a waste of time and a trial to the temper to have to struggle with bits of twisted wire or knotted string. In urban districts, padlocks are advised.

Field Feeding

During spring and summer, varying somewhat according to the district and the latitude, horses living out will need no food other than grass, although they will appreciate a salt or mineral lick. Eating the bark of trees and chewing fences are not habits the horse indulges in simply to annoy its owner; they usually mean it is short of minerals, which can be supplied by the lick.

When it becomes necessary to feed hay, it should be put into the rack in the field shelter. Alternatively it can be given in haynets, or in racks similar to those used for feeding cattle. It is wasteful to feed it on the ground as it perpetually gets trodden and dunged on, becomes a sodden mess in wet weather, and blows away in wind.

The easiest way to feed concentrates out of doors is in a long, solid wooden trough. If given in the shelter, horses tend to fight and bully one another, but they will generally eat together quite peacefully along either side of a fairly long trough. Feeding from buckets is wasteful – of feed, which will be spilled and trodden on, and of buckets, which will be tipped over and kicked. Buckets set in holders are available, guaranteed impossible to tip over. For just two horses fed together, these are satisfactory; if more, they may lead (as bucket feeding often does) to in-fighting between the greedy, quick eaters, and the less greedy who nevertheless will defend their feed. Portable mangers, which can be hooked on to the top bar of a gate, or the rail of a post and rail fence are excellent, but not suitable for hooking on to wire fences.

It's not possible to specify exactly how much feeding, either of concentrates or of hay, any individual horse kept out will need during a winter. It will depend on the weather (the colder it is the more concentrates needed to create body warmth) and on the size and type of horse. Mountain and Moorland ponies are proverbially 'good doers', and will need relatively less than non-native types of the same sizes. The age of the horse is also relevant: young horses, under five, and elderly ones, over 15, will need rather more than the mature and middle-aged group. So is the amount of land which is being grazed: four animals in an extensive, well-sheltered pasture with varied herbage, may eat no more during a winter than two in a small, exposed paddock. Roughly, however, 1 tonne (1 ton) of hay can be estimated per animal per winter. If winter starts early, it may need more: conversely, if the climate is mild, less. Horses themselves are good

guides as to when to start feeding hay, and how much to feed, because if there is any good grazing around, they prefer it. In autumn, if they are spending a lot of time just standing about, probably near the gate, you can take it that the grazing is poor and they need hay. If they eat up every wisp within half-an-hour of its being put out, it was not enough. If they leave some, and wander off to graze again, it's been more than they need. By mid-winter they will probably get through from 7·9 kg (16–20 lbs) per day per horse. Make particularly sure they have enough in cold, wet and windy or frosty weather.

Flaked maize is a good winter addition to a horse's concentrate ration, but it should be mixed with bran, and cubes or oats or barley; on its own it is pleasantly warming, but somewhat lacking in fibre. Boiled barley, well mixed with bran and fed warm is an excellent feed for cold winter mornings, and bran and molasses mashes are good for the digestions when there is little or no green food about.

The fly fringe, a specially-designed browband, effectively wards off irritating flies in summer, but for some highly-strung horses the fringe itself may prove to be as much of an annoyance as the flies.

In mild, open winter weather, one concentrate feed a day is enough, with hay, to keep horses in good condition. In very severe weather, a morning and evening feed is better. Pregnant mares must be fed well if out-wintering, and to ensure they get all the vitamins and minerals necessary, it is safest to feed balanced stud cubes. Weaned foals should always be brought in at night during the first winter of their lives (two can share a loose box), given a feed when they come in and another in the morning, and plenty of hay overnight. It is difficult in later years to compensate for under-nourishment at this time so make sure that foals get all they need.

Worming

Worming is important for all horses; but particularly for those living out as their dung continually re-infects the pasture. If, in spite of regular three-monthly wormings, an animal has a pot-belly, is a bit 'ribby' and has a rough, staring coat, it should be given another dose. Fields on which horses graze benefit from being grazed occasionally by cattle, which will not only eat up the rougher grasses the horses reject, but consume the worm larvae, to which they are impervious.

Daily Care

Horses and ponies living out and not working should still be visited every day, firstly, to check they are all present. If many are kept in a big pasture, they will probably form into groups, and may graze quite long distances apart. If one is missing, check to see it is not caught in a fence, or lying down in a corner, in which case is it sick, or just resting? Alternatively it may have jumped out, pushed its way through the fencing or broken a gate. Check that all horses are sound and look over each for cuts, scratches or lumps. Grooming is not necessary, but it will be appreciated if twigs or burrs caught in manes and tails are removed. In late winter and early spring, manes, the roots of tails and any feather on the legs should be closely inspected for lice which can attack any horse. A heavy daily dusting with a proprietary louse powder every day for a week should eliminate them.

Horses and ponies not required for work can have their shoes removed, although it may be better to leave front shoes on those with brittle, shelly feet. The farrier should inspect feet every eight weeks, to trim and shape as necessary. Check the feet during the daily visit; hoofs that are splitting or becoming mis-shapen, need attention.

The Grass-kept Working Horse

Spring and Summer
The best time to bring in a working horse that lives out is early in the morning, so it can have a feed while owner or groom has his breakfast. From then on, the routine is very similar to that of the stabled horse. It will need a box with bedding, equivalent to the day-bed of stabled horses, from which droppings must be removed, and haynets taken out and refilled. It will need grooming, although not so thoroughly as its stables counterpart, as too much grease (which gives natural protection from inclement weather) should not be removed from the coat. If it is to be ridden it can be tacked up at once; if not wanted until later it can be untied after grooming and left.

On return from work, or at about 12.30, it will be time for a second feed and a small haynet. If the horse has been ridden, it should have its feet picked out, be lightly brushed over the saddle patch, and dried off, if it has sweated, either by putting on a

sweat rug or rubbing with a straw wisp.

If required for work in the afternoon, the horse can be left in peace until some ten minutes before the ride starts. Then it must be tacked up, and droppings should be removed from the box before going out. The procedure described above should follow the ride, and a third feed given. There is no need to give a haynet now, as when the feed is finished, the horse can be turned out. The box will then be cleaned, haynet refilled and hung up, water bucket refilled, the yard tidied and tack cleaned.

The amount of concentrate feed a horse kept in this way needs will depend, as ever, on the work he is doing, his temperament, and the capabilities of his rider, or riders. The principle of dividing it will be the same as for stabled horses; the total weight however, being divided into three portions instead of four. The last portion is still the largest. In spring and summer a total weight of about 5·5 kg (12 lbs) of food other than grass could be the average for the horse turned out at night. Morning and noon haynets need only therefore contain about 1·5–2 kg (3–4 lbs) each.

On days when a horse is not needed to work in the afternoons, it can either be left in to rest, or turned out after the second feed. If the grass is very good and the horse is inclined to carry a lot of flesh, it is better left in until after the third feed, when a smaller one can be given. This feed will not be so fattening as an afternoon's grazing would be, but will ensure plenty of energy for the next day.

For the private owner who cannot ride every day, after the morning feed the horse should be brushed over to remove dust and dirt, and his feet picked out, before being returned to the field. The box can then be set ready for the next day. With practice, this will only take about half-an-hour, provided the field is near the house.

Winter
Apart from having to muck out the box, little extra time and trouble is involved in keeping a horse in at night, and it has many

Most horses need hay and extra feed in the winter. Haynets must be tied high enough to prevent the horse's feet getting entangled, but not so high that seeds fall in his eyes.

advantages. If a gale blows up in the night, there's no need to worry because the horse is out without a rug and no need to go out to the field with hay and a feed.

The routine for winter should be to give a feed and haynet, and muck out, before breakfast. After breakfast, groom and prepare for riding as in summer, followed by the second feed and second small haynet at midday. When the horse has finished its second feed it is turned out. If it is to be ridden in the afternoon and not the morning, it should be turned out after breakfast, brought in about 12.30 for the second feed, groomed and prepared for riding.

If not required for riding at all, the horse can be turned out after breakfast with a haynet in the field and brought in before dark, to a good feed, a haynet, and a groom-

A New Zealand rug, waterproof and warmly lined, makes it possible to clip a horse which is kept at grass during the winter. The rug must be carefully fitted.

ing. As in winter this will be about 4.30, the horse will need a big haynet later in the evening, and a final feed, the contents of which will depend on what is expected of him next day. For private owners who may have little time to ride during the week in winter, cubes are better than oats. If the horse is going to have an energetic weekend, he can have oats on Friday evenings, and over the weekend, decreasing the amount on Sunday and going back to cubes during the week. Whenever a horse is only doing very light work, its oat ration should be cut down; if off work through lameness or injury, oats should be cut out altogether; but the bulk (hay) increased to keep the balance of weight.

Horses that are going to work hard in winter, even if only on certain days, will need to be clipped. If they are living partly out-of-doors, a trace clip will be enough; but this will mean that when they are turned out, they must wear a New Zealand, or a modern light-weight waterproof rug. The majority of horses turned out during the day in winter are better rugged even if not clipped. Whether they also have to be rugged at night will depend on the weather, the cosiness of their boxes and the thickness of their coats. Some horses grow very dense, winter coats; others simply grow somewhat longer hair than in summer. Unless the weather is exceptionally cold, few horses that spend part of their days outside in winter will ever need more at night than a single wool-lined jute rug. The important thing to remember about rugging is that once rugged the horse must stay rugged till spring.

A horse's ears are guides to whether or not he is cold; cold ears mean a cold horse. If a horse comes in cold and wet in winter, from work or from the field, drying the ears with a stable rubber will help to restore warmth, as will putting a layer of clean straw along the back and putting a rug (inside out) on top.

Snow is no hardship to horses when it has fallen and is crisp, and the day if fine and sunny. What they find hardest to endure are cold wet winds, and driving rain or sleet; this kind of weather can take condition off them quickly, unless they have plenty of food and plenty of shelter.

Saddlery

A DISTINCTION should be made between the words 'saddlery' and 'harness', the latter, in particular, being often misused. Saddlery refers to the equipment of the riding horse, whilst harness is used to describe the accoutrements of the driving horse. To confuse further the uninitiated, horsemen will frequently refer to both as 'tack' (i.e. tackle).

In general terms, saddlery is concerned with the saddle and bridle and their accompanying auxiliaries, such as girths, leathers and martingales. It can extend to cover all items made of leather; even if some of those items, e.g. muzzles, headcollars etc., are applicable to both riding and harness horses. Bandages, rugs and blankets, however, are grouped under the composite term 'horse clothing'.

The early horse peoples managed their horses with the minimum of equipment, concentrating, naturally enough, on methods of control. Initially, control of the horse may have been achieved by a form of noseband encompassing the lower jaws and fitted above the nostrils. Illustrations of Syrian horsemen of the fourteenth century BC show this rudimentary form of bridle quite clearly. There is, however, evidence of a more sophisticated bridle, involving the use of a bit, used at an earlier date. On the tomb of Horenhab of Egypt (dated circa 1600 BC) a horseman is depicted on an obviously spirited horse ridden in a snaffle bridle of surprisingly modern design.

As the use of mounted horsemen increased and selective breeding, combined with hand-feeding (i.e. with corn, an energizing feedstuff) produced horses of more quality and spirit, so a greater emphasis was placed on the means of control through the agency of the bridle. By the time the Assyrians had emerged as a major horse people, a bitting arrangement had been devised that gave to the rider a very acceptable degree of control over his mount. Two hundred years later, when the Persians of the sixth century BC had superseded the Assyrians as the leading nation of horsemen, the bridle had become an even more forceful instrument, largely because of a notable change to a heavier type of horse.

These horses would have certainly been corn-fed and they are depicted in various sculptures in a heavily collected posture with the head over-bent, a carriage that would certainly give more control to the rider. The bits used to effect this imposed balance were the familiar phallic-cheeked snaffles combined with a noseband which

seems to have been set with knobs or spikes (like the Spanish *careta* still used today), and with the addition of a strap fastened below the bit that is very similar to our modern drop noseband. There were however exceptions to the obsessive interest in control. The Numidian cavalry which marched with Hannibal, for instance, managed their small ponies without resort to a bridle of any sort, steering their mounts with a switch applied to the appropriate side of the head. History does not reveal how the halt was effected.

Nonetheless, in general terms, the trend towards stronger bits, capable of exerting a greater mechanical force, and thus allowing the horseman to position and restrain his horse more effectively, continued. From the sixth century BC onwards, bits became increasingly severe, with both Greeks and Persians using mouthpieces that incorporated sharp rollers and spikes. Somewhere around 300 BC the Celts of Gaul produced the curb bit, an instrument that was to develop to monstrous proportions in the centuries that followed.

The curb bit of the armoured knights of the Middle Ages, which existed in only slightly altered form well into the eighteenth century and even later, was made necessary by the sheer size and strength of the heavy horses that were needed to carry a fully armoured man and his weapons, as well as the weight of their own protective armour. To control such an animal, and more particularly to put him in a state of balance which would facilitate the manoeuvres required in battle, or later at the joust and tournament, a mechanical force of some power was needed if the animal's weight was to be placed over the hindquarters and the forehand lightened in

Saddlery or 'tack' on sale at an auction. The saddle and bridle are the basic pieces of equipment needed for an ordinary riding horse and there are many different types; which ones to use depends not only on the type of horse but also its stage in training, the use to which it is being put and the ability of the rider.

consequence.

The use of the bit to place the horse in balance persisted well into the Renaissance period which marked the beginnings of the 'classical art'. The early Masters, like Federico Grisone in Naples and his pupil Pignatelli, did, however, stress the importance of preserving the lightness of the mouth, achieving their object by the use, once more, of the spiked noseband. Even so from a study of their books (Grisone's *Gli Ordini di Cavalcare* was published in 1550) it is clear that little emphasis was placed on the suppling of the horse and the development of his posture by a progression of exercises, whilst great store continued to be set on breaking the animal's resistance by forceful means. During this period the prototype of the modern double bridle emerged with the addition to the curb bit of a thin bridoon, the 'flying trench', which was operated by a second rein. Recognition of the fact that flexion at the poll has to be accompanied by a corresponding relaxation of the lower jaw, was marked by the occasional use of metal 'keys' fitted to the centre of the mouthpiece to encourage the horse to play with the bit and create saliva in the mouth. The Greek general Xenophon had, in fact, used the same device on a snaffle bit some 1800 years previously and the modern straight-bar 'mouthing' bit used in the

breaking of young horses, and similarly fitted with keys, varies only slightly in detail from that used by the Spartan horseman.

The curb bit, however, with its cheek-pieces often as long as 37 cm (15 in) held its place as the chief weapon in the horse-man's armoury until, at the beginning of the seventeenth century, the later classical Masters, like Pluvinel and Newcastle, encouraged the individual study of horses and more patient and gentler methods were advocated in their training.

By the following century the art of classical riding had become established, largely through the teachings of the Frenchman François de la Guérinière, who is known as the 'Father of Classical Equitation', and whilst the curb bit continued as a predominant influence, it ceased to be regarded as an instrument of coercion.

From that point on, the tendency was towards milder bits, but the obsession with the positioning of the head and the control of the horse through the bit continued to occupy the minds of horsemen right up to our own century, despite the increasing frequency and volume of the exhortation 'legs before hands'.

The nineteenth century and the first part of the twentieth, produced a huge variety of bits, all of which were acclaimed (at least by their ingenious inventors) as the panacea for all equine ills. However, the passing of the individual craftsmen, forging bits by hand, the considerations of modern commercial practice and methods of mass production, together with an increasing knowledge of equestrian theory, has resulted in the past 30 or 40 years in a much simplified range of bitting

devices. So much so in fact, that the modern horseman is restricted, essentially, in his choice to one of five basic groups or families of bits, of which, if his horse has been correctly schooled, he will only rarely need to employ more than two.

These five groups comprise: the *snaffle*, in its various forms; the *double* bridle, i.e. curb bit and bridoon (the latter is, in fact, a light version of the ordinary snaffle but changes its name, for no very good reason, when used with a curb bit); the *Pelham*, a hybrid derived from the curb bit and attempting to produce the same result as the double bridle with the use of a single mouthpiece; the *gag snaffle*, a gadget borrowed from the harness horse, and, finally, the *bitless bridle*, frequently termed a *hackamore*, which relies solely on pressure exerted on the nose for its effect.

Of these the *snaffle* is the mildest form of bitting, the most simple and the most common. It is made in a variety of weights, ranging from the pencil thin to the much more acceptable thick mouthpiece, described by the Irish as 'soft'. The principal division within the group however, is between those with a jointed mouthpiece and those made without a joint in a 'half-moon' shape known as a mullen mouth, the latter being the mildest of the two.

The action of the snaffle depends upon the position of the horse's head and, therefore, upon the stage of training that has been reached. In the young, relatively unschooled horse, carrying his weight on the forehand with a correspondingly low head carriage, the action is upwards against the corners of the lips. In the case of the horse in a more advanced state of training more weight is carried on the quarters, the forehand is therefore lightened and the head raised to a point where the nose is held a little in advance of the vertical. The snaffle then acts across the lower jaw, lying over the tongue and placing more pressure on the bars of the mouth (i.e. the area of gum between the incisors and the cheek teeth).

The snaffle can become a stronger means of control by variations being made

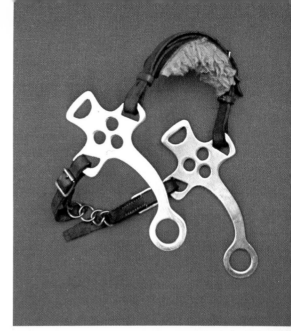

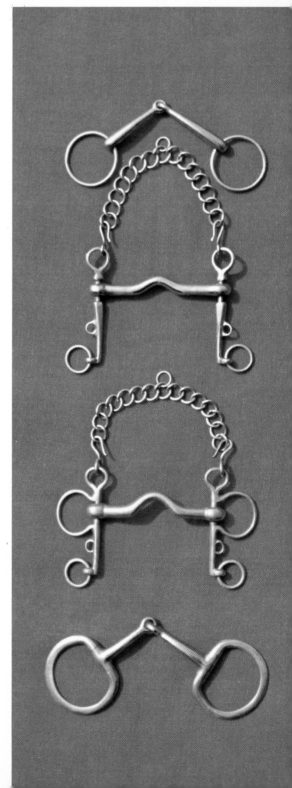

Above right The hackamore – a bitless bridle in which the reins act, via the cheekpieces, on a band over the nose, instead of a metal bar in the mouth.

Right The three basic bit patterns used for the riding horse. *bottom*: The snaffle; this one has a jointed mouthpiece. *top*: The double bridle consisting of a thin snaffle, or bridoon, and a curb (Weymouth) bit. *middle*: The Pelham – an attempt to combine both actions of the double bridle in one bit by providing an extra ring in line with the mouthpiece for a bridoon rein; the port in the centre of the mouthpiece makes it more comfortable over the tongue than the usual straight-barred version. Double bridles and Pelhams are both worn with a flat-linked curb chain. This is fitted in the chin groove under the horse's lower jaw, and is attached to hooks on the top rings of the bit cheekpieces. It is sometimes kept in place by a leather lip strap which is passed through the spare centre link on the chain and attached to the small dees on the cheekpieces.

to the mouthpiece. This can, for instance, be twisted, or serrated, so as to give a sharper pressure on the mouth, or it can be fitted with rollers, set horizontally within the mouthpiece or round its circumference. The action of the bit can also be altered and/or assisted by the use of auxiliaries such as drop nosebands or martingales.

A drop noseband, the nosepiece resting some 7 cm (3 in) above the nostrils and the rear strap fastening below the bit, fulfils a number of purposes. By closing the mouth it prevents evasions of the bit's actions caused by the horse opening the jaws or attempting to cross them. It helps, also, to maintain a correct position of the head by exerting a downwards and backwards pressure on the nose, transmitted to it through the action of the rein. The result of a correctly positioned head, allowing the rider's hands to be higher than the mouth, is to give a greater degree of control. A certain, if slight, restriction of the breathing, is involved in the use of the drop noseband – a violent upward movement of the head being countered by a momentary increase of pressure upon the nasal passages.

The use of martingales is also concerned with the maintenance of an acceptable head position. The two principal types are the standing martingale attached to a cavesson noseband (never to a drop), thus restricting any upward movement of the head, and the 'running' type achieving the same result through pressure on the

Below A running martingale in action. The running rings exert a downward action on the bit when the horse raises its head too high, but careful fitting is required to ensure reasonable freedom of movement.

mouth. The running martingale comprises a bifurcated strap, each end of which is fitted with a ring through which the rein is passed. Thus pressure is put on the mouth to effect a lowering of the head.

The double bridle, with its curb bit and bridoon, lies at the opposite end of the spectrum in comparison with the snaffle. It is the most sophisticated of the bitting arrangements and within the province of only the educated rider and the educated horse, permitting the former to *suggest* a positioning of the head with a far greater finesse. The snaffle, or bridoon, acts to raise the head, whilst the curb when it assumes an angle of about 45 degrees in the mouth, induces a lowering of the nose, flexion of the lower jaw and of the poll. The mouthpiece of the curb is most usually a straight bar made with a central hump, called the port. The purpose of the port is to accommodate the tongue, thus allowing the bearing surfaces of the mouthpiece, on either side of the port, to come into direct contact with the bars. If the mouthpiece was made without a port, the bit would bear more upon the tongue than the bars and would, therefore, be rendered less efficient and direct in its action.

The severity or otherwise of the curb bit depends upon the length of the cheek below the mouthpiece, the longer the

The two most commonly used types of bridle. *above left*: The snaffle bridle complete with drop noseband, which prevents the horse opening its mouth and evading the bit. *above*: The double bridle with the two bits and double reins, used mainly on show horses and ponies, and for dressage.

cheek the greater being the possible leverage. The length of the cheek *above* the mouthpiece, which incorporates the 'eye' to which the headpiece of the bridle is attached, is, however, of almost equal significance. A long cheek will cause a greater downward pressure on the poll as the 'eye' moves forward in response to the application of the rein, transmitting that pressure through the cheekpiece to the head-strap.

The Pelham bridle is something of a compromise between the extremes represented by the snaffle and the double bridle (the two basic bridles used in the correct schooling of the horse). With one mouthpiece, usually of the half-moon type, and a cheek which incorporates an additional ring for the fixing of a bridoon rein, it attempts to reproduce the effects of the latter. In practice, the snaffle action of the bit will predominate when the bridoon rein is held outside the little finger and the opposite result will be obtained when the position of the reins is reversed and the

curb rein is held in a similar manner.

The 'gag' bridle, on the other hand, is little more than an extension of the snaffle, accentuating the upward, head-raising, action of the latter by its peculiar construction. In the gag, the bit rings are made with two aligned central holes in the ring through which a cheekpiece of rounded leather is passed, the rein being attached to a ring on the bottom of the latter. This arrangement enables the bit to move upwards in the horse's mouth exerting very considerable pressure on the corners of the lips. In fact, of course, the action produces contradictory pressures, one upwards on the mouth and one downwards on the poll. Nonetheless the gag is held to be a useful aid in controlling an impetuous horse and perhaps, more particularly, for one that approaches his fences rather faster than is considered desirable, whilst holding his head firmly between his knees.

The last of the bridle groups is that which gives control through pressure on the nose alone. This type is often called a 'hackamore', the name deriving from the Spanish *jaquima* – a noseband, used by the *domador* (trainer) in preparing the horse for the 'spade' bit (a curb bit with a solid high port resting on the tongue and sufficiently long to act against the roof of the mouth) which was used by the trainer or 'reiner' of the advanced horse, the *arrendador*. This bitless bridle is part of a sophisticated method of schooling originating in the Iberian Peninsula and passing from there, by means of the sixteenth century *conquistadores*, to the Americas. There it remains integral in Western riding, but it has also achieved a more general use in recent years. Many riders employing the European system of training use, or more frequently misuse, the bridle, mistakenly supposing it to be a 'kinder' form of control. In fact, in the wrong hands, the bridle is a very severe instrument.

The development of the bridle began early in the history of man's association with horses and in comparative terms it was not long before a satisfactory form of harness evolved. Perhaps surprisingly, the saddle and more particularly the stirrup, was a much later introduction. Most of the pre-Christian horse peoples used coverings and pads, some of the latter being quite elaborate, on the backs of their horses, although Xenophon (430–355 BC), possibly because he was a Spartan, decried the practice maintaining that the bare legs of a man wrapped around the sweating coat of his horse gave more security.

The limitations of cavalry operating without the security afforded by a saddle and stirrups would seen to be obvious. Primarily, of course, it prohibited the cavalry soldier from closing with the enemy, but it was not until the fourth century that a saddle constructed on a wood foundation, the 'tree', was in use and it took almost another 100 years before the stirrup was invented and made possible the cavalry charge against bodies of infantry.

Charles Chenevix Trench, author of *A History of Horsemanship* and a contributor

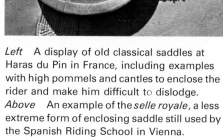

to this book, has this comment to make: 'It is surprising that horsemen took 1500 years to think up something so simple. One is reluctantly driven to the distasteful conclusion that we are not really a very bright set of people'.

It is probable that it was the Sarmatians, a people later absorbed by the Goths, who used a tree and produced a saddle built high at the pommel and cantle to enclose the rider. Credit for the stirrup goes to the Huns of Attila and a Chinese officer writing in 477 AD confirms its use by these Mongolian horsemen.

The same type of enclosing saddle served the mediaeval knight, whose long stirrups were hung well forward so as to allow the rider to brace himself against the cantle. This position prevented his being thrown forward and enabled him to withstand the impact of the charge against infantry without departing unceremoni-ously over his horse's rump. That saddle exists in recognizable form today as the Western saddle. The *selle royale*, still used at the classical schools of Saumur and Vienna, the home of the Spanish Riding School, and those saddles currently in use in Portugal and Spain are its direct descendants and little different from the saddles of the late Renaissance period. The only major alteration is in the positioning of the stirrup bars, which are placed further to the rear than in the saddle of the mounted knight. In turn, the modern dressage saddle, although considerably more streamlined in appearance, has its origins in these saddles. Like that of the armoured knight, the dressage saddle is ideally suited to its purpose, fulfilling the rider's requirements in this particular and specialized branch of equitation.

Dressage involves movements demanding a state of collection, the horse moving with the head held high and the greater part of the weight being carried over actively engaged quarters. In order to remain in-balance with the horse it is necessary for the rider's body weight to be positioned as nearly as possible over the centre of balance of the horse. In the horse at rest, this can be taken to be at the junction of an imaginary vertical line, drawn from some 15 cm (6 in) behind the withers to the ground, and a horizontal one drawn from the point of the shoulder to the rear. In movement the horse's centre of balance shifts forward, its position being governed by the attitude of the head and neck which act as the balancing agent of the body mass. In the galloping horse, which stretches out its head and neck, the point moves forward. At the opposite extreme, when the horse is in a state of collection, the elevated head carriage and lowered croup cause the centre of balance to move

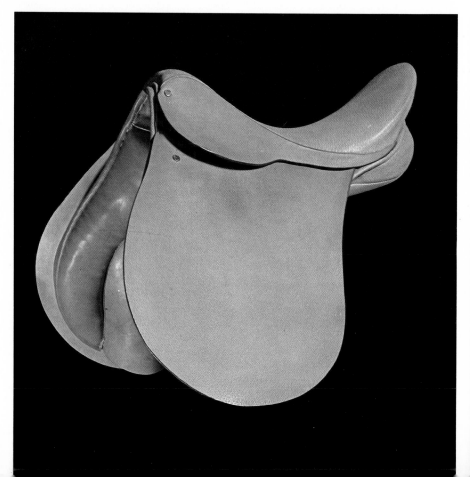

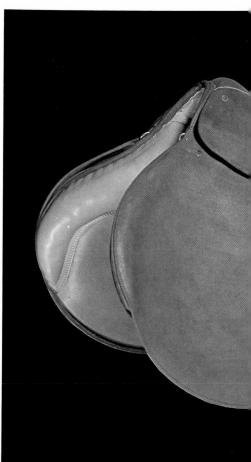

to the rear. The dressage rider, sitting centrally in a relatively dipped seat and with a long leg which can be accommodated by a nearly straight cut saddle flap, is ideally positioned in relation to that centre of balance. But that seat and that saddle would be of little use to the show-jumping or event rider, who operates at a much faster pace and is concerned with a different balance. In those instances the centre of balance will in general be further forward and on occasions considerably further forward. For a rider to remain in-balance he must employ a shorter stirrup leather and use a saddle which, by the position of its bars, over which the weight will be carried, and the advancing shape of its flaps, allows for the shorter leather and assists the rider in maintaining his body forward over the horse's point of balance.

The incentive for the production of such saddles, the modern jumping and general-purpose saddles of today, was provided by an Italian cavalry officer, Federico Caprilli (1868–1908) whose theories resulted in the 'forward system' of riding, often referred to as the 'forward seat'. Up to Caprilli's time the classical influence, directed at the production of the collected horse schooled in indoor arenas, had dominated European equestrian thought,

Below Three modern saddles designed for different jobs. *left*: The dressage saddle, with a straight flap and a dipped seat which enables the rider to sit deep into the centre with a long, almost straight leg. *middle*: The general purpose saddle (this one is made of deerskin) which is comfortable for almost any type of riding. *right*: A forward cut jumping saddle with knee rolls to help the rider keep the correct position in relation to the horse's centre of balance whilst it is jumping.

in the vanguard of which were the military schools. Cavalry troopers rode with a 'full' seat (i.e. one firmly implanted in the saddle at all times) and with a long leg, using saddles corresponding to that position.

Caprilli, holding that the role of cavalry was reconaissance, involving crossing over a country and the natural obstacles presented by it at speed, thus discarded formal school training. In its place he used the actual type of terrain over which cavalry might operate as a schooling ground, compelling his horses to adjust their own balance and allowing them to do so by being given complete freedom of the head and neck. He made his riders 'perch' teachings, even though nearly half a century went by after his death before a thoroughly satisfactory article was made.

In the intervening period, of course, many saddles were designed that purported to be in accordance with the Caprilli theory. Saddles were built with forward-cut panels and flaps to accommodate the use of the shortened stirrup. Some even incorporated the now familiar 'spring' tree, mady by laying two strips of tempered steel on the under sides of the tree from front to rear to give greater resilience. None however found general acceptance – a fact above the saddle with the seat slightly raised and they used a shortened leather to position themselves forward over the point of balance. The principal was that of non-intervention.

Caprilli's system has not survived in its entirety; competitive riding today is too demanding for that. Instead his system and the classical one has melded. Modern riders practise the dressage on the flat that he discarded, but follow him in sitting forward across country and over fences. Modern saddles, however, are the result of his

which may be taken to uphold the rightness of Mr. Chenevix Trench's comment.

The breakthough came in the post-war years as a result of the work of a Spanish horseman, Count Ilias Toptani, a trainer of the Caprilli persuasion who schooled the South American show-jumping teams. In brief, Toptani increased the depth of the saddle seat, narrowed the waist or 'twist' of the saddle so as not to spread the thighs of the rider and brought the stirrup bars forward by sloping the head (pommel) of the tree. By so doing he ensured that the rider's weight was positioned forward. The lower body was anchored by the provision of rolls on the panel, supporting the lower thigh just above the knee, and was cut well forward in line with the slope of the head. He used a spring tree to give resilience to the seat and so afford greater comfort to the rider and the horse – the tree 'giving' to the movement of the latter's back.

Toptani's saddle was ideal for jumping but not quite so effective for cross-country riding since it placed the rider rather too far forward. A modification, slightly less exaggerated in shape, coming somewhere between the pure jumping saddle and the dressage saddle, resulted in the now ubiquitous 'general-purpose' saddle. These three are the principal types in use today, outside of racing and the show-ring saddle (the latter a scaled down, flatter-seated version of the dressage saddle).

If we reflect that alongside the precision riding developed by the Western horsemen there existed another and opposite form exemplified by the eleventh century Moors and Mongols, themselves following the style of the earlier Huns in riding short and adopting a very forward position, we may reach another conclusion – that there is very little new in the world.

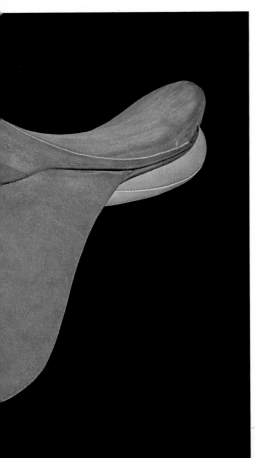
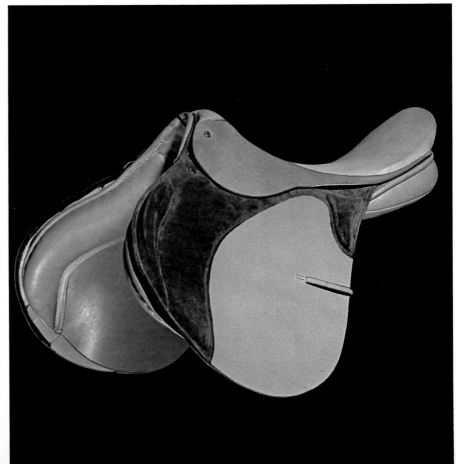

The Health of the Horse

Good health is something which many people take for granted. In the horse, it is usually regarded as synonymous with normal function, that is the ability to perform the purpose for which the animal is kept. In common terms, a healthy horse is a sound horse; conversely, an unsound horse is one in which usefulness has been diminished, either temporarily or permanently, by some disease or unhealthy condition.

The interrelationship of soundness and disease sums up the horseman's approach to the subject; and it is a practical approach. However, there are certain aspects that lie outside this particular concept. For example, a horse may have a disease, such as a mild infection or a condition of bone, such as a 'splint', yet be able to carry out a useful function.

At this point, there has to be a more strict definition of disease, albeit practical. Disease is any condition where body structure is abnormally altered. This alteration has a cause (etiology), a course of development and recovery (pathogenesis), a likely outcome (prognosis) and a means of treatment or control. These criteria can be applied to all conditions, from whence they can be broken down into finer divisions of knowledge such as, is the cause infective, or does the condition have an underlying (predisposing) cause?

It is necessary to classify disease both for the purpose of description and so as to develop a better understanding of the subject. The following is a broad classification of those diseases which anyone concerned with the welfare of horses could expect to find: infective diseases, parasitic diseases, diseases and conditions of bone, diseases of the alimentary tract, diseases of the liver, diseases of the genital organs, infertility, diseases of pregnancy, diseases of the newborn foal, diseases of the older foal and yearling, diseases of the urinary system, diseases of the nervous system, diseases of the cardio-vascular system, diseases of the respiratory tract, diseases of the eye and diseases of the skin.

Infective Diseases

Infective diseases are those caused by micro-organisms (germs or microbes). There are three main groups of microbes – virus, bacteria and fungus. Each group is subdivided into families, genera and species, just as mammals are classified according to their particular characteristics. Thus within the group of bacteria there are *Streptococci*, *Staphylococci* and

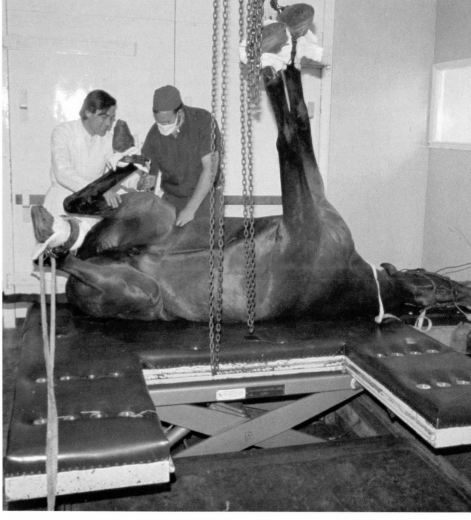

Above Modern equine veterinary practice is well-equipped to handle such problems as manoeuvering an anaesthetised horse on the operating table.
Below Examples of microbial infections. *left*: An angleberry on the inside of the thigh – a semi-malignant tumor, caused by a virus, which requires special treatment for successful eradication. *middle*: Spasm of the third eyelid when the side of the face is lightly tapped with the finger is a symptom of tetanus (lockjaw). *right*: Cracked heel – an infection of the skin in the hollow of the pastern.

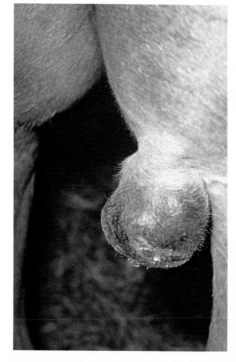

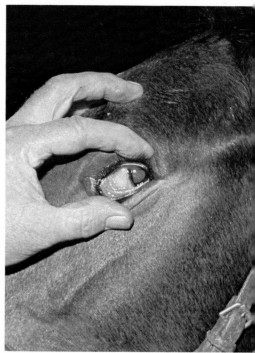

Klebsiella, according to the characteristics that these microbes display under microscopic, cultural, biochemical, serological and other means of examination which help to distinguish even the most closely related forms from one another.

Microbes can live on the surface of the skin or on the mucous membranes lining the various body cavities such as the mouth, vagina, etc. They can also invade the tissues and live within the various body structures, such as the bones, liver or kidneys. Not all microbes are harmful and some exist within the body in a state of mutual benefit, such as the bacteria in the colon and caecum which digest the cellulose and fibre in a horse's feed. Between those that do cause disease, and the host there exists quite a complicated relationship. Each type of microbe has a more or less developed capacity for invading the body and causing damage. This property is known as virulence and is recognized in practice, by the severity of the illness it causes, and the ease with which the condition spreads through the horse population. For example, the bacterium *Streptococcus equi* which causes the disease Strangles, is associated with a feverish condition which spreads rapidly through the inmates of stud or stable. On the other hand its close relative *Streptococcus pyogenes* is more often associated with localized conditions, such as infection of the uterus, which are peculiar at any given time to an individual.

Virulence can be variable according to the environmental circumstances. For instance the bacterium known as *E. coli* is ubiquitous and is found in large quantities in the gut and faeces of horses. It also lives in the soil and rarely causes problems. However, it is sometimes responsible for foal diarrhoea and during epidemics of this condition, its virulence may increase as it passes successively through one case after another, resulting in a corresponding increase in the severity of the epidemic. One of the chief factors here is the lack of

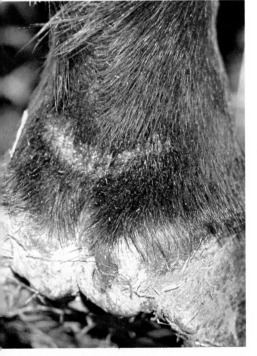

Table 1 – BACTERIAL DISEASES

Disease	Chief Symptoms	Cause
Acne*	Small boils and/or weeping sores in skin	*Staphylococcus aureus*
Brucellosis**	Lameness; poll evil and fistulous withers	*Brucella abortus*
Glanders**	Nasal catarrh; fever; oedematous swellings; pneumonia	*Leofflerella mallei*
Leptospinosis**	Fever; jaundice; anaemia	*Leptospira pomona*
Lockjaw*	Painful spasms	*Clostridium tetani*
Salmonellosis*	Diarrhoea, usually blood-stained; sudden death	*Salmonella typhimuriun* *Salmonella enteritidis*
Sleepy foal disease*	Weakness and fever in newborn foal	*Actinobacillus equuli*
Strangles*	Fever; nasal discharge; abscesses in glands, mainly of head and neck	*Streptococcus equi*
Tuberculosis**	Wasting; stiffness of the neck	*Mycobacterium tuberculosis*

* Common diseases
** Less common diseases

Table 2 – DISEASES CAUSED BY VIRUSES

Disease	Chief Symptoms	Virus
Epidemic cough	Cough; fever	Influenza
Sporadic or stable cough	Cough; nasal catarrh; sometimes fever	Rhinovirus Herpesvirus Adenovirus
Pneumonia	Fever; difficult or abnormal breathing (especially in foals)	Adenovirus Herpesvirus
African horse sickness	Pneumonia and enteritis	Reovirus
Warts	Small discrete cornified growths usually around muzzle	Papova virus
Angleberries (sarcoids)	Proliferating growths with tendency to ulcerate and bleed	Papova virus
Spots (coital exanthema)	Small ulcers on vulva of mare and penis of stallion	Equid herpesvirus
Equine infectious anaemia	Fever; anaemia; swellings on legs and dependent parts	Unclassified

Table 3 – DISEASES CAUSED BY FUNGUS AND OTHER MICROBES

Disease	Symptoms	Microbe
Ringworm	Scab covered circular lesions on skin peeling off to reveal ulcer	Fungus: (*Microsporum*) (*Trichophyton*)
Broken wind	Heaves, cough	Various species of fungus
Abortion	Thickened placenta	
Guttural pouch mycosis	Haemorrhage down nose	
Biliary fever (Piroplasmosis, Babesiosis)	Fever; anaemia; jaundice	Protozoa (species of *Piroplasma*)

resistance of a foal, which does not have the same immunity against bacterial infections as has usually been developed by adults.

Immunity is another factor in the relationship between microbe and host. An individual gathers immunity by the capacity of special cells in the body to produce protective substances (antibodies) which neutralize the invading microbe. The antibody must of course be specific to the microbe, or it will have little or no effect in preventing it from becoming established in the body tissues. For example there are two strains of influenza virus which are popularly called the Miami and Prague strains. The horse may be immune to the Prague strain, because it has experienced this infection before and is capable, therefore, of producing Prague-strain antibodies, but the same individual may be susceptible to the Miami strain because the body has had no previous experience of it. The same difference would exist if the individual had been vaccinated with one, but not the other strain.

Vaccines illustrate another way in which an individual may develop immunity. In this case the immunity is artificial, but the principle of naturally developing immunity is similar. Protein, in the form of the whole or part of the microbe, enters the body and is recognized by the host tissues as foreign. The protein is known as antigen and is capable of stimulating the production of antibody. The immunity varies with the microbe and the vaccine, which is solid and lasting in some cases and weak or limited in others. In the case of influenza or tetanus (lockjaw), booster doses are required following vaccination, since immunity gradually decreases.

Quite apart from immunity, individuals vary in their response to infection because of predisposing factors, which make the body susceptible. For example a mare that takes air into the genital tract because of faulty perineal conformation, causes the uterus to become more prone to bacterial infection.

The common equine diseases caused by microbes are shown in Tables 1, 2 and 3.

Parasitic Diseases

Parasites are organisms which live at the expense of another, but which do not necessarily harm it, nor do they usually cause death. They are therefore distinct from microbes, although some parasites do produce severe effects, which may have fatal consequences. An example is the redworm, *Strongylus vulgaris* and *S. edentatus*, the life cycle of which includes a larval phase spent in the blood vessels in the former case and in the peritoneum in the latter.

Parasites may spend part of their development in a free-living state, that is, unassociated with the host. Their parasitic existence may be spent inside (endoparasites), or on the surface (ectoparasites) of the body. The main endo- and ectoparasitic diseases of the horse are shown in Tables 4 and 5.

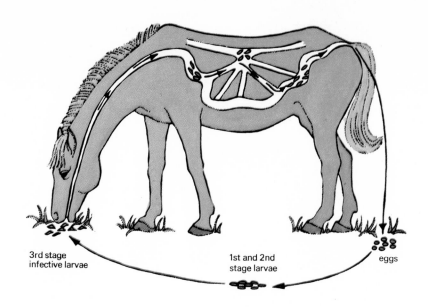

Above The life cycle of *Strongylus vulgaris*. Infective larvae (third stage only) are eaten by the horse and in the gut they burrow into blood vessels and migrate to the main arterial root where they develop further. Adults return to the intestine and lay eggs which are passed out to repeat the cycle. *Right* Maggots of the bot fly in the stomach. Eggs, laid on the hairs by the adult flies, are licked off by the horse and hatch in the stomach. The maggots attach to the stomach wall and large infestations may rupture it.

Table 4 – ENDOPARASITIC DISEASES OF THE HORSE

Disease	Symptoms	Parasite
Strongylosis	Diarrhoea; loss of condition; colic; anaemia	*Strongylus vulgaris* *Strongylus edentatus* *Strongylus equinus*
Ascariasis	Diarrhoea in foals; colic; broncho-pneumonia	*Parascaris equorum*
Oxyuriasis	Rubbing tail	*Oxyuris equi*
Tapeworm	None	*Anoplocephala perfoliata*
Bot maggot	Gastritis; perforation of the stomach; rectal haemorrhage	*Gastrophilus intestinalis*

Table 5 – ECTOPARASITIC DISEASES OF THE HORSE

Disease	Symptoms	Parasite
Lice	Irritation; rubbing; loss of hair	*Bovicola equi*
Ticks	Irritation; carry disease such as encephalomyelitis	Ixodidae and Argasidae species
Mange	Scabs; intense irritation; loss of hair; thickened skin	*Sarcoptes* and *Psoroptes*
Ear mange	Head shaking; stamping; rubbing	*Chorioptes equi*
Autumn itching	Pimples and scabs on legs	*Trombicula autumnalis* (harvest mites)

Diseases and Conditions of Bone

Bone disease, as such, is rare in the horse, and is confined mainly to disorders of growth in horses up to the age of about two years old. In older horses, it may occur in cases of nutritional imbalance. From the horseman's viewpoint, these are conditions of enlargements (sometimes painful) around the fetlock and above the knees or hocks in foals and yearlings caused by inflammation of the growth plate (epiphysitis), or recognizable in older horses as 'big head' in which the bones of the head become softened and distorted.

Most conditions affecting bone in horses, apart from nutritional disturbances, can be traced to trauma or infection. A better understanding is achieved by recognizing that bone is not a static structure, nor can it be regarded in isolation from its relationship with joints or from its attachment to ligaments and muscle (see The Body of the Horse). Bone is lined by a fine membrane known as periosteum on its outer surface and endosteum on its inner surface. These two membranes mould the shape of the bone by building and breaking down the bony substance which is nourished by blood vessels and is composed mainly of calcium and phosphorus laid down in a system of canals or spaces surrounded by bone cells.

In practice, we become aware of bony disorders in the form of lumps which may be painful or painless, small or large, and may or may not cause lameness. These are known as 'splints', high and low ringbone, osselets, bone spavin, sore or bucked shins, pedal ostitis or, as the veterinarian would say, exostoses, i.e. bony outgrowths. Collectively, they are the result of inflammation of the periosteum and the raising up of the fine membrane from the surface of the bone. The reaction usually spreads to neighbouring tissues causing a fibrous swelling which precedes the laying down of new bone beneath the periosteal lining. This reaction is seen at its most typical in the development of 'splints'. Here the ligament binding the splint to the cannon bone may become affected and a fibrous reaction develops, which can be seen displacing the skin outwards over the site of reaction. After a time new bone is laid down and the splint becomes calloused, gradually diminishing in size over quite a long period of time.

'Splints' may also be caused by fracture of the slender shaft of the bone, which results in a callus, that is new bone developed in the fibrous reaction between the severed ends of the shaft. The callus fixes and re-unites the fractured part, as also occurs when larger bones are fractured, providing the ends of the bone are immobilized. Sore and bucked shins are often the result of stress fractures of the cannon bone. Resembling nothing more than cracks in china, they are difficult to demonstrate on X-ray. Nonetheless they evoke a reaction of the periosteum and a painful enlargement at the site of fracture.

The lower parts of the legs, where the bone is close to the skin, are the regions where exostoses commonly occur. These show as bulges through the skin. Areas likely to be affected on the foreleg are shown below.

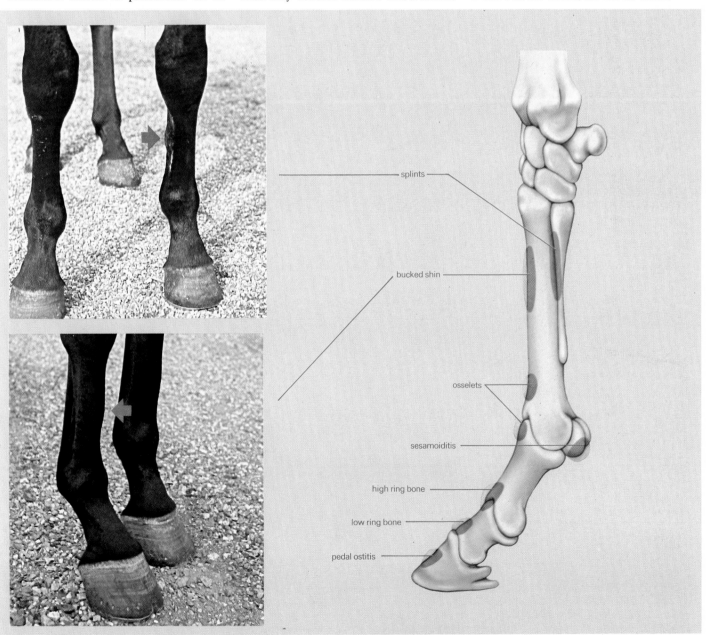

splints

bucked shin

osselets

sesamoiditis

high ring bone

low ring bone

pedal ostitis

The periosteum may become damaged when ligaments or joint capsules are torn at the point where they insert into the outer lining of the bone. Osselets and sesamoiditis are examples. In these cases the reaction takes much the same course, typified by heat, pain and swelling.

Arthritis means inflammation of a joint and the symptoms are swelling, heat and pain when the joint is moved. Joints are composed of several structures, one or more of which may be damaged, thus giving the symptoms of a sprained joint, but requiring veterinary investigation to determine the exact nature of the condition. For example a swollen, painful fetlock joint may be caused by a sprain of the joint capsule, a supporting ligament, or of the articular surfaces of the joint.

The surface of the bones forming a joint is lined by cartilage, which is softer than bone and is able to replace the cells that are lost through wear. Any process which damages the surface, such as infection or trauma, sets up an inflammatory reaction, i.e. arthritis. The swelling of arthritis is caused by an increase in synovial fluid (joint oil) which makes the capsule bulge. A soft swelling is produced and this can be felt at certain points around the joint. The arthritic area on the joint's surface may be likened to an ulcer. It can heal or become progressively deeper until it reaches the bone beneath, which may respond by producing new bone in an effort to repair the damage. However, this new bone is usually too fragile or too profuse to achieve functional repair of the joint. The consequence is seen as bony outgrowths from

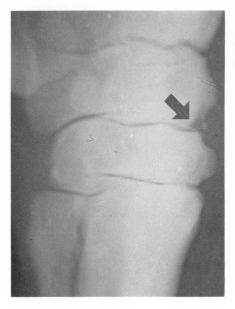

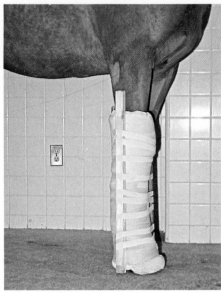

the joint surface from which small pieces become detached. These pieces lie free in the joint cavity and are commonly described as joint mice.

Fractures

Any bone in the body may be fractured, but those most commonly affected are the pastern, pedal, sesamoid, carpal, cannon and pelvic bones. Fractures may be simple or compound and the broken pieces widely separated or comminuted – that is protruding through the skin. Treatment of fractures consists of immobilizing the part by bandage or plaster support or by internal fixation.

Above left An x-ray of the hock, showing a joint mouse lying in the joint cavity between the tarsal bones.
Above right A horse with a broken leg is usually put down because the chances of its being sound after the fracture has healed are small but treatment may be worth while in the case of stud stallions and brood mares. This horse has a fractured cannon bone; the leg has been encased in plaster and a wooden support is incorporated.
Below A split pastern, which may be caused by jumping, can be treated by screwing the pieces together. *left*: An x-ray of a split pastern viewed from behind. *right*: The same leg, viewed from the side, after treatment.

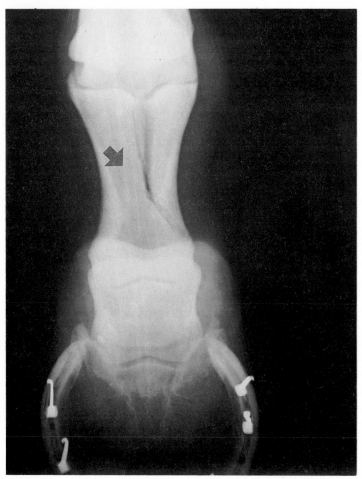

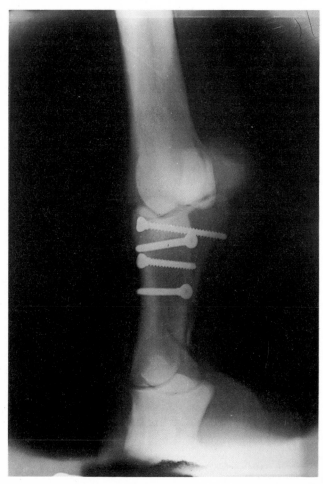

Diseases of the Alimentary Tract

Colic is the condition most frequently encountered in this category in stud or stabled horses. In this context, it implies pain arising from a disturbance in the alimentary tract. The pain causes the horse to show certain symptoms such as sweating, pawing the ground, looking round at the flanks, rolling or lying on the ground (flat out, on the brisket or on the back), refusing to eat and passing dungs of abnormal quantity (usually decreased) or quality (hard, mucous-covered, soft, smelly or diarrhoeaic).

The veterinarian distinguishes a number of differing types of colic, according to the symptoms and based on the results of examinations of abdominal sounds (borborygmi) resulting from peristalsis, blood, rectal temperature; palpation of the abdominal contents *per rectum* and examination of peritoneal fluid obtained by needle puncture through the 'belly' muscles may also aid diagnosis.

The chief types of colic are:

(i) Simple stoppage (impaction) caused by partially-digested food accumulating in the lumen of the gut. There are certain sites where this is most likely to occur, namely in the pelvic flexure of the large colon, in the caecum and where the last part of the small intestine (ileum) enters the caecum. The quantity of food involved depends on the site of obstruction. In the ileum it is small, but in the colon or caecum, large quantities may accumulate.

(ii) Tympany, caused by gaseous distention of the gut which may be a result of fermentation or over-production of gas by bacteria not normally present in the gut. Tympany may involve enormous quantities of gas or be confined to a small part of the gut, but in either case the wall of the gut is stretched, causing pain.

(iii) Spasmodic colic implies an over-activity of the gut wall, and this irritability results in painful spasms which are accentuated by local accumulations of gas.

(iv) Thrombo-arteritic colic follows the blocking of a small or large branch of the arteries which supply blood to the wall of the gut. These arteries travel in the mesenteries by which the gut is suspended in the abdominal cavity. The most common sites affected are the small intestine and the caecum, and the most frequent cause of thrombus is damage caused to blood vessels by the larval forms of the redworm parasite *S. vulgaris*.

The severity of this last form of colic depends partly on the area of wall which is deprived of blood, which in turn depends on the size of the artery in which the clot lodges. However, the sequence of happenings is much the same in all cases, namely the deprived area becomes inflamed and then, if an alternative blood supply cannot be developed from neighbouring blood vessels, the affected part 'dies' in a state

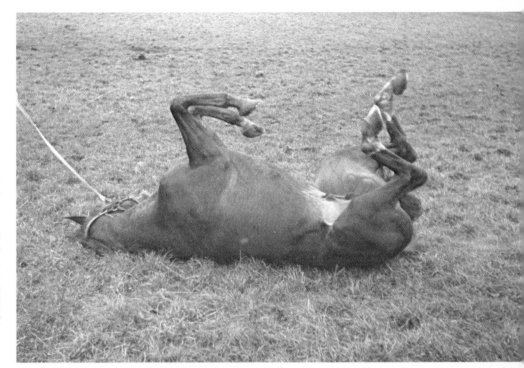

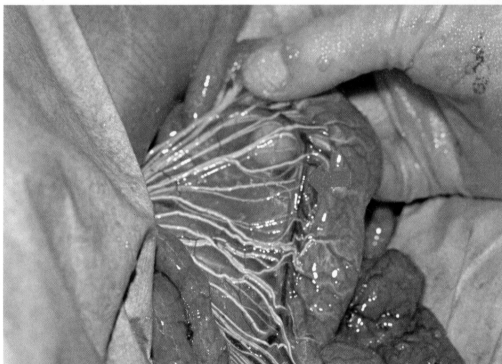

similar to gangrene. Inflammation (peritonitis) of the outer lining of the gut causes acute pain and may result in two loops of bowel becoming adherent to one another (adhesions).

Damage of this nature causes an acute obstruction because peristalsis (the movement of the gut which propels the food along the alimentary tract) does not cross the affected part or produces a reflex paralysis of considerable lengths of bowel. The severity and duration of colic depend on the extent of the damage. In some cases it may resolve, but in others it may lead to profound disturbances in fluid and salt content of the blood and culminate in a state of shock and heart failure.

Twisted gut (volvulus) is another example of an acute obstruction. Portions of the

Abdominal pain, arising from a variety of causes, is termed colic. *top*: Prolonged rolling is a typical symptom. *bottom*: Part of the small intestine, exposed during an operation, showing the blood vessels which can become blocked due to damage by redworm; deprived of its blood supply the gut becomes inflamed and colic pain results.

intestines become 'tied' in a knot or entangled through tears in the mesentery, with similar consequences to cases of arterial blockage by thrombus. A ruptured gut may be the sequel to any type of colic, but is most frequent following tympany, damage from thrombus or the activity of parasites. The stomach may rupture because of tympany, but the caecum and colon are more prone to the consequences of parasitic damage.

There are specific conditions in which colic is the predominant sign, such as grass sickness. The cause of this disease has not been established, despite intensive research since it was first reported as occurring in an army camp in Scotland at the turn of the century. Current opinion favours the hypothesis that it is caused by a toxin in the grass or other feed, which damages the nerves of the sympathetic system supplying the gut, causing paralysis of the alimentary tract.

Colitis X is the name given to a severe and usually fatal condition in which the wall of the large colon becomes thickened and haemorrhagic. This condition is thought to be caused by a toxin produced by bacteria in the hind gut. Death comes about by shock and gross disturbances in the electrolyte and fluid balance of the body.

Treatment of colic depends on the diagnosis, but it is largely symptomatic. Simple impactions are treated with oily lubricants and salt solutions administered by stomach tube. Pain is controlled by administering suitable drugs; fluid and electrolyte may be transfused into the blood stream to counter unfavourable balance that results from more severe forms of alimentary obstruction. Abdominal surgery is used to correct twists and other anatomical obstructions which cannot be relieved by medical therapy.

Choke

This condition is encountered in horses of all ages, including foals. The most dramatic symptom is the sudden profuse discharge, down both nostrils, of saliva, coloured green or brown according to the nature of the diet at the time. The affected animal usually has an anxious expression and may stand with its head over its water supply, perhaps swilling water through its mouth, but not swallowing. The condition is caused by a dry bolus of food or an object such as a piece of wood becoming lodged in the gullet or oesophagus. Treatment with tranquilizing type drugs is usually successful.

Diseases of the Liver

The liver has an enormous number of functions. It filters blood carrying the products of digestion from the gut and thereby plays a strategic part in assimilating the protein, carbohydrate and fats of the diet; it de-toxicates, or works on toxic substances of food (or of drugs administered by mouth or injection), changing them from harmful to innocuous compounds. It forms part of the defence mechanism of the body; helps to regulate the protein level in the bloodstream; produces bile which is a means of treating unwanted pigments as well as playing a vital part in the digestive processes of the gut; it acts as a store for sugar in the form of glycogen; and it is a source of enzymes which enter into innumerable metabolic systems forming the basis of life.

Damage of any kind (from infection, toxins, poisons etc) may impair one or

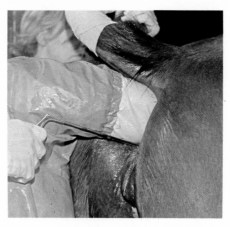

Above Diagnosis of uterine infections may require a biopsy specimen. The vet inserts his arm into the rectum to press the uterine

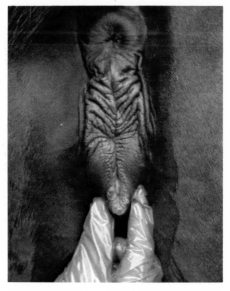

Above Coital exanthema in the mare. This is a virus infection which affects both mare and stallion and is contracted during mating.

Right Mastitis is a bacterial infection of the udder. Treatment involves introducing antibiotic through the teat canal.

more of the liver's functions, thereby causing symptoms of disease. Jaundice, for example, may occur because of haemolytic disease in which excess red blood cell pigment is released into the blood stream because of bacterial or viral infection, or because of iso-immune disease (see haemolytic jaundice of the newborn foal), thus flooding the liver which normally excretes these pigments in the bile. Instead the pigment returns to the bloodstream, albeit in an altered form, and saturates the tissues and membranes, turning visible parts yellow. The liver itself may be damaged by infection or poisons and consequently become unable to deal with normal quantities of pigment reaching it in the bloodstream. This also causes jaundice, but in addition it may interfere with a number of liver functions which may lead to wasting and nervous disorders, as the liver fails in its digestive and detoxicating powers. Equine infectious anaemia and ragwort or metal poisoning are examples.

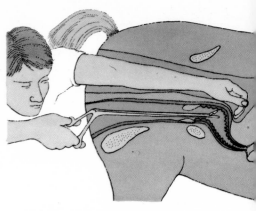

wall into the jaws of the biopsy forceps. A small piece of tissue is removed and prepared for microscopic examination.

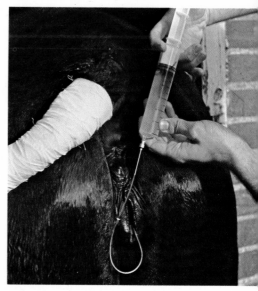

Above Uterine infections may be treated with antibiotics administered through a catheter which remains in position throughout the illness to simplify each treatment.

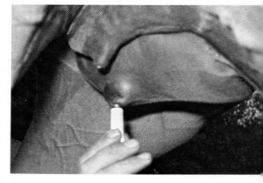

Inflammation of the liver is known as hepatitis.

Diseases of the Genital Organs

The Mare

The genital organs of the mare comprise the ovaries, fallopian tubes, uterus, cervix, vagina, vulva and mammary glands. Primary disease of these organs is comparatively rare, but secondary conditions are common. Tumours of the ovary and uterine infections with *Klebsiella* or *Pseudomonas* species, and coital exanthema (spots) are examples of the first group. Uterine infection with *Streptococci* and other bacteria usually follows predisposing factors such as poor conformation of the vulva and perineum which allows air to enter the genital tract.

Mastitis, i.e. inflammation of the mammary glands may occur, but without the artificial milking to which cows are subjected, it is quite rare. Barren mares seem to be as frequently affected as mares with a foal at foot or those which have recently been weaned. Maiden mares, yearlings and, even, foals may be affected. In most cases one half of the udder becomes swollen and painful with symptoms of discomfort, or in severe cases, hind limb lameness. Oedematous swellings develop in front of the gland or in an upwards direction between the hind legs. Cases may be treated with antibiotics administered by intra-muscular or intra-mammary routes.

The Stallion
The stallion's genital organs consist of the testes, epididymis, vas deferens, accessory glands, scrotum and the penis and its sheath. Again primary conditions are rare, consisting of tumours of the testes or infection due to *Klebsiella* species. The stallion may be affected by coital exanthema (spots) which is a venereal infection, and is caused by a Herpes virus infection spread at coitus with an infected mare. Small vesicles which break to reveal small ulcers, develop on the penis. Sexual rest for about ten days is necessary, during which time the ulcers heal. If the stallion is used, the ulcers may coalesce and become exceedingly painful.

The external genitalia are exposed to injury, especially since the coital act is controlled by management, so there is a risk of the stallion being kicked by a mare that is not properly in heat. Haematomas of the penis are the most common injuries, although blows to the scrotum may occur and result in oedematous swellings which necessitate prolonged periods of rest.

Infertility

Infertility implies a relative reduction in the expected efficiency of breeding and its origins may be traced to the mare or the stallion. The definition depends to some extent on an arbitrary approach; for example, that a mare may be expected to breed every year and to conceive in the selected

months of March to June inclusive. Some mares may, for physiological reasons, fail to conceive every year or during the arbitrarily selected breeding season. Such mares are not biologically infertile and their failure can be sought in managerial rather than pathological reasons. There is, of course, no clear dividing line between the reasons for this type of 'infertility' and pathological infertility which may cause a mare to be more difficult to 'get in foal', perhaps for reasons of mild infection of the uterus, or because of being mated with a stallion, whose quality of semen is not sufficiently high to ensure conception.

Sterility implies the complete inability to conceive and this may be caused by chromosomal abnormalities, senility, indurated conditions of the uterus, blockage of the fallopian tubes or tumours of the ovary.

Infertility in the stallion may be temporary (perhaps following injury) or permanent. Symptoms include low libido (e.g. reduced ability to achieve erection, mounting, intromission or ejaculation) or low-quality semen (in terms of low sperm count, motility or increased abnormal forms). Similarly to the mare, the stallion may be infertile in certain circumstances, such as if overworked or mismanaged in other ways, yet fertile if used under optimal conditions. Most stallions should be capable of achieving over 70 per cent of conceptions in a group of 40 mares, at a rate of about 2·5 services per mare, per stud season. Less productive rates may be experienced to every level, until the individual is incapable of achieving conception in any mares presented to him, and is therefore defined as sterile. However, for practical purposes, stallions that cannot achieve rates of more than 20 per cent fertility are regarded as completely infertile.

Diseases of Pregnancy

Pregnancy in the mare normally lasts 320 to 360 days. Foals born between 300 and 320 days are described as premature, and are usually small, weak and have difficulty in surviving. Foals born before 300 days are said to have been aborted, and have no chance of survival.

Abortion can be caused by infection from bacteria, virus or fungus. These microbes 'attack' the placenta and/or the foetal organs and body, thus destroying the capacity to live or to develop normally.

Non-infective reasons for abortion are less well understood. They include possible genetic, immunologic, hormonal or circulatory disturbances, but an absence of detailed knowledge on the subject provides us only with a theoretical approach to diagnosis. Thus a proportion of aborting cases remain undiagnosed each year.

There is now only one common form of epidemic abortion, namely that caused by Equid Herpesvirus 1. This virus primarily infects the respiratory system and the reason why it causes abortion in relatively few cases is unknown. Abortions occur most often in the seventh to ninth month of pregnancy, but some cases occur later even up to full term. The abortion is usually spontaneous without premonitory mammary development and the foetal membranes are expelled with the foal or shortly afterwards. Affected foals born close to full term show signs of septicaemia (i.e. increasing weakness), and die within about four days of birth. In these cases the mare may have normal mammary development and colostrum in the udder.

The most common single non-infective cause of abortion is twins. The mare's placenta covers the whole of the uterine surface and there is, therefore, competition for area of attachment if two foetuses are present. There are three types of situation resulting in twins of equal or disproportionate sizes. In the majority of cases, one twin dies and causes the abortion of both, between the seventh and tenth months of pregnancy.

Mycotic (fungal) abortion is most common in about the ninth month. The placenta is grossly thickened with a brownish sticky exudate on its surface. The fungus spreads slowly over the placental surface, gradually destroying more and more placenta and causing the foetus to become under-nourished and emaciated. Abortion occurs because the foetus is weakened or dies, and therefore is expelled from the uterus. However, any factor which can cause such a disturbance may operate

The conception of twins is a common cause of abortion. The foal's birth weight is proportional to the surface area of its placenta and twins are always smaller than singletons. Twin foetuses may be equal in size or markedly unequal. Undernourishment of the twins may cause death of one or both in the uterus and abortion follows. Abortion of both foetuses occurs in about 65% of all twin pregnancies.

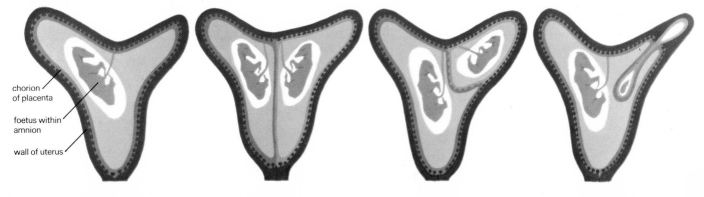

chorion of placenta

foetus within amnion

wall of uterus

SINGLETON   EQUAL SIZED TWINS   UNEQUAL TWINS   MUMMIFICATION OF SMALLEST TWIN

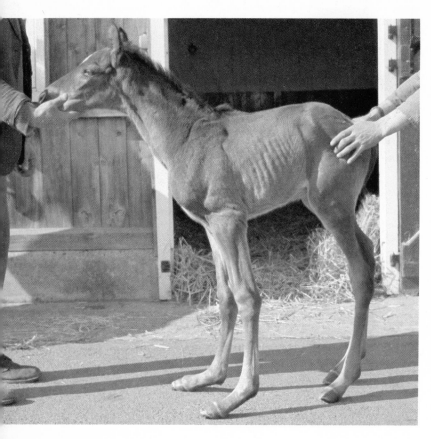

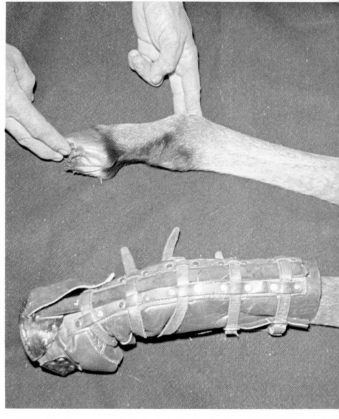

Group 3 abnormalities in the newborn foal. *left*: Weakness of the pasterns and fetlocks (hypoflexion), which in this case was self-correcting. *right*: Hyperflexion of the fetlock (knuckling over) is treated here by fitting a corrective boot.

beyond the 300th day and be responsible for foals that are born premature or, if born at full term, suffering from conditions recognizable as septicaemia or debility, which reduce their chances of survival outside the maternal uterus.

Diseases of the Newborn Foal

The first four days after birth are termed the neonatal period, for this is the time that the major adjustments, except for feeding, are established to enable the foal to exist independently of the mare. Symptoms of diseases peculiar to this period also become apparent now. As we have already seen, many of these conditions owe their origin to intra-uterine existence.

Neonatal disease can be conveniently divided into four groups, the latter three of which are non-infective:

(i) *Group 1:* Infective conditions caused by bacteria or viruses. Symptoms include gradual loss of the suck reflex, developing weakness and inability to hold the suckling position; culminating in eventual coma, convulsions and death.

(ii) *Group 2* includes the neonatal maladjustment syndrome (NMS) when gross behavioural disturbances are displayed. These include convulsions, loss of the suck reflex, and inability to recognize and follow the mare. Older terminology describes these cases as 'barkers', 'wanderers' or 'dummies'. The condition is associated with damage of the brain through haemorrhage or oedema; with profound biochemical and respiratory disturbances and with secondary effects from the deranged behaviour and metabolic status.

Meconium colic caused by alimentary disturbances during the passage of the first dung (normally voided within three days of birth) is a relatively simple condition included in Group 2.

(iii) *Group 3:* Anatomical abnormalities including parrot jaw, cleft palate, ruptured bladder, contracted tendons and a variety of deformities of the head, body or limbs. These conditions may

Below A joint ill swelling on the hock, caused by bacteria which enter through the foal's navel; the needle is to enable the removal of joint oil for analysis. *Below right* Epiphysitis of the right hock.

be inherited or developed through disturbances in foetal growth brought about, probably, by virus infection nutritional errors or the administration of drugs. These causes have been incriminated in many species, but evidence on the subject is still generally lacking, making the cause of equine anatomical defects mostly speculative at present.

(iv) *Group 4:* Haemolytic jaundice of the newborn foal, also known as Isoimmune disease, is an uncommon condition characterized by massive destruction of the foal's red cells by antibodies that it receives from the mare's colostrum. These antibodies (anti red cell substances) develop in the mare's blood stream because of an hereditary factor in the foal's red blood cells. Some of these cells cross from the placenta into the mare during foetal development, and act in a manner similar to a vaccine, stimulating

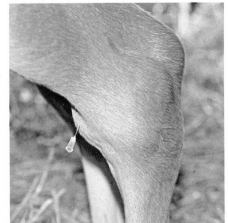

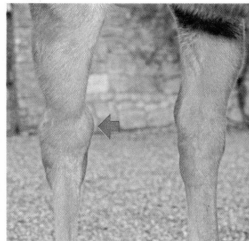

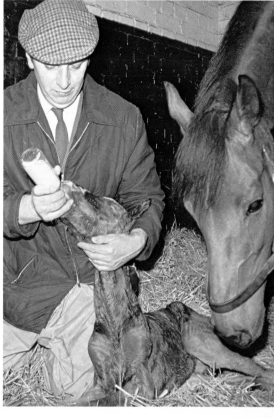

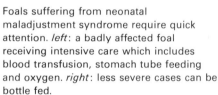

Foals suffering from neonatal maladjustment syndrome require quick attention. *left*: a badly affected foal receiving intensive care which includes blood transfusion, stomach tube feeding and oxygen. *right*: less severe cases can be bottle fed.

the maternal tissues to produce anti-body specific to the foal's red cells. The anti-bodies become concentrated in the colostrum, together with those of a protective nature, and are absorbed through the small intestine after the first feed following birth. The foal develops an increasing jaundice with rapid heart and respiratory rates on exertion and, in most cases, unless treated, the foal dies within three days of foaling. If it is known that the foal is likely to be affected, the condition can be prevented by witholding colostrum during the first 24 hours of life. During this time the foal is muzzled and fed colostrum from another mare, followed by artificial milk. The foal may be allowed to suck from its dam after 24 hours because, by this time, the small intestines have lost the ability to absorb antibody into the foal's blood-stream.

Treatment of neonatal conditions is mostly by symptomatic means, for example, loss of the suck reflex is countered by feeding through a stomach tube; the inability to get up, by help from attendants and general nursing, (the inability to get up to suck is dealt with by feeding from a bottle); dehydration, by intravenous fluid therapy and transfusions of whole blood or plasma; and the inability to maintain body temperature, by heating the foaling box. Specific treatment includes antibiotics for infections, surgical repair of a ruptured bladder, and the transfusion of red cells in cases of haemolytic jaundice.

Health problems of the neonatal foal are discussed further on page 220.

Diseases of the Older Foal and Yearling

Foals up to the time of weaning may suffer from conditions peculiar to this age group, such as infective arthritis (joint ill) and diarrhoea caused by bacteria, rotavirus, fungus or parasites (chiefly *Strongyloides westerii*).

Foals and yearlings are particularly prone to diseases of bone, because during the first 18 months of life, the long bones of the limb are developing rapidly. They are therefore particularly vulnerable to disturbances of growth caused by nutritional imbalance, to infection and from certain actions of management, e.g. over-feeding and under-exercise. Some young horses may have an inherited susceptibility to these bone disorders, which include contracted forelegs (straightness of the forelegs and knuckling over), crooked legs and epiphysitis.

Epiphysitis usually occurs when the growth plate at the end of the long bones is due to close. For example, the growth plates of the lower end of the cannon bone close when the foal is six to nine months old, and those in the lower end of the forearm and second thigh at 18 to 24 months old. Symptoms of epiphysitis are firm, painful swellings over the growth plate, more commonly encountered on the inside of the limb, just above the fetlocks or above the knee and hock. There are various theories concerning the cause of epiphysitis, such as concussion, especially in foals and yearlings which are over-weight, or a disturbed calcium phosphorus ratio of the diet, in particular an excess of phosphorus.

Cerebella hypoplasia is a disease, thought to be inherited, which affects Arab and some other breeds. Symptoms include 'nodding' of the head and increasing incoordination of the limbs.

Foals are particularly susceptible to viral pneumonia and to infection of the lungs with *Corynebacterium equi*, the cause of summer pneumonia.

Further information on diseases of the older foal is given on page 222.

Diseases of the Urinary System

The horse is not as prone to urinary disease as many other animals. Horsemen often suspect 'kidney trouble' when a horse has apparent difficulty in staling or is tender in the back region. However, these conditions are usually attributable either to certain types of colic or injuries to the lumbar muscle or spine. Newborn foals may suffer from infection of the kidney with *E. coli* or *Actinobacillus equuli* (BVE) causing multiple minute abscesses and symptoms of 'sleepy foal' disease. Stones and infections in the bladder or urethra are uncommon. When they do occur symptoms include repeated attempts at staling and passing urine containing protein, pus cells and/or blood.

Diseases of the Nervous System

Areas of the body may be paralyzed or suffer from loss of sensation through injury to nerves. The most common conditions are:

(i) Radial paralysis, where there is difficulty in advancing the limb.

(ii) Facial paralysis, in which the upper lip is pulled to the side opposite from that affected by paralysis.

(iii) Suprascapula paralysis in which there is wasting of the shoulder muscles.

(iv) Laryngeal hemiplegia manifested by roaring or whistling and caused by impaired function of the recurrent nerve supplying the laryngeal muscles. There is increasing evidence that this condition has an hereditary basis.

(v) Wobbler disease, a form of incoordination that affects the hind and, sometimes, the forelimbs, caused by compression of the spinal cord as it passes through the neck vertebrae. The condition is incurable and may be caused by injury or a congenital defect in the vertebral bones.

(vi) Shivering, a condition of the hind limbs, characterized by shaking movements of the hind limb and tail when the leg is flexed and lowered to the ground. Stringhalt is a nervous disorder in which there is an exaggerated snatching-up movement of the hind limb. Both conditions are regarded as an unsoundness, but their cause is unknown.

Diseases of the Cardio-Vascular System

Horses do not usually suffer from heart attacks in the same way as humans, that is from a clot (thrombus) blocking the coronary arteries and causing acute illness or sudden death. The most common catastrophe in horses is the rupture of an artery which causes fatal haemorrhage. This may occur in any part of the body, but is most frequently encountered as epistaxis (nose-bleed) resulting from bleeding from the lungs or one of the two guttural

pouches; rupture of the aorta as it passes through the chest or abdomen, often as a consequence of parasitic larval activity; and, during foaling, rupture of the arteries supplying the uterus and/or vagina. Recent reports have indicated that horses suffer from obliterative type lesions in small arteries, causing abnormal changes in the bones of the forelimb, and, in particular, the sesamoid bones of the fetlock and navicular bones of the feet.

Cardiac arrhythmias, such as partial heart block and atrial fibrillation, are common. The significance of partial heart block is unknown and the condition is probably of no functional consequence, but atrial fibrillation seriously affects performance by diminishing the pumping effectiveness of the heart. Arrhythmias are diagnosed by using an electrocardiogram. Heart murmurs are also frequently heard in horses of all ages, and their significance is often difficult to interpret in the absence of other signs of cardiac disease. Murmurs are graded according to loudness, to the place they occupy in relation to the two major heart sounds – 'lubb-dup' – as systolic or diastolic, and to the position on the chest relative to the underlying parts of the heart, i.e. mitral, aortic, tricuspid or pulmonary (terms which refer to the heart valves).

Diseases of the Respiratory Tract

Diseases of the respiratory system are referred to as pneumonia, bronchitis, broken wind, cough and roaring or whistling. Coughing may be caused by a large variety of viruses, including those of influenza, herpes and the rhino groups, followed by secondary bacterial infection causing symptoms of nasal catarrh. Coughs may also occur through allergies from mould dust of hay and straw and the

cough may be the only obvious signs of broken wind, which in its best known form, results in severe respiratory embarrassment with a marked double expiratory (breathing out) effort, a condition also known as heaves.

Diseases of the Eye

The horse's eye is vulnerable to injury causing ulcers on the cornea which may penetrate to the interior. If this happens, fluid is allowed to escape which can lead to the collapse of the eyeball. Alternatively the ulcers may heal leaving a scar or corneal cataract. Cataracts of the lens result from trauma or, possibly, from hereditary or infective causes. Periodic ophthalmia (moon blindness) is a condition of recurring attacks in which the pupillary structures become inflamed. The condition is progressive and usually results in loss of sight in the affected eye. The third eyelid is a common site for growth of a malignant tumour.

Diseases of the Skin

Inflammation of the skin is known as dermatitis and horses can suffer from infective, parasitic and allergic types. Ringworm from fungal infection, and acne or spots from *Staphylococcus aureus* infection are common in stabled horses. Small hard lumps, large weals and eczema may result from allergy-causing substances in feed or bedding, and from midge bites.

Below left The circular lesions typical of ringworm, a fungal disease of the skin which is contagious and is readily transferred from horse to man.
Below Corneal inflammation (keratitis) can be caused by trauma or infection; local application of antibiotics and corticosteroid drugs may completely cure the condition.

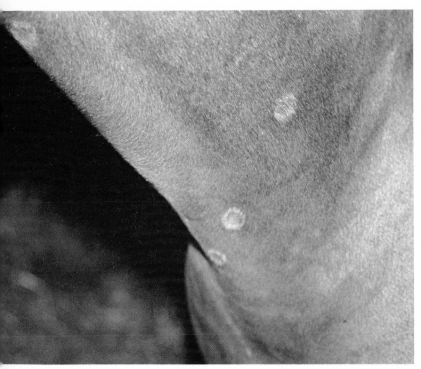

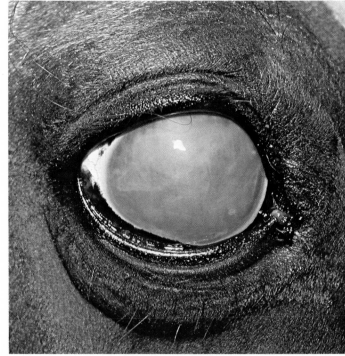

Breeding

Stallion Management

This quality stallion, wearing his covering tackle, is a credit to his handler. In the peak of condtion, he is relaxed and happy.

There are two predominating factors that enable a stallion to stand at stud, namely the prevailing laws and permits of the country in which he will stand, and the facilities available for the purpose. The former must be carefully checked at the outset, as they normally take effect when the colt is two years old, and the latter are decreed by circumstances or finance.

Defects barring a stallion from stud duties are: cataract, roaring or whistling, sidebone, spavin, navicular disease, stringhalt, and imperfect genital organs. Conformation and action should be as near perfect as possible, as the stallion is required to improve on the mare's short-comings. It is the turf records of racehorse stallions that are important; conformation is secondary.

The genital organs of the stallion must be functional and normal in appearance. The testicles should both be visible, lying level, laterally placed and of equal size. If one is retained in the body of the horse he is considered unfit for stud duties. Known as a rig, he is usually infertile, and if he does reproduce, the resultant male stock tend to inherit the defect.

The stallion's requirements are a loose box, an exercising paddock or yard and a covering area, with trying or teasing equipment. Necessarily, he requires an experienced leader, or handler who in his turn requires capable help with the mares. Once a partnership has been established, it is a good policy to keep the same leader and stallion together for the entire season, as the two soon learn to work together, anticipating each other's movements.

The stallion's stable management is of prime importance. The more 'amidst his family' he lives the happier he will be, even if he cannot participate in the general routine. Where possible he should be treated in similiar fashion to his stable companions, although certain restrictions regarding too close proximity to other horses during the covering season must be borne in mind. It is not always wise or safe to include the stallion within every yard, particularly the highly strung Thorough-bred who may not relax under such cir-cumstances, but the stallion who is shut away, banned from all company except for routine covering, is often frustrated, lonely and unhappy. This will make him difficult to manage.

The stallion's quarters should be kept scrupulously clean, for long hours spent standing on soiled litter can cause thrush and contraction of the feet. He should be strapped and groomed daily to keep his coat gleaming, his muscles in trim, and his pores unclogged. Boiled linseed, as well as being a great conditioner, gives a beautiful sheen to the coat.

Thoroughbred stallions and those of the larger breeds require a high protein diet, with up to 7 kgs (16 lbs) of crushed oats daily for maximum fertility. Good quality hay is a further necessity. On this type of diet regular exercise – apart from stud duties – is essential, to keep him fit without getting fat. Overfatness is a prime cause of sterility and can also lead to laminitis – a very painful condition of the feet.

Many smaller stallions can be ridden or driven, and their inherent intelligence tells them immediately the difference between exercising tack and the covering bridle. If impeccable manners are insisted upon from the beginning, most stallions will accept that sexual desire is definitely out of order during exercise. Stallions on Thoroughbred studs are rarely ridden and should be given one to two hours leading exercise daily, with some lunging if they are overfresh. Where possible, all stallions should have access to the freedom of a paddock for out-of-season months, or days devoid of stud duties and many stud grooms believe that daily fresh grass keeps up a stallion's fertility. Strong, high double fencing, a horse's length apart, will deter even the most determined from jumping or breaking out. Many small pony stallions can run in adjoining fields with a single fence.

Covering tackle consists of a bridle with a straight, metal mouth-piece, and a strong chain about 45 cm (18 ins) long. This is buckled to a long leather or webbing lead, of lunging length, and is run through the nearside bit ring, under the jaw and clipped to the offside ring. When pressure is applied on the lead the jaw is held in a vice, which being painful, generally keeps the stallion's desires under control. If the anticipated covering renders the stallion difficult to bridle, a headcollar with brow-band can be left on during off-duty hours, and a bit buckled to the side rings when he is required. A long lead is necessary as some stallions rear and plunge before their energies have been expounded. The leader should carry a short, strong stick.

The stallion and mare are introduced from either side of teasing gates, rails or boards. This is for the stallion's safety and also to prevent him from plunging at the mare and mounting her before she has been teased or prepared with hobbles (see Mating). Some stallions are too virile and over-excitable to be used for teasing a mare to establish her readiness for service, so for this purpose a 'teaser' is kept on a busy stud. He is usually an inferior stallion or a rig, whose job is to flirt with the mares, under supervision, enabling the stud groom to ascertain which mares are ready for service proper.

A two-year-old colt can usually take about six mares for his first season, but ideally his early services should be to mat-rons, who, being flaccid, simplify his entry. They will also generally stand quietly dur-ing his clumsy and unsuccessful early attempts. Colts will often throw them-selves at a mare, with no erection of the penis, clambering all over her to no useful effect, but a good stud groom will keep the colt teasing until he is just right. The mare handler can then back her round the teas-ing apparatus and up to the colt at the optimum moment. With the co-operation of willing mares, a youngster will soon learn providing his confidence is not pre-maturely shattered by a vicious young maiden.

At three, the young stallion can take about 20 mares, and at four, his full complement of 60. This is providing he is in good, hard condition and the mares are spread judiciously over the season, coming to him clean and veterinarily inspected for covering at the optimum time in their oestrus cycle, thus economizing on his number of services (see Mating).

Particular service problems can arise with individual stallions. Occasionally the extremity of the penis of an over-enthusiastic stallion distends prematurely, becoming too enlarged to penetrate the vulva and enter into the vagina of the mare. In this situation the leader must restrain the stallion from mounting, or if he has already done so, pull him off forcefully to prevent misplaced ejection of his semen, which would render the service useless. The stallion must be led away from the mare until his proportions have returned to normal, at which time a second attempt can be made.

Some stallions are notoriously slow in showing erection, and are even less keen to mount. A little cunning with the mare is required, shifting and moving her about to taunt the stallion into aggression. An improved diet with extra vitamin E (the fertility vitamin) is also beneficial. Other stallions will refuse to cover a certain mare, however well bred, yet cannot wait to jump a piebald pony of doubtful lineage! Again, cunning is required, and stallions have frequently covered a previously ignored mare in a white or coloured rug by moonlight, or a switched mare in the dusk!

A stallion who takes a dislike to a mare, or one who is nervous of mounting, should be treated with caution, for he will not be averse to laying back his ears and spinning

Above A 'teaser' – usually a rig or an inferior stallion – is introduced to mares to establish whether or not they are ready to be covered and what their behaviour when mated is likely to be.
Below All stallions need exercise and some freedom of movement. Leading in hand and lunging, and even riding smaller stallions, are forms of exercise to be used as well as letting them out to grass.

round on her, kicking out violently. Some stallions will bite the neck of the mare during service, holding it in a vice and breaking the flesh and muscle. A padded guard over the neck protects the mare, and will prevent the pain making her hump and attempt to kick during the vital 'seeding' time. A further hazard is the stallion who, thoroughly spent in his efforts, drops to the ground behind the mare, leaning on her quarters. As many mares give an automatic kick after service, the leader must pull him away as speedily as possible, while the mare handler immediately raises her head and turns her so that her quarters swing away from him.

Particular care should be taken to prevent the horse's genital organs being kicked. Cuts may ulcerate and be slow to heal, keeping the horse away from his duties, and a severe blow on the testicles can render a stallion irrevocably sterile.

When a stallion's job is to run with the mares, it is wise to wait for each individual mare to come into season before turning her with him. After a service in hand they will settle more quickly and safely.

Many stallions remain active until into their twenties, although they will be able to cover fewer mares as they get older. When a stallion's duties are finally done, and senility sets in, it is kinder to have him humanely destroyed on his own territory, than for him to become a decrepit shadow of his former self, no longer enjoying his dominion.

Mating

The ultimate successful mating of a mare begins well before she is actually covered. Essentials of finance, facilities, her suitability and the search for a favourable partner must first be carefully considered, followed by preparation of the mare before service, in order that the project will prove fruitful.

The finances demanded will involve veterinary treatment, travelling expenses, stud and groom's fee, livery charges, possible alterations and extension of existing facilities, as well as extra feeding and the rearing costs of the eventual foal. (Facilities and feeding are dealt with in Pre-Natal Care of the Mare).

The type, temperament, conformation and action of the mare must be related to the intended appearance of the offspring, and the purpose for which it is intended. With these points in mind, the most suitable stallion can be chosen. Breeding should not be attempted at all if the mare is bad tempered, severely faulty in conformation or unsound from weakness or hereditary defects, or if there is no certain future for the foal.

It is through judicious choice of a stallion that a few imperfections in mare's conformation or action can be improved upon in the foal. The stallion should be extra good where the mare fails and should have

a good reputation or show record, or the foal may turn out to be disappointing. A Thoroughbred or Arab stallion will add quality or scope to the cob-type mare, while for breeding up, a larger stallion is used – (vice versa if a smaller animal is required). Colour and stamp are harder to determine,

Above A mare being led away from the covering yard of a large, well-equipped stud. It is always advisable to put a mare to the best possible stallion available.
Below A mare and stallion being introduced on either side of teasing boards. From the mare's reactions, the handler will be able to gauge what precautions will need to be taken when the time comes for the mare to be covered.

unless both parents are of pure breeding and similar colour, their ancestry having been likewise for several generations. Stamina usually comes from the mare, speed from the stallion and the best jumping blood from French lines. Talent is a bonus, but temperament is hereditary from both sides. Racehorses are generally line bred, from and by stock with exceptional turf records. The stallion's management and the efficiency of the stud staff are also important considerations and will have a direct bearing on the success of the mating (see Stallion Management).

The healthy, relaxed mare is the ideal for stud purposes, particularly if her condition is improving. Pregnancy is more difficult to obtain both in overfat mares and those in hard, fit condition. Really thin mares, in poor condition, will have an impaired reproductive system. So the obese should be slimmed down, and the ailing built-up with extra protein and a vitamin/mineral supplement.

To avoid delay in getting the mare covered and in foal, prior to sending her to stud, her reproductive anatomy and genital organs can be checked by a vet experienced in equine gynaecology. This will determine if she is free from all inflammatory or bacterial conditions. Infection of the genital tract leading to inflammation of the womb may cause infertility. Damage to the vulva and tract from a previous foaling, or bad conformation in this area, can cause an infection, either through broken tissue,

allowing air to enter, or from faeces or urine collecting at the entrance. These conditions can be dealt with surgically. A maiden mare, tight and resisting in the vaginal tract, can be stretched manually by a skilful vet, thus easing the situation for the stallion. A persistent hymen in such a mare may need to be broken down, also surgically. Mares going to stud should be free from worms and be unshod, and before covering, most studs will require a swab to be taken during oestrus for laboratory examination.

An established and correctly synchronized oestrus (sexual) cycle is vital for reproduction, and the mare should come into season at regular intervals of 18 to 21 days. The duration of her time in season, or 'horsing', and the days between each heat period should be noted, as the information is valuable to the stud when arranging her covering sessions to coincide with ovulation. Mares with abnormal cycles will need treatment, and for those that do not come into season when required, a saline wash is commonly used, resulting in oestrus five or six days later. A hormone injection may be necessary to achieve the same result by dissolving certain cysts in the ovaries which are preventing oestrus.

Where the ovaries are completely inactive, a different hormone injection can be given. Lack of evidence of the oestrus cycle in familiar, home surroundings need not mean that the mare does not ovulate regularly. She may have a silent heat, and a change of scenery in the proximity of a stallion usually establishes whether or not she is normal.

In some studs, once the mare is known to be in season, through the attentions of the teaser, a vet will establish the time of ovulation, which is when the ripe egg is ready for fertilization. The covering service is then arranged at the optimum time to promote pregnancy. Without this assistance the mare should be covered on alternate days in the second half of her period, this being when ovulation generally occurs. The life of the stallion's spermatozoa cannot be guaranteed for longer than 48 hours, and an isolated service too long before ovulation is a wasted one.

The stallion and mare are introduced to one another, either side of teasing rails, gates or boards and the mare's reactions should be closely observed. Maiden mares will probably be nervous, as most stallions trumpet loudly and prance about, eager for mating. She may well strike out with her

For the actual mating, the mare may need to be specially dressed. This one is wearing hind hobbles to prevent her kicking the stallion once mating is complete, as well as a twitch and the protective neck guard in case the stallion attempts to bite her. After service the mare and stallion should be firmly pulled away from each other.

front feet, through nerves or temper. Should she appear ready for covering, by standing still (often almost sitting), opening the vulva spasmodically and micturating liquid, she can be lead to the covering area. Twitching a mare is normal routine, unless she is familiar and known to be absolutely reliable against kicking. For the mare who shows an inclination to kick, a front hobble strap can be fixed on the leg until the stallion has mounted, and for those who are obviously going to strike out viciously hind hobbles and kicking boots must be employed.

When the mare is dressed and ready, the stallion approaches her from behind, usually with much eagerness and virility. A nervous mare or maiden should be calmed and held firmly at his approach, the handler being prepared for her to leap forwards and upward, attempting to kick. Her head should be held as high as possible and, as soon as the stallion has mounted and his organ is *in situ*, the leg strap must be quickly released. While he thrusts at her, often violently, she must be kept as still as possible, particularly when his semen is being ejected (see Stallion Management). The stallion usually spends one to two minutes on the mare.

After service the twitch and hobbles are removed and the mare led round and away from the horse for ten minutes, her handler discouraging her from staling.

If the mare to be covered has a foal at foot, it should be shut away during service. Its presence will make the mare possessive, and often resentful of the stallion's attentions. A mare comes into season seven to ten days after foaling, this being termed her foal heat, although some mares are bi-annual and will not breed with a foal at foot.

Should the mare return into season, in accordance with her usual cycle, she is assumed not in foal and must be covered again. A further return at six weeks decrees re-examination for infection, and the problems concerning hormone deficiency explored. Feeding extra vitamin E will also prove beneficial.

Pre-Natal Care of the Mare

The brood mare is considered to be in foal if she does not come into season again three weeks after her final service, and she should be thoroughly tested during the entire week that she would normally be 'horsing'. Most owners feel reasonably confident that discontinuation of the oestrus cycle at this time confirms their hopes, although others consider that six weeks is a safer period, particularly if the mare has failed to breed previously on the three week basis. Certainly mares can break at six weeks, returning again into season. Some may go nine or ten weeks and then show again. In these cases nature has usually disposed of the embryo (barely large enough to be noticeable), and the mare begins her cycle over again, in a way similar to that following foaling.

For this reason the mare requires careful watching on her return from stud, and signs of sexual interest or behaviour of an abnormal manner, should be treated with suspicion. A clever vet will be able to ascertain whether the mare is in season again, or if the cervix of the womb is open or distended, indicating a miscarriage. If no experienced vet is available, the mare can be taken back to the stallion for testing, or if he is too far away, a strange gelding or a local young colt can sometimes be used. If a miscarriage is suspected, it would be necessary to test her eight to ten days after the assumed date of the disaster.

Mares returning from stud should only be turned out with familiar companions, ideally a quiet pony mare, a donkey or aged hunter. Mares are preferable for company, unless a gelding companion has never been known to arouse her and her heat periods have previously passed unnoticed. Any gelding who has shown signs of worrying her in the past should not be used. Young horses, who are prone to fooling about playfully, kicking and galloping in high-spirited fun, are not good companions, and if hounds are meeting nearby, the mare should be brought in from pasture and kept as calm as possible.

A pregnant mare should have quiet, familiar company and not be subjected to excessive excitement. A pet donkey or elderly pony is the ideal companion.

All the vitamins are necessary for the building of the embryo, each playing its own vital role, and they are complemented by certain essential minerals, such as calcium (for bone building), potassium and iron. Where the quality of the food offered the mare is suspect, extra vitamins and minerals can be supplied in powder form as a supplement in the feed. These additives are manufactured and distributed in most countries where the welfare of the horse is considered important, and distributed through veterinary suppliers or comprehensive stable stores.

Rations given depend on temperament, and the amount of grazing available. A quiet sensible pony mare, of native or mixed blood requires little else than good grazing until late summer, when 1 kg (2 lbs) of oats or stud cubes mixed with 0·5 kg (1 lb) of bran can be fed daily. When the grass has faded and contains meagre nutriment, up to 3·5 kg (8 lbs) of hay should be given at night. If the pony appears rounded and in good condition, these rations should suffice until spring arrives. Should she appear hungry or begin to lose weight, then an additional morning feed of the same quantity should be given and the hay ration increased to 5·5 kg (12 lbs), providing she eats it all. The pony on sparse grazing which has little value, should have two feeds plus hay from the time she returns from stud, the amount varying according to her overall condition. A pregnant mare should not be too fat, but the protein ration should remain constant, with the hay and bulk in the diet fluctuating to suit her figure.

The same rules apply to the large or Thoroughbred mare, although the quantities of food should be raised according to size. The 17 h.h. Thoroughbred requires about 3·5 kg (8 lbs) of oats, 2 kg (4 lbs) of stud cubes and 2 kg (4 lbs) of bran divided into two feeds daily, with up to 6·5 kg

Mares can be tested for pregnancy 45 to 100 days after the final covering by a blood test, and after 120 days lapse with a urine test. It is also possible to confirm a pregnancy after 12 weeks by internal rectal examination. One of these tests is advisable before the winter commences so that facilities and diet can be brought into line with the mare's condition.

Assuming the mare returns from stud in late spring or early summer, she must be fed according to her home environment. If she is looking well and has access to an extensive range of grazing, which is clean and nutritious, then she can be turned out after a worm dose until early autumn. Good grazing will supply all the necessary ingredients in her diet for the first four months, and the relaxation and peace will give her a calm and settled outlook, but remember pastureland must be safely fenced.

Should the pregnant mare's grazing be restricted to a few patches of land that are constantly overgrazed, it will be necessary to consider supplementary feeding immediately on the mare's return. For the foetus a complete new bone structure, internal system, body and sensory organi-

Above In fine weather a pregnant mare should spend as much time as possible out at grass during the day, as she will benefit from the fresh air and exercise.
Right Quality mares will need to be stabled at night and in bad weather.

zation has to be made up of substances acquired through the mare, while her own condition must also be maintained. She will draw these building materials from the items of which her diet is composed, namely proteins, starches and fats, fibrous roughage and the various mineral salts and vitamins.

The part proteins play in the gradual building of the foetus is the formation of tissue and muscle. As the mare also requires replacement for muscular wastage, high protein foods such as oats, maize, linseed and beans are essential. Good hay and lucerne (alfalfa) are also high in protein.

Fibrous roughage or bulk must form between one-half and two-thirds of the mare's total intake, and they enable her to absorb the protein and other food constituents. Bulk foods consist basically of hay, chaff and bran.

(14 lbs) of good hay during the winter months, or if there is no grazing available. When pasture is abundant and of good quality she is also better left out during the summer, the feeds beginning and increasing in amount as the supply of grass diminishes in both quality and quantity, and the weather turns cold.

Although mares of calm outlook, who are usually the 'good doers', can take oats, and benefit from doing so, a flighty temperamental mare will be more relaxed if these are replaced by flaked maize, rolled barley, extra linseed or high protein nuts. Some countries produce milk pellets, formulated specifically for horses. These are high in protein vitamins and minerals, but have a calming effect on the animals who consume them and are ideal for a nervous, unrelaxed mare. (Milk powder is often more easily obtained than the pellets.) For the lean type of mare, who requires building up, soaked sugar beet pulp, boiled barley or molassine meal added to the feeds will help improve condition.

The feeding of the brood mare can be summed up by saying that as the protein in the grass fades, it must be replaced with protein foods, and as the quantity of grass diminishes, hay and bulk should be given in the feeds. A pony requires from 8–9 kg (18–20 lbs) overall food intake daily, one third of which should be protein and a horse requires from 9–11 kg (20–24 lbs) overall intake, 3·5 kg (8 lbs) of which should be protein. As the feeds are made up of the various components and are not entirely protein, the daily intake required is divided into two halves, one half being given as short feeds and the other as hay. The protein ratio will then be one third of the total.

Although the tough mountain and moorland bred pony often lives out happily during the winter, the brood mare of this type will benefit from a field shelter to make conditions more comfortable. Mares of the majority of other breeds and types, and definitely the Thoroughbred, need to be stabled at night from early winter until foaling.

The loose box for the brood mare should be large and comfortable, and if possible roomy enough to foal down in, so that when her time comes she will be in familiar surroundings. A full size mare requires a foaling box of dimensions 3·5 m × 6 m (12 ft × 20 ft).

The mare should be turned out daily, after the morning feed and allowed to graze and exercise herself during the day. Fresh air and exercise are vital for the pregnant mare, helping to prevent overfatness and encouraging oxygen to travel through the bloodstream to the placenta. Exercise also helps to prevent a sluggish system and water retention. She can be brought back in during the late afternoon for an evening feed and her haynet. If grazing and space are not available, the mare should have up to two hours walking exercise daily, preferably split into two sessions. The bedding should be clean and fresh and a constant and clean water supply always available. If the box is to be used for foaling it should be

absolutely draught proof and have electric lighting, be free from all dangerous protrusions and, if possible, be near a telephone and a supply of hot water.

It is not necessary to groom the mare every day, and indeed, she will need the grease in her coat to protect her against inclement weather. A brush over once a week is all that is required, to remove dried mud and matted hair and to keep the pores unclogged. Her feet should be regularly trimmed and she should be wormed every three months if on ample, clean grazing or with cattle, or every six weeks if on restricted grazing with other horses. It is not usually necessary to rug a brood mare, but if she is particularly thin-skinned and feels the cold, she will maintain better condition in a jute rug and blanket at night and a New Zealand rug in the daytime during the coldest months.

If a mare has been ridden prior to service and is only away for a short while, gentle hacking with a light rider will not harm her or the unborn foal. Essential considerations are that she must never be overexerted, allowed to sweat, or become short of breath by being asked to do fast work or climb steep hills. Jumping is not advised and all riding should be discontinued at the commencement of the seventh month.

The gestation period of the brood mare is officially eleven months and four days,

Whatever the weather, fresh air will benefit the mare. If it is cold and wet she should be well rugged up.

although the time varies considerably and a mare can have a healthy foal at ten or twelve months. Fillies usually come before colts, but not invariably. After the tenth month it is advisable to handle and massage the maiden mare's udder and adjoining regions, to prevent resentment when the foal first nuzzles around in its effort to obtain sustenance.

After the tenth month, the udder will begin to spring, the teats becoming clearly defined. As foaling approaches it will appear quite large and swollen, globules of wax appearing on the teat extremities. At this stage, the mare should be watched closely, as foaling generally occurs within 24 hours. When the globules drop off and milk appears, and when the muscles of the quarters sag on either side of the croup, her time is nigh. The vulva will soon distend, indicating that she will shortly come into labour.

The mare's udder is a good indicator of her nearness to foaling and should be carefully watched. *left*: An udder prior to four weeks before foaling. *right*: An udder just before foaling is well rounded and has wax globules plugging the teat canals.

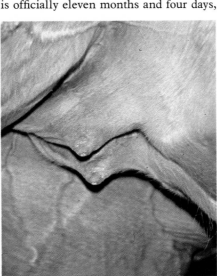 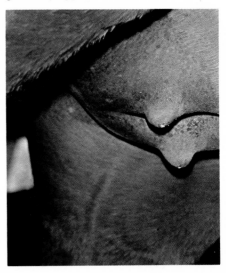

Foaling

The birth of a foal, or the act of parturition, usually occurs between 335 and 350 days after the female ovum has been successfully fertilized by the male sperm. A useful and quick mental method of anticipating the foaling date is to count eleven months and four days from the last service. Thus a mare covered on the fourth of May one year, is likely to foal on the eighth of April the following year. During this time the foal floats in a bag of waters surrounded by the placenta in the womb of the mare, and it is fed and nourished through the placenta and the attaching umbilical cord until ready for birth.

This sequence illustrates the various stages in a normal birth of a foal. When the mare is healthy and the pregnancy has not had complications the birth should go smoothly, though it is always advisable to have an attendant on hand in case help is needed, and to tell the vet when the mare goes into labour so that he is ready if necessary.

Natural birth is when no outside assistance is involved, and should be aimed for as nearly as possible, within the limits of hygienic preparation and a straightforward presentation.

Native ponies and the coarser bred type of mares, who have foaled previously, are often better left to foal outside, providing the weather is dry and warm. Some ponies are distinctly unhappy foaling indoors and will delay foaling for several days until they are let out. Those having their first foal, Thoroughbred types and mares due to foal in unsettled, cold or wet weather, or particularly early in the season, will benefit from coming into a loose box. Within the stable walls, the birth can be observed, help is at hand if required and mare and foal can be left in safety when it is all over. A difficult birth in the dark, in inclement conditions, will often go unnoticed until a dead foal is found the following morning.

A suitable loose box must be carefully prepared, and it has to be large enough for the mare to walk around with ease. It must be weatherproof, draught-proof and thoroughly cleaned and disinfected. An electric light is necessary for watching the mare's progress during the hours of darkness. The floor should be covered deeply with straw or other suitable bedding and there must be nothing on which a distressed mare or an ungainly foal could knock or cut themselves. Portable mangers and water containers should be removed at the first signs of foaling, or after the final observation of the night has been made. A sliding panel, peep hole or other means of watching the mare, while she is unaware of the fact, are useful, and for this purpose a very dim, shaded light can be left on permanently. Where possible the mare should be thoroughly used to the box well before she is due to foal.

Labour is conveniently divided into three stages. Stage one involves involuntary uterine contractions, with resultant positioning of the foetus for expulsion, and gradual relaxation of the cervix and associated structures. Stage two is the voluntary expulsive effort as the foetus enters the pelvis of the mare and passes through the cervix. Uterine contractions are amplified by the voluntary expulsive effort. The expulsion of the foetal membranes (afterbirth) comprises stage three.

▼ The mare's raised tail is a clear indication of incipient labour.

▼ Looking round at her flanks is a sign that contractions have begun.

Immediately before the birth ▶ begins, the mare's waters break.

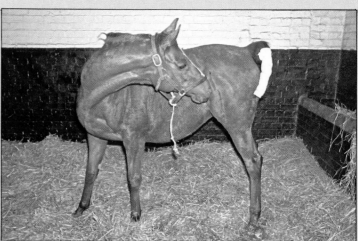

▼ Once the foal's shoulders are free of the mare, the membranes round the nose can be cleared.

▼ The mare looks round at her newborn foal which is still attached to the placenta by the umbilical cord.

The pattern of natural birth and behaviour of the mare follows this sequence:

(i) The mare paces around the stable or section of the field, swishing her tail and showing discomfort at regular intervals. Often she looks round at her sides in a manner similar to the approach of colic. These reactions are caused through the first contractions of the womb, and will continue at lessening intervals until they come every few minutes. The mare lies down and gets up again several times as the contractions become stronger and more painful, and she may start to sweat. This stage can continue from one to eight hours. (Occasionally these symptoms may be transitory, the mare returning to normal and not foaling for two or three days.)

(ii) A sudden gush of water is emitted from the vagina, either when the mare is standing or lying down. This indicates the rupture of the water bag and escape of allantoic fluid.

(iii) The mare lies down and begins straining, often emmitting loud grunts.

(iv) The forefeet of the foal, covered with membranes, appear between the distended lips of the vulva. At this stage the mare may get up, pace round the box and then lie down again for the next contraction.

(v) The foal's head appears, lying on its forelegs, while the mare continues to strain. If progress is slow after this point, and the mare appears to be having trouble shifting the foal, a little help can be given by clasping each of the foal's forelegs firmly above the fetlock, and pulling *downwards*, but only as the mare strains. As soon as the head and shoulders of the foal are free of the passage, the membranes over the nose can be broken and the nostrils cleared to allow free passage of air into the lungs when breathing commences. Premature clearance of the membrane, before the foal's shoulders are clear is dangerous, as the mare may get up again and the foal slip back temporarily into the passage, enabling fluid to enter the nose and lungs.

(vi) Once the shoulders are through, the foal slides out comparatively easily and is partially covered in membranes. It will be very wet and still attached to the placenta by the umbilical cord. It should be left alone, until it struggles free of its own accord or the mare moves, enabling the cord to break in exactly the place that nature intended. During this time nature's 'blood valve' will close, forbidding exit of blood from the foal but still allowing the foal to glean the maximum from the placenta.

(vii) The mare may remain lying down for up to half-an-hour, recovering her strength. She will probably whinny softly in delight when she realizes she has a foal, and will shortly get up and begin to lick the foal and mother it.

(viii) At this stage part of the foetal membranes or afterbirth are seen hanging from the passage, and the mare experiences further contractions in an effort to expel it. It generally comes free within an hour or two. No effort should be made to pull the

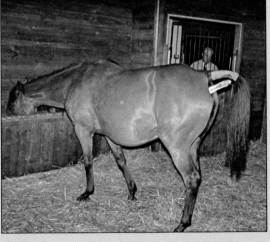

After the forelegs have appeared ▼ the mare may pause and even get up for a mouthful of hay

Lying along the forelegs, the ▶ foal's head emerges.

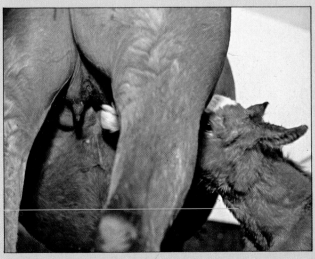

▼ The hungry foal takes its first drink of the essential colostrum.

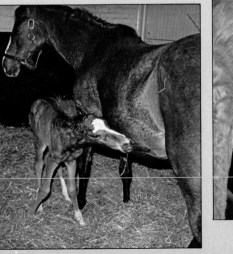

The mare's licking and nuzzling ▼ encourages the foal to struggle to its feet.

Guided by instinct along its ▼ mother's flank, the foal searches for the udder.

membrane away, as this could result in it breaking, in which case a part is likely to remain within the mare. If this is not dealt with it can cause fever and septicaemia. Should the mare not cleanse independently within eight hours of foaling, veterinary attention must be sought. After every birth the afterbirth must be inspected by a vet to ensure it is complete. It should never be thrown away without the inspection, or the mare's health may be endangered.

(ix) The foal usually attempts to rise to its feet after half-an-hour or so, and pitches and falls about alarmingly. If it does not manage to remain upright long enough to take a drink after a further half hour of struggling, it should be gently helped and guided to the mare's udder. Any attempt at forcing it, however, will be resented by both mare and foal, and as far as possible the foal should be left to follow its instincts. It is important that the foal takes the colostrum (mare's first milk) within about two hours of being born.

Problems During and Immediately Following Foaling

Normal parturition follows the pattern of events described and occurs in the majority of cases. However problems can occur, in which case skilled veterinary assistance is required. The accent is on skilled, for unskilled interference will greatly increase the hazard to both mare and foal, and should never be given.

If foaling does not progress as previously described, veterinary assistance should be sought immediately. Attempts to correct abnormal presentations should be left to those qualified to do so! If, however, the vet is delayed for any reason, the assistant should thoroughly disinfect and lubricate an arm and examine the abnormality to decide if it is possible for him to straighten a limb between contractions. The risk of putting a knee or hock through the tense roof of the uterus is considerable and no manipulations requiring force should be attempted. Pending the arrival of the vet, plenty of hot water, soap and a suitable disinfectant, plus a towel, should be made ready.

The foal is normally presented coming head first on extended fore-feet and any diversion from this constitutes an abnormal presentation. In a posterior presentation, when the hind feet and tail are presented first, the foal can be delivered without further manipulation. In this position speed is necessary to overcome the common occurence of asphyxia of the foal as it drowns in the foetal fluid. Help is given by pulling down on the hind fetlocks during contractions, and freeing the nose from mucous at the first opportunity.

To sum up, in any case other than normal presentation, or possibly posterior presentation, veterinary assistance should be called immediately. The complications of

The milt is held in the foal's mouth until birth. Its function is supposed to be to prevent fluid entering the lungs during gestation.

parturition are the vet's province, and the extent of his specialized knowledge, cannot come within the range of the practical mare owner.

Occasionally the umbilical, or navel, cord does not break naturally, and in cases where it stubbornly remains intact, (although it should be given every chance to rupture of its own accord) it may be necessary to cut it. This is done by tying a piece of sterilized cord tightly round it, about 4–5 cm (1½–2 in) from the belly, and again 2·5 cm (1 in) further away. The cut is then made between the two knots with a sterilized knife or scissors. The raw end should be treated with iodine, an antibiotic powder, or aerosol spray such as aureomycin gentian violet. Joint ill (see page 222) in the foal is the result of germs entering the exposed end of the cord.

A foal in difficulty with breathing should be shaken, head downwards to clear any fluid remaining in the passages. The foal who makes no attempt to breathe, should be slapped with a wet towel or massaged energetically. Blowing down one nostril whilst keeping the other shut, as mouth to mouth resuscitation, can also be employed.

Prolapse, otherwise known as 'throwing down the foal bed' is caused by the mare overstraining during and after a difficult confinement. The womb appears as a huge, pear-shaped, bright red mass, and may, in severe cases, hang down almost as far as the hocks. The slightest sign of the womb appearing between the lips of the vulva demands the immediate attention of the vet. Whilst awaiting his arrival, any weight can be relieved by taking a clean,

The feet of a newborn foal, showing the fringe of soft horn which protects the bag of waters from being pierced by a sharp hoof before birth. These soft flaps soon wear off.

warm and wet sheet or piece of towel and supporting the womb as near to the vulva as possible. The vet will administer methods of retention once it is replaced within the body of the mare, possibly by stitching and sedation.

Sometimes it appears impossible for the foal to take its first meal. This may be because of weakness, as it is unable to struggle to its feet for long enough to take the first steps to the mare's udder. The foal may be able to wander about, but appears quite devoid of any instinct regarding the position of the udder or its purpose. Often a strong foal, with every intention of gaining sustenance will be baulked by a ticklish, unhelpful mare who will not stand still to endure its useless first fumblings. In cases where weakness is the cause of failure, the mare's first milk or colostrum should be taken and fed to the foal by a sterilized bottle and teat. This first milk is vital for the foal as it removes the black meconium present within its digestive system at birth. After two or three feeds at two hourly intervals, the foal will gain strength and it can then be guided to the udder, which should be made wet with the mare's milk. Milk should also be encouraged to flow on to the foal's nose and lips. Once it has sucked naturally, it will continue to do so, and no further help will be required.

When the mare is at fault, she should be held firmly up against a wall, with one foreleg raised to restrict her movement, and forced if necessary to stand while the foal sucks. If she is very resentful measures including twitching should be employed, as the foal's welfare is at stake. Once the mare has allowed the foal to suck on three or four occasions, she may only need holding by the headcollar, and finally not at all. A difficult maiden mare indicates the necessity of indoor foaling, as she may otherwise be uncatchable or even fierce, allowing no outside assistance for the foal.

Once the foal is up and either sucking happily or has at least had his first feed, and if no complications with the mare have arisen, both can be left in peace in a dim light or undisturbed stable.

An interesting aspect of foaling is the milt, melt or melch which is present in the foal's mouth at birth, and which is quickly rejected. Similar in appearance to a piece of liver, its purpose is supposed to be to prevent water entering through the mouth before and during birth. In many cases it is never found, but according to country lore, when it is, it should be dried and kept in the clothing of the person who finds it, or placed on the roof of the stable. It is claimed to hold magic powers, destroying all evil forces that pursue the carrier or the inmates of the stable. A further point of interest is the formation of the feet of the newborn foal, which have a flaky fringe of soft, spongy horn round the extremities, giving the appearance of being frayed. This is another of nature's protective measures, ensuring that the hooves are not sharp enough to pierce the bag of waters whilst the foetus is still *in situ*. The flakes soon harden and come away when dry, and the feet then assume a perfect appearance.

After a careful veterinary inspection to ensure that all is well, mare and foal will benefit from being left to relax.

Post-Natal Care

Following natural birth and a rest period, the vet should be asked to visit and inspect the mare and foal during his normal working hours. Before his arrival, the mare's rear external parts can be washed with warm soapy water, to remove stains, mucous and dried fluid.

The vet will inspect the foal for any congenital defects, such as contracted tendons and limb abnormalities, as well as for hernias, hare lip, parrot mouth or other malformation. Proper functioning of the bladder and the passing of the meconium (foetus faeces) must be established, and the foal should have routine injections for the prevention of joint ill and tetanus.

If any abnormal behaviour is noticed during the hours following the vet's first visit, he should be recalled. Disorders such as jaundice or rupture of the bladder may not be obvious immediately after foaling, but are definitely the vet's province.

Any tearing of the mare's passage or vulva should be stitched – the sooner after parturition, the less painful it will be and the quicker it will heal. This must not be overlooked, as failure to stitch where necessary will be detrimental to the mare holding to future services, as air and foreign bodies may enter the passage and set up infection.

It is imperative that the preserved afterbirth is examined for completeness. If a shred of it has been retained within the body of the mare, an attempt must be made to remove it manually; an antibiotic pessary should be inserted into the mare and antibiotic injections given.

Post-Natal Problems and Diseases

Inflammation of the Vagina
Severe bruising of the vagina with possible haematoma or blistering of the lining membrane, will cause the lips of the vulva to swell and the vagina to appear dark red to black in colour. This again is a case for the vet. Antibiotic and anti-inflammatory cover may be necessary to prevent infection becoming established. If veterinary advice is not sought, a repugnant smelling discharge may develop, and the mare may have difficulty in micturating. The temperature and pulse of the mare will fluctuate, indicating infection.

Inflammation of the Womb

This condition occurs from two to ten days after foaling, when the womb has not contracted normally, usually following retention of a part of the afterbirth. Other causes of faulty contraction are an overlarge foal leading to overstraining of the uterus and loss of muscle tone, intra-uterine haemorrhage during labour and the excess blood being retained, or infection entering through an assisted foaling not covered by antibiotics.

If infection is established, the mare will become stiff in her movements and will show complete loss of appetite. Her coat will stare and she will exude a discharge from the vagina, at first pale pink and thin, becoming thicker, darker and evil smelling as the condition progresses. There will be an increase of temperature and pulse rate and pressure on the loins will be painful. Her milk supply will dry up and laminitis may occur. If the inflammation is not checked in the early stages by removal of the offending deposit, followed by thorough cleansing and the administering of antibiotics, death will follow. This condition is caused entirely from lack of care during and following foaling and infection will not occur if all the precautions previously suggested are strictly adhered to.

Mastitis or Inflammation of the Udder

Mastitis can occur at any time during the sucking period of the foal and immediately following weaning. It is caused by an abundant supply of milk, an energetic foal with sharp front teeth, the mare lying on cold, wet or hard floors, or injuries or obstruction in the teats. Swelling and enlargement of the udder is noticeable, and if the milk is drawn, it will be found to be clotted and blood stained. The mare will also show acute pain when the udder is handled. As in all cases of inflammation, the vet's advice must be sought, and the foal prevented from reaching the udder initially, at least until the acute phase is over, being fed meanwhile as for orphan foals (see next page). The udder will need to be stripped by hand until the condition has cleared, in the hope of getting the milk supply back to normal. Strict hygiene

During a bout of mastitis the pressure in the udder must be relieved by hand. This needs to be continued until the milk is clear.

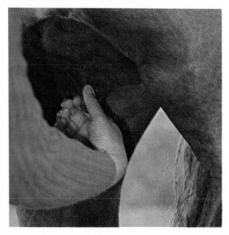

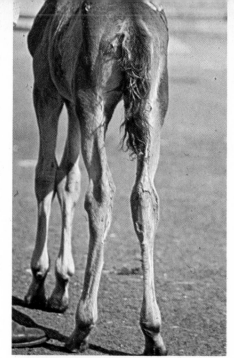

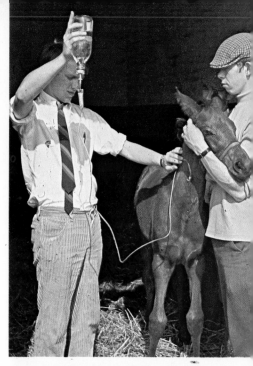

Veterinary help is needed for the ailments from which foals may suffer. *top*: A foal suffering from diarrhoea, and *top right*: treatment with an intravenous fluid to combat the consequent dehydration. *bottom left*: Typical symptoms of meconium colic are signs of discomfort, straining and rolling. *bottom right*: Synovial fluid being withdrawn for diagnosis in a case of joint ill, or infection of the navel, a distressing and frequently fatal ailment which can be prevented by a routine injection.

should be practised, and the bedding and floor of the box kept scrupulously clean and disinfected. Warm bathing, intra-mammary antibiotics and systemic treatment under veterinary care will be necessary once the condition has been diagnosed.

Joint Ill or Infection of the Navel

Infection of the foal's navel is termed joint ill or blood poisoning, and the disease is mainly caused by lack of attention to this part immediately following foaling. However, the infection can also be lying latent on a stud where the condition has been previously established. It can also take effect when colostrum from the mother's milk has been delayed or is not available for building up natural resistance. In these instances wide spectrum antibiotics will be needed. A newborn foal should always be given a routine antibiotic injection against joint ill.

Symptoms include swelling and suppuration in the navel area, often resulting in abscesses. If the foal is not treated in the early stages, it becomes stiff, loses the will to suck and eventually loses the use of one or both hind legs, the joints becoming swollen, stiff and painful.

Abscesses on the joints may form and rupture, causing discharge and joint oil to flow. As poisons infuse the blood stream, the condition worsens until the foal cannot move. Death will follow, coming as a blessing at this stage as anybody who has ever attempted to save a foal suffering from joint ill, will know. It causes immense distress and yet a little trouble at the right time could well prevent it.

Retention of Meconium and Constipation

If the meconium present in the foal's system is not expelled soon after birth and the first milk intake, the foal will show signs of colic and discomfort, rolling on to its back instead of lying in the normal relaxed position. It will also strain without result. An enema will be necessary to effect clearance, and a tablespoon of castor oil poured gently down the throat will help. If the condition does not improve, the foal must be inspected by the vet for possible blockage.

White Scour

Caused by the presence of a microbe in the digestive tract, this is an infectious form of diarrhoea. Scouring commences two or three days after birth, liquid of a yellowish-grey or dirty white colour, with a repulsive foetid odour, being emitted with

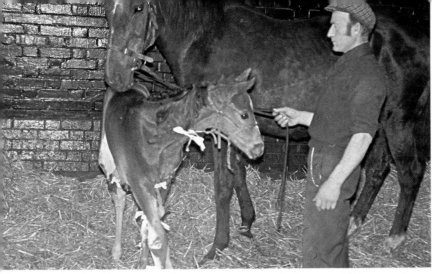
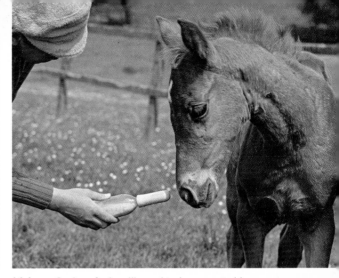

great force. The foal's rear end soon becomes a filthy, sticky mess requiring constant washing in warm soapy water, and careful drying. Cream should be applied to prevent chapping of the skin. Veterinary treatment is required from the outset as the organism will have to be classified, a sensitivity test done and the most effective antibiotic found to eliminate the particular bacteria. Drenching with antibiotics will be necessary. As the disorder is infectious, the mare and foal should be isolated and the foal kept quiet, warm and comfortable. All parts of the stable must be kept clean and disinfected and all dirty and soiled litter should be burned. Foals suffering from this condition rapidly become dehydrated and may need replacement fluid given by the vet.

Simple diarrhoea must not be confused with white scour. The former is not infectious and can be caused by an overabundant supply of milk, or the foal being chilled. Ill health in the mare which affects her milk can also lead to the condition. In an older foal, improper early feeding is a probable cause. Treatment consists primarily of drenching with a preparation formulated specifically for drying up the trouble and obtainable through the vet.

Foals will often scour when the dam is in season, particularly during the foal heat. This is of no consequence, and will terminate with, or soon after, the heat period.

Lack of Milk

A few mares give barely enough milk to sustain the foal and certainly not enough to ensure its growth. An udder that looks small does not always signify lack of milk, but if the foal appears constantly hungry

and does not thrive, shortage should be suspected. Supply can often be increased by an improved diet. Within the dictates of the season, high quality and abundant grazing should be sought, as nothing is better for encouraging milk production. In cases where no grass is available, milk pellets or powder added to ample rations of oats and flaked maize should be given, as all are high in the protein required for milk production. A constant supply of clover or meadow hay should be fed, and where available any green or succulent food added to the rations, including lucerne, comfrey and roots. Clean water in constant supply is essential. Should the milk quantity not improve, the foal will require supplementary feeding (see Orphan Foals), but should not be discouraged from taking what is available from the mare, as constant sucking induces further supply.

Orphan Foals

In the sad cases where the mare dies during or after foaling, and the foal survives, every effort should be made to find a foster mother. When the mare in question has recently foaled, the orphan foal can be smothered in her afterbirth or discharge before being introduced. Taking the skin from a dead foal and placing it over the orphan's body is often successful in inducing a bereaved mare to accept it. Some mares will accept a foal and mother it without any fuss, others will not tolerate a strange foal at any price, and will show dangerous resentment that threatens to damage it. If difficulty is encountered in the early stages, the two should live side by side, with a partition between them, so that they can see each other at all times. The

Orphan foals will need to be accepted by a foster mother or else be fed from a bottle. *left*: This orphan has been draped in the skin of the mare's stillborn foal in the hope that she will accept it as her own. *right*: A great deal of patience is needed to persuade an orphan to accept the bottle.

mare should be milked to keep the supply flowing, and this can be bottled and fed to the foal. A few mares will accept and mother a foal quite happily without having been pregnant and with no milk at all. A 'nanny' of this type can be useful as caretaker to the foal, who can then run out at pasture with others whilst being guarded from danger. She will also 'keep him in order', allowing him to grow up naturally, his mentality developing along normal lines. Such a foal must of course be bottle fed until the time that he would normally be weaned. A mare with a very young foal and an abundant milk supply will, with encouragement, occasionally feed two foals.

Where no foster mother or nanny can be found, the foal must be reared on a bottle. Although the distribution of a milk replacement powder, with a composition specifically for foals, is not yet universal, it is available in some countries and can be obtained through a vet. The powder is easily mixed according to the manufacturer's directions, and is fed at blood heat from a sterilized bottle and teat. Where powder is unobtainable, useful substitutes are: goats milk, either fed by bottle or taken straight

A healthy mare and her equally energetic foal exult in the freedom of the paddock on a fine day.

223

be sufficient.

Mares who have lost their foals at birth should be kept on low protein diet of hay and daily bran mash until the milk has dried up. There are also veterinary products to aid the drying up process. The mare must have as much exercise as possible, but should not be turned out on good grazing and the udder will need constant observation for signs of mastitis. Drawing the milk is only recommended in cases of severe over-supply, as nature will endeavour to replace the milk that has been taken.

Feeding and Exercise

Following natural birth with no associated complications, and providing the weather is reasonably mild and dry, the mare can be turned or led out for exercise with the foal after a day of recuperation. In the case of native ponies or animals of mixed blood, foals born in May and June can be turned out at night as well after the first three days. Those born outside at this time and in warm, settled weather can remain outside throughout the summer. Thoroughbred foals, and those born indoors early in the season, must be treated with consideration in inclement weather conditions, and brought in at night until the situation improves.

Mares and foals on abundant grazing of high quality will require little else, other than good grass during the summer. Where herbage is sparse a high protein diet of crushed oats, flaked maize and stud cubes mixed with a little bran, and given to the mare with a liberal supply of good hay, should keep the milk supply flowing. Foals need exercise for growth and muscle development and should not be restricted, the company of other foals being a bonus to their playful instincts.

Both mare and foal require constant observation from birth until weaning. A foal's natural inquisitive nature is often likely to get it into trouble. A foal slip placed on its head within a week of birth, and gentle fondling of the head every so often, will simplify halter breaking. Foals should receive their first anti-tetanus injection at weaning time.

Foals are usually weaned at six months if the mare is in foal again, but can be left until eight months if she is barren and looking well. The best procedure is to separate them completely in safe quarters, out of sight and earshot for three weeks, that is providing the foal was eating well before weaning.

Where foaling has been normal and trouble-free, with no bruising, stitching or discharge, a mare can be covered on her foal heat for another foal the following year. Seven to ten days after parturition is the normal duration of this heat period, but if missed she can be covered during the week following her 27th day. As some mares are difficult to get in foal whilst feeding one at foot, the foal heat should not be missed where conditions are favourable, as this is the time when she is most likely to conceive.

Above A foal that is handled from birth is unlikely to prove awkward when a foaling slip is fitted. The slip should be fitted with care to avoid any possibility of discomfort, and should be adjusted as the foal grows.
Below Being at liberty in good quality pasture will benefit both dam and foal.

from the goat by the foal; cows milk, diluted with one third the quantity of warm boiled water and sweetened in the proportion of 20 gms of brown sugar to 1 litre (approximately ⅔ oz to 1 quart).

In all cases strenuous efforts should be made to obtain colostrum immediately, but if it is not available the foal should first be fed glucose and water to clear the system of meconium, and prevent constipation. Several days of antibiotic cover will be necessary to replace the protective colostrum.

For the ensuing bottle feeding, meals should be regular, at first every two hours, followed by every four hours in two or three weeks depending on progress, and continuing with longer intervals between feeds. At four or five months, when the foal is eating well, two milk feeds per day will

IT is a strange fact that while most people are capable of buying themselves suitable clothes, furniture, or even houses, without having to be professional tailors or dressmakers, joiners or estate agents, few people who are not professionally connected with horses can buy themselves a suitable mount, particularly if it is their first buy. More remarkable still, is that whereas everybody is only too eager to seek and take expert advice if they are in any doubt about the worth of a material object, the novice horse buyer *may* ask for advice, but he seldom takes it. This is particularly true of those buying a horse or pony for a child, when all too often the purchase is way beyond the child's riding capability. To buy a horse that suits one's capacity as a rider is extremely important, for nobody's riding will be improved by a horse that is really too great a handful. The results are far more likely to be a loss of confidence, possibly a few broken bones and a ruined horse.

The tendency is for novice horse buyers to over-rate their capabilities, but worse still, they do not always seem to realize that they are buying a living creature. Horses may not have so much intelligence as humans, but each has a character and a temperament as individual to it, as those of each human being. Presumably the private person wants to own a horse because he likes riding and he will enjoy his riding very much more if the horse he buys is not only the right make and shape for him, but has a temperament not incompatible with his own.

Before deciding to buy a horse, it is as well to examine the reasons for wanting to own one. Horse-owning is not something to be embarked upon lightly. The domestic horse is not a self-sufficient animal; it is unable to hunt and provide for itself if neglected. A horse-owner must not only enjoy riding, but also like horses enough to be willing to give up time to care for his animal. The worst reason for wanting to own a horse is to 'keep up' with other horse owners. A horse should never be thought of as a status symbol.

When buying a pony for a child, it is the child's needs and riding ability that must be considered, and not what others will think of the pony. Buying a top-class, expensive animal does not automatically ensure first place in the showing line or jumping ring, unless the child is really

It is important to buy a pony of the right type for the child's experience. This young owner is obviously delighted with her pony.

talented and is having regular, good instruction. Children are generally competitive up to a point, but they should not be encouraged by their parents to think that winning prizes is more important than the enjoyment of riding, and the companionship of their ponies.

Preparing to Buy

Before starting to look for a horse, decide on the maximum amount you are prepared to pay, then look at animals offered for sale around that price. Don't be in a hurry. With patience, you will find the right animal. Buy the wrong one and you will probably find difficulty, and financial loss, in reselling it – that is if you have not become too fond of it in the meantime to want to sell it at all.

Consider the amenities you have for its keep, the time available to spend on its care, and the climatic conditions. If the horse is to live out, or partly out, in a cold climate, it must not be too highly bred. If it is to be stabled, and you are a competent rider, the choice is wider.

Relate your height and weight to the height and type of horse you need. Remember that a big horse, in height, is not necessarily a weight carrier; conformation and bone are more important. Nor is a big horse necessarily any faster or a better jumper than a smaller one. Moreover, too big a horse can be awkward for mounting or dismounting. A good cob is probably better for a rather heavy rider than a so-called heavy-weight hunter which can be a bit common. The best heavy-weights, which have a bit of class, will cost a great deal of money.

Don't buy a young horse because it is cheaper, and attempt to bring it on yourself, unless your riding is really up to professional standard, or you live where you can have constant expert instruction.

Another trap is to think that a horse over 12 is automatically too old. This is not

necessarily so; horses that have been well looked after all their lives can work happily into their twenties. It may be best to look for something between five and eight years old, but don't reject a suitable sounding animal just because it is a little older. For a novice rider, in particular, a horse in its teens can give a lot of pleasure, increase the rider's confidence – and it costs a lot less to buy.

Before actually looking for the horse, have some sort of picture in your mind of what you want. Don't be dogmatic about colour, or about sex, unless you've ridden a lot and have developed a preference for either mares or geldings. Financially, however, a nice mare, particularly if she's known to have had a foal, drops less in value with age than a gelding.

In buying a pony for a child, particularly a first pony, temperament is all important. Looks are unimportant, just so long as the pony is not so wide the child can't get its legs round it! This is one reason why Shetlands do not always make good first ponies. Children get as much pleasure and fun from looking after and being with their ponies as they do from riding them. A first pony should therefore be patient and amiable, but not such a slug when ridden that it walks about with its head practically on the ground. Never get a young pony, with the idea that both it and the child can learn together. They can't.

Ponies for older, more advanced children may be of no particular breed, or they can be pedigreed ponies of one of the many native breeds. The cost of these will depend to a certain extent on the fashion of the moment.

Each native breed has its own very individual characteristics; all have charm and quality, are hardy and can live out because they grow dense winter coats, and the majority have highly developed equine intelligences. Many are well up to carrying adults as well as children, and these make good 'family' ponies. Before choosing a

particular breed, it's a good idea to find out more about them and perhaps go to one of the big shows, where they can be seen, both in hand, and being ridden. Children should always ride and handle ponies (i.e. tack and untack them) before a decision is made to buy them.

How to Buy

If you have been going regularly to a reputable riding school, your instructor should be the best person to fit your riding ability to the right horse. There may be nothing suitable in his stable at the moment of asking, but he will probably have a good idea of the horsey doings in the neighbourhood, and will be able to advise you where else to go. The accent of course is on 'reputable'; no riding establishment with a reputation to uphold would risk damaging it by selling you some old 'plug' they didn't want. On the contrary, it is to their advantage to find you the right animal. If there is a horse you have been riding regularly which you would like to buy, find out as much about it as you can by handling it in its box, and seeing if it is as pleasant to handle as it is to ride. If you like what you find, ask if it is for sale, without being *too* eager.

If a horse is suggested to you as being suitable, don't feel you have to buy it if you don't like it, even if it gives you a nice ride. If you are going to own a horse, you will be spending quite a lot of time with it, so it is essential you like it as a personality.

If there is no riding school to contact, try a reputable dealer in your neighbourhood. There tends to be an unjustifiable prejudice against dealers. A good dealer, like a good riding school, has a reputation to uphold; so he, too wants to satisfy his clients. However, never go to a dealer pretending you know more than you do. He will take a lot of trouble to suit a genuine, acknowledged novice, horse buyer, but who can blame him if now and then he takes advantage of ignorant show-offs?

Finding a horse through an advertisement in the paper or a horsey magazine is a possibility, but keep a sense of proportion – and of distance. If a horse you like the sound of is a long way away, it is going to cost you a fair amount of time and money to go to see it. Moreover, for some reason it tends to be more embarrassing to say 'no' to a private seller than to a professional. Try and find a suitable sounding animal nearer to home, and having made an appointment to see it, make sure you keep that appointment, or telephone if you want to cancel it. It is never advisable for the novice to buy a horse at a public auction or sale, unless he has been able to try the animal and handle it beforehand.

Above Weighing up a prospective purchase. The question to ask is: 'Will we get on well together?' It is as important to like your horse as to know he has quality.
Below Buying horses from auctions and horse fairs, like this one at Stow-on-the-Wold, Gloucestershire, can be a bit risky unless you have a good deal of experience.

You must, of course, try any horse you ever think of buying, but ask the seller to ride it for you first. It may not have been ridden for some days, or even weeks, and if it's going to be a bit fresh, rather the current owner on its back than you! If it appears to be rather more of a ride than you feel you can cope with, say so.

Not many people are prepared to let horses go out on trial, except some good dealers. If a seller can be persuaded to part with the horse on a week or a fortnight's trial, so much the better. If he is not happy to do this, suggest that you return and have another ride before making a final decision. Always handle a horse you think of buying, not only when he is tacked-up and ready, but when he is taken back to his stable. See how he behaves in his box. See if he will let you lift his feet. Ask whether or not he is easy to shoe.

If you see a privately-owned horse, which having tried, you think is suitable, don't hand a cheque over there and then. Proclaim your interest, but say you would like your veterinary surgeon to have a look at it, and that, if his report is satisfactory, you will buy it. If there are several other people interested, and you really want the horse, you can offer a 10 per cent deposit on the understanding that if the vet's report is unsatisfactory, it is returned.

Always get *your* vet – not the seller's – to check the horse. He should examine its heart, wind, limbs and eyes, and will tell you its age. Over eight years old, a horse is called 'aged', because after that it is not easy to be accurate to within a year or two. The unwary, however, can be caught by the unscrupulous selling a two-year-old as a five-year-old, as a two-year-old has a full mouth of baby teeth, and a five-year-old, of adult ones.

A vet's report will include any blemishes and technical unsoundness he may find during his examination. If these include splints, it is of no great concern. Many horses have these small bony enlargements on the inside of the front cannon bone between the knee and the fetlock, or occasionally on a hindleg, but once formed, they seldom cause lameness.

Unless you know a great deal about the conformation of the horse, it is better to think of the animal as a whole, and the picture that whole presents to you. Stand back from a horse you're considering buying and see what kind of picture he makes.

It should be pleasing, and in proportion. Legs should not seem either too long, or too short, for the body, which should be compact, not elongated or perhaps with a hollow back. The shoulder should be sloping; an upright one will give a short-striding, not so comfortable, ride. The neck should be curved but not exaggeratedly crested, and the head should look 'well set on'; with clean lines. Watch carefully as the horse walks; he should stride out freely, hind feet tracking well up and coming down in advance of the print left by the forefoot. He should carry his head well, and, when looked at from the front, his forelegs should move in a straight line, not swing out sideways. He should not appear to be very narrow in the chest, with forelegs

Above It is most important to have a trial ride before buying a horse or pony, as well as asking to see it being ridden.
Below Before you finally decide to buy, make sure your horse is inspected by a vet.

very close together. Remember, however, that no horse is perfect, and unless you want a horse or a pony for showing, one or two small shortcomings are not too important, providing the horse gives a good ride, has a pleasant temperament, and is the right price.

That all-important 'temperament' should perhaps be considered further. Some horses are nervous and highly strung and they should certainly be avoided by nervous and highly strung riders. Some are more excitable than others and an excitable rider will make them more so. Nervous people should choose placid horses, who will help them overcome their own nervousness. Calm people will be able to soothe nervous horses.

While it is sometimes possible to buy inexpensively, a good horse that is in very poor condition, this is not really a good idea for the novice. It is not generally easy to tell what can be made of such a horse and it will also take time and expert management to effect the transformation.

Briefly, here are some basic rules to bear in mind when buying:

Buy within your means; not only what you can afford to pay for, but also what you can afford to keep. The more highly bred, the more expensive the keep will be.

Buy according to the amenities you have, and the time you can spend on looking after a horse.

Buy what you enjoy riding *now*; not what you hope you will be able to manage one day.

Always ask for, and take, the advice of an experienced person before you sign the cheque.

Progressive Training

THE key word in the title of this chapter is 'progressive', because unless the training of the horse is progressive there will be no logical pattern and, therefore, no clearly defined objective. There is no way of communicating the objective to the horse, but the logical pattern of progress is vital if he is to understand and react willingly to the wishes and demands of his trainer.

In human terms the horse is an incredibly simple soul and so it is essential that any method used or applied for the purpose of teaching him anything must be reduced to the simplest possible terms. By now we know a good deal about his body and the way it works, but beyond that we really know very little. We do not truly know whether he can 'think' or certainly what form thought takes. We know nothing of the intellect or powers of reasoning of the horse, although there are fragments of evidence which suggest he may have one or both.

As the trainer, we must be constantly aware that it is impossible for us to think or behave in any manner other than human; we have no wish to become horses and we have no right to expect horses to become humans, or even human-like. Anthropomorphism presents a considerable barrier in the training of animals. Such books as *Black Beauty, Wind in the Willows* and the works of Walt Disney are undoubtedly charming and yet, with a sad irony, they have done a great deal to retard the progress of understanding and communication between humans and animals. On the other hand, it is far worse to consider that animals are incapable of thoughts, feelings, and emotions. As usual there is a middle course, and it is this that the serious trainer must continuously seek.

Once the horse has reached about four years old and has been backed, introduced to the 'aids' and shown that he is willing and able to walk and trot with a rider on his back, he is ready to begin 'progressive' work. From this moment on, and for ever more, the trainer must have clearly uppermost in mind that there are three things required of every ridden horse on the move. These are:

Controlled, free, forward movement

The correct bend

An even rhythm at all paces at a tempo chosen by the rider

The three requirements are of equal importance and can be equally as correctly stated in any order. They form a trinity by which the horseman must live, for it is a fact that if *any* one of the three requirements has deteriorated or disappeared it is *impossible* for the horse to make a change of pace or direction correctly. Their importance cannot, therefore, be underlined too strongly.

The wording of the requirements is carefully chosen and deserves closer scrutiny. In 'controlled, free, forward movement', the word 'controlled' alludes to the horse in that he is exercising self-control whilst eagerly awaiting the wishes of his rider. Every horse should come out of his stable yearning to run and jump and play, but such is his training that he will control himself, channelling his desires to those of his rider. The better and more established his training, the more self-control he will display. The word 'free' alludes to his limbs, joints, and muscles. They must move freely and easily over each other, co-ordinated and, above all, without tension. 'Forward', apart from the obvious physical sense, alludes to the horse's mental attitude. He must show clearly in his behaviour and way of going that he is 'thinking forward' and has an unmistakeable desire to go there. 'Movement' is self-explanatory.

Having 'the correct bend' means that the horse will be uniformly shaped throughout his entire length, i.e. from poll to tail, so that, seen from above, his body conforms exactly to the line along which he is moving. On a straight line, therefore, he is straight and on a circle, or part of a circle, the curve of his body will coincide with the arc of whatever size circle is being attempted.

It is important to understand what the horse has to do to comply with this requirement in the light of the fact that, in most horses, the section of the spine from the withers to the croup, has very little ability to bend and in a number of horses, none at all. It follows, therefore, that he has to manipulate his limbs and muscles in a manner which does not come naturally to

The object of training a horse is to make him happy to be ridden and a pleasure to ride, no matter what the pursuit.

him. When a horse is curved (i.e. bent) the distance between the shoulder blade and the hip joint is shortened on the concave side, or inside, and increased on the outside. If he could bend his spine, these variations in distance would come about automatically, but as this is not the case it means that the inside shoulder must deliberately be drawn back and the inside hip pushed forward independently of the spine, whilst still keeping an even rhythm of his steps. Among other things, there has to be compression of the ribs and flat muscles on the inside and stretching along the outside.

A deeper study of the horse's anatomy would reveal a considerable number of additional difficulties, but enough has been said to illustrate why horses so frequently resist bending. It also shows why the 6 m circle is so much more advanced than the 20 m, and why trainers must be careful and sympathetic in their demands.

Rhythm should be *metronomic* in its evenness and consistent regularity, at all paces. Anything else would lead to unequal physical development, causing one or more muscle or limb to become stronger and/or more flexible than its partner, which would result in one-sidedness. Another very important reason for a regular rhythm is the effect it has on the horse's mind. It has a distinctly calming influence and contributes greatly to his ability to concentrate. When a horse loses concentration, the rhythm will at once alter or become erratic, and, conversely, if the rhythm is allowed to deteriorate, he will lose concentration and become easily distracted. This last factor gives the key to the importance of keeping the rhythm when making alterations within the pace, i.e. passing from collection to medium or extension and vice versa, for these are especially vulnerable moments with regard to balance and concentration. Once the tempo (the speed of the steps, or the number of footfalls per minute, which must be chosen and set by the rider) has been established, the rhythm must be rigorously maintained.

One-sidedness in a horse can come about through a number of causes: a mental reluctance to move one way because of a bad experience on that side as a foal or youngster, probably caused by an inept or clumsy handler, or a spoilt mouth, perhaps from careless fitting of side-reins when lunging or from bad riding. A spoilt mouth commonly occurs when a young horse is changing his teeth, the mouth becomes inflamed and hyper-sensitive in some part or parts, so that he naturally, resists contact in that area. Too often this resistance is mistakenly interpreted by the trainer as wilful disobedience and the ensuing coarse insistence can create a one-sided mouth in a very short time. Unequal muscular development, either from working with an erratic rhythm or simply by working too much in one direction, is an obvious cause. Many riders have a natural preference for one direction and, quite unwittingly, work much more on that rein. Not changing the diagonal fre-

quently when rising at the trot is also a strong contributor to rendering a horse one-sided.

When one-sidedness is encountered, the horse should *not* immediately be worked more on his bad side. The work should be equal in quantity in both directions, but related in quality to his bad side. If, for instance, the horse can easily move around a 10 m circle to the left, but cannot manage less than 20 m to the right then he must only be worked on the larger circle on both reins. As his bad side improves and he can work on an 18 m circle on that rein, then the circles on his good side are reduced by the same amount. To pursue tight work on the good side and open work on the stiff side – even though the stiff side be worked five times as much – will not achieve the desired result and, more often than not, will magnify the problem in the mind of the horse, rider or both.

Lunging the young horse as a precursor to backing and riding is both necessary and desirable, provided it is done well. If a young horse is correctly and thoroughly lunged it will produce benefits, which will stand him in good stead for the rest of his life. It is equally true that careless and inadequate lunging, especially at this critical time, can do severe, if not irreparable damage. So many people take trouble and pains to learn to ride competently, and then proceed to 'break' young horses, having had little or no tuition in lunging. Then they wonder why they encounter so many problems and difficulties in the saddle.

The objectives of lunging, prior to backing should be clearly understood so that a young horse is not asked to deal with more than he is able and so that the relevant lessons are thoroughly learned. Full

opportunity should be taken to establish confidence and trust in his trainer in particular, and in humans in general. If he has been kindly handled from a foal the task should be easier, but it must also be remembered that over-confidence and careless behaviour by the trainer at this time can undermine the horse's trust, so he feels betrayed. In addition, he may well resolve never to be fooled again by that two-legged monster! With the horse that has had previous bad experiences, however, this lunging period is a golden opportunity to reverse his poor view of humanity.

A major objective in lunging is to teach the horse an understanding of, and an obedience to, the verbal commands to walk, trot and halt. He should learn these to such a degree that he will obey them in any order, on either rein and in response to different voices. The person who teaches him on the lunge may not be the first one to ride him, and to have a different voice issuing the word commands from his back could cause confusion. The words used *must* be clearly distinguishable from each other. In England, for example, it is common practice to say 'whoa' (pronounced 'wo') instead of 'halt'. It must be delivered shortly and clearly, not drawn out, so it resembles the command 'walk', which is and should be drawn out. The canter has no place on the lunge until the horse is much more mature and quite advanced.

A young Swedish horse being introduced to his first pieces of lunging equipment. He will be handled from the ground with a special cavesson noseband and long rein prior to being ridden. Note particularly the attention being given to gaining the horse's trust and confidence.

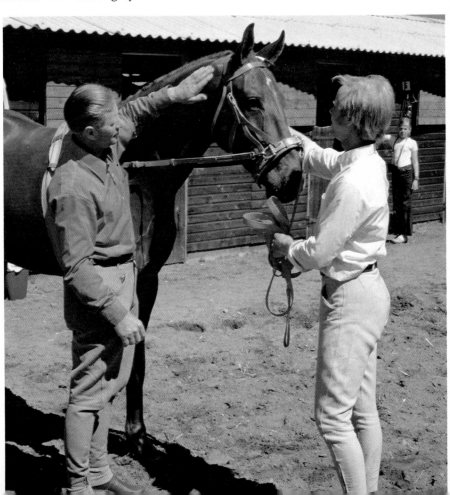

Lunging will *not* make a horse strong. It will make him more healthy and his joints more flexible, *preparing* them and the muscles for weight-carrying work. After two or three months of good lunging the horse will *look* bigger and stronger than he actually is, and the most vulnerable of all in this regard, is the beautiful big four-year-old of 16·2 h.h. or more.

The horse must be lunged on as large a circle as possible. More irrevocable injuries to hocks and backs and necks have been sustained by lunging on too small a circle, than from any other cause – including accidents. The trainer should be working to impose the three basic principles referred to earlier, but they will be more difficult to maintain on the lunge than under saddle. It is very difficult indeed to achieve a uniform bend throughout the horse (which is another reason for the circle to be as large as possible), but certainly he must not be allowed to bend to the outside. At this age and stage he will not show much self-control but he should learn that to go freely forward without playing the fool is what pleases his trainer the most. Rhythm is, however, more readily achieved, and if it is painstakingly and consistently demanded the rewards will be enormous in the months to come.

The calming influences and associations picked up by the youngster in these early days of lunging will frequently come in useful in later years when he comes to competition work. It is possible, for instance, to calm a fit eventer prior to his dressage test by lunging, thus avoiding having to ride him for hours and risk sapping his strength for the speed and endurance tests.

Before going on to describe the ridden work it is a good idea to consider the area where the work is to be undertaken. Large open spaces are, if not essential, highly desirable for the proper development of the horse's body and mind. They stimulate the joy and freedom of movement that is the essence of his beauty and our aim is to preserve that essence so that it will always show in his work, no matter how artificial the surroundings may be. Nevertheless, there will be a period each day when he has to be put to discipline: taken, as it were, to the classroom for his lessons.

Educators of humans have always considered it necessary to consider carefully the design and layout of their classrooms. Logical though it would appear to apply the same to the training of horses, this is not always done. More is the pity, because there can be no doubt that a carefully marked-out school will enhance progress enormously. Expense is certainly no excuse for, providing the ground is flat and comfortable to tread upon, the horse will give his all just as willingly amongst oil-drums, poles, and cardboard as he will under chandelier and marble.

The accuracy with which school figures are ridden can be an end in itself, although there are relatively few riders to whom such an aim appeals. To use accuracy as a means, however, is something to which all riders should aspire, for it is the only means we have of really measuring progress. It is of great importance that exercises and movements taught to horses, are not only done *how* we want them, but also, *where* we want them. A transition, for example, may be perfect in all respects, but if it was achieved a metre before or after the spot where the rider had intended it to happen, then the whole exercise has failed. It means that his signals were badly timed, or the horse anticipated them or was slow to obey, or even (heaven forbid!) that the rider had no clear intention in the first place. Whatever the reason, control was lost.

As we have seen, circles play a major role in training the horse, but unless they are as near perfect as possible, they are not only useless, they can even retard progress. It is impossible to maintain an even rhythm around an irregularly-shaped circle, whereas a true circle is one of the very best exercises for promoting it. It is impossible to have the correct bend at all times on an irregular circle since the radii are constantly varying. The horse's steps will therefore be a little shorter at times, and then a little longer and his bend will vary from acute to non-existent. All this can only lead to anxiety, confusion and loss of balance. A true circle is incredibly difficult to ride and it is a fact that few riders in the world can perform it consistently without the aid of guides or markers.

The description of the working area that follows is based on the standard dressage arenas used throughout the world. The actual measurements are not vital, although they will be found to be very convenient and will suit horses of almost any

Further training on the lunge, which will continue after he has been backed. On the left the young horse is being exercised over slightly raised poles to strengthen and flex his joints. On the right, more athletic exercises over a jump. In both cases calmness and trust are being linked with athletic agility.

size and shape. The proportions however are very important, and the surface must be flat, with as little slope as possible. The area is 40 m long and 20 m wide – that is composed of two squares side by side, each measuring 20 m × 20 m. Since the 20 m circle is the foundation of all future work, the advantages of having these carefully marked squares become obvious.

The diagrams show how and where the letters and marks are situated. The letters are those used in dressage arenas and schools all over the world: any letters in any order could be used but it is probably better to use the accepted ones so that the rider becomes thoroughly familiar with using them. If the spots and lines and letters are easy to read and fully understood the rider soon begins to use them instinctively and so is able to devote the proper degree of concentration to the performance of the horse. Incidentally, no-one seems to know how the letters came about, nor do they appear to have any logical sequence.

By having the spots or marks on the wall in differing colours one quickly becomes accustomed to their relationships to each other and to the perimeter of the school. This means that having decided to ride a circle, or part of a circle of any size, the exercise can be commenced just about anywhere in the school and there will always be at least one mark by which to measure the accuracy, and therefore the success, of the movement. This accuracy is always integrated with the three basic principles and becomes, as it were, a fourth dimension. Clearly it will serve no useful purpose to ride faithfully from tangent to

Right Diagram showing the ideal layout of a 40 metre × 20 metre schooling area (also called a *manège*) and examples of utilising the letters and marks in riding accurate circles; the lines within the area linking various points are included here to show the relationships of opposite marks, but obviously are not required to be marked on the actual schooling surface.

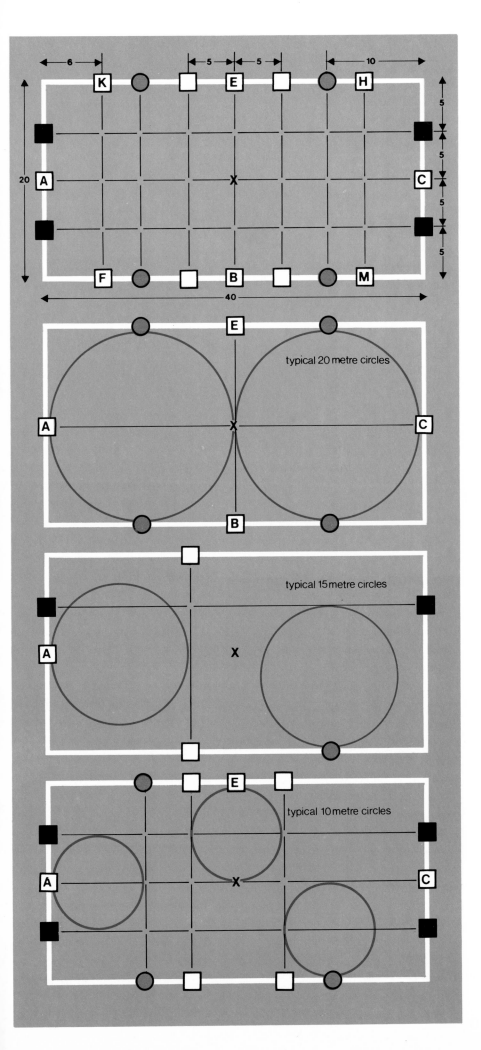

tangent if the bend or rhythm or forward movement are lost in the process.

Before embarking on the training of a horse it is important that the trainer has a proper understanding of the paces so that not only are the objectives clear, but the various criteria being applied and sought for are recognizable and progress may be measured. It is impossible to work on the Walk or the Trot or the Canter if the trainer is not sure whether the horse should be over-tracking, or tracking-in, or under-tracking; whether he should have the head and neck raised or stretched; whether he should have some bend or none at all and so on. For a clear description of each of the paces and of what is required in them, one can hardly do better than to refer to the authoritative view of the Fédération Equestre Internationale (F.E.I.). The following extract is the official English translation as published by the British Horse Society (B.H.S.) in Part III of its 'Dressage Rules' (1975 Edition).

F.E.I. DEFINITIONS OF PACES AND MOVEMENTS

Object and General Principles

1. The object of Dressage is the harmonious development of the physique and ability of the horse. As a result, it makes the horse calm, supple and keen, thus achieving perfect understanding with its rider.

2. These qualities are revealed by:

(a) the freedom and regularity of the paces;

(b) the harmony, lightness and ease of the movements;

(c) the lightness of the forehand and the engagement of the hindquarters;

(d) the horse remaining absolutely straight in any movement along a straight line and bending accordingly when moving on curved lines.

(3) The horse thus gives the impression of doing of his own accord what is required of him. Confident and attentive, he submits generously to the control of his rider.

4. His walk is regular, free and unconstrained. His trot is free, supple, regular, sustained and active. His canter is united, light and cadenced. His quarters are never inactive or sluggish. They respond to the slightest indication of the rider and thereby give life and spirit to all the rest of his body.

5. By virtue of a lively impulsion and the suppleness of his joints, free from the paralyzing effects of resistance, the horse obeys willingly and without hesitation and responds to the various aids calmly and with precision.

6. In all his work, even at the halt, the horse must be on the bit. A horse is to be 'on the bit' when the hocks are correctly placed, the neck is more or less raised according to the extension or collection of the pace, the head remains steadily in position, the contact with the mouth is light and no resistance is offered to the rider.

7. The position of the horse when 'on the bit' depends on the conformation as well as on the degree of training of the horse.

The Halt

1. At the halt, the horse should stand attentive, motionless and straight, with the weight evenly distributed over all four legs, and be ready to move off at the slightest indication of the rider. The neck is raised, the poll high, the head a little in front of the vertical, the

mouth light, the horse champing his bit and maintaining a light contact with the rider's hand.

2. The transition from any pace to the halt should be made progressively in a smooth and precise movement.

The Walk

1. The walk is a marching pace in which the four legs of the horse follow one another in four time, well marked and maintained in all work at the walk.

2. When the four beats cease to be well marked, even and regular, the walk is disunited or broken.

3. It is at the pace of the walk that the imperfections in dressage are most marked. The pace will suffer if the degree of collection is not in accordance with the stage of schooling of the horse, but is precipitated.

4. The following walks are recognized: medium, collected, extended and free.

(a) Medium walk. A free, regular and unconstrained walk of moderate extension. The horse should walk energetically but calmly, with even and determined steps, distinctly marking four equally spaced beats, the hind feet touching the ground in front of the footprints of the forefeet. The rider should keep a light and steady contact with the mouth.

(b) Collected walk. The horse moves resolutely forward, with his neck raised and arched. The head approaches the vertical position, the light contact with the mouth being maintained. The hind legs are engaged with good hock action. The pace should remain marching and vigorous, the legs being placed in regular sequence. Each step covers less ground and is higher than at the medium walk because all the joints bend more markedly. The hind feet touch the ground behind the footprints of the forefeet. In order not to become hurried or irregular the collected walk is slightly shorter than the medium walk, although showing greater mobility.

(c) Extended walk. The horse should cover as much ground as possible, without haste and without losing the regularity of his steps. The hind feet touch the ground clearly in front of the footprints of the forefeet. The rider lets the horse stretch out his head and neck without, however, losing contact, the head being carried in front of the vertical.

(d) Free walk. The free walk is a pace of rest in which, the reins being stretched to their utmost, the horse is allowed complete freedom of his head and neck.

The Trot

1. The trot is a pace of two time on alternate diagonals (near-fore and off-hind and vice-versa) separated by a moment of suspension.

2. The trot, always with free, active and regular steps, should be gone into without hesitation.

3. The quality of the trot is judged by the general impression, the elasticity and regularity of the steps and the impulsion, while maintaining the same cadence.

4. The following trots are recognized: working, medium, collected and extended.

(a) Working trot. This is a pace between the medium and the collected trot in which a horse, not yet ready or trained for collected movements, shows itself properly balanced and, with a supple poll remaining on the bit, goes forward with even, elastic steps and good hock action. The working trot is not part of the official Dressage tests – St. Georges, Intermediaire and Grand Prix (Ride-Off) – where a higher degree of collection is demanded.

(b) Medium trot. This is a pace between the extended and the collected trot and more rounded than the extended trot. The horse goes forward freely and straight, engaging his hind legs with good hock action, on a taut but light rein, his position being balanced and unconstrained. The steps should be as even as possible. The hind feet touch the ground in the footprints of the forefeet.

The degree of energy and impulsion displayed at the medium trot denotes clearly the degree of suppleness and balance of the horse.

(c) Collected trot. The neck is raised, thus enabling the shoulders to move with greater ease in all directions, the hocks being well engaged and maintaining energetic impulsion, notwithstanding the slower movement. The horse's steps are shorter but he is lighter and more mobile.

(d) Extended trot. The horse covers as much ground as possible. He lengthens his stride, remaining on the bit with light contact. The neck is extended and, as a result of great impulsion from the quarters, the horse uses his shoulders, covering more ground at each step without his action becoming higher.

5. The collected trot is executed 'sitting'. The working, medium and extended trots are executed 'sitting' or 'rising' as indicated in the test. In the official Dressage tests (Prix St. Georges, Intermediaire and Grand Prix) all movements at the trot must be executed sitting.

The Canter

1. The canter is a pace of three time. In the right canter for instance, the sequence is as follows, left hind leg, left diagonal (right hind leg and left foreleg), right foreleg followed by a period of suspension with all four legs in the air before taking the next stride.

2. The following canters are recognized: working, medium, collected and extended.

(a) Working canter. This is a pace between the medium and the collected canter in which a horse, not yet ready or trained for collected movements, shows itself properly balanced and, with a supple poll remaining on the bit, goes forward with even, light and cadenced strides and good hock action. The working canter is not part of the official Dressage Tests – St. Georges, Intermediaire and Grand Prix (Ride-Off) – where a higher degree of collection is demanded.

(b) Medium canter. This is a pace between the extended canter and the collected canter. The horse, perfectly straight from head to tail, moves freely, with a natural balance. The strides are long, even and the pace well cadenced. The quarters develop an increasing impulsion.

(c) Collected canter. At the collected canter, the shoulders are supple, free and mobile and the quarters very active. The horse's mobility is increased without any loss of impulsion.

(d) Extended canter. The horse extends his neck; the tip of the nose points more or less forward, the horse lengthens his stride without losing any of his calmness and lightness.

3. Counter canter (false canter). On the circle, this is a suppling movement. The horse maintains his natural flexion at the poll to the outside of the circle, in other words, remains bent to the leading leg. His conformation does not permit his spine to be bent to the line of the circle. The rider, avoiding any contortion causing contraction and disorder, should especially endeavour to limit the deviation of the quarters to the outside and restrict his demands according to the degree of suppleness of the horse.

4. Simple change of leg at the canter. This is a change whereby the horse is brought back into a walk and, after one or two well defined steps, restarted into a canter with the other leg leading.

5. The horse changes leg 'in the air' in a single stride while cantering. This change of leg is termed 'flying' (or 'in the air') when it is executed in close connection with the suspension which follows each stride of the canter. Flying changes of leg can be executed in series, for instance at every fourth, third, second or at every stride. The horse, even in the series, remains straight, calm and light with lively impulsion. The degree of collection in the series should be slightly less than in the collected canter.

The Rein Back

1. The rein back is a kind of walk backwards. The legs being raised and set down simultaneously by diagonal pairs, the hind legs remaining well in line and the legs being well raised.

2. The horse must be ready to halt or move forward without pausing at the demands of his rider, remaining at all times lightly on the bit and well balanced.

3. Any signs of hurrying, evasion of the hand, deviation of the quarters from the straight line or spreading and inactivity of the haunches are serious faults. Violent influence on the part of the rider may be detrimental to the joints of the hindquarters.

4. A horse that is not obedient to the aids of the rider in the rein back is insufficiently suppled, badly schooled or badly ridden.

5. If, in a dressage test, a trot or a canter is required after a rein back, the horse must strike off immediately into this pace without an intermediate step.

The Submission

1. At all paces, a slight flexion of the jaw, without nervousness is a criterion of the obedience of the horse and of the harmonious distribution of his forces.

2. Grinding the teeth and swishing the tail are signs of nervousness, tenseness or resistance on the part of the horse and must be taken into account by the judges in their marks for the movements concerned as well as in the collective mark no. three.

The Transitions

1. The changes of pace and speed should always be quickly made but be smooth and not abrupt. The cadence of a pace should be maintained up to the moment when the pace is changed or the horse halts. The horse remains light in hand, calm and maintains a correct position.

2. The same applies to transitions from the passage to the piaffe and from the piaffe to the passage.

The section goes on to give a number of other definitions which are not relevant at this stage, but they are highly recommended to a serious student at any level. It puts simply and very concisely a great deal of information that it is *essential* to know and, because it does not state how anything is achieved, it is free from controversy or confusion.

There are a number of exercises for the horse to carry out in each of the paces described. If these are performed correctly, progressively, and regularly they will improve the pace, at the same time as contributing to the other states and paces. One of the earliest and most valuable lessons a horse receives is in making smooth transitions up and down from one pace to another. The lessons are limited at first to the halt, the walk, and the trot, and much patience and understanding is required from the trainer. If a horse responds quickly and smoothly to a signal from his rider he has shown an act of obedience to the wishes of the rider, and that is, of course, valuable and important. In addition, however, he has shown something of equal if not more value and importance, in that he has developed a mental and physical co-ordination *in himself*.

Once the horse understands that a restriction on the reins coupled with gentle pressure from the rider's legs and seat means slow down or stop, and that a relaxation on the reins coupled with pressure from the rider's legs means move off or go faster, he is ready to begin transitions. Take a simple example of changing from trot to walk. The horse is trotting along, when he feels a deliberate pressure on his bit which he knows to mean 'slow right down'. Unless he is a rogue (and there are very, very few of them) he will say, in effect, 'certainly, at once, – but just wait a moment whilst I sort my legs out!' There is thus a delay between the action on the bit and the reaction of the horse and this is often misinterpreted as a disobedience or, at least, a reluctance to obey. What has actually happened is that mentally the horse obeyed his rider immediately, but his body did not obey his mind so quickly. In other words, his mind and body are not yet coordinated and it is in this, that he needs lots of time and patient practice. This explains, in part, why a horse finds upward transitions much easier than downward. In nature the horse's primary defence mechanism is 'flight'. He is equipped mentally and physically to 'get away' quickly and easily, whereas to be able to stop or slow down has no part to play in his ability to survive. The theory may easily be tested by watching young horses at play: there upward transitions are always beautiful and, in dressage terms, very correct, but when slowing down they are often careless and even clumsy. It follows, therefore, that the trainer can be quite demanding with upward transitions, but should be very patient with the downward ones.

When the horse begins to show signs that his mind and body are coordinating better, the trainer can introduce exercises to heighten and improve this coordination. One of the most useful of these is performed at the walk and is called a 'turn about the forehand'. (This exercise is commonly known as a 'turn *on* the forehand' but I refuse to speak, or even think, of any movement being done *on* the forehand.) In carrying it out the horse walks his forefeet around a small half circle. Each step is taken side-by-side and there is no crossing or widening of the front legs. His body is held straight from poll to croup which necessitates his hind legs crossing one in front of the other. On completion he will have described two half-circles, one with his forefeet and a larger one with his hind feet, concentric to each other and both having about the same centre point. Progress is gradual, and the

exercise should begin by walking the forefeet around a half-circle of 6 m in diameter and gradually reducing it to 1 m or a little less. There is no advantage in attempting to turn about the forehand on the spot and, with the young horse, it can be positively harmful.

The rider's inside leg *must* remain at the girth and the outside rein is used to keep the horse straight and regulate the steps. As mentioned, through being kept straight whilst moving along a curved line the horse will be obliged to cross his hind legs but there must be no question of the rider pushing the quarters out by drawing back his inside leg.

The exercise may be done at the walk without stopping, although it will be easier for the horse at first if the walk is slowed down a little just before the moment of entry. It may also be done *from* the halt but not *at* the halt. Having halted, the horse is moved straight forward for a step or two and then into the turn-about. This is often useful with horses that walk very boldly or are a little impetuous, and for young riders whose timing is still in doubt.

The foundations of agility and mutual trust are well illustrated here. Progressive training on the flat is essential before obstacles like this can be tackled safely. Note the exemplary position of the rider which is in no way impeding the horse.

A study of the aids for this exercise, shows that whilst the inside leg pushes for maintained or slightly increased impulsion the reins are guiding and gently discouraging forward movement, thus obliging the horse to yield part of himself (his quarters) laterally to the applied leg. In doing so he will stretch the muscles and ligaments in his quarters and hind legs in a sideways direction and so it has value as a modest gymnastic exercise. More important, however, is the lesson he learns in coordination. For the first time in his life, he feels the rider's legs and hands being

used at the same time and yet making apparently contradictory demands. He will be puzzled at first and make mistakes which should not be misconstrued as evasions. By a steady application of the aids without the smallest compromise of the rider's position, the horse will soon understand what is wanted and his body will learn to obey him. This first realization is always a great thrill to the sensitive rider, and it is a major moment in the horse's life. Provided there has been no force or impatience from his rider, it will have a tremendous influence on his willingness to learn new and strange things from that moment on.

It should take about one month for the horse to become competent at the turn about the forehand, not because he is unable to learn it faster but because it is better to spread it over a series of very short practices each day. The trainer should be quick to reward the most modest signs of progress as they occur. The appropriate form of reward in this case would be to trot vigorously forward with lots of patting on the neck and vocal noises – anything to let the horse know beyond doubt that he has done well.

Considerable stress has quite deliberately been laid on the importance of this exercise because, properly learned and thereafter properly carried out, its spectrum of influences on other work is very broad indeed. It will greatly improve transitions and gymnastically, it has a marked influence on the trot. If, during a lesson for instance, when the trot appears to be fading or is becoming choppy, the horse is brought to a walk and asked to do two or three turns about the forehand, the difference in the ensuing trot will be quite remarkable. This exercise is also invaluable as part of the preparation for the rein back; lessons in striking off into canter from walk or halt will be greatly assisted if the canter is asked for on the last step of a turn about; and it is obviously valuable as an introduction to leg yielding and shoulder-in.

Recognition of the far-reaching effects and influences of one exercise on other work is really the key to progressive training and it is important to observe which aspect of any exercise will be useful to the horse in learning or carrying out another. A good example is the way in which the 10 m circle can teach the horse about collection if it is carried out in the following manner:

Put the horse to a good working trot on a 20 m circle at A or C, paying strict attention to the three basic principles, especially the evenness of the rhythm. Once these are established reduce the circle to 15 m from the same starting tangent and when that circle is going well reduce to 10 m, again using the same tangent, so that every circle has begun and ended at the same point. If the impulsion and rhythm have been strictly maintained throughout, the horse will have no alternative but to shorten his steps and lift his feet higher, i.e. become more elevated, and so, with no extra or unfamiliar aids from the rider, the

reaching the quarter line tangent, ask for a transition straight into the lengthened trot (or medium trot when the time comes) as he proceeds down school on the quarter line. The downward transitions from medium or extended into working or collected are very difficult and must be approached with care, but at the same time, the strong paces must not be allowed to just fade away. The lessons described for achieving collection and extension at the trot may be reproduced exactly for the canter when the time comes.

The above procedure then is a good example of how carefully chosen exercises will bring about a desired result as a *natural* consequence, which is so much better than a lot of complicated interference by the rider. To sum up what has been achieved so far, we see that the horse is making good transitions through halt, walk, and trot; he has an understanding of the rider's leg and hand to the extent where he will advance or retard his paces to quite a competent degree of collection and extension, and he will yield his quarters laterally, willingly but under control. The rider, however, has done nothing more than to ride him forward consistently and to guide him carefully.

Lateral work should be approached with much the same attitude. There is nothing complicated or mysterious about the aids used here *but* they must be applied from a secure and correct position and their timing is critical. The first of the sideways movements is called Leg-yielding. It is carried out at working trot, with no collection and no bend, and is taught in two distinct stages. When the second stage is established, both forms will be used thereafter at various times for various reasons.

The first phase is best described as Leg-yielding from line to line. There are five main longitudinal lines used in the school; the two outer tracks which run close to the boards down each long side; two quarter lines, each 5 m in from the track; and the centre line marked at each end by A and C. There are, in fact two more – one on each long side, which run 1 m in from the outer track and these are called the inner track. The inner track is a much neglected line which should be used a lot more than it generally is – especially in indoor schools.

The two lines chosen for the first lessons of Leg-yielding are the quarter line and the inner track. The horse is going to be asked to move from the quarter line to the inner track without changing direction, and he will remain parallel to both lines throughout the movement. In other words, his forefeet and hind feet will leave the quarter line at the same moment and they will arrive at the inner track simultaneously. The reasons for choosing these two lines should be understood from the start.

For some unknown reason the boards have a magnetic effect on horses and it is always easier to ride towards them than away from them, thus for the first attempts of this new lesson the horse is asked to move in a direction that he is more willing to go. Because of that very attraction, however, he is only allowed to go as far as the

---

horse has *collected himself*. After two or three (three at the most) of the 10 m circles the horse is returned to working trot and taken out of the circle, before being rested and rewarded. The next phase is to go through the same procedure but instead of going large into working trot the rider holds the collection achieved, at first to about halfway down the long side and gradually for longer until he can maintain it for a full circuit of the school.

It will not be too long before the rider can dispense with the large circles and put his horse an a 10 m circle anywhere in the school whenever he wishes to achieve collection. At this stage the rider should always give the horse clear warning that he is about to be asked to circle by the use of half-halts just before he leaves the track. It is better if these half-halts are just a shade more clearly defined than usual but take care not to jar or startle the horse. From there it is simple and logical to be able to achieve collection through a 10 m half-circle and then a quarter-circle (which is the same as passing through a corner), and finally anywhere in the school, without any change of direction. Later on, more advanced collection can be developed by reducing the circle to the volte (a volte is automatically a circle of 6 m diameter).

Lengthening the stride with a view to medium and, ultimately, extended trot

More and more racehorses are being given progressive training to develop their strength and stamina, which at the same time promotes greater trust in their riders. Note the lovely sympathy shown by the position of the leading jockey's fingers; the horse has struck the hurdle and could well have fallen without full freedom of his head and neck.

will, of course, have been practised all the time that the above shortening work has been going on. By the time the third phase (dispensing with the larger circles) has been reached the horse should be capable of a number of even, long-strides – bordering on medium – without losing his balance. He will have been allowed to stretch into these progressively from working trot with the first few steps smoothly getting longer and longer. Now the time has come for him to learn to make a proper transition in the long strides (it will not yet be a fully developed medium trot) and for this he will need the collection that he is currently learning and at which he is already modestly proficient.

If the 10 m circle of collection is centralized at A or C, its side tangents coincide with the quarter lines running the length of the school. Every so often, then, instead of going into working trot at A and going large, the rider should hold the collection for a further quarter-circle and, upon inner track, so that it is always the rider who stops the sideways movement and never the boards. The procedure for the first phase of Leg-yielding therefore, is as follows:

At the short end of the school, ride a 15 m half-circle and proceed down the quarter line. Ride the line absolutely straight once or twice to test and, if necessary, check any tendency by the horse to drift over toward the boards of his own accord, for he must not go until asked. Next time hold the straightness down the quarter line until roughly opposite E (or B), at which time apply the inside leg firmly, but not suddenly at the girth. The horse's reaction will be to try to go faster or stronger (quite understandably because that is what he has been taught to do), and you should anticipate this reaction by a clearly defined steadying influence down the outside rein *before* applying the inside leg. Continue to exert this influence on the rein until reaching the inner track, at which point, soften the outside hand, and apply the outside leg to stop the sideways movement. Use the other leg to drive him forward, so that in the moment of driving forward both legs are being firmly applied at the girth. The horse should remain straight from poll to croup throughout.

It is not a difficult exercise and, provided the ground work has been thorough, horses perform it remarkably well in a very short time. The second stage is perhaps slightly more difficult. It is called Leg-yielding on the line, which means that although the horse is making a sideways movement, his body is placed at an angle to the original line and his hind feet never leave it. It is usually performed on one of the longitudinal lines but it can be done on any straight line including diagonally or across the school.

The aids here are exactly the same as in the first stage, but carried out in the following manner:

Put the horse on to the chosen line (preferably *not* the outer track) and, after a few horse's lengths to check straightness and give the warning signals, take the forehand little by little to the inside, until the outside forefoot is stepping in front of the inside hind foot (in other words until he is moving on three tracks). As before the horse remains absolutely straight from poll to croup and the movement is ridden from the inside leg at the girth into the steadying outside rein. As he becomes competent, the angle can be increased to between 30° and 40° which means, of course, that he will be moving on two tracks; that is to say that whilst both hind feet remain on the original line his forefeet are moving on a separate parallel line of their own.

The pitfalls to watch out for are allowing the horse to bend, usually in the neck, and fall out or escape through his outside shoulder, (almost certainly caused by neglect of the outside rein, or alternatively, by too much inside rein); tilting of the horse's head caused by an over restraining and backward feeling hand; and quarters going out into the movement instead of the forehand coming in (probably a result of the rider drawing back his inside leg). This last point needs particular emphasis, for on *no* account should the rider draw the inside leg back behind the girth in Leg-yielding or in Shoulder-in. Not only will it result in sending the quarters out, but loss of impulsion will almost certainly ensue and it will very likely cause confusion to the horse when the time comes for him to learn the half-pass. All of these are very serious mistakes and must be extremely carefully guarded against.

Lightness, gaiety and obedience are clearly apparent in both these fully trained horses. Whilst the final objectives are very different the basic education of this advanced dressage horse and this showjumper has been along very similar lines.

Once Leg-yielding has developed to the stage where the horse is moving clearly on two tracks it becomes a gymnastic exercise in the true sense of the term, and it will exert considerable influence on improving the working trot. At the same time, the horse will have been practising smaller circles and collection, so we now have a horse who is capable of moving laterally at working trot, bending easily, and of carrying himself to a more or less modest degree of collection. Together these three things – that is lateral movement plus bend plus collection – comprise the Shoulder-in. Shoulder-in is, in principle, the same as Leg-yielding on the line but with the added dimensions of collection and a uniform bend. These extra dimensions have been learned and practised as separate entities and it follows that the more thorough the lessons have been, the fewer problems will arise when the horse is asked to combine two or more of the results in the one movement or exercise.

Herein lies the essence of progressive training. It is in having a clear intention of the aims and objectives, coupled with a knowledge of the criteria to be applied. It is in recognizing the benefits and qualities inherent in one lesson which will contribute to the easier learning of the next. It is in developing a feel for the way in which a horse will probably react in the future in the light of the way he is reacting now. It is in the determination of the rider to adopt the correct posture on the horse and never to compromise that position in order to get a result.

The lessons that have been described here as examples have shown, it is hoped, that by building carefully on a secure foundation of knowledge and understanding, a sound and lasting structure *will* result. Advanced work is the direct product of early work, each lesson is entirely dependent on its predecessor for its success. There are no short cuts.

Careers with Horses

WHEN the internal combustion engine began to drive horses off the roads along which they had carried man through the ages, and off the land which they had helped him to cultivate, many thought it would lead to the gradual extinction of the species.

This is not the case, however. There are probably as many horses in the world today as there were when the horse was man's indispensable helpmate. The difference is that in this age of technology, he has become an indispensable part, not of man's work, but of his leisure. In most civilized countries, more and more people are taking up recreational riding, becoming horse-owners or starting studs – with the result that every year, more trained and knowledgeable people are needed to look after horses, to handle and break youngsters, to manage stables, and to teach riding to the constant flow of novices.

For those who want a career with horses, provided they are willing to train and qualify, there is a great variety of openings. It is not possible here to give detailed information on careers throughout the world. The examples which follow all relate to Great Britain but much the same opportunities exist in other countries.

The most urgent needs in the horse world of today are for good instructors, and for responsible and skilled stud workers. For each of these careers there is an official governing body, or society, which sets the necessary graded examinations, and whose qualifications are accepted as guaranteeing certain standards of knowledge and efficiency. In Great Britain, for the training of instructors and stable managers, it is the British Horse Society; and for stud workers, the National Pony Society. The examinations offered by these societies are recognized as career training by most Education Authorities, and those wishing to train for them can generally obtain Further Education grants.

Training is necessary because in any profession it is advisable to obtain the qualifications offered by that profession's 'establishment'; but there are other reasons, too. Horse owners and breeders can hardly be expected to pay a wage to someone who doesn't know even the rudiments of the job, however much that person may like horses. Horses are valuable animals and cannot be left in the care of someone inexperienced. In addition, riding, stable management, handling breeding stock and breaking young horses are not techniques one acquires by the light of nature. A career with horses is as serious a one as any other. No one would dare to call themselves a doctor, or a lawyer, if they had no qualifications to show for it; the same applies, if one is to be successful, in the horse world of today.

There are careers to be made in the various forms of racing, and in Hunt service. And there is the profession of veterinary surgery in which, once qualified, it is possible to specialize in horses. Two ancillary professions, or crafts, are farriery and saddlery.

It is important to remember that all active careers with horses involve a considerable amount of hard physical work; that none offers the joys of riding without the inevitable chores of stable work, at least, not until one is successful enough, and probably old enough, to be able to employ help and train others. A career with horses consists of a great deal more than learning to 'look nice' on a horse, and performing in jumping competitions before an admiring public!

British Horse Society Examinations

In Great Britain, the British Horse Society is recognized as the official body responsible for setting and maintaining the standards of both riding and teaching. The

Mucking out is one of the less glamorous aspects of a career with horses, but all working pupils in stables will have to join in when it is time for such chores.

Society offers four graded examinations and anyone wishing to teach riding should aim to take as many of these as are within their capabilities.

The examinations are: the Assistant Instructor's, which can be taken at the age of 17; the Intermediate Instructor's; the Instructor's, for which one must be 22, and the Fellowship. Because it takes intelligence to be a good instructor, before starting to train for the first of these, it is necessary to have four 'O' levels, or four CSE Grade 1 passes (unless the candidate is over 20, when extra maturity is held to make up for a possible lack of scholastic achievement). It is, therefore, not necessary to start training immediately on leaving school.

Rather than give the exact syllabus for the first exam, it is enough to say that it consists of four sections, and that one must achieve a 'pass' standard in each section. These are: Riding, Stable Management, Minor Ailments, and Powers of Instruction. The standard of riding calls for a competent, correct rider, who can jump fences up to 1 metre (3 ft 3 ins), ride without stirrups, and ride different horses. Stable Management covers feeding, grooming, rugging, bandaging, trimming, plaiting, and the general care of horses, both stabled and at grass. Minor Ailments is a written paper, its title being self-explanatory. In Powers of Instruction, the candidate is expected to know not only what, and how, to teach but also how to control a ride.

It should be obvious that to pass this exam, it will not be enough just to have ridden and looked after one's own horse or pony. To be successful, it is essential to learn what the examiners want. It is almost always necessary, therefore, to go for a period of training to a recognized Riding Establishment: one that is on the recommended list of the British Horse Society. The most economical way to train is as a 'working pupil' and most establishments accept working pupils provided they stay for at least a year. As the name suggests, work is expected in return for training. The alternative is to be a paying student, for whatever length of time it may take to reach examination standard. Some establishments allow students to bring their own horses, provided they pay for their keep. The British Horse Society will send on request a list of approved schools, as well as the examination syllabus. It is advisable to visit several before making a final choice.

The point of these examinations is to produce riding instructors, but for those who are genuinely not interested in teaching, there are two other examinations: the Certificate of Horsemastership and the Stable Manager's Certificate. The first of these is really exactly the same as the Assistant Instructor's without the teaching section. In the second, there is more accent on general horsemastership, and the business side of running a yard. After passing one examination, it is advisable, if possible, to take a position in a riding school that will help to train you for the next one. It is also sometimes possible to

Above Strapping or grooming is another daily task essential to the horse's health and well-being. Pupils working for National Pony Society examinations have to spend time on an approved stud where they will learn about all aspects of breeding as well as stable management.

Right First steps in teaching. Instructing forms a major part of British Horse Society exams, and candidates from all over the world study in the U.K. to qualify as official instructors.

get a further grant for training for the higher examinations.

Some knowledgeable private owners take people into their stables to train, but it will probably be necessary also to take a short course at an official school, for however good private teachers may be (and many are excellent), they may not know exactly what the examiners are looking for. Nor may they have an indoor school in which a candidate must get used to riding before exam day.

The address of the British Horse Society is: National Equestrian Centre, Kenilworth, Warwickshire, CV8 2LR.

The National Pony Society Examinations

To many, training for stud work means training for the most rewarding of all careers with horses. This is because the stud – the stallions, mares, foals and young animals – is the foundation of every other horse activity; and also because it is the handling, breaking and schooling of the young animals that can make or mar the thousands of foals born every year. Far too many young horses and ponies are spoilt as

a result of ignorance or of no proper early training, for although there are today many knowledgeable breeders, there are not nearly enough knowledgeable handlers and breakers. It is unlikely that any foal is born vicious, or a rogue, it is incorrect human handling – sometimes too rough, sometimes too sentimental – that produces warped equine temperaments.

Working in a stud, where animals spend a lot of their time at liberty, tends to give a far deeper insight into the true nature of the horse than working only with those that are stabled or partly stabled. The behaviour patterns of horses at liberty are fascinating to watch and help towards a greater understanding of horse psychology.

The National Pony Society offers two examinations: the Stud Assistant's Certificate, and the Stud Assistant's Diploma. The first can be taken at the age of 16, although it is doubtful whether anyone so young could have had enough experience. For the second, the candidate must be over 22 years old. Both exams can be taken with or without riding. To take them with riding obviously offers a wider choice of future jobs, but there are many people who are not particularly keen, or skilled, riders who nevertheless have the right temperaments for dealing with breeding stock and young horses. Since a great deal of a young horse's early work is done 'on the ground', people not interested in riding should not be put off taking stud training because they

do not wish to ride. The standard of riding asked for is high, needing knowledge of backing, schooling and bringing on a young horse.

To take the Stud Assistant's examination, it is necessary to have at least a year's experience at one of the studs recognized by the Society as a student training centre. This is how long it takes to cover the stud's full activities and all the stages of a mare's foaling cycle.

The address of the National Pony Society is: 7 Cross and Pillory Lane, Alton, Hampshire. The Secretary will send on request a syllabus of the examination and a list of the studs which accept pupils for training.

Although the examinations are offered by the National Pony Society, this of course does not mean that the qualifications are only for working with *ponies*. For the highly specialized work of bloodstock breeding, however, the Thoroughbred Breeders' Association, 168 High Street, Newmarket, Suffolk, CB8 9AJ, can advise on studs which might be willing to accept students.

Flat Racing, National Hunt Racing

There is no short cut to becoming a jockey, even if one is small and already a good rider! The way in, to anyone interested in this as a career, is through apprenticeship. Apprentices are often taken on straight

from school, but are usually asked to work for a trial period before being finally 'indentured': that is, before signing on to remain with a particular trainer for three, five, or seven years.

A limited number of courses for apprentices and would-be apprentices are held each year at the National Equestrian Centre. These are mainly filled by trainers' nominees, but Schools' Careers Officers or parents can apply for a place for a pupil or child by writing to the National Equestrian Centre, Kenilworth, Warwickshire, CV8 2LR.

Not every apprentice makes a jockey, and not every jockey makes the top grade. But if it is a life's ambition to ride races on the fastest horses in the world, then it is worth making the effort to realize it. There are, however, other openings in racing stables. An ordinary 'lad' need not remain so forever. If he is good, he can work his way up the ladder and become Senior Lad, or Travelling Lad, maybe Head Travelling Lad – perhaps eventually reaching the highest position in any yard, that of Head Lad, the person who, under the trainer, is responsible for the running of the yard, the welfare of the horses and the supervision of the staff.

The wages of lads when they start are tied to the minimum agricultural wage of the time, although some trainers pay more. Wages rise with experience, and there are usually quite a number of 'perks', given by grateful owners to the lads who 'do' their horses when the horses win or are placed in races. Also, many good Senior Lads, Travelling Lads and all Head Lads will be provided with a house.

For many years, a great many lads have, in fact, been 'lasses', and there is nothing to stop a girl going right to the top of the ladder in racing stables. Until recently, it was not possible for girls to become apprentices, because girls were not allowed to ride races under rules. This is now changed, but what the future holds for girl apprentices and women jockeys remains to be seen.

The easiest way to get into racing stables, as an apprentice or as a lad, is to write to a trainer – if there is one in the neighbourhood – and ask for an appointment to see him. Trainers are always on the lookout for good lads, and apprentices who may one day make good jockeys. If there is no training establishment in the district, write to the Jockey Club, 42 Portman Square, London, W.1. They will provide a list of trainers who may be able to help.

In considering a career in National Hunt stables, with the idea of perhaps becoming a steeplechase jockey, it is important to remember that the profession of National Hunt race riding is an extremely tough one, calling for an extra allowance of nerve. It is also hazardous; a jump jockey during his career will probably break most of the breakable bones in his body and will, moreover, often ride in the next race after a fall which would have kept lesser mortals out of the saddle for days, if not weeks.

Most National Hunt trainers take on lads rather than apprentices, for while almost everyone can be taught to stay attached to a horse on the flat, it takes considerable riding talent to become good over fences. As most National Hunt lads ride their horses at work (the better ones over fences too), trainers are quick to spot talent, when a lad will be given the better horses to ride and school, and probably also the chance to ride in some of the 'Opportunity Races' which are specially organized for would-be jump jockeys. There are similar chances to climb the hierarchical ladder in the yard as there are in flat-racing stables, and the wages, and the 'perks', are similar. The way in to National Hunt Stables is the same as the way into flat-racing: contact a trainer directly or write to the Jockey Club.

Hunt Service

This is a wonderful career for someone who wants a country life as well as a life with horses.

The openings into Hunt Service are naturally limited by the number of Hunts in existence, but all Hunts take on new staff from time to time, and most will take people straight from school if they are keen and willing to learn. Hunt horses are easier school-masters for the learner-rider than racehorses. When they come up from grass in the late summer, they need a lot of slow exercise, and even when they are hunting fit they are in regular work and consequently seldom so ebullient. A career in Hunt Service begins with being a sort of general 'dogsbody' around the stables. There may be anything up to about 25 horses stabled, which makes a lot of work. From 'dogsbody' one graduates to groom, or 'strapper', with two or three horses to look after. The next step, provided one is a good enough rider, is to become Second Horseman, then Second Whipper In, First Whipper In, and finally, Huntsman, who hunts hounds, or Kennel Huntsman, who in the absence of the Master is in charge of the field. The Huntsman is in overall charge of the stables, kennels, and all employed therein. This is a responsible and well-paid position and good Huntsmen are widely sought after.

Wages start with the minimum agricultural and progress upwards. An important 'perk' is that all riding clothes are provided

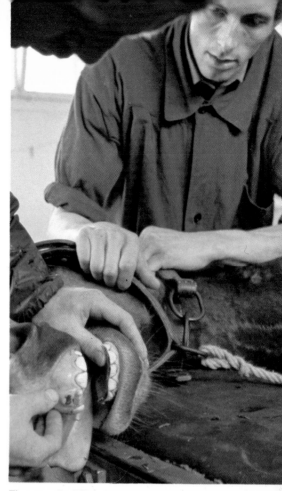

Three totally different careers connected with the horse world. *left*: A young apprentice trains for the jockey's trade, a tough and competitive career with long hours and relatively small reward except for those at the top. *middle*: Working with hounds entails long hours too, and in all types of weather, but this young hunt servant is undismayed. *above*: Training to be a veterinary surgeon is arduous, and high academic qualifications are required for a university degree course, but the career can provide substantial financial reward for hard work.

by the Hunt. To enter Hunt Service, the personal approach is best: if there is a local Hunt, find out where the kennels are (the stables are there too), go to see the Huntsman and ask if there is a chance of being taken on. If not, he may know of another Hunt looking for a trainee, or may be able to give a definite date for starting in the future. The life of the Hunt servant has many advantages, not the least being the chance to live in, and become part of, a country community and a particular countryside.

Veterinary Surgery

However much anyone wanting to become a veterinary surgeon wants also to specialize in horses, it is necessary first, as it is in human medicine before specializing, to take the general qualifying degree: to 'become a vet'. This is not easy, any more than becoming a doctor is easy. It takes at least five years to qualify and needs high academic standards. 'A' levels are called for, or Scottish 'Highers', emphasis being on biology, physics and mathematics. There is great competition to enter the profession; all Veterinary Colleges have more applicants each year than they have

places for, but there is no sex discrimination. Women should remember, however, that because they are usually smaller and not so strong as men, that when it comes to practice they are often better in 'small animal' practices.

In Great Britain, the controlling body of the veterinary profession is the Royal College of Veterinary Surgeons, 32, Belgrave Square, London, S.W.1. The College recognizes the degrees granted by the six Veterinary Colleges in the United Kingdom, each of which is a part of the parent University. In England, these are London, Bristol, Liverpool and Cambridge; and in Scotland, the Glasgow Veterinary College, and Royal(Dick) Veterinary College, Edinburgh. The usual student grants are obtainable for veterinary courses, at the end of which the first degree is that of Bachelor of Veterinary Medicine and Surgery (BVMS). The holder of this degree is entitled to become a Member of the Royal College of Veterinary Surgeons (MRCVS) and can start practice.

The main difference between the veterinary and the human medical courses is that during the former, a specified time has to be spent each vacation doing practical work. For the first two years, this should be

spent on a farm learning about animal care and feeding; during the last three years, vacations must be spent as a student working with a practising veterinarian.

On going into practice, it will be necessary for those who wish to specialize in horses to choose a district where horses abound. Although it will not be possible in general practice to deal with horses only, it will be possible to earn a reputation as a 'good horse vet'. But by no means all who qualify in veterinary medicine go into general practice. Many study for postgraduate degrees in special subjects, for example, veterinary radiology or veterinary anaesthesia; or they take courses in laboratory research. For any of these, further grants can usually be obtained. There are also openings in Government Service in, for instance, the Animal Health Division of the Ministry of Agriculture. This is responsible for the prevention, and control if they occur, of all notifiable diseases, and for the inspection of markets, abbatoirs and ports of entry into the country.

The best start, however, for anyone wishing to specialize in horses, would be to try to get into one of the big veterinary practices near Newmarket, or any other major training centre.

Animal Nursing

This is a subsidiary profession to that of veterinary surgery, and could appeal to many who may have left it too late to get the academic qualifications necessary to become veterinarians. The full title of a qualified animal nurse is: Registered Animal Nursing Auxiliary (RANA). The scheme to train and keep a register of animal nurses was started by the Royal College of Veterinary Surgeons in 1961. There is a big demand for RANAs, some veterinary practices employing several, not only to help during operations, but for post-operational care, and the care of animals kept in for long-term treatment.

A trainee must be 17 years old, or over, and have three 'O' levels, one of which must be English, and one of the others either mathematics, or physical or biological science. It takes two years to train for the necessary examinations but training need not be consecutive. It can be taken working as a student nurse to a veterinarian, when the trainee will receive a wage. It is also possible to train at a Veterinary College, attending lectures and gaining practical experience from the animals in for care or operation. The curriculum for the examinations is comprehensive; it includes anatomy, physiology, anaesthesia, and detailed knowledge of the care and feeding of different animals in sickness and in health.

Once trained as a RANA, it is a career that can be carried on part-time, if that is all circumstances allow. And, like human nursing, it is one which can be pursued wherever one is living.

The Royal College of Veterinary Surgeons will send a booklet called 'Animal Nursing Auxiliaries' to anyone interested, together with a list of places where it is possible to train.

Farriery

Farriery is one of the most vital of all professions connected with horses. If there were no farriers, the entire horse world would come to a stop, except perhaps for a few fortunate individuals lucky enough to be able to ride always and exclusively on grass. Even they would find it hard to keep their mounts going sound and true if there were no one to trim, shape, and generally care for, their feet.

Contrary to popular imagination, it does not take enormous strength to become a farrier. A combination of knack and know-how is required, as probably anyone who has struggled to remove a loose shoe, taking ages over what takes the farrier a few seconds, will have discovered. What it does take, as does every profession connected with horses, is a real interest in and feeling for the animal itself, and the right kind of temperament – calm and patient, but firm. A hot-tempered, impatient person, who hits the horse if it makes the slightest movement, will never be a good farrier; nor will the nervous person who picks up a foot as though it were made of eggshells. It also takes intelligence, for farriers have to be registered and to become registered they have to prove through examinations that they know a lot more than just how to make shoes, and put them on and take them off a horse. They must know about corrective

'No foot, no horse' is a well-worn phrase, but a relevant one, explaining why farriers are such important people in the horse world. Though little more than a lad, this farrier knows exactly what he's doing, as the horse's serenity makes clear.

shoeing; about the anatomy of the horse, in particular the workings of the tendons, ligaments and joints of the legs; about diseases of the foot and the structure of the foot; how a horse should stand correctly in natural balance and how the feet should be shaped or trimmed to enable him to 'bear evenly' on all four. Qualified farriers are really 'veterinarians of the feet': the word 'farrier' means 'horse-doctor' as well as 'shoeing smith'.

There is in fact much more to the profession of farriery than is probably imagined from watching a farrier at work trimming, fitting and nailing on shoes with such apparent ease. With the tremendous contemporary upsurge of interest in riding, there is today a very good living to be made as a farrier. For those who like to think of being their own masters, it is a most satisfying profession, for the majority of farriers are just that – they can work when they like, for as long as they like, on whatever days of the week they like. Alternatively, there are a number of salaried positions for farriers. Many racing stables, studs and large showing establishments like to have their own resident farriers.

The procedure for training is to find a Master Farrier willing to take on a trainee. This is not always easy but the Schools Careers Officer can sometimes help. If he cannot, the local Small Industries

Organizer, if there is one, should be able to assist. The Youth Employment Bureau may also be able to help, and the local Education Authorities can be approached. If in difficulties, write to The Worshipful Company of Farriers, explaining any problems, and asking for the apprenticeship application form. The address is: The Field Officer, 58 Hall Park Drive, Lytham West Park, Lytham, Lancashire.

To become a Registered Shoeing Smith (RSS) takes four years of training, or apprenticeship. With the approval of the Company, Registered Shoeing Smiths can take on and train apprentices. There are two further certificates that can be attained: Associate of the Farriery Company of London, and Fellow of the Worshipful Company of Farriers.

A major difference between farriery today and in the past is that whereas then everyone took their horses to the forge, most people now expect their farriers to come to them. Most farriers therefore find it necessary to have a small portable forge as well as their home one, where they make the shoes.

Saddlery

The Worshipful Company of Saddlers is the oldest of the present-day Livery Companies of the City of London. The earliest document in the Company's possession goes back to 1160, in which there is already mention of 'customs of old', which makes it appear that the Company was originally an Anglo-Saxon Craft Guild. The first Charter was granted to the Company by Edward I in 1272, and the Incorporation Charter by Richard II in 1395. The provisions of this were amended or ratified by subsequent monarchs until James I, whose Charter of 1607 is in force today.

Although much contemporary saddlery is more or less mass produced, and many so-called saddlers little more than retailers, there is still a great need for craftsmen and women. There are many Master Saddlers, capable of making every conceivable article of tack (metal work excluded) that any horse might need. The best way to learn the craft is to work with such a saddler, as a learner-worker, or as an apprentice. A learner-worker will get a wage, small at first, and rising as he progresses. An apprentice will sign on to remain for a stated number of years, probably paying an apprenticeship fee. It is usually possible to get an Education Grant to train in this way.

Training in the workshop of a Master Saddler is complete and comprehensive. Starting work with the simplest of stitching repair jobs, it progresses through to making, as well as repairing, most articles of tack, except perhaps saddles. Even then it will have been necessary to have learnt all about the anatomy of saddles, so they can be restuffed or relined, or taken apart for the trees to be checked. Training will also include how to run a saddlery business, or shop, so as to make a profit; which wholesale firms are the best to deal with, and which extra goods it may be profitable to stock. As most working saddlers do a fair amount of second-hand trade, training will include how to run this aspect so as to be fair both to the business and the client. There will also be clients who ask the saddler to bring saddles out to them to try on their horses for correct fit, so this side of the successful saddler's craft will be learnt as well.

There are other ways of learning the craft of saddlery. The Cordwainers Technical College, 182, Mare Street, Hackney, London, E8, runs a Rural Saddlers' Course. Those who pass the theoretical and practical examinations at the end of the course can often get a bursary from the Worshipful Company to continue training. Both the City and Guilds of London Institute, and the Walsall School of Arts and Crafts run courses in saddlery and

Training schemes in the highly specialized trade of saddlery are available in Britain to both boys and girls, like these trainees at the bench of a Master Saddler's workshop.

leatherwork; again, those who pass the necessary examinations at the end of the courses can be helped to further training by the Worshipful Company, which will also sometimes pay full apprenticeship fees for those who cannot afford them, or who have been unable to get educational grants. Whatever method of training is considered it is always a good thing to write to the Company, asking for their advice and help. The address is: The Worshipful Company of Saddlers, Saddlers' Hall, Gutter Lane, London, EC2V 6BR.

Although a saddler does not have to be a rider, the more he knows about horses and riders, and their often very different needs, the better. Naturally, many of his clients will be experienced people who know exactly what they want. But many will be novices knowing little more than that in order to ride a horse, they need a saddle and bridle. They therefore need, and their horses will appreciate, a good saddler's advice.

APPENDIX

GLOSSARY

OF

EQUESTRIAN TERMS

Account for to kill a fox.

Acey Deucey riding with one stirrup leather longer than the other, a style sometimes adopted by jockeys in the U.S. to help them keep their balance on sharp bends.

Acting Master a person appointed temporarily to organize a hunt, either for a day, or for a longer period pending the appointment of a permanent master.

Against the Clock in show-jumping – a competition or jump-off decided by time, the winner being the competitor with the least number of faults in the fastest time.

Aged a horse which is seven years old or more.

Aid any of the signals used by a rider to give instructions to his horse. See also ARTIFICIAL AIDS, NATURAL AIDS.

Air above the Ground any of the various high school movements performed either with the forelegs or with the fore and hind legs off the ground. See also BALLOTADE, CAPRIOLE, COURBETTE, CROUPADE, LEVADE.

Albino a colour type, rather than a breed, comprising pure white hair, pale skin and pale translucent eyes.

All on a hunting term normally used by the whipper-in to let the huntsman know all hounds are up with the pack.

All-round Cow Horse a horse which is skilled at carrying out all the duties required of it by a cowboy.

Also-ran any unplaced horse in a race.

Alter to castrate a horse or colt, thus rendering it sterile.

Amble a slow gait in two time in which the horse's hind and foreleg on the same side are moved forward together.

Ante-post Betting the placing of bets on a race, at an agreed price prior to the day of the race.

Anvil (a) a heavy iron block with a smooth flat face, usually of steel, on which horseshoes are shaped. (b) (Western U.S.) a horse, particularly one which is shod, which strikes the forefeet with the hind feet.

Appointment Card a card sent out to interested parties by the hunt secretary informing them of the time, date and place of forthcoming meets.

Apprentice a youth who is being trained as a jockey and serves an indentured apprenticeship of five to seven years.

Apron a covering made of strong horse-hide worn by farriers to protect the front of the body whilst shoeing a horse.

Arena the area in which a horseshow or show-jumping competition is held.

Artificial Aids items such as whips, spurs and martingales which are used by the rider to help convey instructions to the horse.

As Hounds Ran the distance covered in a hunt by hounds.

Asking the Question asking a horse to make a supreme effort when it is being pushed to its limit in competitive events, such as racing, show-jumping or combined training.

At Bay the position of hounds when kept off the quarry.

Automatic Timing an electrical apparatus used for show-jumping events. The horse breaks an electronic ray as it goes through the start, triggering off the mechanism which starts the clock. As it goes through the finish it breaks a similar device which stops the clock.

Autorisation Spéciale a pink card issued to a rider by his national equestrian federation permitting him to compete in an international dressage, show jumping or combined training event.

Autumn Double the Cesarewitch Stakes and the Cambridgeshire Stakes – two racing events held annually at Newmarket, England in the autumn.

Back to place a bet on a horse.

Backer a person who places a bet on a horse.

Back Hander a polo stroke in which the player travelling forwards hits the ball backwards in the opposite direction.

Back Jockey the stop skirt of a Western saddle.

Badge of Honour an award presented by the F.E.I. to riders competing in Prix des Nations competitions with points given as follows: Bronze–five, Silver–25, Gold–50. Competing in an Olympic Games is counted as competing in five Prix des Nations.

Bag Fox a fox kept temporarily in captivity until it is required for a hunt.

Ballotade an air above the ground in which the horse half rears, then jumps forward, drawing the hind legs up below the quarters, before landing on all four legs.

Band a group of horses.

Bang-tail a horse.

Bareme any of the three tables of rules set by the F.E.I. under which show jumping competitions are judged.

Barrage a jump-off.

Bareback Riding riding a horse without a saddle or blanket on its back.

Barrel the part of the horse's body between the forearms and the loins.

Barrier (a) the point at which a race starts. (b) in a rodeo arena the barrier behind which the roper or steer wrestler's horse wait until the stock is far enough out of the chute.

Bay (a) a dark skinned horse with a dark brown to a bright reddish- or yellowish-brown coat, with a black mane and tail and normally black markings on the legs.

(b) the noise made by a hound.

Bayo Coyote a dun horse with a black dorsal stripe.

Beaning disguising an unsoundness in a horse.

Bed Down to put down a bed for a horse in a stable or loose box.

Bell as rung in show-jumping competitions to signal competitors to start, restart or stop, or to indicate elimination.

Bet (a) a wager placed on a horse in a race. (b) to make a wager.

Betting (a) the quotation of the wager prices of horses in a certain race. (b) to place a bet on a horse.

Betting Shop a licensed bookmaker's establishment, not on a racecourse, which takes bets on horseraces, etc.

Big Race the principal race of the day at any race meeting.

Bit a device, normally made of metal or rubber, attached to the bridle and placed in the horse's mouth so as to regulate the position of the horse's head and to help control the pace and direction of the horse. It is manipulated by use of the reins.

Bitch Fox the name given to a female fox.

Bitch Hound a female hound.

Bitless Bridle any of a variety of bridles used without bits, pressure being exerted on the nose and the curb groove instead of the mouth.

Black a horse with a black coat, mane and tail with no other colour present, except possibly white markings on the face and/or legs.

Black Saddler a saddler who specializes in making items of saddlery for riding horses.

Blacksmith an artisan whose medium is iron and amongst other things makes horse shoes.

Blemish any scar left by an injury or wound.

Blind Bucker a horse which bucks indiscriminately, heading into anything, when ridden.

Blinkers a pair of leather eye-shields fixed to the bridle or on a head covering used to prevent a horse from looking anywhere other than in front of it.

Blood the amount of blood in a horse's body is made up of approximately one-eighteenth of its total body weight.

Blood Horse the English Thoroughbred.

Bloodstock thoroughbred horses, particularly race and stud animals.

Blow a Stirrup to lose a stirrup iron. If this happens in a rodeo contest the rider is disqualified.

Blow Away to send hounds after a fox by blowing a given signal on the hunting horn.

Blow Up (a) a term used in the dressage arena or the show ring when a horse either breaks from the pace at which it is meant to be going or misbehaves generally. (b) (U.S.) to start bucking.

Body Brush a tightly-packed, short bristled brush used to remove dust and scurf from a horse's coat.

Bog Rider a cowboy whose job is to rescue cattle which have got trapped in mud or marshland.

Boil Over to start bucking.

Bookie an abbreviated term for a bookmaker.

Bookmaker a professional betting man who is licensed to accept the bets placed by others on horses, etc.

Boundary Rider station (ranch) worker whose task it is to ride round all the fencing on the huge Australian cattle and sheep properties, to find holes and to repair them.

Bran a by-product of grain milling, which, when freshly ground and dampened, acts as a mild laxative and aids digestion.

Break the initial training of a horse for whatever purpose it may be required.

Break Down to lacerate the suspensory ligament or fracture a sesamoid bone, so that the back of the fetlock drops to the ground.

Breastplate a device usually of leather, attached to the saddle to prevent it from slipping back on the horse.

Breeder (a) the owner of a mare which gives birth to a foal. (b) the owner of a stud farm where horses are bred.

Breeze In to win a race very easily.

Bridle the part of a horse's saddlery or harness which is placed about the head.

Bronco an unbroken or imperfectly broken wild horse.

Bronco-buster a person who breaks and trains broncos.

Bronc Riding one of the standard rodeo events. The only piece of tack worn by the horse is a wide leather band round its middle, from which a leather handhold protrudes.

Bronc Saddle a saddle used in breaking broncos.

Browband the part of the bridle which lies across the horse's forehead below the ears.

Brumby Australian wild horse.

Brumby Runner Australian bush horseman who captures wild horses.

Brush the tail of a fox.

Buck a leap into the air by a horse keeping its back arched, and coming down with its forelegs stiff and its head held low.

Buckaroo (a) a cowboy. (b) a bronco-buster.

Bulldogging see STEER WRESTLING.

Bulldogging Horse horse used for steer wrestling.

Bull Riding one of the standard events in a rodeo, in which the contestant has to ride a bull equipped only with a rope round its middle, which the rider may hold with only one hand.

Bumper (a) an amateur race rider. (b) an amateur race.

Bush Track an unofficial race meeting in the United States.

By sired by.

Bye-day an extra meet held by a hunt, usually during the Christmas school holidays or to compensate for days lost through bad weather.

Calf Horse a specially trained horse used for calf roping.

Calf-Roping one of the standard events in a rodeo in which the rider ropes a calf and then swiftly dismounts to tie the calf by three legs.

Call Over the naming of the horses in a race, when the latest betting odds on each horse are given.

Camera Patrol equipment for the filming of a race while it is in progress.

Camp Drafting a uniquely Australian rodeo contest in which a rider separates a large bullock from a group of cattle and drives it at the gallop around a course marked with upright poles.

Canter a pace of three time in which the hoofs strike the ground in the following order: near hind, near fore and off hind together, off fore (leading leg): or off hind, off fore and near hind together, near fore (leading leg).

Cap the fee payable by a visitor for a day's hunting.

Capriole an air above the ground in which the horse half rears with the hocks drawn under, then jumps forward and high into the air, at the same time kicking out the hind legs with the soles of the feet turned upwards, before landing collectedly on all four legs.

Catchweight the random or optional weight carried by a horse when the conditions of a race do not specify a weight. Except in matches, this does not occur now.

Cavalletti a series of small wooden jumps used in the basic training of a riding horse in order to encourage it to lengthen its stride, improve its balance and loosen up and strengthen its muscles.

Cayuse an Indian horse or pony.

Certainty a horse regarded as certain to win a particular race (may or may not be the official favourite).

Chaff meadow hay or green oat straw cut into short lengths for use as a feedstuff.

Charley a fox.

Check a halt in hunting when hounds lose the scent.

Cheekpiece (a) the leather part of the bridle to which the bit is attached at one end and the headpiece at the other. (b) side pieces of a bit to which the reins are attached.

Chef D'Equipe the manager of an equestrian team responsible for making all the arrangements, both on and off the field for a national team competing abroad.

Chestnut a horse with a gold to dark reddish-brown coat, usually having a matching or slightly lighter or darker mane and tail, or sometimes with a flaxen coloured mane and tail.

Chime hounds giving tongue in unison when on the line of the quarry.

Chukka a period of play in polo lasting seven and a half or eight minutes, depending on which country the game is being played in.

Classic any one of the five chief English flat races for three-year-old horses: that is, the Derby, the Oaks, the St. Leger, the 1,000 Guineas and the 2,000 Guineas.

Clear Round a show-jumping or cross-country round which is completed without jumping or time faults.

Cob a type rather than a breed. A short legged animal with a maximum height of 15·1 h.h. with the bone and substance of a heavy weight hunter and capable of carrying a substantial weight.

Co-favourite one of two or more horses equally favoured to win a race and given the same shortest price in the betting odds.

Colic sharp abdominal pains often the symptom of flatulence, an obstruction created by a mass of hard food, or faeces in the bowel, and which can lead to a twisted gut.

Collection shortening the pace by a light contact from the rider's hands and a steady pressure with the legs to make the horse flex its neck, relax its jaw and bring its hocks well under it so that it is properly balanced.

Colt an ungelded male horse less than four years old.

Combination Obstacle in show-jumping, an obstacle consisting of two or more separate jumps which are numbered and judged as one obstacle.

Combined Training Competition a comprehensive test of both horse and rider, consisting of the following three phases: dressage, cross-country and show-jumping, held over a period of one, two or three days depending on the type of competition.

Contact the link between the rider's hands and the horse's mouth made through the reins.

Corn bruising of the sole in the angle between the wall of the hoof and the heel.

Corral a pen or enclosure for animals, usually made of wood and always circular in shape, so that the animals cannot injure themselves.

Country the area over which a certain pack of hounds may hunt.

Couple two hounds.

Courbette an air above the ground in which the horse rears to an almost upright position, and then leaps forwards several times on its hind legs.

Course (a) a racecourse. (b) in show-jumping and cross-country a circuit consisting of a number of obstacles to be jumped in a particular order within a specified time limit. (c) for hounds to hunt by sight rather than by scent.

Course Builder the person responsible for designing and building a show-jumping or cross-country course.

Course Designer (a) a person who designs a show-jumping or cross-country course and may or may not actually build it as well. (b) (U.S.) a course builder.

Covert a hunting term for a thicket or small area of woodland.

Cowboy a man who herds and tends cattle on ranches, doing his work mainly on horseback.

Cow Horse the horse which a cowboy rides while working cattle.

Croupade an air above the ground in which the horse rears, and then jumps vertically with the hind legs drawn up towards the belly.

Cry the noise made by hounds when they are hunting their quarry.

Cub a young fox.

Curb Bit type of bit used in conjunction with a snaffle bit in a double bridle consisting of two metal cheekpieces and a mouthpiece with a central indented section (called the port).

Curb Chain a metal chain which is fitted to the eyes of a curb or pelham bit and lies in the curb groove of the horse's jaw.

Curb Groove the groove of the lower jaw just behind the lower lip.

Curry Comb a piece of grooming equipment used to remove dirt and scurf from a body brush. It has a flat back, while the front consists of several rows of small metal teeth.

Cut to geld or castrate a colt or stallion.

Cutting Horse a horse especially trained for separating selected cattle from a herd.

Dam the female parent of a foal.

Dandy brush the long-bristled brush for removing the surface dirt or mud from a horse's coat.

Dark Horse in racing, a horse whose form is little known outside its own stable.

Dead Heat in racing, a tie for first, second or third places.

Declaration a statement made in writing by an owner, trainer or his representative, a specified time before a race or competition, declaring that a horse will take part.

Dirt Track a race track, the surface of which is a combination of sand and soil.

Dividend the amount paid to a person who has backed a winner or a placed horse on the totalizator. In the U.S. called the pay-off.

Dog Fox a male fox.

Dog Hound a male hound.

Dope to administer drugs to a horse, either to improve or hinder its performance in a race or competition. It is an illegal practice and carries heavy penalties in all forms of equestrian sport.

Double (a) the backing of two horses to win in separate races, the winnings of one race being carried as a stake on to the second. If either horse fails to win the bet is lost. In the U.S. known as the DAILY DOUBLE. (b) in show-jumping a combination obstacle consisting of two separate jumps.

Double Bridle a bridle consisting of two bits, a curb and a snaffle which are attached by means of two cheekpieces and may be operated independently.

Drag an artificial scent for a hunt made by trailing a strong smelling material such as a piece of sacking impregnated with aniseed or a fox's dropping over the ground.

Draghound a hound trained to follow a drag.

Draghunt a hunt with a drag or artificial scent.

Drain an underground pipe, ditch or watercourse in which a fox may hide.

Dressage the art of training horses to perform all movements in a balanced, supple, obedient and keen manner.

Drover Australian horseman who herds cattle or sheep over long distances.

Each Way in racing, to back a horse to win and to finish in the first three.

Earth the lair of a fox which it digs below ground level or in the side of a bank.

Elimination the excluding of a competitor from taking further part in a particular competition.

Engaged a term applied to a horse entered in a particular race.

Enteritis inflammation of the intestinal or bowel lining which may be set up by bacteria, chemical or vegetable poisons, or mouldy or damaged food containing harmful fungi.

Equestrian (a) of, or pertaining to, horsemen or horsemanship. (b) a rider or performer on horseback.

Equestrienne a female rider or performer on horseback.

Equine (a) of, or pertaining to, the horse. (b) a horse.

Evens in racing, the betting odds given on a horse when the person who places the bet stands to win the same amount as his stake. In the U.S. known as even money.

Event Horse a horse which competes or is capable of competing in a combined training competition.

Exacta a type of wagering in which the better must select the first and second place finishers in exact order.

Fall a horse is considered to have fallen when the shoulders and quarters on the same side touch the ground. A rider is considered to have fallen when there is separation between him and his horse which necessitates his remounting.

Fancied said of a horse likely to win a particular race. In the U.S. called favourite.

Farrier a person who makes horseshoes and shoes horses.

Fault in show-jumping, a scoring unit used to record any knockdown, refusal or other offence committed by a competitor during his round.

Favourite the horse in a race having the shortest odds offered against it.

F.E.I. the Fédération Equestre Internationale (International Equestrian Federation) which is the governing body of international equestrian sport and was founded in 1921 by Commandant G. Hector of France. It has its headquarters in Brussels. The F.E.I. makes the rules and regulations for the conduct of the three equestrian sports which comprise the Olympic Equestrian Games; show-jumping, three day event and dressage, as well as international driving competitions. All national federations are required to comply with these rules and regulations in any international event.

Fence (a) any obstacle to be jumped in steeplechasing, cross-country, show-jumping or hunting. (b) in racing, to jump over an obstacle.

Field (a) the mounted followers of a hunt. (b) in racing, (i) all the horses running in a particular race; (ii) all the horses not individually favoured in the betting.

Filly a female horse less than four years old.

Finish a horse is said to finish a race when it passes the winning post mounted, providing, in the case of a steeplechase or hurdle race, it has jumped all the obstacles with its rider.

First Jockey the principal person engaged by an owner or trainer to ride for him.

Flapper a horse which runs at an unauthorized race meeting.

Flapping an unofficial race meeting which is not held under the rules of racing.

Flat Racing racing in which there are no obstacles for the horses to jump.

Foal a young horse up to the age of 12 months.

Forehand the part of the horse which is in front of the rider: that is the head, neck, shoulders, withers and forelegs.

Form the past performances of a horse in racing.

Fox a carnivorous animal of the canine family.

Fox Dog a foxhound.

Foxhound one of a breed of swift, keen-scented hounds bred and trained for hunting foxes.

Foxhunting the hunting of the fox in its natural state by a pack of foxhounds, followed by people on horses or on foot.

Full ungelded.

Full Mouth the mouth of a horse at six years old, when it has grown all its teeth.

Furniture any item of harness or saddlery put on a horse.

Fuzztail Running the act of herding and catching wild horses.

Gad a spur.

Gag Bridle a severe form of bridle: cheekpieces are made of rounded leather and pass through holes at the top and bottom of the bit rings, before attaching directly to the reins.

Gall a skin sore usually occurring under the saddle or girth.

Galloway an Australian show ring category based upon an animal's height: a Galloway measures from 14 to 15 h.h. (in Australia ponies are under 14 h.h.).

Garron any native pony of Scotland or Ireland.

Gate frequently used as an upright obstacle in show-jumping competitions.

Gelding a male horse which has been castrated.

Gestation the period between conception and foaling, normally about eleven months.

Get the offspring of a stallion.

Girth (a) the circumference of a horse, measured behind the withers round the deepest part of the body. (b) a band, usually of leather, webbing or nylon, passed under the belly of the horse to hold the saddle in place.

Give Tongue for hounds to bark or bay when in full cry after a quarry.

Going the condition of a race track or other ground over which a horse travels; variously classified as soft, good etc.

Gone to Ground a fox having taken refuge in an earth or a drain.

Good Mouth a horse with a soft, sensitive mouth.

Go Short said of a horse which is lame or restricted in its action.

Green (a) a horse which is broken but not fully trained, an inexperienced horse. (b) a trotter or pacer which has not been raced against the clock.

Grey a dark skinned horse with a coat of black and white hairs mixed together; the whiter ones becoming more predominant with each change of coat.

Groom (a) any person who is responsible for looking after a horse. (b) to clean the coat and feet of a horse.

Grooming Kit collectively, the brushes and other items of equipment used to groom a horse.

Ground to let the reins touch the ground after dismounting so that the horse will stand without having to be tied up.

Ground Money in a rodeo the entry fee and purse money split equally among all the contestants in an event when there is no outright winner.

Gymkhana mounted games, most frequently for children under sixteen, many of which are adaptations of children's party games.

Habit the dress worn by a woman riding side-saddle consisting of a jacket and matching long skirt or shaped panel which is worn over the breeches and boots.

Hack (a) a riding horse for hire. (b) a pleasure ride.

Halter a hemp rope headpiece with lead rope attached, used for leading a horse when not wearing a bridle, or for tying up in the stable.

Hand a linear measurement equalling 4 ins (10 cm) used in giving the height of a horse, the fractions being expressed in inches.

Handicap (a) the weight allocated to a horse in a race. (b) a race in which the weights to be carried by the horse are estimated so as to give each horse an equal chance of winning.

Haunches the hips and buttocks of a horse.

Haute Ecole the classical art of equitation.

Hay grass cut and dried at a particular time of the year for use as fodder.

Head one of the measurements of distance by which a horse may be said to have won a race: the length of a horse's head.

Head Collar a bitless headpiece and noseband, usually of leather, for leading a horse which is not wearing a bridle, or for tying up a horse in a stable.

Heavy Horse any horse belonging to one of the breeds of large draught horses, such as Clydesdale, Percheron, Shire or Suffolk Punch.

Height the height of a horse is measured in a perpendicular line from the highest part of the withers to the ground.

High School the classical art of equitation.

Hitch Up to harness a horse or horses to be driven.

Hit the Line for hounds to pick up the scent of the quarry.

Hog's Back in show-jumping, a spread obstacle in which there are three sets of poles, the first close to the ground, the second at the highest point of the obstacle and the third slightly lower than the second.

Holloa the cry given by a person out hunting to indicate that he has seen the fox.

Hood (a) a fabric covering which goes over the horse's head and ears and part of its neck, and is used when travelling, most usually in cold weather. (b) blinkers.

Hoof (a) the insensitive horny covering which protects the sensitive parts of a horse's foot. (b) a term used to describe the entire foot.

Hoof Pick a hooked metal instrument used for removing stones and dirt from a horse's foot.

Horse (a) the general term for an equine animal, whether it be a stallion, mare or gelding. (b) a stallion or uncastrated horse. (c) to provide a person with a horse to ride. (d) to ride on horseback.

Horseman (a) a rider on horseback. (b) a person skilled in the training and management of horse. (c) a farm labourer who works with horses.

Horserace a competition for horses ridden by jockeys which takes place on the flat or over obstacles within a given area and over a prescribed distance, under the control of appointed officials.

Horseshoe a shaped metal band nailed to the base of riding and harness horses, hoofs to protect them and prevent them from splitting.

Horse Show a meeting at which competitions are held to test or display the qualities and capabilities of horses and their riders.

Horse-tailing taking charge of the band of horses used by drovers when herding cattle or sheep over long distances.

Hull a term for a saddle.

Hunt Button a button with the symbol or lettering of a particular hunt on it.

Hunter a horse bred and trained to be ridden for hunting.

Hunter Trials a type of competitive event held by most hunts, and other organizing bodies during the hunting season, in which horses are ridden over a course of obstacles built to look as natural and similar to those encountered out hunting. The course has to be completed within a specified time.

Hunting the sport of following different types of hound, either mounted or on foot, in pursuit of the fox, the stag or the hare or an artificially laid drag line.

Hunting Cap a velvet-covered protective riding hat.

Hunting Horn a cylindrical instrument, usually 23–25 cm (9–10 ins) long, made of copper with a nickel or silver mouthpiece, used by huntsmen to give signals, both to hounds and to the field.

Hunt Livery the distinctive coat of a particular hunt worn by the staff of the hunt.

Hunt Secretary a person who carries out the normal duties of a secretary in connection with the hunt; is also responsible for keeping close contact with farmers and landowners within the area of the hunt, and collects the cap money at the meet.

Hunt Servant any salaried employee of a hunt, such as the huntsman, kennel huntsman or whippers-in.

Huntsman the person in charge of hounds during a hunt, whether the master or someone employed by the master.

Hunt Subscription the fee payable by a person who is a member of a hunt.

Hunt Terrier a small short-legged terrier kept by a hunt and used to bolt foxes from earths, drains or other places which are inaccessible to hounds.

Hurdle one of a series of wattle fences over which a horse must jump in hurdle racing. In the U.S. the fences are made of brush.

Hurdle Racing horseraces over a course of hurdles.

In Blood said of hounds having made a kill.

Inbreeding the mating of related individuals, such as brother and sister, sire and daughter or son and dam.

Independent Seat the ability to maintain a firm, balanced position on a horse's back, without relying on the reins or stirrups.

In Foal pregnant.

In Full Cry a pack of hounds in strong pursuit of the quarry and giving tongue.

In-Hand Class any of various show classes in which the animals are led, usually in a show bridle or head collar, but otherwise without saddlery (except for draught horses which are often shown in their harness), and are judged chiefly for conformation and/or condition.

In the Book accepted for, or entered in, the General Stud Book.

Irons stirrup irons.

Jiggle the ordinary gait of a cow horse averaging about 8 km/h (5 m.p.h.).

Jockey (a) a person engaged to ride a horse in a race. (b) formerly a dealer in horses, especially a disreputable one.

Jog a short-paced trot.

Joint-master one of two or more people who share the mastership of a pack of hounds.

Jumper any horse trained to compete over jumps, such as a steeplechaser or showjumper.

Jump Jockey a jockey who races horses over hurdles or steeplechase fences.

Jump-off in show-jumping, a round held to decide the winner of the competition from competitors who have tied for first place in the previous round.

Keep a grass field which is used for grazing. Known as pastures in the U.S.

Kennel Huntsman a person employed by a hunt which has an amateur huntsman to manage the hounds and to act as first whipper-in on hunting days.

Kennel Man a person who works in hunt kennels under the supervision of a huntsman or kennel huntsman.

Kennels the buildings and yards where a pack of hounds is housed.

Lad (a) a boy or stableman who works in a stables of any kind. (b) a girl who works in racing stables. Known as a groom in the U.S.

Laminitis inflammation of the sensitive laminae which lie between the horny wall of the hoof and the pedal bone. It is a very painful condition.

Lawn Meet any meet of a hunt held at a private house by invitation of the owner.

Length one of the measurements of distance by which a horse may be said to win a race; the length of a horse's head and body.

Levade a high-school movement in which the horse rears, drawing its forefeet in, while the hindquarters are deeply bent at the haunches and carry the full weight.

Light a term meaning to dismount.

Light Horse any horse, except a Thoroughbred, used or suitable for riding such as a hack or hunter.

Line the direction in which a fox is travelling with hounds in pursuit.

Linseed the seed of flax generally used in the form of linseed jelly, oil or tea, both as a laxative and to improve the condition and gloss of the coat.

Livery Stable an establishment where privately owned horses are kept, exercised and generally looked after, for an agreed fee. Called Livery in the U.S.

Loriner a person who makes the metal parts of saddlery and harness such as bits, curb chains and stirrup irons.

Lunge Rein a piece of cotton or nylon webbing, usually about 2·5 cm (1 in) wide and 7·5 m (25 ft) long, which is attached by a buckle and leather strap to one of the side rings on a breaking cavesson and is used in training horses.

Maiden a horse of either sex which to date has not won a race of any distance.

Maiden Mare a mare which has not had a foal, though she may be carrying one.

Maiden Race a race in which only horses which have never won a race may be entered.

Mane the long hair growing on the top of a horse's head and down the neck.

Mane and Tail Comb small long-toothed metal combs used for cleaning or pulling the mane and tail.

Mare a female horse aged four years or over.

Martingale a device used to help in keeping a horse's head in the correct position. It generally consists of a strap, or arrangement of straps, fastened to the girth at one end, passed between the forelegs and, depending on the type, attached at the other end to the reins, noseband or directly to the bit.

Mask the head of a fox.

Master the person appointed by a hunt committee to have overall responsibility for the running and organization of all aspects of the hunt.

Match a race between two horses, on terms agreed by their owners. There is no prize awarded.

Meet (a) the place where the hunt servants, hounds, followers, etc. assemble before a hunt. (b) the hunt meeting itself.

Mixed Meeting a race meeting at which both flat and steeplechase or hurdle races are held on the same day.

Mixed Stable a racing stable where both flat race and National Hunt horses are kept.

Montura (a) a riding horse. (b) a saddle.

Mount (a) a horse used for riding. (b) to get up on to the back of a horse.

Mount Money the money paid in a rodeo to a performer, who is riding, roping or bulldogging in exhibition but not in competition.

Muck Out to clean out a box or stall in which a horse has been stabled removing the droppings and soiled bedding.

Mudder a racehorse which performs well on a muddy track.

Mud Fever an inflammation of the upper layer of skin, caused by subjection to muddy and wet conditions.

Music the cry made by hounds when they are hunting.

Mustang a wild horse.

Nap (a) a horse is said to nap if it fails to obey properly applied aids, as in refusing to go forward or to pass a certain point. (b) in racing a good tip.

National Federation the governing body of equestrian affairs in any country affiliated to the F.E.I.

Natural Aids the body, hands, legs and voice as used by the rider to give instructions to the horse.

Near Side the left-hand side of a horse. This is the side from which it is usual to mount a horse.

Neck one of the measurements of distance by which a horse may be said to win a race; the length of a horse's head and neck.

Nose the shortest measurement of distance by which it is possible for a horse to win a race.

Noseband the part of a bridle which lies across the horse's nose consisting of a leather band on an independent headpiece which is worn below the cheeks and above the bit. Also known as a cavesson in the U.S.

Numnah a pad placed under the saddle to prevent undue pressure on the horse's back. Cut to the shape of the saddle, only slightly larger, it may be made of felt, sheepskin or cloth covered foam rubber.

Oats a cereal crop used as part of a horse's feed. May be given either whole, bruised or boiled.

Objection in racing, an objection may be made against any of the placed horses, and must be heard by the stewards at the meeting where it was raised.

Odds the betting quotation on a horse in a particular race.

Odds On betting odds of less than even money.

Off Side the right-hand side of a horse.

On its Toes said of a horse eager and keen to move on.

On Terms said of hounds able to keep hunting steadily because there is a strong scent.

One-Day Event a combined training competititon consisting of dressage, show-jumping and cross-country phases and completed in one day.

Opening Meet the first meet of the regular hunting season.

Outfit (a) a ranch with all its equipment and employees. (b) the personal equipment of a cowboy.

Outlaw a horse which is particularly vicious and untameable.

Outsider a racehorse which is given long odds in the betting as it is thought to have little chance of winning the race.

Owlhead a horse which is impossible to train.

Owner the person in whose name a racehorse runs, irrespective of whether that person is the sole owner of the horse or is a member of a syndicate.

Pace a lateral gait in two time, in which the hind leg and the foreleg on the same side move forward together.

Pacemaker in racing, a horse which takes the lead and sets the speed for the race.

Pad the foot of a fox.

Paddock (a) a grassy enclosure near a stable or house in which horses can be turned out. (b) the enclosure at a racecourse in which the horses are paraded and then mounted before a race.

Pancake an English riding saddle.

Parabola the arc made by a horse from the point of take-off to the point of landing as it jumps an obstacle.

Parallel Bars a type of spread fence used in both show-jumping and cross-country courses, consisting of two sets of posts and rails.

Parimutuel the U.S. and continental equivalent of the totalizator; a form of betting in which the total amount wagered, after a deduction of a percentage for costs, etc., is divided among the holders of the winning and place tickets. An electro-mechanical apparatus is used for recording the number and amount of bets staked by this method.

Passage one of the classical high school airs, comprising a spectacular elevated trot in slow motion. There is a definite period of suspension as one pair of legs remains on the ground with the diagonal opposites raised in the air.

Pelham Bit a bit designed to produce with only one mouthpiece the combined effects of the snaffle bit and the curb bit. Normally made of metal, vulcanite or rubber and used either with two reins, or one rein, in which case a leather couplet is used to link the two rings of the bit.

Penalty in racing, an additional weight handicap carried by a horse, usually imposed when it has won a race since the weights for the race in which the penalty is given were published.

Perfecta a type of wagering in which the better must select the first and second place finishers without regard to the actual order in which they pass the post.

Photo-finish the result of a race photographed by a camera with a very narrow field of vision situated at the winning post on a race-course. A camera was first used for recording a photo-finish in 1890 by John Hemment at Sheepshead Bay in the United States.

Piaffe a classical high school air, comprising a spectacular trot with great elevation and cadence performed on the spot.

Picnic Races meetings held in Australia's Outback, when amateur riders and their grass-fed mounts compete against each other for small prizes on primitive bushland racetracks.

Piebald a horse whose coat consists of large irregular and clearly defined patches of black and white hairs.

Pinto a piebald or skewbald horse.

Pirouette in dressage, a turn within the horse's length, that is, the shortest turn it is possible to make. There are three kinds of pirouette – the turn on the centre, the turn on the forehand and the turn on the haunches.

Place to finish second in a horserace.

Planks a show-jumping obstacle made up of painted planks about 30 cm (1 ft) wide.

Plug any slow or broken down horse.

Polo a mounted game, bearing a resemblance to hockey played between two teams of four a side. Popular in many parts of the world, it is recorded as having been played as long ago as the reign of Darius I of Persia (521–486 BC).

Polocrosse Australian mounted game which is rather like a horseback version of lacrosse: the ball is scooped up in a small net at the end of a long stick and is then carried or thrown.

Pony (a) a horse not exceeding 14·2 h.h. at maturity. (b) the sum of £25 in gambling.

Pony Speed Test the racing of ponies ridden by light boy riders around the quarter-mile circuit at showgrounds in Australia.

Post (a) either the starting or winning post in racing. (b) to rise from the saddle at the trot.

Post and Rails a type of obstacle in show jumping and cross country courses consisting of upright posts between which are laid a number of horizontal posts. In show-jumping the rails are simply supported by the posts, whereas in cross-country events, they are fixed to the posts.

Price the odds quoted by a bookmaker at a race meeting for a particular horse.

Prix des Nations an international team show-jumping competition held at an official international horse show. Four members compete in each team jumping the course twice, the three best scores of the team are counted in each round. In the event of equality after the two rounds a jump-off is held in which faults and time are totalled to give the final result. Again only the three best scores and times are counted.

Punter a person who bets regularly on horses.

Quarters the area of a horse's body extending from the rear of the flank to the root of the tail and downwards on either side to the top of the leg: the hindquarters.

Race Card the printed programme of a race meeting giving information, including the name and time of each race, and the names of all horses, their owners and trainers and the weights to be carried.

Racecourse a race track properly constructed for flat and/or steeple-chasing and hurdle racing, together with all the relevant facilities, such as grandstands, paddock, stables, office buildings, etc. and administered by appointed officials.

Racehorse a horse bred and trained for racing, either on the flat or over hurdles or steeplechase obstacles.

Race Meeting (a) a meeting at a given place for the purpose of holding a fixed number of horseraces. (b) the period during which this meeting takes place.

Racing Plate a thin very lightweight horseshoe used on racehorses.

Racing Saddle a saddle designed for use on racehorses, which may range from the very light type of less than 1 kg (2 lbs) used for flat racing, to the heavier more solid type used for hurdling and steeplechasing.

Rack the most spectacular movement of the five gaited American Saddle Horse, it is a very fast even gait in which each foot strikes the ground separately in quick succession.

Range Horse a horse which is born and brought up on the range, and is never handled until it is brought in to be broken.

Rear for a horse to rise up on the hind legs.

Red Flag a marker used in equestrian sports to denote the right-hand extremity of any obstacle. It is also used to mark a set track and must always be passed on the left-hand side.

Red Ribbon a piece of red ribbon tied round the tail of a horse, especially when hunting, to indicate that it is a known kicker.

Refusal (a) in racing, the failure of a horse to attempt to jump a hurdle or steeplechase fence. (b) in show-jumping and combined training, either the act of passing an obstacle which is to be jumped, or stopping in front of it.

Rein Back to make a horse step backwards while being ridden or driven.

Reins a pair of long narrow straps attached to the bit or bridle and used by the rider or driver to guide and control tis horse.

Renvers a dressage movement on two tracks in which the horse moves at an angle of not more than 30 degrees along the long side of the arena with the hind legs on the outer and the forelegs on the inner track, looking in the direction in which it is going and being bent slightly round the inside leg of the rider.

Rep a cowboy employed to search for and round up cattle which have strayed from the ranch of his employer. Such cattle would be recognizable by their brand.

Resistance the act of refusing to go

forward, stopping, running back or rearing.

Ride Off in polo, to push one's pony against that of another player in order to prevent him from playing the ball.

Riding School an establishment where people are taught to ride and horses can be hired for riding, or may be taken for livery, or both.

Ringer a horse entered in a race under the name of another horse, the object being to win bets illegally on a good horse, which the public and bookmakers believe to be an inferior one.

Roan a horse having a black, bay or chestnut coat with an admixture of white hairs (especially on the body and neck), which modifies the colour.

Rope Horse any horse which is especially trained and used for roping cattle.

Run Mute said of hounds which are running very fast and thus have no time to speak.

Runner any horse taking part in a particular race.

Run Out (a) in show-jumping and combined training, to avoid an obstacle which is to be jumped by running to one side or the other of it. (b) in racing, to avoid an obstacle which is to be jumped or to pass on the wrong side of a marker flag.

Saddle a seat for a rider on horseback, made in various designs according to the purpose for which it is required.

Saddle Bronc Riding one of the standard rodeo events. The rider has to use a regulation saddle; he is allowed to use only one rein attached to a simple halter and is not allowed to touch the saddle, the horse or himself with his free hand. He must remain mounted for 10 seconds and is judged according to how hard the horse bucks and how well he rides.

Saddle Furniture the metal parts of a saddle.

Saddler a person who makes or deals in saddlery and/or harness.

Saddlery the bridle, saddle and other items of tack used on a horse which is to be ridden as opposed to driven.

Scent the distinctive odour of the fox which is given off by the glands under the tail and from the pads.

School (a) to train a horse for whatever purpose it may be required. (b) an enclosed area, either covered or open where a horse may be trained or exercised.

Scratch (a) to withdraw a horse from an

equestrian event after it had been officially entered. (b) (U.S.) to spur vigorously.

Scrub Dashing galloping after half-wild cattle in timbered country in Australia in order to round them up into a herd.

Selling Race a race immediately after which, any runner, if a loser, may be claimed for a previously stated price, or, if the winner, must be offered for sale at auction.

Service the mating of a mare by a stallion.

Shoeing the act of putting shoes on a horse. Normally a horse needs its shoes renewed every four to eight weeks depending on the type of work it is required to do, whether it is worked on soft or hard ground and how fast its feet grow.

Show (a) to compete in a horse show. (b) (U.S.) to finish third in a race.

Show Class any of various competitions held at horse shows in which the animals are judged for their conformation, condition, action and/or suitability for whatever purpose they are used, or intended to be used.

Shy for a horse to swerve away suddenly in fear (or occasionally from mere high spirits) from an obstacle or sound.

Side Saddle a saddle designed for women on which the rider sits with both feet on the same side, normally the nearside. On that side, the saddle has two padded projections placed diagonally one above the other. The rider hooks her right leg over the upper one and places the left leg under and against the lower one resting her left foot in the single stirrup iron.

Silks the peaked cap and silk or woollen blouse, both carrying the colours of the owner, worn by a jockey in racing.

Sire the male parent of a foal.

Skate a horse of poor quality.

Skewbald a horse whose coat consists of large irregular and clearly defined patches of white and of any other colour, except black.

Sleeper a horse which unexpectedly wins a race having previously shown poor form.

Slow Gait one of the gaits of the five-gaited American Saddle Horse. It is a true prancing action in which each foot in turn is raised and then held momentarily in mid-air before being brought down. Similar to the rack and also called the single foot.

Snaffle Bit the oldest and simplest form of bit, available in a variety of types, but consisting chiefly of a single bar with a ring at each end to which one pair of reins is attached.

Snaffle Bridle the bridle used in conjunction with a snaffle bit.

Sound said of a horse which is free from any illness, disease, blemish, physical defect or imperfection which might impair in any way its usefulness or ability to work.

Speak the bark or bay of a hound on finding a scent.

Splint a bony growth which gradually forms between a horse's cannon bone and one of the splint bones as a result of excess strain or concussion.

Spread Fence in show-jumping and cross-country events, any of various obstacles which are wide as opposed to simply high, such as a hogs back, parallel bars, triple bar or water jump.

Sprinter a horse which is able to move at great speed over a short distance but is seldom able to maintain the pace over a long distance.

Spur a pointed device strapped on to the heel of a rider's boot and used to urge the horse onwards, etc.

Stable (a) a building in which one or more horses are kept. (b) a collection of horses belonging to one person, such as a racehorse owner or riding-school proprietor, or kept at one establishment.

Stale Line the line of a fox which has passed some time previously.

Stallion an ungelded male horse aged four years or over.

Stallion Hound a male hound used for breeding purposes.

Standard Event any of the five rodeo events recognized by the governing body, the Rodeo Cowboys Association. These are bareback riding, bull riding, calf-roping, saddle bronc riding and steer wrestling.

Starter's Orders when the starter of a race has satisfied himself that all runners are present and ready to race, a flag is raised to show that the horses are 'under starter's orders'.

Stayer a term applied to a horse which has great strength and power of endurance and is therefore likely to be successful over a long distance.

Steeplechase a race over a certain course of a specified distance and on which there are a number of obstacles to be jumped.

Steer Wrestling one of the standard events in a rodeo. The contestant rides alongside a running steer, and jumps from the saddle on to the head of the steer, the object being to stop the steer, twist it to the ground, and hold it there with the head and all four feet facing in the same direction.

The contestant completing the event in the shortest time is the winner. Also called bulldogging.

Steward an official at a race meeting appointed to see that the meeting is conducted according to the rules.

Stirrup Iron a loop, ring, or similar device made of metal, wood, leather, etc., suspended from a saddle to support the rider's foot.

Stirrup Leather the adjustable strap by which the stirrup iron is attached to the saddle.

Stock (a) a white neckcloth worn for hunting and formal occasions. (b) the handle of a whip.

Stock Class a show class for stock or ranch ponies.

Stock Saddle the high-pommelled, high-cantled Australian cowboy's saddle which has long flaps.

Straight Fence in show-jumping and cross-country courses, any obstacle which has all its component parts in the same vertical plane, such as a gate, post and rails or planks.

Strangles an infectious and highly contagious disease caused by the organism *Streptococcus equi* and occurring most commonly in young horses. The symptoms include a rise in temperature, a thick nasal discharge and swelling of the submaxillary and other lymphatic glands of the head in which abscesses eventually form.

Strike a Fox to find a fox.

Stud (a) an establishment at which horses are kept for breeding purposes. (b) any large establishment of racehorses, hunters, etc., belonging to one owner. (c) (U.S.) a studhorse or stallion. (d) a metallic head screwed into a horseshoe to give the horse a better grip on a slippery surface.

Stud Groom a senior groom, especially at a stud farm.

Surcingle a webbing belt usually 6 to 8 cm (2½ to 3 ins) wide, which passes over a racing or jumping saddle and girth and is used to keep the saddle in position, or which can be used in place of a roller to secure a day or night rug.

Sweat Scraper a curved metal blade with a wooden handle used to scrape sweat from a horse.

Sweet Itch a dermatitis usually found in horses that are allergic to a particular pasture plant, and therefore most likely to occur in the spring and summer months. It particularly affects the crest, croup and withers causing intense irritation and producing patches of thick scaly, sometimes

ulcerated skin, which the horse often rubs bare in its attempts to get relief.

Tack saddlery.

Tail the tail of the horse includes the dock together with all the hair which is usually allowed to grow about 10 cm (4 ins) below the point of the hock.

Technical Delegate the person at an international horse show or three-day event who is responsible for seeing that the competition is run according to international rules and that the course is correct. He is usually from a country other than the host nation.

Teeth when fully mouthed the horse has 40 teeth: 12 incisors (6 in each jaw), 4 canines (1 in each side of the upper and lower jaw), and 24 molars (6 above and 6 below on each side). Females lack canines.

Temperature the normal temperature of a horse is 38°C (100·5°F).

Tetanus an infectious, often fatal, disease caused by the micro-organism *Tetanus bacillus* which lives in the soil and enters a horse's body through wounds, especially of the foot. One of the first visible signs is that the horse will stand with its head pointed forwards, its front legs wide apart, its hind legs straddled with the hocks turned outwards and its tail raised. If made to move the animal will walk stiffly. As the disease advances the horse may become nervous and excited and the facial muscles become so rigid that the animal is unable to open its mouth.

Three-Day Event a combined training competition completed over three consecutive days. It consists of a dressage test, a cross-country section, which includes a steeplechase course and two circuits of roads and tracks as well as a course of cross-country obstacles, and finally a show-jumping event.

Throat Lash a strap which is part of the headpiece of a bridle. It fastens under the horse's throat so as to prevent the bridle from slipping over the head. Known more correctly as Throat Latch.

Thrush inflammation of the frog of a horse's foot, characterized by a foul smelling discharge.

Time Allowed the prescribed period of time in which a competitor must complete a show-jumping course if he is not to incur time faults.

Time Limit the prescribed period of time in which a competitor must complete a show-jumping course if he is not to be eliminated.

Tipster in racing, a person who makes a business of providing information or tips about the chances of horses in races.

Totalizator An electromechanical apparatus used for a form of betting in which the total amount wagered, after a deduction of a percentage for costs, etc., is divided among the holders of winning and place tickets.

Trail Horse a horse trained, bred or used for cross-country rides.

Trainer a person qualified to superintend the training of a horse for a particular sport or pursuit.

Training Tracks concentric tracks inside the racecourse proper at Australian racetracks, on which the great majority of Australian racehorses are trained.

Travers a dressage movement on two tracks in which the horse moves at an angle of not more than 30 degrees along the long side of the arena with the forelegs on the outer and the hind legs on the inner track, looking in the direction in which it is going and bent slightly round the inside leg of the rider.

Treble in show-jumping, a combination obstacle consisting of three separate jumps.

Triple Bar in show-jumping, a spread fence consisting of three sets of poles built in staircase fashion with the highest at the back.

Trot a pace of two time in which the legs move in diagonal pairs but not quite simultaneously.

Turf (a) any course over which horse-racing is conducted. (b) in the U.S. turf races are held over grass courses as opposed to dirt tracks. (c) the world of horseracing in general.

Turn on the Forehand a movement in which the horse pivots on the forehand while describing concentric circles with the hind legs.

urn on the Quarters a movement in
h the horse pivots on the hind legs
e describing concentric circles with
relegs.

d said of a hound which has not
a cub hunting season.

orse which has not yet taken

ider who has in some way
f the saddle.

rse which has any defect
unable to function prop-

o buck.

Volte in dressage a full turn on the haunches: the smallest circle a horse is able to execute on either one or two tracks, the radius being equal to the length of the horse.

Walk a pace of four time in which the hoofs strike the ground in the following sequence: near hind, near fore, off hind, off fore.

Walking Horse Class any of various competitions held for Tennessee Walking Horses at horse shows in the USA.

Walkover a race in which only one horse has been declared to start. To qualify for the prize money the horse has to be saddled, paraded in front of the stand and then has to walk past the winning post.

Wall (a) an upright show-jumping obstacle made of hollow wooden blocks which are painted and stacked to look like a brick wall. (b) a cross-country obstacle built of brick, concrete blocks, sleepers or stone. Such obstacles are usually built as uprights, but dry stone walls may be as wide as a narrow topped bank.

Wall of the Hoof that part of the hoof which is visible when the foot is placed flat on the ground. It is divided into the toe, the quarters (sides) and the heel.

Water to provide a horse with water to drink.

Water Brush (a) a brush used to wash the feet and to dampen the mane and tail. (b) in show-jumping, a small sloping brush fence placed in front of a water jump to help a horse take off.

Water Jump a spread show-jumping obstacle consisting of a sunken trough of water with a minimum width of 4·2 m (14 ft) and a length of up to 4·8 m (16 ft). A small brush fence is usually placed on the take off side.

Weigh In in certain equestrian sports where a specified weight has to be carried, such as racing, combined training and show jumping, the rider has to be weighed immediately after completion of the race, or his round in the competition, to ensure the correct weight was carried throughout the event.

Weighing Room the place on a racecourse where the jockeys are weighed.

Weigh Out in certain equestrian sports where a specified weight has to be carried, such as racing, combined training and show-jumping, the rider has to be weighed before the race or competition to ensure the correct weight is carried.

Weight Allowance a weight allowance in racing which may be claimed by a jockey or apprentice who has not ridden a certain number of winners.

Weight Cloth a cloth carried under the saddle on a horse. It is equipped with pockets in which lead weights may be inserted to achieve the correct weight.

Weight for Age a method of handicapping horses in a race by their age, the older horses carrying more weight than the younger horses.

Weights blocks, normally of lead, placed in the weight cloth and used by a rider who is not heavy enough to make the specified weight for an event.

Whipper-in the huntsman's assistant with a pack of hounds.

White Flag a marker used in equestrian sports to mark the left-hand extremity of an obstacle. It is also used to mark a set track and must always be passed on the right.

Wind a Fox for hounds to smell the scent of a fox.

Windgall a puffy elastic swelling of a horse's knee or fetlock joints caused by an over-secretion of synovia, a fluid similar to joint oil.

Windsucking a harmful habit in which a horse draws in and swallows air, causing indigestion.

Wing one of a pair of upright stands with cups or similar fittings used to support the poles or other suspended parts of a show jumping obstacle.

Win in a Canter to pass the winning post first at an easy pace, being so far ahead of the rest of the field.

Winner's Enclosure the place on a racecourse reserved for the first three horses in a race and to which their riders have to return mounted immediately after the end of the race.

Winter Horse a horse which is kept at a home ranch for use during the winter.

Winter Out for a horse to be left out in the field during the winter rather than to be brought into the stable.

With a Stain a well bred horse but having some common blood.

Withers the highest part of a horse's back: the area at the base of the neck between the shoulder blades.

Wrangle to round up, herd and care for horses.

Young Entry the name given to young hounds before the start of the cub hunting season when they are unentered. During cubbing they are trained to hunt the quarry so that by the time the hunting season starts they are entered, usually at about 18 months of age.

INDEX

Page numbers in italics refer to
illustrations or their captions

Entries in the Glossary (pp 242–251)
are not included in this index

ACKNOWLEDGMENTS

The publishers would like to thank the following individuals and organisations for their kind permission to reproduce the photographs in this book:

Alpha/Zimmerman 129; All-Sport (Tony Duffy) 103, 111, (Don Morley) 112, 177 above right; American History Picture Library 26; Ardea Photographics 72, (J.P. Fererro) 198 above left, (K.W. Fink) 19, (P. Morris) 73 above, (Su Gooders) 14 above, (Su Gooders/Fores Ltd.) 121, (Su Gooders/T. Hoskinson) 99 below inset; Aspect Picture Library 75 centre; Australian Information Service 152 below; Barnaby's Picture Library 50 centre, 66 below; Bio-Arts 180, 182, 185 below, 191 above and below, 192, 195 above and below, 215; British Museum 16 left and right, 17 left, (M. Holford) 26–27; Bulgarian Tourist Agency 53 below; G.L. Carlisle 162; Bruce Coleman Ltd. 63 below, (J. Burton) 12–13, (Rex Coleman; 108 below left, 113 right, 235 right, (George Laycock) 123 below, (C. Osborne) 151 above, (Hans Reinhard) 24–25, 34–35, 41, (J. Van Wormer) 148; Colorsport 88–89, 97 right, 104, 114 left, 115 below right, 116 above and below, 136 above, 234; G. Cranham 95, 100 above, 107 above right, 108–109 above, 109 below, 110 above and below, 117, 123 above, 127 above and below, 216 below; From the 1902 Edition of The Sears, Roebuck Catalogue © 1969 Crown Publishers Inc. Used by permission of Crown Publishers Inc. 30 below; Anne Cumbers 130 above, 141 above left, above right and centre, 141 below right; Findlay Davidson 105 above; M. Edwards 76 above; R. Earle 132; Bob Estall 62 below; Mary Evans Picture Library 20 above, 22 above left, 23 above left and above right, 31 above, 119 inset; James Fain 61 below; John Fairfax 152 inset; Alan Foley Photo Library 13, 152 above right; Werner Forman Archive 15 above, 17 right; Fox Photos 126; F.P.G. 164, 224 below, (Alpha) 65 below, (Alpha/Niki Collins) 176–177, (Cal Harbert) 31 below, (Ward Allan Howe) 159, (R. Meek) 147 below right; Tim Graham 2–3; Luther C. Goldman 83 above; Susan Griggs Picture Agency (Michael Boys) 124 below, (Horst Munzig) 136 below left and below right, (Mike Sheil) 157, (A. Woolfit) front endpapers, 98–99 below; Robert Harding Associates 37, 137 centre, (T.E. Clark) 161 inset, (Tim McGarry) 806, (Singer) 84 below, (Trevor Wood) 118–119, 119 inset; Brian Hawkes 14 below left; The John Hillelson Agency Ltd. (E. Lessing) 96 below, (E. Lessing/Magnum) 21, (Fred Mayer) 176, (R.S. Michaud) 15 below, 142 below; Jacana Agence de Presse (Trouillet) 48 below; Betty Kellock 22 above right; Keystone Press Agency 87 below; Paolo Koch 18 above, 32 below, 139, 140, 145, 146 below, 147 above; E.D. Lacey 93 below right, 101 above, 105 below, 106, 107 above left, 108 below right, 114–115 below, 115 above, 217 above, 233; Leslie Lane 94 above; Claire Leimbach 147 below left, 178 above, 227 above 228, 240; Mansell Collection 20–21, 22 below, 23 below, 66 above, 99 above inset, 120, 142 above, 143 above; Jane Miller 74 centre, 87 above; Missouri Fox Trotting Association 63 above; John Moss 14 below right, 107 below, 134–135, 135 above and below, 154 inset, 196 above; N.H.P.A. 101 below; Novosti Press Agency 39 right, 68 below, 69 below, 177 below; Pictor International Ltd. 6–7, (Pictor/Alpha: Tony Frissell) 102 below; Picturpoint Ltd. 28, 124 above, 125 left, 149 158, 221, 227 below; (Gordon de Lisle) 152 below; Racetrack Magazine, Australia 153; Radio Times Hulton Picture Library 134; Minette Rice Edwards (Charles Barieau) 131 above left and below, (Martin Rice Edwards) 130 below, 131 above right; S.W. Rickets 204 above right, 210 right; J. Rigby 183, 230 left and right; Mike Roberts 40 above right and below, 90–91, 100 below, 144, 154–155; Peter Roberts 93 below left; Peter D. Rossdale 200 above, below left and below right, 201, 202, 203 above left and below right, 204 above left, below left and below right, 205 above and below, 206 above left, centre left, centre right and below, 208 above left, above right, below left and below right, 209 left and right, 210 left, 213 below, 217 below left and below right, 218 above left, above right, below left and below right, 219 above left, above centre, above right, below left and below centre, 222 above left, above right, centre left and centre right, 223 above left; W.W. Rouch (Guy Wilmot) 45 above; Society for Anglo-Chinese Understanding 85 above; S & G Press Agency Ltd. 50 below right, 94 below; Spanish Riding School, Vienna 93 above; Spectrum Colour Library 6 centre right, 38 above, 82 above, 96 above, 143 below, 181 above, 194–195, 197, 226 below, 238; Syndication International Ltd. 97 left, 113 left, 152 above left; Sally Anne Thompson 6 above right, 36, 128, 133, 141 below, 156 above, below and centre, 160 inset, 181 below, 184, 185 above, 186 above left, above right and below, 187 above and below, 188, 189 left, centre and right, 191 centre, 193 above and below, 198 below, 198–199, 222 below, 223 above and below, 225, 237 below, 239 left, 241, (Z. Raczkowska) 55 above; John Topham Picture Library 138, (Parkhouse) 10–11, (Topham/R.G. Foord) 190 above; Transworld Feature Syndicate (UK) Ltd. (Tim Graham) 137 below; Fiona Vigors Ltd. 211, 212 below, 213 above; VLOO (Adams) 214, (Danton) 160–161, (Lacz Lemoine) 172 below left, (Montferrand) 235 left, (Camille Pelletier) 178 below, (Jean-Louis Staicq) 102 centre, (D.H. Tassaux) 25, (A. de Vomecourt) 179; Warner Bros. 29; E. Weiland 4–5, 6 above left, 7 above and centre, 48 above, 58 above, 85 below, 92, 102 above, 122, 137 above, 166–67, 173 below, 196 below, 198 above right, 212 above, 216 above, 219 below right, 220 above and below, 226 above, 229, 237 above, 239 right; Western Americana Picture Library 27, 30 above, 33, (Tex-Tan Western Leather Co.) 32 above; Wyoming Travel Commission 7 below, 8–9, 146 above left and above right, 165 above and below; ZEFA (UK) Ltd. (Deckhart) 81 centre, (K. Hakenberg) 71 below, (Janoud) 65 above, (K.A.W.) 163, (Studio Keresztes) 18 below, (H. Lutticke) 78 centre, (G. Mabbs) 236, (S. Masser) 78 below, (P. Park 150, (Hans Reinhard) 6 below left, 79 above, (R.G. Theissen) 125 right, (M. Thonig) 6 centre left, (J.P. Wienke) 190 below, (H. Wiesner) back endpapers.
Pictures in the Breeds section (pp 42–87 inc.) not acknowledged above were supplied by Sally Anne Thompson.

The publishers would also like to thank the following illustrators for supplying the drawings:

Frank Kennard 169–175, 203; Trevor Lawrence 231; David and Thea Nockels 168, 207; Lorraine Richardson 202, 206.